Progress in Learning Disabilities

OTHER BOOKS BY DR. MYKLEBUST

Progress in Learning Disabilities

VOLUME IV

EDITED BY

Helmer R. Myklebust

Grune & Stratton

A Subsidiary of Harcourt Brace Jovanovich, Publishers

New York   San Francisco   London

Grune & Stratton, Inc.
111 Fifth Avenue
New York, New York 10003

Distributed in the United Kingdom by
Academic Press, Inc. (London) Ltd.
24/28 Oval Road, London NW1

Library of Congress Catalog Number 67-24545

International Standard Book Number 0-8089-1128-7

Printed in the United States of America

Contents

Contributors

Enoch Callaway, M.D., Professor of Psychiatry in Residence and Chief of Research, Langley Porter Neuropsychiatric Institute, University of California, San Francisco, California.

Lee Elliott, Ph.D., Professor of Psychology, California State University, Stanislaus, California.

Joan M. Finucci, Ph.D., Assistant Professor, Department of Pediatrics, The Johns Hopkins University School of Medicine, Baltimore, Maryland.

John T. Guthrie, Ph.D., Director of Research, International Reading Association, Newark, Delaware.

Roy Halliday, M.A., Research Specialist, Langley Porter Neuropsychiatric Institute, University of California, San Francisco, California.

Pamela Evans Hook, Ph.D., Coordinator, Learning Disabilities, Boys Town Institute for Communicative Disorders, Omaha, Nebraska.

Doris J. Johnson, Ph.D., Director, Center for Learning Disabilities and Professor of Learning Disabilities, Northwestern University, Evanston, Illinois.

James R. Killen, Ed.D., Assistant Professor, College of Education, University of Illinois at Chicago Circle, Chicago, Illinois.

Alan Leviton, M.D., S.M. Epid., Department of Neurology, Children's Hospital Medical Center, Boston and Harvard Medical School, Boston, Massachusetts.

Helmer R. Myklebust, Ed.D., Visiting Scholar, Center for Learning Disabilities, Northwestern University, Evanston, Illinois.

Byron P. Rourke, Ph.D., Professor of Psychology, University of Windsor, and Consultant in Neuropsychology, Windsor Western Hospital Centre, Windsor, Ontario, Canada.

Helen Shaner Schevill, Ph.D., Graduate School of Education, University of Pennsylvania, Philadelphia, Pennsylvania.

Jane Schulman, M.S., Research Assistant, Department of Neurology, Children's Hospital Medical Center, Boston, Massachusetts.

Mary Seifert, M. Ed., Research Specialist, International Reading Association, Newark, Delaware.

Preface

The broad range of attention devoted to the question of how children learn to read is an indication of the deep concern in our society about this aspect of learning. It is of foremost concern in American education and in many other fields as well. Since initiation of the concept of learning disabilities, with its emphasis on language disorders, a new concentration has emerged with respect to concepts of why some children are unable to learn to read. This new concentration involves several disciplines, with the result that knowledge of the processes in learning to read and why some children fail, is growing rapidly.

There are basic interactions between reading and learning disabilities. Although many children who are unsuccessful in learning to read do not have a learning disability, a significant number of them do. A major purpose of this volume is to explore the various relationships between reading and learning disabilities. Another purpose, perhaps of equal importance, is to signify that learning to read entails complex psychologic and neurologic processes. It is revealing that most of the contributors do not single out the psychologic and neurologic processes but study them one in relation to the other. This is especially gratifying inasmuch as such emphasis was a primary objective when this series was inaugurated in 1968.

Although an immediate goal of Volume IV of Progress in Learning Disabilities is to provide discussions beneficial to those responsible for treating and educating learning-disability children, we are interested also in presenting new concepts as represented by data gained from ongoing research. We are delighted that each of the authors report new findings directly related to the question of how all children learn to read, with emphasis on how their results pertain to why some find this task so difficult. Also, many suggestions are given that pertain to procedures, methods, and approaches useful in teaching children with reading disabilities.

The range of topics, according to plan, is broad, but there is an underlying theme. All the authors, from their respective points of view, present challenging data and discussion of the fundamental psychoneurologic prerequisites for learning to read. Throughout there is an overriding concern with the complex issues involved in how reading is achieved, especially as they relate to short-term memory, imagery, auditory, visual, verbal and nonverbal cognitive processes, and the underlying brain functions that make such cognition possible.

Perhaps the most basic theme is cognition and the types of disturbances responsible for reading failure. Reading disabilities not caused by such disturbances are not included. There is the clear suggestion, however, that cognitive disturbances not be overlooked when screening for reading disabilities.

Like the previous volumes, this volume is intended as a text, mainly for advanced classes in language pathology, reading disabilities, clinical child psychology, neuropsychology, and related courses. As a reference work, it will be useful in areas of child psychiatry, pediatric neurology, psycholinguistics, special education, and neuroscience.

I am grateful to the authors for their interest and cooperation and for their willingness to present original discussions of their concepts and research findings. The fields of reading disabilities and learning disabilities will benefit accordingly. Again, with gratitude, I acknowledge the painstaking editorial assistance provided by my wife.

Helmer R. Myklebust

I. Toward a Science of Dyslexiology

HELMER R. MYKLEBUST

An extensive, concerted approach to study and treatment of persons having dyslexia is evolving. This is fortuitous, even inspiring, because it embodies all facets of knowledge allied with learning to read. Encompassed in this area of specialization is scientific investigation, clinical insight and ingenuity, innovative remedial teaching, as well as expert guidance and counseling. As a significant phase of human behavior and learning, the area of dyslexia is of wide concern nationally and internationally. Although not generally recognized as an area comprising a body of knowledge, as a field in and of itself, it is one which requires investigation. It has its own issues, questions, and concepts—spanning disciplines such as psychology, language pathology, psychiatry, neurology, pediatrics, ophthalmology, electroencephalography, psycholinguistics, genetics, and education. Medical science, neuroscience, behavioral science, and pedagogical science have critical roles and obligations to be fulfilled if we are to meet the challenge of dyslexic children and adults. For these purposes, we propose the term *dyslexiology* to designate the field of professional specialization necessary to accomplish these objectives.

During the past few years the term *aphasiology* was adopted to specify the phases of knowledge relevant to disorders of spoken language. Since adoption of this term, attention has been concentrated on the problems sustained by aphasics by forming special committees, academies, organizations, and professional journals to provide a forum for exchange of ideas, all crucial to advancement of knowledge. As an appellation, dyslexiology is analogous to aphasiology. We anticipate that its adoption will foster coordination of effort from several disciplines and enhance developments.

More precise terminology with an improved nosological structure is necessary for growth of the field of dyslexia. Without such terminology, new conceptualizations are impeded and old confusions persist. Moreover, advancement of knowledge requires extensions of terminology if that which is new is to be adequately interpreted and communicated. The term *language pathology* serves as an illustration. When this term came into use several years ago, it stimulated investigations, clinical and scientific, and enhanced conceptualizing language disorders in a more meaningful way. Much was gained. However, this term is inclusive and does not meet the specialized interests represented by the two major types of language disorders, aphasia and dyslexia. Aphasiology and dyslexiology are considered subspecialities within the area of language pathology.

Because of the need for professional effort and knowledge pertaining to language and language disorders, specialization within a speciality seems warranted. The term dyslexiology is intended to encompass all phases of dyslexia, congenital and acquired, at all age levels. The types discussed in this chapter are inner-language dyslexia, auditory dyslexia, visual dyslexia, and intermodal dyslexia.

DYSLEXIA: A COGNITIVE DISORDER

During the past few decades modifications have occurred in the theories advanced in psychology and education. The behavioristic approach has limitations, especially as propounded by early learning theorists. Nowhere is this more evident than in the area of dyslexia. Serving as a background for these changes are contributions of cognitive

1

psychologists, neuroscientists, and behavioral neurologists (Neisser, 1967; Teyler, Raemer, Harrison, et al., 1973; Kinsbourne, 1975). Emphasis on brain function in learning is a powerful impetus for extending the conceptualizations of cognitive psychology.

Throughout this discussion we rely heavily on the endeavors of neuroscientists and information-processing psychologists (McKay, 1969; Rumelhart, 1977). One cannot be concerned with learning in relation to language and language disorders and avoid feeling the impact of contributions such as reported by Teyler et al. (1973). They have shown, for instance, that evoked brain potentials are different when the subject is presented with the word *rock,* depending upon whether this word is used to mean a stone, a type of music, or a rocking chair. The brain codes and classifies, not on the basis of *rock* as a vocal utterance, nor as a *word* on a page, but on the basis of the meaning being conveyed.

The implications of these contributors are of immeasurable importance for a model of dyslexia, providing a foundation for the concept of inner language—for the concept of language as representational behavior, for language as verbal symbolic behavior (Mowrer, 1960; Langer, 1972). John, Karmel, Corning, et al. (1977) present similar evidence:

> The brain seems to use representation of recent experience to generate expectations about future events. Match-mismatch operations are involved in response to novelty, focusing attention, habituation, and organization of memory, as well as in cognitive processes involved in comparisons of word meaning. . . . Different averaged evoked waveshapes are elicited when the same spoken or printed word is embedded in syntactical content as a verb or a noun. (p. 1396).

These neurometric, neurophysiologic data, demonstrating the significance of *meaning* in relation to information processing, are critical to a cognitive model of dyslexia.

Meaning and Inner Language

The cognitive mechanisms consequent to acquisition of language—inner, receptive, expressive—have not been well defined in psychology or in education. Specific emphasis on meaning and inner language as essential components of language learning in human beings is infrequent and vague, but expositions that include mediation processes and intersensory perception are of value (Mowrer, 1960; Birch and Belmont, 1965). In our studies we stress that meaning is the dominant feature in language learning, and forms the basis of the verbal code. It is symbolization that makes coding possible. Language is the result of transforming sensory information into meaningful symbols.

Although we will not review the various ways in which language has been defined, the definition presented in the *Webster's Third International Dictionary* (1963) is useful because it focuses on meaning: "Language is a systematic means of communicating ideas or feelings by use of conventionalized signs, sounds, gestures or marks having understood meanings." This definition recognizes that symbolic representational learning is of two types, verbal and nonverbal. Our discussion is mainly concerned with verbal symbols but it is relevant that nonverbal images also are used representationally. Strictly speaking, inner language comprises two symbolic forms, one verbal and the other nonverbal (Paivio, 1971; Myklebust, 1975). Some handicapped children (those deaf from early life, the profoundly retarded, and the autistic) seem to use nonverbal symbols extensively. The consequence of symbolic representational behavior in the evolution of the human mind has been reviewed by Langer (1972).

Words and Meaning

The concept of language as verbal-symbolic-representational behavior is critical to understanding childhood dyslexia. This feature, if ignored, results in overlooking the most salient characteristic of language. Nevertheless, investigators frequently report studies and discuss data as though words have no symbolic meaning. We must recognize that symbolization, this phenomenal aspect of human learning, necessitates that information, as it progresses cognitively from reception to expression, be transduced into representational units and coded on the basis of meaning. This is the essential element which characterizes learning in human beings. It is also the principle element to be taken into consideration in definition and treatment of dyslexia.

Meaning has received wide attention from neurologists; they evolved the concepts of aphasia, dyslexia, dysgraphia, agnosia, and apraxia (Goldstein, 1948). Moreover, frequently they are successful in relating these conditions to specific dysfunctions in the brain. In more recent years, this effort has forged ahead through contributions by neuroscientists using computerized neurometric procedures, with the result that the relationships that exist between brain function and language behavior have been greatly explicated. Through their work and through the efforts of information-processing psychologists and behavioral neurologists, we have entered a new era of awareness of the "meaning of meaning" in understanding inner language (MacKay, 1969; John, 1977). In the study of dyslexia it is necessary to assess the role of meaning relative to the cognitive processes essential in learning to read, because in dyslexia the symbolizing process has been disturbed.

Each child acquires verbal meaning according to his age, abilities, and experience. The mechanisms by which this is achieved is the fundamental question. Acquisition of meaning concerns cognitive, integrative processes, a primary component of which is ability to transform incoming sensations into verbal symbols, in turn making it possible to code, store, and retrieve experience. Only to the extent that experience becomes symbolically representational does it become meaningful. The brain processes meaningful information differently compared to meaningless information (Myklebust, 1967; John, 1977). For example, when a child recognizes a picture of his father, he has a nonverbal, symbolic coded image of him which cognitively represents his father. Thereby he can match this image with the one in the picture and identify it—it has meaning.

Similarly, when the child hears and comprehends the word *father,* he relates this verbal, representational symbol with the coded image *father,* with the proper unit of experience, and gains the intended meaning. In like manner, when the child initially learns to read the word *father,* this printed symbol is related to the auditory, spoken word and hence to the appropriate unit of experience. Again, the intended meaning is gained.

These processes comprise inner language and its functions and must be further clarified if we are to meet the urgent needs of a large number of dyslexic children. There are a number of unresolved questions but, fortunately, definitive information is forthcoming year by year pertaining to the cognitive-neural processes involved in learning to read. Golinkoff (1975–1976) has proposed a theory which would specify units of measurement for determining the level of meaning attained. He shows how the reader goes beyond linguistic information and constructs a representation of the message based on inference. Poor readers were found to be identifying words, whereas good readers read at least a phrase at a time.

Meaning is the result of relating incoming information to information previously coded, classified, and stored. Such inner language processes require cognitive manipulation of verbal and nonverbal symbols representationally. It is symbolic representation that makes simultaneous identification possible, as it does the comparison and recognition of information being received. Incoming, or internally evoked sensations, become meaningful to the extent that they evoke already meaningful representational symbols. Information cannot be processed cognitively and become meaningful unless it evokes symbolic representations of similar or related events. Therefore, information processing requires ongoing utilization of memory, of previously coded and stored experience. Indeed, learning can be regarded as the process of acquiring a greater and greater range of symbolically represented experience in an ever-increasing range of specialized, unique combinations and relationships, thereby attaining a greater and greater range of significance as it relates to the total composite of meaningfulness in daily living.

These intriguing cognitive, inner-language functions relate directly to assessment of cognitive disturbances as found in childhood dyslexia. Assessment usually requires a complex of procedures because various cognitive processes are involved and there are varying levels of meaning. For example. most learning necessitates more than simple matching of one unit of information with another learned previously, as matching a picture of father with the coded representational image of father. The matching level of learning, including matching of the name of an object with the object itself (naming level) is the most concrete level of learning, and characterizes learning in early infancy. Our studies of written language indicate that this level also characterizes the learning of profoundly retarded children, and to some extent the learning of the profoundly deaf, the blind, deaf-blind, and autistic (Myklebust, 1964, 1965, 1973).

Abstraction and Cognition

Abstract learning requires cognitive processes other than those used in simple matching. This type of learning is expected of most children year by year, as well of most adults—even into advanced age. The cognitive processes entailed in learning to use words (spoken, read, and written) in ways that make metaphorical and analogical reasoning possible are in need of further investigation. Our intent, however, is to note that there are levels of meaning as seen in inuendo, connotation, inference, parable, and proverb. In this sense, too, meaning is critical to reading.

The unique manner by which meaning is derived is emphasized by MacKay (1969), who states,

> The mechanical *energy* of the message must be sufficient to do the mechanical job that eventually resets the brainlevers; but the selective job, of determining which levels shall move, depends on the *form* of the message, and the state of your brain before you hear it. There is where the meaning of the message comes in. As long as we think only of what actually happens, we may be able to make do with explanations solely in terms of physical energy. It isn't until we consider the range of other states of readiness, that *might have been selected but weren't,* that the notion of meaning comes into its own. A change in meaning implies a different selection from the range of states of readiness. A meaningless message is one that makes no selection from the range. An ambiguous message is one that could make more than one selection. . . . Defined in this way, meaning is clearly a relationship between message and recipient rather than a unique property of the message alone. (p. 24)

Norman (1972), making a comparable observation, writes,

The meaningful component of language is completely isolated from the physical aspects of the signals that are used to communicate that language. The persuasive arguments put forth to support a system of decoding by means of an analysis-by-synthesis require that the meaning of the physical input be determined simultaneously with the decoding of the symbols that comprise that input, for the two aspects of decoding and understanding cannot be separated from one another. (p. 284)

A deficiency in ability to gain meaning, especially in relation to abstract thought, is the most significant consequence of a handicap or a disability, including dyslexia. To be unable to gain abstract meaning is to be stimulus-bound, to be unable to deduce, infer, and profit from connotation. It is to be limited to the observable. In comparison, to engage in abstract thought is to detach oneself from the immediate and observable, to categorize and to conceputalize on the basis of commonalities and principles. These capabilities require a richness of inner language because conceptualizing necessitates exclusion of immediately observable features and inclusion of features not observable in the concrete. In other words, conceptualization assumes identification of generalizations and implications, which in turn must be integrated symbolically with other broad commonalities of experience.

As Gibson and Levin (1975) have observed,

Meaning is a psychological concept which precedes language. Meaning begins with the real things in the world, their distinctive features, and events that have been observable and predictable relations among things and people and actions. Although children are aware of meanings in a real environmental context at an early age, before speech has developed to any great extent, it is a long time before they generalize meanings in a systematic way to the semantic aspects of language, both spoken and written. (p. 77)

Concept formation

Even though there are differences in detail, generalized experience is coded and categorized on the basis of similarities in meaning; in turn, this generalization is recognized and identified as a new unit of experience. This is abstract learning. It can be accomplished only by submersion of obvious, concrete meanings, of matching or descriptive responses (maintaining these only as background experience), while abstract, conceptualized meanings are projected as foreground experience.

Cognitively this process is basic to concept formation because concepts themselves are not observable in the concrete; they exist only in the mind. The concept *furniture* exists only as a symbolic representation of a generalized experience. The generalized experience itself is not immediately observable. Only the subjects that make up the category can be perceived through the senses; there is no object that can be designated *furniture*. This designation can be applied only to experience gained from a number of objects, all of which—because of the inherent relationships among them—form a category. There are features in common so the category itself has a unique meaning. This generalization of meaning comprises a concept, and it is inner language, symbolic processes that make possible its formation.

John (1972) studied meaning in relation to memory, using neuroelectric techniques, and showed that readout components were not elicited by meaningless stimuli, but appeared when the stimuli became meaningful. He concluded that learning occurred when activation and release of specific memory occurred:

Different brain regions come to share a common mode during learning. When an experienced organism receives a novel and meaningless stimulus and generalization occurs, this new afferent input in a familiar context activates the representational system in such a way as to cause release of a common mode of activity like that stored during the learning experience. (p. 864)

Metaphor

Before considering dyslexia more specifically, we recognize another example of symbolic behavior—use of metaphor—which further illustrates the phenomenal manner in which representational behavior makes it possible to manipulate experience. When used metaphorically, the word or phrase does not have literal meaning. Instead, language is used to suggest an inferred meaning. The significance of metaphoric language usage in relation to language disorders and perception of meaning has been all but overlooked. Teachers of dyslexic children often observe how difficult it is to explain the generalized meaning of words. Even the simple word *run* has a variety of meanings. It may refer to the act of rapidly moving one's legs to move from one place to another, or it may refer to running water, running for office, or running a corporation.

Metaphors encompass even more abstract meanings. When we say, ''He has a chip on his shoulder,'' none of the words comprising this sentence should be interpreted literally. The intended meaning pertains neither to chips nor to shoulders. As an utterance, we are conveying a fact, an observation of a person to the effect that he is quarrelsome, antagonistic, and hostile in attitude. To communicate metaphorically, to use representational symbols in this way, may be the highest level of abstract behavior yet attained by man. It requires use of symbols figuratively, parabolically, emplematically, and referentially. As Langer (1957) states, ''The nature of metaphor . . . cannot be properly understood without a symbolistic rather than a signalistic view of language'' (p. 132). She also observes that ''metaphor is our most striking evidence of abstractive seeing, of the power of the human mind to use representational symbols'' (p. 141).

The intent of this discussion has been to affirm the complex nature of inner language processes and their consequence in understanding a language disorder, such as dyslexia. To have a childhood dyslexia is to be limited in these processes, with concurrent loss of meaning. Thus, there is a psychology of dyslexia which needs greater emphasis and further investigation, including the psychology of language as representational behavior. It even entails meaningful use of the designation *childhood dyslexia*. It is from this frame of reference that this disorder in ability to symbolize is further delineated.

DYSLEXIA: A LANGUAGE DISORDER

In achieving verbal behavior, the child goes through five stages of language development. First, inner language must be established (initially at a rudimentary level) because this cognitive process makes meaningful symbolic representational behavior possible. In addition to inner language, there are two forms of auditory language and two forms of visual language. Auditory language, following inner language, is the most basic form acquired by man. For communication with others, it was the first acquired phylogenetically and is the first acquired ontogenetically. Therefore, there is a sequential relationship between the auditory and visual language forms, between the spoken and the read. Developmentally the auditory is first, with the read form acquired later and superimposed on the auditory. This relationship between auditory and visual language is emphasized by Fries (1962), who states,

> Learning to read is *not* a process of learning new language signals. He [the child] is learning to put the visual on the signal he already has. The language signals are the *same*. The difference is in the modality relating to other nervous system functions. So the process of learning to read is learning to transfer from the auditory already learned to new signs for the same signals. (p. 15)

As suggested by Fries, reading must be understood as a cognitive process. Such understanding is critical to definition and precise characterization of all language disorders, including dyslexia. One of our greatest gains has been the realization that both auditory and visual cognitive abilities are involved in learning to read. No longer can reading be perceived only in terms of vision, or even only in terms of visual cognitive processes. Deficits in either auditory or visual cognitive processes can cause serious disruptions in reading achievement. Together with the role of memory, these processes must be further clarified.

But even with intensified interest in the psychology of reading, the relationship between the auditory and visual forms often is overlooked. When sequential cognitive-interneurosensory processes are ignored (the auditory being first and the visual second), there is confusion of the issues which embody child language. The role of auditory language in learning to read is dramatically revealed by children deaf from early life. The model presented in Figure 1 evolved from studies of deaf children. They have no auditory cognitive processes, no auditory language form, so they must learn to read by visual cognitive processes alone. These studies substantiate that to do so is extremely difficult,

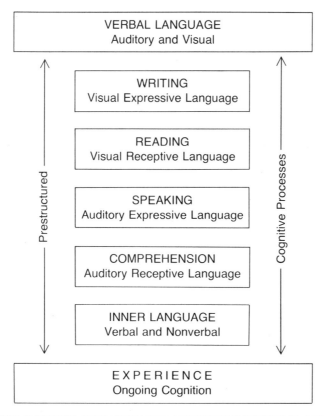

Fig. 1. DEVELOPMENTAL HIERARCHY FOR ACQUISITION OF VERBAL LANGUAGE.

representing perhaps the most difficult learning task encountered by any group of children (Myklebust, 1964).

Prestructured Processes

The intriguing question is, Why can we not teach reading more successfully by using visual processes alone? McKeachie's (1976) observations are highly relevant. He states that research results secured from several disciplines attest that the brain is *prestructured* to operate in certain specific ways. This observation reflects precisely the circumstances found in acquisition of auditory and visual language. Because the brain is prestructured to process information in specific modes, it is naive to expect children to learn well when instructed by methods contrary to these modes. To do so not only is disappointing but can be harmful. The prestructured neuro-cognitive systems include operations of both of the distance senses, hearing and vision. Audition is nondirectional, mandatory, and exceedingly suitable for language acquisition. Therefore, auditory language, the language most basic to survival, develops first, with visual-read language being attained later.

Witelson and Pallie (1973) have presented pertinent evidence, especially as it applies to language. They measured the cerebral hemispheres in adults and newborns. The left planum was significantly larger than the right in both groups. They observed that, "The anatomical asymmetry found in neonates favoring a left temporal area of known significance in reception of language in adults supports the hypothesis that the human newborn has a pre-programmed biological capacity to process speech sounds" (p. 645).

Because of better understanding of brain processes, we can relate the ways in which the brain is prestructured to the concept of childhood dyslexia. It is because of this prestructuring that deaf children find it so difficult to bypass auditory cognitive processes and learn to read by visual cognitive processes alone. There are similar circumstances in childhood dyslexia because it is the brain that learns; there is both a neurology and a psychology of learning. Certain brain systems are specialized to serve certain cognitive functions, so it is possible to relate these systems to each of the five stages, or levels, of language development, as shown in Figure 1.

Penfield and Roberts (1959) first suggested that the centrencephalic system was responsible mainly for processing information integratively so meaning can be attained. The neurologic systems serving principally auditory language are more readily understood (Geschwind, 1972). The systems requisite to processing receptive auditory language are not the same as those serving expressive auditory language, as is true also for visual-verbal language. There is a system for processing output (writing) and one for processing input (reading). Using this cognitive model, the five primary types of language disorders are inner language, receptive aphasia, expressive aphsia, dyslexia, and dysgraphia.

Specialization by Hemisphere

The relationship between brain function and cognition is apparent in other ways, particularly by the different means in which each of the brain hemispheres serves cognition and learning (Geschwind, 1975; Kinsbourne and Smith, 1974; Galaburda, LeMay, Kemper, and Geschwind, 1978). Broca (1861) was one of the first to show that the hemispheres were functionally different. His discovery that spoken language was served by a system within the left hemisphere often has been verified, a fact that in itself is a foundation for the neuropsychology of language. There is no more significant facet of our model than the one that emphasizes differences in information processing by hemisphere; cognitive functions vary by hemisphere, with language processed mainly on the left and nonverbal information mainly on the right. By implication, for man to be man, neuro-cognitive functions must be specialized by hemisphere to a high degree. In one study we found that the more profound the mental retardation, the less the specialization. These differences by hemisphere pertain directly to childhood dyslexia, as well as to all other phases of language pathology (Kinsbourne, 1975). Vital to this construct is that these variations of hemisphere, existing from birth (Witelson and Pallie, 1973), provide further evidence that the brain is prestructured and preprogrammed to operate in specific ways. This observation is essential to understanding the sequential relationship between auditory and read language, and thereby crucial to conceptualizing childhood dyslexia.

Witelson (1977), in an ingenious study, revealed that developmental dyslexia can be associated with bihemispheric representation of spatial abilities. When nonverbal functions become unduly represented on both hemispheres, they interfere with development of the specialized functions normally found on the left and result in deficient linguistic-cognitive learning. Witelson advises that this pattern of cognitive deficits seems to compel the child to read by a spatial-cognitive strategy instead of by a phonetic-sequential strategy. Because of this lack of normal development on the left hemisphere, a developmental dyslexia ensues.

Prerequisites for Reading

Normal language development assumes normal cognitive functions. When cognitive functions are disturbed or deficient, as in the mentally retarded or in other types of exceptional children, language acquisition often is affected. However, as experience is gained and integrated, cognitive processes are ongoing and rudimentary inner language gradually develops. Initially it consists of nonverbal imagery, which is used representationally in early life by normal children; it persists into later life when conditions like deafness or profound mental retardation are present. Normally, nonverbal images and auditory words exist side by side (Paivio, 1971). There is diminution of nonverbal imagery as auditory verbal comprehension grows, although use of nonverbal symbols is retained throughout life (Ferguson, 1977).

As a cognitive process, inner language is requisite to language development. However, disorders of inner language continue to be complex and equivocal in evaluation and identification. The most observable symptom in the auditory form is *echolalia* (Myklebust, 1957). The child repeats words, phrases, or sentences without knowing the meaning of what he is saying. In reading, a similar occurrence is *word-calling;* the child "reads" words, phrases, or sentences but is unable to attach meaning to what he reads. These disorders affirm that language is more than input and output. In between reception and expression falls the discerning process of coding, of relating information to referents—to specific units of experience—and thereby permitting attainment of meaning. As foreseen by Vygotsky (1962), a word without meaning is not a word.

As the child gains ability to relate the spoken word to units of experience (the experience *father* with the word *father*), he is acquiring auditory receptive language; the more words used representationally, the more he comprehends. Other than inner language, this is the first verbal system—comprehension of the spoken word; he does not first learn to read. The reasons for the first language being auditory have been discussed elsewhere (Johnson and Myklebust, 1967), but it is clear that audition rather than vision is prestructured as a modality more suitably for language learning. Even prehistoric man evolved and acquired spoken language, whereas the visual-read form is of recent origin.

As might be anticipated, a disturbance of cognition affecting auditory receptive language results in a severe limitation on other levels of language to be acquired. If the spoken word is not comprehended, as in *receptive aphasia,* the child does not speak; there must be auditory inner verbal language and ability to comprehend before the spoken word can be used expressively. Also, if auditory, verbal comprehension is not acquired, it is exceedingly arduous for the child to learn to read because the visual word cannot be converted into its auditory equivalent. But this deficit in learning to read is not a dyslexia. It is a receptive aphasia which secondarily affects learning to read; the deficiency in reading is reciprocal to the auditory receptive language disorder, second only to disorders of inner language (Myklebust, 1954, 1971a).

Experimental evidence based on studies of both normal and exceptional children is leading to new insights and conceptualizations of the essential role of auditory cognitive processes in learning to read (Gibson and Levin, 1975). There is recognition of the brain being preprogrammed so that acquisition of auditory language should precede acquisition of the visual-read form. Learning to read begins with acquisition of auditory language. Only after this verbal-symbol system has been established can the read form be attained in the normal manner.

Childhood Dyslexia: The Inherent Characteristic

Reading assumes a written language form. Studies of the development and disorders of written language are basic to consideration of all types of reading disabilities (Myklebust, 1965, 1973). Gelb (1963) refers to the alphabet as one of the greatest achievements of the human mind. Alphabetologists have added immeasurably to knowledge of language behavior, especially in regard to reading. There is realization that childhood dyslexia is more common than assumed, being a significant factor in the composite of the learning disabilities associated with all types of exceptional children, as well as being the common denominator in many children without other handicaps.

Of the language disorders in children, dyslexia has presented unusual obstacles to acceptance by educators. But this situation is changing. There is more agreement as to the nature of this disorder than ever before. There is more emphasis on research, on definition, diagnosis, and program planning (Kavanagh and Mattingly, 1972; Guthrie, 1976). This is fortunate because clarification of issues leads to more effective intervention. Albeit, as one analyzes developments covering a period of more than a century, one is impressed by the ingenious clinical observations but dismayed by disagreements as to the precise disorder inherent in this reading disability. If this issue can be resolved, there would be enormous benefit to a large group of children.

Dyslexia is a language disorder, a deficit in ability to verbalize symbolically. But as one analyzes reports on reading disabilities, seldom does one find ability to symbolize being differentiated from other disorders. Inability to symbolize the read form of language is the paramount feature—the inherent factor in dyslexia—in both children and adults. This feature, the inability to transduce printed words into meaningful symbols, must be differentiated from other reading disabilities. There is now a perspective from which this can be done. This perspective derives mainly from cognitive psychology and the neurosciences (Weimer and Palermo, 1974; Thatcher and John, 1977). These constructs provide a basis for a functional definition, as well as a basis for a concept of the psychoneurology of learning as it relates to childhood dyslexia.

How can dyslexia be differentiated from other types of reading disabilities? This is not a simple question, but most disagreements could be avoided if the concept of reading as a language process is not overlooked. The essential feature of dyslexia encompasses its being a cognitive disorder involving the read form of language. Other reading disabilities do not entail cognitive, symbolic processes. Although nonlanguage reading disabilities can affect language acquisition and reduce the reading level, they are not deficiencies in ability to symbolize. Dyslexia is a disorder in symbol-making behavior; other reading disabilities are not. But often those who consider issues relating to dyslexia do not refer to language, nor to deficiencies in ability to use words representationally.

An example is a study by Taylor, Satz, and Friel (1977), who compared children designated as dyslexic with reading-disability children designated as nondyslexic. Language is not mentioned. Classification as dyslexic was based on teacher judgment and on scores on a test of reading. It is unlikely that most teachers can distinguish between dyslexic children and those who fail to learn to read for other reasons. Moreover, failure on a reading test, like failure on any other type of test, does not in itself constitute a basis for diagnosis. One is not astonished, therefore, that these investigators found no differences between the groups of poor readers; scores on a reading test indicate the extent of the failure in learning but are not necessarily criteria for distinguishing dyslexia from other factors which influence success in learning to read.

This study manifests the point at issue; consideration must be given to whether ability to use symbols representationally is disturbed or whether other factors are causitive. Before dyslexia can be differentiated from these factors, criteria must be established for ascertaining what it is that comprises this specific language disorder. This assumes precise definition.

DEFINING CHILDHOOD DYSLEXIA

Language is the essential component in the definition of dyslexia. From this vantage point, it is helpful to review the definition proposed by the World Federation of Neurology (1968), which does not use the term *language,* nor does it refer to deficits in verbal, symbolic processes. Rather, it states that "Dyslexia is a disorder manifested by difficulty in learning to read despite conventional instruction, adequate intelligence, and sociocultural opportunity. It is dependent upon fundamental cognitive disabilities which are frequently of constitutional origin" (p. 22). This definition is limited because it does not include the principle criterion comprising dyslexia, the deficiency of language. On the other hand, three other essential criteria are included: ability to learn, opportunity for learning, and the presence of cognitive disturbances.

Dyslexia, a language disorder, must be distinguished from other reading disabilities on the basis of this criterion. Critical to so doing is the fact that words, to be words, are meaningful symbols. One might be proficient in hearing and seeing "words," or even in writing them, but be unable to symbolize them. In addition, this cognitive disturbance must be attributable to brain dysfunction. Thus, the definition should include both psychologic and neurologic aspects. This rationale is highlighted by neuroscientists (Teyler et al., 1973; John, 1977), who have shown that the brain differentiates between meaningful and meaningless information.

Poor Reading: Not Dyslexia

Perhaps when attempting to read, the brain in dyslexic children reacts as it does in normal children who are confronted with meaningless information. The differentiating factor is whether there is a deficit in gaining meaning from the written word. If there is not, the reading disability should not be designated a dyslexia. Among the conditions that cause poor reading achievement are lack of opportunity, inadequate teaching, low intelligence, emotional disturbance, poor hearing or vision, and bilinguality.

Another deficit that must be differentiated from childhood dyslexia is an inability to learn to spell. Poor spelling ability characterizes the written language of dyslexics but spelling disorders per se are not necessarily the result of dyslexia. On the other hand, as shown by Boder (1973), analysis of types of spelling errors often reveals the type of dyslexia present—whether the dyslexia is predominantly auditory or visual (Johnson and Myklebust, 1967). Savin (1972) states that "The difference between reading and spelling is analogous to that between recognition and recall, acknowledged by psychologists to be different processes" (p. 333).

Likewise, although clinically revealing, punctuation errors do not constitute a basis for establishing the presence of dyslexia (Myklebust, 1965, 1973). Other misconceptions pertain to reading skills (Gates, 1950). Deficiencies in skill are not necessarily due to a language disorder. Although dyslexia obviously affects reading skill, many skill factors do not entail reading as a language form. For example, reading rate encompasses reading skill, but being a slow reader does not mean that one is dyslexic, although as dyslexic children learn to read, usually they do so very slowly. Level of complexity of the material being read also must be considered. Material so difficult as to be outside of the child's realm of experience cannot be read meaningfully. Everyone, child and adult, encounters material which is readable but not meaningful because it cannot be associated with previous experience; it does not evoke referents. Children with deprived backgrounds might achieve poorly in reading because of limitations experientially. This could be an issue of considerable magnitude, one in need of careful investigation. However, this is not a language disorder, hence, does not involve dyslexia.

Developmental Readiness

Developmental immaturity also can cause retardation in learning to read. Children who are developmentally immature, who have not achieved reading readiness, are unable to begin reading at the expected age. Although some authorities discount the importance of the readiness concept, evidence suggests that it is a significant cause of failure in learning to read. Ilg and Ames (1965), who studied school readiness from several points of view, found that as many as 20% of children were unduly immature and not ready for the learning expected of them when school placement was based on the factor of chronological age alone. Moreover, if children were placed in a grade on the basis of mental age alone, many were developmentally immature in other respects so they could not perform at the expected level educationally.

Developmental readiness might be altered as a result of a variety of circumstances: genetic traits, parental oversolicitation, sociocultural deprivation, childhood illnesses, lack of schooling, and frequent displacement from one school to another. More recently, neuroscientists have implicated developmental immaturity of the left brain hemisphere as a significant involvement in delayed language acquisition, including a delay in learning to read (Kinsbourne, 1975). Although such neurologic immaturity can result in dyslexia, usually it does not. As growth and maturation are achieved, although at a slower than average rate, reading is accomplished; there is no disorder in verbal-symbolic learning. Nevertheless, determining hemispheric lateralization is essential when assessing reading failure (Witelson, 1977).

Emotional Aspects

Emotional well-being is consequential to all learning. In the field of reading dis-abilities, this phase has received wide attention—sometimes to the exclusion of other considerations. But children must be properly motivated to learn. Severe negativism, autistic withdrawal, and hysterical reactions do alter ability to learn. Children who sustain such emotional disturbances, and even though they interfere with learning to read, should not be referred to as dyslexia. Their behavioral disorder is not one which causes disturbance in verbal-symbolic cognitive processes. Moreover, emotional and developmental immaturity often overlap. We found that a group of severely emotionally disturbed children were developmentally immature, presenting a pervasive pattern of which the behavior disorder was but one aspect. As they approached 17 years of age, they acquired facility in use of read and written language at the normal level (Myklebust, 1973).

Reading in Black Children

Black children sometimes are less successful in learning to read than white children. This does not suggest a higher incidence of dyslexia in Black children. Other circumstances contribute to their failure. According to our model, some Black children find it hard to learn to read because of the dialectical form of their spoken language (Gibson and Levin, 1975). Any dialect, like having a foreign language as one's native tongue, increases the difficulty of relating the written language form with the auditory. Written English, though not entirely phonetic, is more readily converted to the auditory the more one speaks the common form of English—the more it is equated with the written, including grammar syntax, sentence length, and vocabulary. When Black children find reading arduous, it is necessary to appraise their spoken language and assist them by pointing out how their spoken form varies from the written. As in other areas of reading retardation, it is advantageous to begin training at the auditory language level. Although not a dyslexia, the model we propose indicates the sequential hierarchy for remediation helpful for many children with reading retardation.

Reading Epilepsy

Reading epilepsy, a neurogenic condition, is found in some children and adults. As shown by Forster (1975), the act of reading sometimes stimulates the brain in a way that produces a seizure; this is a dramatic illustration of the relationship between cognition and brain disturbances. The incidence of this form of epilepsy is not known but it is encountered often in clinics for learning-disability children. Obviously, there is a direct effect on learning to read, but typically these children are not dyslexic. Even though reading, as a cognitive process, serves as an irritant in the brain and causes seizures, the disorder is not one of language.

Auditory Agnosia

Psychologists, special educators, speech pathologists, and audiologists frequently see children who can hear, see, say, or write words but who cannot attach meaning to them. This inability to attach meaning to what is heard, seen, or touched is referred to as *agnosia;* Freud (1953) was the first to use this designation. More specifically, when sounds are not comprehended, the involvement is known as *auditory agnosia.* Receptive aphasia is a form of auditory agnosia because the spoken word is heard but not understood. The individual hears what is said but cannot convert what is heard into words; the speech sounds cannot be symbolized so meaning is not gained. This is a language disorder, an inability in use of the spoken word.

Visual Agnosia

Visual agnosia, an analogous disorder, is an inability to attach meaning to what is seen. Dyslexia is a form of visual agnosia. The words on the page can be seen but cannot be coded; no meaning is gained. This is a *verbal-visual agnosia.* A similar disorder is encountered in deaf children who see the lip movements of the speaker but cannot attach meaning to these movements (Myklebust, 1964). A corollary of auditory and visual agnosia is *tactile agnosia;* meaning is not gained from what is touched. This might take the form of a verbal agnosia, as seen in some blind children who cannot learn the meaning of braille symbols.

Apraxia

Disorders in language affect not only receptive processes but often disturb expressive functions as well. When verbal-symbolic expressive language is disturbed, the disorder is designated *apraxia*. Expressive aphasia is a form of apraxia; the individual knows what he wants to say, but because of a symbolic disturbance he cannot utter the words. The analogous condition in written language is *dysgraphia* (Myklebust, 1965, 1973). There is no paralysis. An apraxia effects ability to convert symbols into their equivalent motor form. Therefore, it is a language disorder—a disturbance of verbal-symbolic behavior. Expressive aphasia and dysgraphia are verbal apraxias.

Other Considerations

Before defining childhood dyslexia more specifically, we again turn to the hierarchy of language development, as shown in Figure 1. This hierarchy is applicable only to phonetic language—to languages of the Western world. In the Orient, where alphabets are not used (the spoken and written forms are not directly related), the sequences of language development are not the same as in cultures where alphabets are the mode for the written form. When we first presented our model for language development, we had found it useful in studying cognitive processes in deaf children; they are markedly limited in acquisiton of language, spoken and read (Myklebust, 1964; Hughes, 1971). Since then it has served as a basis for studying all forms of language disorder (Myklebust, 1965, 1973).

This developmental hierarchy conforms to the way in which the brain is prestructured to process verbal information. So, for language, the normal manner is to process information from auditory to visual. Unless the auditory form is sufficiently intact so that auditory information can be processed, having the visual form is of little advantage. Reading specialists who study normal children report results showing this sequential relationship. Hardy, Smythe, Stennett, et al. (1972) investigated phoneme-grapheme and grapheme-phoneme correspondence and found developmental trends in mastery of visual-auditory equivalents. Processing from phoneme to grapheme was easier than processing from grapheme to phoneme.

When analyzing the dependence of visual language on the auditory, and the prestructured cognitive processes, audition is more critical to daily life and more efficient for verbal learning. It is both permissive and mandatory. It is ongoing so that language learning can occur while the child is engaged in a host of other activities involving his vision and his hands. Auditory language impinges on the child from all directions—in the dark, around corners, and even through walls. Moreover, less neuro-cognitive maturity is required for acquisition of auditory language; studies of the mentally retarded demonstrate that greater psychoneurologic maturity is required for learning to read and to write (Myklebust, 1973).

DEFINITIONS

Study of childhood dyslexia and its definition has a long history. A pioneer, Hinshelwood (1917) defined childhood dyslexia as a congenital defect occurring in children with otherwise normal and undamaged brains, characterized by a disability in learning to read so great that it is manifestly due to a pathologic condition and where attempts to teach the child by ordinary methods have completely failed. This definition incorporates aspects which cannot be ignored but because of greater understanding of reading as a process, especially in relation to brain function, we now can be more specific in stipulating criteria for assessing dyslexia in children.

Silver (1970), who has been concerned with dyslexic children for a number of years, refers to their deficiency as "A profound defect in spatial and temporal perception . . . visual and auditory modalities and with difficulties in the intermodal integration" (p.9). Many such definitions have been presented but they are overly inclusive, not specific to dyslexia. A child might sustain disorders of spatial and temporal perception without reading being affected. Moreover, intermodal aspects of information processing are not necessarily involved. Intramodal disturbances, either auditory or visual, might be more common.

Eisenberg (1975) defines specific dyslexia as "the failure to learn to read with normal proficiency, despite conventional instruction, a culturally adequate home, proper motivation, intact senses, normal intelligence and freedom from gross neurologic deficit" (p. 218). Although language and ability to symbolize is not mentioned, success in this aspect of learning is implied by the phrase *failure to learn to read*. Other essentials are included but it is necessary to be more definitive. For example, Vellutino, Smith, and Steger (1975) investigated the perceptual deficit hypothesis in relation to age and found that "specific reading disability is not attributable to visual-spatial disorders" (p. 492). A more appropriate rationale, they conclude, is that reading disabilities occur because of a disorder in verbal mediation.

Definition of a deficit in language to some extent depends upon one's area of specialization and the purpose for which the definition is intended; more than one definition of childhood dyslexia could be advantageous. Nevertheless, some aspects are preemptory and should not be omitted from any definition. As stressed throughout this discussion, learning to read is the fourth stage in acquisition of language developmentally. Accordingly, reading achievement can be disturbed by disruption of any one of the steps that precede it—mainly by disturbances at the level of inner language and comprehension of the spoken word. Expressive language disorders (expressive aphasia and dysgraphia) have little effect on learning to read.

We define childhood dyslexia as *a language disorder that precludes acquisition of meaning from the written word because of a deficit in ability to symbolize. It may be endogenous or exogenous, congenital or acquired after birth. The limitations in read language are demonstrated by a discrepancy between expected and actual performance in reading. These limitations derive from dysfunctions in the brain, manifested by disturbances in cognition. They are not attributable to sensory, motor, intellectual, or emotional impairment, nor to inadequate teaching or deprivation of opportunity.*

Inner Language Dyslexia

Childhood dyslexia can be further defined by delineating it into its major types. The most severe form is *inner-language dyslexia*. This deficiency has been recognized for many years, often being referred to as *word-calling*. Usually there are deficits in both auditory and visual verbal processing. The child perceives graphemes and transduces them into their auditory equivalents, evidenced by his ability to "read" aloud. But despite these perceptual and transducing skills, he cannot learn to read because cognitively the level of meaning is bypassed. So far as input and output are concerned, information is processed well, but language is more than input and output. The information must be coded, and coding assumes meaning. In inner-language dyslexia the break occus at this level in the information-processing system. Because information cannot be coded, what is read is not words; there is no meaning. It appears most commonly in autistic and educable mentally retarded children but its existence in children who are otherwise less handicapped should not be overlooked.

Auditory Dyslexia

Over a period of many years attention has been focused primarily on the visual aspects of dyslexia, as illustrated by early use of the term *word-blindness* (Hinshelwood, 1917). Visual-verbal information processing is critical to learning to read, and deficits at this level of cognitive processing can cause dyslexia. However, a more basic type of information-processing deficiency seems common and more disruptive of success. This deficit is the one that affects the auditory cognitive processes involved in learning to read—the ability to relate phonemes to graphemes in formation of words. We have emphasized the developmental significance of auditory functions in learning to read. Here we more specifically consider the relationship between auditory and visual language.

When the child learns to read he must be able to both visualize and auditorize words. Essentially, these two cognitive processes are accomplished simultaneously. Gates (1950) observed a long time ago that in the early stages of learning to read the child often moves his lips, saying the words to himself—sometimes even saying them aloud. He both "hears" and "sees" the words. A dyslexia can occur because of a disorder in either, or both, the "seeing" and "hearing" phases of the reading process; the visual dyslexic cannot cognitively visualize graphemes properly and the auditory dyslexic cannot cognitively auditorize them properly. The deficit is in ability to symbolize and code the read words. This deficiency in auditory processing is not a receptive aphasia because the disorder is in the auditorizaion of graphemes and does not involve comprehension of spoken language.

In an extensive investigation of the nature of learning disabilities in public school children we evaluated both visual and auditory cognitive functions in relation to successful learning (Myklebust, 1973a). One test measured ability to syllabicate. Syllabication requires that visual words be put into the auditory form, in the form necessary for pronunciation. Harris (1970) states, "A syllable is an uninterrupted unit of speech containing one vowel phoneme, forming either a whole word or a part of a word; also the grapheme or graphemes which represent the spoken syllable" (p. 336). The graphemes as they are identified visually must be associated with their respective phonemes, syllable by syllable, according to the sequence that forms the word. Perhaps, because this is a complex cognitive process and closely related to success in reading, the test of ability to syllabicate was the most powerful indicator of success in learning; 49 test scores were compared. Facility in relating the auditory characteristic of the word with the graphemic is a basic type of information processing and must be achieved if visual words are to be coded and attain meaning as words (Myklebust, 1973).

The psychology of reading increasingly requires clarification of the auditory processes necessary for learning to read. This trend assists us in recognizing that these deficits can be the basis of an *auditory dyslexia*. For example, Menyuk (1976), in studying the relations between acquisition of phonology and reading, found that speech perception and production did not follow identical order patterns, indicating that articulation was planned on the basis of syllable rather than smaller word segments. Her conclusion was that speech is not perceived as individual elements, grouped into syllables and then into words. Rather, the child analyzes speech into syllables and then identifies the phonemes that make up the syllable. In so doing, the focus of attention is on meaning. Moreover, in learning to read, the process is not one of simply transforming the auditory into the visual. Although such transformation is necessary, the process of doing so is complex, with each of the auditory and visual cognitive processes having differing qualities and its own rules.

Schilder (1944), too, concluded that dyslexia is a primary disturbance of the sound structure of the written word. Kinsbourne (1976) expands this observation by stating that the reading process has visual, auditory, and associative components. In evaluating deficits, he breaks reading into functions of form, orientation, and sequence, and the auditory functions into ability to repeat words, match phonemes to whole words, hold three phonemes in mind, and synthesize a three-letter word. In beginning reading he says the primary task is to decode visual symbols into their auditory-verbal referents, but he also stresses the role of attention and memory, differentiating these factors by stating that attention disorders are not processing disorders. By factor analysis he found the primary component to be auditory, followed by visual discrimination and visual recognition. In studying the effect of remediation, Kinsbourne found that improvement of auditory functions increased ability to read but improved visual functions did not.

Vogel (1972) approached the question of auditory cognition by investigating the syntactic abilities of normal and dyslexic children, her basic assumption being that syntactic ability was related to reading comprehension. Syntax was defined as comprising five factors: melody pattern, grammaticality, comprehension of syntax, sentence repetition and morphology. She found significant differences between the dyslexic and normal readers on three; the dyslexics were inferior on melody pattern, sentence repetition, and expressive syntax—all based on auditory functioning. These results are in agreement with results from our studies of written language (Myklebust, 1965, 1973). In a detailed analysis of syntactical abilities, the rules governing syntax derived from the auditory-spoken language form. Moreover, average normal use of syntax is not fully established until approximately 10 years of age, the identical age at which Satz and Sparrow (1970) reported language to be fully lateralized to the left brain hemisphere.

In a study of grapheme-phoneme learning (Marsh, Desberg, and Farwell, 1974), spoken words were more effective than pictures when used as stimuli for learning to read. They concluded that emphasis on the visual aspects of words was ill-advised and suggested that concentration be on increasing the availability of responses. In their conclusions they state, "Prereading children apparently have little difficulty in dealing with letters as stimuli but a great deal of difficulty in dealing with letter sounds as responses" (p. 115).

Auditory cognitive processes in learning to read are being elucidated. In most dyslexic children the primary disturbance seems to appear in these processes. The auditory language form, the most basic form, serves as a foundation for the visual-verbal form. It is exceedingly difficult to learn to read unless the auditory form has been acquired.

Visual Dyslexia

Both auditory and visual cognitive processes must show integrity if reading is to be achieved normally. That a given modality process can be deficient with another remaining intact is expressed by Hebb's (1963) semi-autonomous system concept, which affirms that a modality process, such as the auditory, is not identical to that of another modality, such as the visual. From this conceptual framework, for reading to be achieved, each of these modality cognitive processes and the intermodal processes must be functioning properly. Both modality systems, auditory and visual, might be intact but if a disruption in intermodal cognitive processee exists, reading is not achieved.

Learning to discriminate among letters is fundamental to learning to read (Gibson, 1965); only after so doing can graphemes be transformed into phonemes. The child must learn to recognize each letter by its differentiating characteristics: size, form, straight or curved lines, angle of slant, vertical or horizontal. This ability is necessary because it is at this level some children encounter difficulty; they cannot attain symbolic meaning because letters are not recognized as letters, so there is a visual dyslexia. This form differs from inner language dyslexia in that when the child achieves success in letter recognition (assuming he can transform to the auditory), he is not limited in attainment of meaning. However, the disturbance in letter recognition results in a dyslexia because it affects ability to symbolize, ability to visually code graphemes and form words.

Nevertheless, in assessing the visual processes necessary for learning to read, we go beyond ascertaining ability to recognize letter forms; in this respect Gibson's discussion seems limited. For example, Shankweiler and Liberman (1972) state, "The problems of the beginning reader appear to have more to do with synthesis of syllables than with scanning of larger chunks of connected text" (p. 298). They found that good and poor readers among young children did not differ in strategy or ability to scan but they did differ in ability to deal with individual words and syllables. They concluded that the primary problem of poor readers was at cognitive levels, beyond visual identification of letters.

Samuels (1976) studied the hierarchy of subskills comprising the reading acquisition process and analyzed the benefits of a wholistic versus a part approach. The subskills he identified are as follows: the reader must scan letters from left to right, the letters must be sounded, the letter sounds must be blended to form the word. Similarly, La Berge and Samuels (1974), in an investigation of automatic information processing in reading, found a hierarchy of sequence and progression from distinctive features to letters, letter clusters, and words. In an earlier study, Jeffrey and Samuels (1967) showed that specific training on letter-sound correspondences was superior to whole-word training. Shankweiler and Liberman (1972) reviewed the question of whether the primary problem in poor reading was at the word or context level; reading of connected text was as good and no better than reading individual words.

In agreement with our results for learning-disability children (Myklebust, Bannochie, and Killen, 1971), Guthrie (1973) found good readers had integrated the subskills. Reading ability evolved as one skill. In contrast, poor readers manifested the subskills as separate abilities; they were not integrated, forming one process. This is the highly significant manner in which the psychology of learning for dyslexic children varies widely from that of the normal. Perhaps this is the reason children with deficits in visual-verbal processing often are not identified as dyslexics, especially if auditory processing is intact. On screening or reading readiness tests, their scores might fall within normal limits because they perform well auditorially. But in analysis of test items, their visual abilities are not readily converted into the auditory. Thus, it is necessary to assess each modality process separately, and then to assess the extent to which each of the modality functions can be transformed into the equivalent of the other.

Much emphasis has been given to visual perception as a factor in learning disabilities, including presumed disturbances of visual perception in relation to childhood dyslexia. Fortunately, Vellutino, Steger, and Kandel (1972) studied this "perceptual deficit hypothesis" in reading disabilities. Their results do not support the presumption that visual perceptual disorders are causitive in reading failure. Rather, good and poor readers were equal in ability on visual perceptual tasks, both verbal and nonverbal. They concluded that "reading disability is best viewd as a cognitive rather than a perceptual disorder" (p. 116).

In another study, Vellutino, Smith, and Steger (1975) investigated the "visual perceptual deficit" hypothesis in relation to age. Their previous results were confirmed, with the conlcusion that "specific reading disability is not attributable to visual-spatial disorder" (p. 492). They further suggest a more appropriate rationale is that reading disabiliies occur because of a disorder in some aspect of verbal mediation.

In a third study, Vellutino, Bentley, De Setto, et al., (1977) presented words to the right and to the left visual fields of children in the second and sixth grades. Their results indicated that intrahemisphere deficits are a primary causitive factor in reading disabilities. They concluded that "reading disability in children at both early and later stages of skills development, is attributable to some form of verbal deficiency associated with left hemisphere dysfunction" (p.7).

Other investigators have obtained essentially identical results. For example, Morrison, Giordani, and Nagy (1977) compared reading-disability children on intactness of memory and perceptual processes. In contrast to the opinion that perceptual disorders are a primary cause of reading disorders, they found the quality and quantity of information received by poor readers did not differ from that received by good readers. They state that "reading disability involves some problem in the processing information in stages following initial perception, perhaps in encoding, organizational, or retrieval skills" (p. 79).

Because of the emphasis given to visual perception in relation to dyslexia and other types of learning disabilities, it is noteworthy that this level of information processing is not a significant factor in causing visual-verbal language disorders. According to our conceptual framework, as illustrated in Figure 1, perceptual processes are fundamental to all aspects of learning but they are mainly nonverbal. Children who have visual dyslexia usually can identify letters by name; often they write profusely but what they write is jargon and nonreadable. They are capable of discriminating the letters visually but cannot read them as meaningful words. Therefore, as is true in all dyxlexia, the deficit is in attainment of meaning, in encoding words on the page as words. In this sense visual dyslexia is a *visual-verbal agnosia*. Typically, this is not a disability in differentiating the visual components of words, although such a difficulty is present in some children, but in visualization of them for coding; even though the components are differentiated, they cannot be symbolized. This is a significant form of childhood dyslexia.

Intermodal Dyslexia

Learning to read requires more than facility in intraauditory and intravisual processes. In our studies of the impact of handicaps on cognition and learning, we adhere to the construct that there are three types of learning: intraneurosensory, interneurosensory, and integrative-neurosensory (Myklebust, Bannochie, and Killen, 1971). Thus far in our discussion we have considered inner-language dyslexia, a form that results from deficits at the level of integrative-neurosensory learning, and auditory and visual dyslexia which are sustained by disturbance at the intraneurosensory level of learning. When intraneurosensory language disorders occur, the assumption is that the deficit falls within a given modality process, the auditory or the visual. Hence, an auditory dyslexia can occur without a visual dyslexia, and vice versa.

Many children who have learning disabilities, including childhood dyslexia, are not deficient in intraneurosensory learning. Rather, they do not learn normally because of interneurosensory disorders. Both auditory and visual cognitive processes are achieved, but one cannot be transformed into the equivalent form of the other. Four types of cognitive functioning are necessary for success in learning to read: integrity of auditory processes, integrity of visual processes, integrity of the processes required for transmodal learning, and integrity of the processes required for integrative learning. Killen (1975) has presented an excellent discussion of this concept in relation to a learning systems approach to intervention.

Various investigators have given attention to the learning problems arising when interneurosensory deficits occur. Birch and Belmont (1965) reported evidence for failure in intermodal integration in poor readers. This study has been useful in several respects, although Gibson and Levin (1975) point out that these investigators did not demonstrate their subjects to be intact insofar as intraneurosensory processes were concerned; intermodal deficits can be ascertained only after intramodal processes are shown to function adequately.

Denny (1974) investigated the relationship of three cognitive style dimensions to elementary reading abilities and found that learning to read correlated with ability to visually process information and to encode responses into a verbal channel. Cross-modal development and reading also was studied by Bryant (1975), who has made a revealing statement concerning cross-modal and within-modal processing. After cautioning that to learn about cross-modal functions we first must determine the level of within-modal functions, he states, ''To be able to read one has to make some connection between visual and auditory information. The child must learn that written, and therefore visually presented, letters and words signify particular sounds which themselves are spoken letters, and words'' (p. 195).

In a slightly different context, Savin (1972) contends that the basic feature of learning to read initially is simply learning which letters of the alphabet correspond with which phonemes. However, this cross-modal process, as propounded by Gibson and Levin (1975), is not accomplished on a straightforward one-to-one, or matching basis because it assumes facility to identify and then follow various rules for each of the auditory and visual language forms. Gagné (1965) is one of the few educational psychologists who evolved a theoretical model incorporating this aspect of learning. He states that concept learning appears to be critically dependent on interneural processes of representation. Cross-modal learning also is dependent on such respresentational processes. For a visual word to be transformed into an auditory word, it must be symbolically coded. The same is true of an auditory word as it is being transduced into a visual word.

Advances in understanding biochemic and neuroelectric functions in the brain are extending knowledge of these processes, as shown by Schmitt, Dev, and Smith (1976). They report that ''Intraneuronal and interneuronal transport of various types of substances suggests that the biochemical and bioelectric parameters are functionally interwoven. Through such interactions neuronal local circuits, with their distinctive properties, may play a distinctive role in higher brain functions'' (p. 120).

Further evidence of cross-modal disturbances has been presented by Blank and Bridger (1967), who studied perceptual and conceptual abilities in retarded readers; symbolic mediation was a necessary condition for children to solve tasks temporally presented, regardless of the modality through which the information was received. Retarded readers not only had difficulty in cross-modal transfer but were limited in ability to apply verbal labels. Good and poor readers were equal on perceptual tasks but the poor readers were deficient in language involving abstract concepts. We came to similar conclusions when we studied use of abstraction by various types of handicapped children (Myklebust, 1965, 1973).

Zigmond (1966) compared dyslexic and normal children on intraneurosensory and interneurosensory learning by using the paired associates paradigm; dyslexics were inferior on nine out of nine intrasensory auditory tasks and on one out of four intrasensory visual tasks, implying a hierarchy of the neuro-cognitive processes required for learning to read. The most basic process was auditory, involving intraneurosensory operations. The second most basic process was transformation of auditory information into visual equivalents. The third most basic process was transformation of visual information into auditory equivalents. The last step, according to Zigmond's results, was processing information from visual to visual, another form of intraneurosensory functioning. These results support the theoretical model proposed in this discussion. In learning to read, the child first must have integrity of intraauditory processes, then integrity of intermodal functions, and finally integrity of intravisual processes.

In a similar study, Duff (1968) obtained results showing basically the same hierarchy. Using a different paradigm, she showed auditory-to-auditory processing to be the primary deficit factor in failure to learn normally. The second most critical factor was ability to transduce from the auditory to the visual. However, in comparison with Zigmond's findings, Duff's results were reversed for the two final steps: visual-to-visual and visual-to-auditory.

Although there was moderate disagreement between the results of these studies, they are remarkably consistent; intraauditory processes serve as the fundamental basis for learning to read. But, developmentally visual processes in relation to the auditory must become operational at an early stage. Next is being able to decode the auditory into visual equivalents. From the results of Zigmond, which seem supportive of other investigations (e.g., Bryant, 1975), after the auditory and decoding from the auditory to visual have been established, the task is to learn to reverse this process and decode from the visual to the auditory. Finally, to achieve the highest level of reading, the child must process the graphemes only visually; he must learn to read by processing on a visual-to-visual basis. He must be able to read with only occasional interaction with auditory processes. In the early stages of learning to read there is in essence total dependence on transducing graphemes into their equivalent spoken forms. But gradually the successful reader is less and less dependent on the auditory. Although never achieved with perfection, he is able to bypass the auditory and read by only visual processes.

The nature of the brain dysfunction resulting in a *cross-modal dyslexia* also is being investigated by neuroscientists (e.g., Jonas, 1978; Petrides and Iversen, 1976). Petrides and Iversen (1976) studied cross-modal learning in monkeys by making selective lesions in the prefrontal system and tested them on tactile-visual cross-modal learning. With lesions in the banks and depths of the arcuate sulcus, there was impairment of visual-tactile crossmodal learning. Although these neuro-cognitive systems responsible for interneurosensory information processing have not been clarified in detail, data are forthcoming. Geschwind (1972) has provided many insights into the neurology of these functions, and John, et al. (1977) have demonstrated the significance of neurometric information.

Intermodal disturbances seem characteristic of many children with disorders of read language (Myklebust, 1973). Those in whom the deficits are principally due to auditory involvements are designated as *auditory-intermodal dyslexia*. The analagous form, in which the principle involvements are visual, is designated as *visual intermodal dyslexia*. These are subtypes of auditory and visual dyslexia. The dyslexia occurs because of disturbances in cross-modal processing, not because of deficits in within-modal processes. This distinction is necessary, clinically and scientifically. Only when we recognize these various forms of childhood dyslexia can we provide suitable intervention programs.

DYSLEXIA AND HEMISPHERE SPECIALIZATION

During the past decade specialization by hemisphere, with many clarifications, as it relates to cognition and learning has been demonstrated. Each of the hemispheres carries differing responsibilities—the right having the major role in processing nonverbal information and the left having the major role in processing verbal information (Galaburda, LeMay, Kemper, et al., 1978). In childhood dyslexia we must concern ourselves not only with intra- and intermodality functions, but also with intra- and interhemispheric functions. In our discussion of cross-modal processes we observed that the most basic level of cognition in learning to read is auditory-to-auditory processing. However, much of what we understand as meaning is processed mainly on the right hemisphere. Processing of verbal information can be executed at a high level without attainment of meaning, such as in echolalia and word-calling. The vast amount of experience that occurs without verbalization, but is highly meaningful, must be integrated with language. It is through interaction of verbal and nonverbal units of experience that human behavior and knowledge become unique. Some learning-disability children are severely handicapped, not by the verbal limitations from dysfunctions on the left hemisphere but by nonverbal disorders from dysfunctions on the right hemisphere. This type of learning disability often entails disturbances in learning to tell time, learning directions, and understanding the actions of other people—social perception (Myklebust, 1975).

In study of childhood dyslexia we cannot overlook the impact of disturbances in hemispheric lateralization. It has been suggested that such "cerebral dominance" can disturb abilities concerned with learning to read by becoming fixed too early, as well as by other deviations such as not being established adequately (Kinsbourne, 1975). So, although normal language usage assumes intactness of both hemispheres, with normal communication between them, most children with language disorders manifest dysfunctions on the left hemisphere—the hemisphere most responsible for acquisition of language: spoken, read, and written.

But other factors should be considered. For example, differences by sex in the extent and nature of lateralization by hemisphere have been investigated. Wada, Clark, and Hamm (1975) showed that females consistently showed a smaller degree of anatomic asymmetry in comparison with males. Levy and Reid (1976) found that dextrals used an inverted hand-finger posture while writing, in contrast with sinistrals. They state, "The two traditional measures, handedness and sex, supplemented by our new measure of hand position, allow very simple, rapid, and reliable prediction of hemisphere specialization and lateralization" (p. 339).

Bakker (1973), in his investigation of hemispheric specialization in connection with learning to read, concluded that this relationship was stage-dependent. Early reading seemed to be hampered by dominance, but fluent reading seemed to profit from it. The question of cortical plasticity has been raised by a number of researchers. Such plasticity seems to influence learning, particularly consequent to damage or in circumstances where undue rigidity occurs. Using kittens in their research, Kasamatsu and Pettigrew (1976) concluded that "catecholamine neurohormones may play a major role in maintenance of cortical plasticity" (p. 208) but they did not determine which of the catecholamines, dopamine or norepinephrine, was of greatest effect.

The different functions by hemisphere was a primary focus of a study by Witelson (1976). When the left hemisphere does not provide specialization for language learning but becomes functional for spatial learning, similar to the right hemisphere, learning to read is impeded. In her opinion this dysfunction suggests a neural deficit rather than a maturational lag. Results in support of Witelson's findings have been presented by Levin, Divine-Hawkins, Kerst, et al. (1974). Children low on imagery learning did not profit from instruction on imagery cognitive strategy, but those high on imagery showed gains. Presumably, those high on imagery had right-hemisphere lateralization, having no conflict with the verbal-cognitive processing on the left hemisphere.

A computerized approach, using cortically evoked potentials, has proved advantageous in study of many types of impositions on learning (Thatcher and John, 1977; John, 1977). Using this approach, Connors (1970) performed an ingenious investigation on an entire family, most of whom were dyslexic. There was a close relationship between the dyslexia and the evoked potentials; similar results appeared for other types of learning disabilities. Preston, Guthrie, and Childs (1974) also compared visual evoked potentials for normal and disabled readers. The reading disabled manifested a significantly smaller amplitude eminating from the area of the angular gyrus. Their findings support a neurogenetic construct of reading disability.

Other investigations of the interaction of brain and cognitive processes have been made. Robbins and McAdam (1974) assessed the variations of alpha activity when tasks involved verbal or nonverbal cognitive processes; they referred to it as interhemispheric alpha asymmetry and imagery role. Their findings revealed that alpha activity varies on the basis of the type of information being processed. When the task required recall and processing of verbal material, alpha was reduced on the left hemisphere. In contrast, when the task required imagery in spatial, nonverbal terms, alpha was suppressed on the right hemisphere.

From many sources and a variety of disciplines, we know that learning to read requires intactness of function in the cerebral cortex. As Kinsbourne (1975) has stated so well, the two cerebral hemispheres subserve different cognitive operations. Moreover, there is specialization within each of these hemispheres to serve specific cognitive processes, as suggested by Hécaen (1969). In childhood dyslexia, therefore, the task is to determine whether anomalies in the distribution of these systems in the brain might be responsible for dyslexia. Only when all of these factors are considered can children be given the treatment and remediation required and be benefitted to the greatest extent possible.

MEMORY PROCESSES

Memory processes are a determining factor in learning, as emphasized by experimental psychologists for many years (e.g., Underwood, 1969; Luria, 1976). A comparable emphasis has not been shown by educational psychologists. More recently, through the efforts of information-processing psychologists, the critical role of memory is being elucidated (Rumelhart, 1977).

In discussion of meaning we suggested that storage and retrieval of information is dependent upon coding, and that coding occurs on the basis of the meaning attached to the information received—on the basis of whether the word *rock* refers to a stone or a type of music. According to Rumelhart (1977),

> Linguistic inputs are designed to fit into a general framework and are dependent upon that framework to make sense. We are beginning to find evidence on the nature of the processes that help us tie into previous knowledge. This is a growing area of psychology—new results are generated nearly everyday. These areas, hardly touched upon by psychologists a mere ten years ago are just now beginning to take shape. (p. 169)

The implication is that to be meaningful, information must be related to a framework of knowledge and that acquisition of knowledge is dependent upon memory. This being the case, it should not be unexpected that memory deficits have a substantial impact on learning to read.

Short-Term Memory

In study of memory, it is helpful to distinguish between *short-term memory* and *long-term memory*. In childhood dyslexia, it seems that deficiencies in short-term memory are of immediate consequence, but as shown by Guilford (1967), a distinction also must be made between storage and retrieval processes. He states, "The distinction between memory abilities and production abilities means that retention and retrieval of information are distinctly different operations" (p. 136). One ability might function normally and the other be deficient, as seen clinically in some children who are unable to store facets of the read word and others are unable to retrieve them. Perhaps there is a dyslexia that results from deficits in the cognitive processes responsible for storage, and another that results from a disturbance of the processes responsible for retrieval. Analagous are forms of aphasia that many years ago were noted to result from memory disorders, such as dysnomia, formulation aphasia, and semantic or syntactical aphasia (e.g., Wepman and Jones, 1964; Travis, 1971). It is apparent that there are similar disorders involving language in the read form but they remain difficult to define and to identify.

The question of memory disorders and learning to read concerns the exact nature of short-term memory, especially in relation to the exact role of auditory cognitive processes. Some researchers (Conrad, 1962, 1964) conclude that short-term memory is only auditory, and that it is at this level that visual language is transformed into the auditory form. But Rumelhart (1977) has a broader perspective. He states,

> We have found evidence that primary memory activations are at least partly "sensory" in nature. This follows from the specifically visual and specifically auditory interference observed. However, they are not just "copies" of the original input. In memory span experiments we find evidence implicating *auditory* coding of visually presented information. Moreover, these activations are not even unimodal representations of some input stimulus, but rather they appear to be multimodal and contain at least visual, auditory, and abstract (name) attributes as well. (p. 186).

Rumelhart observes further that we can generate activations from memory specific to either visual or auditory modalities. Also, the longer information is held in short-term memory, the stronger the possibility that it will be stored in long-term memory. There are other considerations. To code information that does not coincide with what we anticipate is arduous. Likewise, we do not remember information well unless it is consonant with experience already stored. The nature of learning, therefore, is that enhancement ensues when we receive what we expect, when understanding embodies what has been experienced previously, and when remembering embraces what we already know.

LaBerge (1972), who focused attention on how we learn to read, says that both the auditory and visual codes make contact with comprehension processes; he suggests that we use the phonological code only as needed. Crowder (1972), on the other hand, states that in short-term memory auditory components exceed the visual: "Visual memory for language items is an extra, derivative process feeding directly into a storage system that is designed for audition" (p. 270). Conrad's (1972) observations also are striking. He describes the relationship between the spoken and read language forms as, "This evidence tells us that normal adults, using vision to take in verbal information, go to what appears to be considerable neurological bother to recode out of the input state" (p. 216).

As vital as memory processes are in learning to read, their exact role remains to be further clarified. But the importance of auditory functions in short-term memory has been demonstrated. Mattingly (1972) views reading as a language based on skill, not as a primary linguistic activity analogous to listening. Though the auditory is the most fundamental symbol system, he says the reader does not use all of the phonological cues, but relies also on others. This seems in agreement with the model we have evolved, which suggests that fluent readers might read visually, at least for brief moments. Because of their fluency they bypass the auditory system, especially when reading simple materials.

In a rather different vein, Calfee (1975) studied memory relative to cognitive skills in learning to read and observed that uncodable visual images fade from memory within less than a second, and that the way information is processed and stored is a principle determinant of subsequent performance. He suggests that acquisition of decoding skills is a major concern in beginning reading instruction; learning to read acquires ability to select, translate, store, organize, and retrieve information, and these processes make major demands on memory. In a revealing comment Calfee states, "You can't remember what you didn't process" (p. 77).

Gradually, the role of biochemical factors in memory also is being clarified, as shown by Drachman (1977). In work concerning the cholinergic brain neurons, he describes the pattern of cognitive deficits produced by cholinergic blockade as closely resembling the memory deficits associated with advancing age. His findings support the position that the cholinergic system is allied with memory and other cognitive functions.

The specific connection between short-term memory and childhood dyslexia remains a troublesome issue. That deficits at this level disturb facility in learning to read no longer can be questioned. The issue is whether these deficits are symbolic in nature. By definition, if they are not—if they do not affect verbal-symbolic processes—they are not a dyslexia. According to Calfee (1975), information must be coded, hence symbolized, if it is to be remembered. Of consequence too is the extent to which short-term memory is auditory—the extent to which it might also be capable of visual storage.

For several years a major focus of our research was the manner in which profound deafness in early life altered cognitive processes (Myklebust, 1964). In deaf children there can be no short-term auditory memory so our goal was to explore the ways in which their memory processes might be altered. In comparison with the normal, deaf children are superior on certain memory abilities and inferior on others; they are superior to the hearing on memory for designs and on memory for movement patterns. They are inferior on memory for digits presented visually (Frisina, 1955; Blair, 1957; Costello, 1957; Fuller, 1959). When the task can be remembered by use of imagery alone, the deaf are unusually competent, perhaps because this is the type of cognitive functioning on which they are mostly dependent. But when the task requires symbolic abilities, such as memory for digits, they are inferior.

Short-term memory, indeed, can be visual in nature; as a function it is not limited to storage of auditory information. Moreover, it can process either nonverbal or verbal information, depending upon the needs of the organism. But this begs the question of whether deficits in short-term memory alter ability to learn to read in such a way that it must be designated a dyslexia. This decision must await further investigation. Dyslexic children often manifest poor short-term memory, sometimes being unable to remember the first parts of a sentence while reading the last. Conceivably this is a deficit in remembering verbal symbols; nonverbal memory usually is not deficient. However, memory disorders should be differentiated from visual and auditory dyslexia because the break in information processing involves storing the coded symbol, not the level of coding itself. Although the read word is coded and meaning is attained momentarily, the words are not remembered. When the child reads the sentence again, it is as though he is reading it for the first time. This is a serious type of reading disability.

Retrieval

Most research on cognition as it pertains to learning to read has been limited to encoding, to learning how to break the code. Our knowledge virtually is limited to input, to receptive processes. This is unfortunate because much can be learned from study and analysis of output, the expressive processes. Success in use of read language can be appraised by having the child write and by having him express himself through the spoken word. In either case, he must retrieve information gained from what he has read. To be able to recall what has been learned is a paramount feature in all learning. In dyslexic children one often finds a disorder described by experimental psychologists as "recognition without recall." The child knows what it is that he wants to recall and recognizes it when the teacher says it for him, but is unable to recall it. This is analogous to *formulation aphasia* in spoken language. In reading, however, this deficiency in retrieval pertains to what has been read, not to what has been spoken; it can involve either the auditory or visual aspects of graphemes.

Again we encounter the question of whether this is a dyslexia. As a disturbance of ability to retrieve information, this deficit is at the level of processing read language after it has been meaningfully coded and stored. It is not at the level of inner-language processing, nor of visual or auditory coding. The disorder is in processing verbal information after these levels have been achieved. Because the information cannot be processed for expressive purposes, it is not available for use in everyday life. Because the dysfunction embodies words, as in the comparable disorder in aphasia, we view it as a symbolic disturbance, and therefore a form of dyslexia. Like other output, or expressive language deficits, this language disorder usually is less debilitating than receptive disorders.

WRITTEN LANGUAGE AND CHILDHOOD DYSLEXIA

In reviewing literature in the fields of reading and reading disabilities, one becomes aware of an unusual phenomenon: learning to read has been viewed almost exclusively as a receptive process. Presumably, this is because reading has not been conceptualized as a facet of acquiring a language form, the visual-verbal system. Written language, the expressive facet of the visual-verbal system, has been minimized. Our conceptual framework includes both the receptive and expressive components of this, the last language form acquired by man.

One wonders why specialists in reading have not embraced the expressive aspect of read language, as has been done by speech pathologists for decades when analyzing spoken language; receptive and expressive disorders are compared. To better understand reading and reading disabilities, it is essential that we study it according to three states, or levels: the receptive, integrative, and expressive. It was from this perspective that we initiated our studies of written language, including development and standardization of the Picture Story Language Test, a developmental test of facility in use of the written word (Myklebust, 1965, 1973). In addition to cross-cultural studies, our research populations have encompassed the socially emotionally disturbed, mentally retarded, deaf, speech handicapped, reading disability, and dyslexic, as well as normal children.

Reading: Input and Output

The concept of incorporating the written form of the visual-verbal system when studying reading processes stresses that if there is no input, there is no output. If the spoken word is not received, there is no spoken language. Likewise, if the read word is not received, there is no written language. If the child cannot read, he cannot write— except in an "echolalic" manner without meaning. (Previously we considered the circumstances in which there is input and output without meaning.) From studies of a large number of children, we found that most of them who have little, or no, facility with the written word are so limited because they have little, or no, ability to read. Usually children are referred to language disorder clinics with the observation that they cannot read or write. Routinely, evaluation of these children reveals that they cannot read, *therefore* they cannot write.

A serious limitation of constructs of childhood dyslexia is that they omit written language. This expressive process provides information crucial to understanding success in receiving and coding the read word. If information is garbled, either in reception or integration, it will be expressed in garbled form. The psychologist, educator, and others can gain vital information by comparing the written language of handicapped children with the developmental patterns from normal children, who acquire this language form in an orderly, developmental manner. For example, one of our measures (number of words written per sentence) shows exceptional linearity with chronological age. Moreover, age by age, the words per sentence score has not changed in more than 50 years (Myklebust, 1965); it is an unusually stable indicator and shows wide variations from normal by dyslexic children, as well as by other handicapped children. It was the characteristic error patterns, seen in the written language of dyslexic children, which first revealed to us that some of them were deficient primarily in visual reading processes and some in auditory reading processes.

There are also theoretical reasons for studying the written form relative to childhood dyslexia. As shown by Figure 1, it is written language that represents man's highest level of verbal attainment. Grammatologists and alphabetologists have shown that writing has a short history, evolving after use of pictographic and ideographic writing. These scripts were forerunners of the alphabet. Taylor (1883) observed that "To invent and bring to perfection the score or so of handy symbols which we call the alphabet, has proved to be the most arduous enterprise of which the human intellect has ever been engaged" (p. 4).

In evolving the alphabet, the intention was for each letter to depict a single spoken sound. Diringer (1962) highlights the importance of this fact when he states,

> Enormous advantages implicit in using letters to represent single sounds are obvious . . . with its 22, 24, or 26 signs, the alphabet is the most flexible and useful method of writing ever invented, and, from its origin in the Near East, has become the nearly universal basis for the scripts employed by civilized peoples, passing from language to language with a minimum of difficulty. No other form of writing has had so extensive, so intricate and so interesting a history. (p. 24)

Written language originated by evolving "signs" to represent speech sounds; a visual form was developed to represent the auditory. Gelb (1963) quotes Aristotle as having said, "Spoken words are symbols of mental experience and written words are the symbols of spoken words" (p. 13). Through studies of the phylogeny of written language, and because of a growing knowledge of its ontogeny, it seems extraordinary that it has not been investigated more intensively in connection with all reading disabilities, particularly childhood dyslexia.

Visual language comprises three primary cognitive functions—reception, coding, and expression—in addition to storing and retrieving. When receptive symbolic processes were found to be disturbed, historically the condition was designated as dyslexia. When expressive, visual-verbal processes were disturbed, the condition was designated as *dysgraphia*. In contrast to auditory language, in dyslexia different terminology was used to designate input and output disorders. This has led to confusion because dysgraphia, like expressive aphasia, is an apraxia and refers only to this symbolic-motor deficiency in writing. But there are a wide variety of deficiencies which can be detected by analysis of the written word; so, clearly, to more fully understand childhood dyslexia, we must evaluate the written language form. In the future, perhaps we will specify the involvements of childhood dyslexia in a manner equivalent to the disorders of spoken language. Then reading disabilities would be assessed in terms of *receptive dyslexia, central, or inner-language dyslexia,* and *expressive dyslexia.* Understanding the reading process and its disorders requires more than study of the receptive phase. Reading is much more than just input.

WRITING OF DYSLEXICS

The written language of dyslexic children shows many variations from normal. A major difference, as determined by the Picture Story Language Test (Myklebust, 1965) was in Productivity, the amount of language given in response to the test situation. These children were deficient in Total Words, Total Sentences, and Words per Sentence. Another difference was in use of Syntax. Normal children achieved their highest level of usage by 11 years of age; the dyslexics did not achieve this level until 15 years of age.

Factor analysis revealed a significant variation relative to cognition. For normal children, the predominant factor in use of written language was Productivity and Abstraction—the ability to abstractly express meanings. The dyslexics were not inferior in use of abstraction but were deficient in Productivity—the predominant factors were altered. This alteration of cognitive processes recurs over and over again for learning-disability children (Myklebust, 1968, 1971, 1975). The written language of dyslexic children is no exception and indicates the effect of this neurocognitive disability. The psychology by which dyslexic children learn to read varies from normal.

To attain success in learning to read, auditory and visual-verbal processes must operate with a high degree of reciprocity. If one or the other is disturbed, the one not deficient becomes the primary avenue through which information is processed. In auditory dyslexia the inability is in coding auditory information so that it can be converted into its visual equivalents. In visual dyslexia the deficit in information processing is reversed; the inability is in coding visual information into its auditory equivalent. The overall debilitative effect of these two types of dyslexia, however, is different. The visual type is less disturbing, less disintegrating behaviorally. When the most basic language, the auditory, is altered the child is more confused, more deficient in social maturity. Nevertheless, caution must be used when making clinical deductions. At present, due to lack of knowledge, we identify only the most severe dyslexic children. We are unable to diagnosis, to identify all degrees of this language disorder—mild, moderate, or severe. Rarely do we recognize those with mild or moderate degrees of dyslexia, although the impact of even minor deficits can be highly significant, particularly when combined with an emotional disturbance or other handicaps.

The child with visual dyslexia must use his best remaining cognitive modality, so he auditorizes words to a remarkable extent; he cannot use the visual and auditory cognitive processes reciprocally so he gains his success through the auditory information-processing system. As a result he writes words phonetically, as illustrated by a story written by a 10-year-old boy (see below). The words most difficult for him are processed auditorially to match the way the word is heard, not the way it looks. His writing is characterized by phonetization because even though he processes graphemes, he does so auditorially. His visual processing is limited to letters that can be auditorized.

Previously we observed that the writing of visual dyslexics usually is readable, as it is in the case of this 10-year-old boy. The writing of a severely involved auditory dyslexic usually is not readable because he produces a meaningless compilation of letters with no conversion to the auditory. There is little resemblance to words.

STORY WRITTEN BY A VISUAL DYSLEXIC

The boy is plaing with the Doll pepel
The BaBe is ribing on a gogo cart
The Boy is plaing with the Dog
The man is gowing to the tabl
The grill is at the tabll
The tabil is set.

To illustrate the writing of an auditory dyslexic, we present a brief review of a boy, 16 years of age (for further details see Myklebust, 1968, 1971, 1975). Although of average mental ability, he was unable to read. He was asked to write words from dictation. For the word table, he wrote *taivl*; for paper he wrote *pator*; for book he wrote *Bokk*; and for woman he wrote *worm*. To further assess his cognitive processes, we dictated these words again, but each of the words was spelled aloud, dictated letter by letter while the boy wrote them, without error.

The diagnostic information elicited by this procedure is essential for ascertaining the type of dyslexia present. The examiner provided only one type of information, the auditory, in the form of the names of the letters needed to correctly spell each word. When provided with this information alone, he produced the visual, written equivalent. His deficit was not in ability to write, he had no dysgraphia. He knew what the letters looked like and wrote them correctly when given their names auditorially; when given only the auditory equivalent, he performed the task perfectly. His cognitive disorder precluded coding the auditory word into its visual form, so he could not symbolize words as seen. There are many children who have this form of dyslexia, albeit often it is not properly diagnosed until adolescence, or even after reaching adulthood.

Spelling Disorders

Spelling disorders are common in dyslexia (Boder, 1971, 1973), but occur also for other reasons. Certain cognitive disturbances cause poor spelling without either aphasia or dyslexia. We worked with a bright boy, 12 years of age, above average in spoken, read, and written language but unable to spell words of more than one or two syllables when dictated in the usual manner. When the words were dictated one syllable at a time, he spelled them correctly. This boy's spelling disability is a dramatic illustration of the importance of analyzing each child's deficiency so that the designation, childhood dyslexia, is not applied promiscuously. He had no dyslexia or any other form of reading disability; he had a serious learning disability. The fact that he had excellent facility in use of all language forms but could not spell is of unusual interest in terms of brain function and information processing.

Spelling, in the written form, necessitates simultaneous visualization and auditorization, if not of each letter, at least syllable by syllable; either of these cognitive processes, visualizing and auditorizing, might cause a spelling disability. The boy in question could retain and retrieve syllables visually but not auditorially; he had a deficiency in auditorially retaining each syllable sequentially, so that he could write the word. When the teacher dictated the word syllable by syllable, when she did the retrieving and serial ordering for him, he spelled correctly. The reason this condition does not affect ability to read is that it does not involve receiving and coding words. He had no difficulty with verbal symbolization; he was not a dyslexic. The deficit was in short-term memory. He could not auditorially retain more than two syllables at a time. When words were comprised of more than two syllables, he was unable to sequentialize and retain them. Children having this type of spelling disorder are in serious need of better understanding and more appropriate remediation. But they should not be confused with dyslexics. Gibson and Levin (1975) suggest that "The syllable is a good unit and facilitates transcription better than the high sequential probability of single letters succeeding one another" (p.312).

THE SCIENCE OF DYSLEXIOLOGY

Learning to Read

The study of childhood dyslexia has added to knowledge of brain function and to the psychology of reading. A major implication of these investigations is that, in learning, information is processed in a structured, coherent manner. The brain is programmed to process information on the basis of hierarchies and according to the sequential relationships among the types of information being received, integrated, and expressed.

Because of the prestructured hierarchies serving as the basis for processing information, inferences can be drawn as to the most effective methods for teaching reading. In beginning reading, there is little rationale for the "Look and See" approach. Rather, the method corresponding most closely to the ways in which information is processed neurocognitively is "Hear, Look, and Say." The child converts the word he has heard into the word he sees and then says it. Essentially, this is the way the normal child processes words on the page as he learns to read, irrespective of the theory an educator may have in mind.

This auditory framework for reading remains throughout our lifetime. No one completely overcomes "reverting" to the auditory, to auditorization. When we encounter difficult words or passages, we auditorize them—sometimes even aloud to gain meaning—and then go on with what we are reading. Also, frequently we auditorize when sequences and retention are important; we say telephone numbers to ourselves to remember them while dialing. The unsophisticated reader, even when an adult, continues to move his lips while reading, as the child does when first learning to read.

To some degree, highly fluent readers read visually, without auditorizing. They do so because they gain meaning without, or with little, need to convert to the auditory; neurocognitively they have acquired ability to bypass auditory processes. They read by using visual-verbal information processes alone. If they auditorize, they do so rarely and with great rapidity. Such information processing serves as the key for speedreading with comprehension; the more one is successful in reading by visual cognitive processes alone, the faster one reads. Although silent reading is variously defined, to read mainly, if not exclusively, by visual-verbal processing alone may be the only true form of "reading silently." Most readers when attempting to gain speed find that there is a point of diminishing returns because often intermittent transducing to the auditory enhances both meaning and retention.

AN INTERDISCIPLINARY SCIENCE

The conceptual framework expressed in this chapter remains to be further validated. Although many scientific investigations have been achieved, one would not contend that a science of dyslexiology has been developed; rather, that such a science is developing. The importance of this undertaking cannot be overemphasized. Reading, as a characteristic, is highly prized in virtually all cultures. Nevertheless, throughout the United States there is increasing concern at all levels of education about poor reading achievement. Illiteracy remains a dire and somewhat embarrassing situation. We do not assume that increased attention to childhood dyslexia would in itself have a major impact on erradication of poor reading levels and illiteracy.

However, as the science of dyslexiology expands, it will have influence far beyond the needs of dyslexic children. Through such a science all issues related to reading will be elucidated. The scientific data and rationales concerning how any child learns to read will be useful and applicable to normal children, to deaf, blind, mentally retarded, to those with reading disabilities as well as to dyslexics. But, interdisciplinary cooperative effort in diagnosis and treatment of dyslexic children is a necessity, as recognized by many professional groups and individuals. These problems are complex, encompassing brain function, learning, cognitive psychology, and pedagogy. It is beyond the scope of this discussion to outline the role of each discipline but brief mention is made of the participation by some that are essential to the science of dyslexiology.

Usually the first professional person to be consulted is the *pediatrician*. It is most important that he not only keep close scrutiny of the child's health but that he recognize that the youngster might have a dyslexia. This initial contact with someone who can advise and recommend ensuing steps is of great help. Often, it can prevent months, if not years, of frustration and conflict for the child and his parents. Vuckovich (1968) has outlined procedures for the pediatric neurologist that have proved beneficial in examination of learning-disability children. In using these procedures and coding the results for computer analysis, we did not find a characteristic syndrome for these children in comparison with the normal (Myklebust, 1973). But, for some, health considerations were of urgent concern.

If dyslexia is suspected, examination and treatment by a *neurologist* usually is of primary value (e.g., Duane, 1977). Although dyslexia is not a disease, associated conditions can be significant in the child's health and well-being. Some have disturbed sleep patterns, are unduly active, and need medication for seizure involvements, irrespective of whether clinical epilepsy is present. However, the chief complaint for most dyslexic children is academic failure. But even in this connection, medication sometimes can foster more effective learning. Gabrys (1977), in a study of boys 6 through 12 years of age, found that methylphenidate caused memory and attention to improve; the measures used were digit-span and coding scores. Connors (1970) also has shown that learning improves through use of stimulant drugs. Medication as a means of enhancing learning in children with brain dysfunctions is being investigated by medical scientists and holds promise for the future (Swanson and Kinsbourne, 1976).

Electroencephalography often reveals disturbances in the electrical output of the brain in dyslexic children (Hughes, 1968, 1971; Connors, 1970; Preston, Guthrie, and Childs, 1974). The clinical electroencephalographist can make a significant contribution to differential diagnosis of childhood dyslexia. Computerized EEG, as used when studying evoked potentials, represents a major advance. Diagnosis has been improved and vital theoretical questions have been clarified, as illustrated by John, Karmel, Corning, et al (1977) in showing that arithmetical cognitive processes seem to be a major responsibility for the right brain hemisphere. Other evidence is being obtained which clarifies cognitive specialization by hemisphere. Disturbances of hemisphere lateralization seem common in dyslexic children. Determination of these disturbances often distinguishes them from children with other types of reading disability and further illuminates the neurogenicity of childhood dyslexia.

When a child fails to learn to read, not uncommonly it is assumed that vision is at fault. An *ophthalmological* examination is advisable because normality of vision should be established. Nevertheless, visual defects are no more common in learning-disability children than in an average population of normal children (Myklebust, 1973). Dyer (1977) suggests that "physicians should realize, however, that ophthalmologic defects are only rarely found to be the cause of learning disabilities. And once correction of any overt defect is made, the pursuit of 'visual training' is fruitless" (p. 52).

Few studies have been made of the emotional characteristics of dyslexic children. An exception is the one by Connolly (1971), who studied a carefully selected population of dyslexic school children using the Rorschach Psychodiagnostic, Rosenzweig Picture-Frustration, and the Human Figure Drawing tests. The results provided no evidence for a "dyslexic personality." The dyslexic children, however, showed emotional immaturity and impulsivity, especially when confronted with emotionally-laden situations.

That *psychiatric* disturbances sometimes are associated with reading disabilities has been observed by several clinicians in child psychiatry. Eisenberg (1975) states that there are at least two indications that psychiatric intervention is needed: impairment of personal development and emotional disturbance that impedes positive responses to remedial instruction.

Berger Yule, and Rutter (1975) found that psychiatric disturbances occurred about three times more frequently in children with specific reading retardation, in both rural and urban populations in England. The predominant disturbance was antisocial behavior, followed by neurotic patterns. As emphasized by Eisenberg (1977), psychotherapy alone usually does not correct dyslexia. However, it can be a critical step in assisting some dyslexic children by making it possible for them to be more effective learners. Psychiatry has a major role, not only in helping those who are dyslexic but in determining the extent to which emotional factors are influential in the total learning deficit. Family counseling also might be required, an aspect to which the geneticist can make a significant contribution (Hallgren, 1950.

Psychology has a major responsibility for dyslexic children, covering diagnostic, theoretical, and remedial aspects. This responsibility is shared by the specializations of clinical child psychology, neuropsychology, pediatric, educational, and cognitive psychology, as well as psycholinguistics. The psychology of learning for dyslexic and other learning-disability children varies from the normal. Perhaps the most serious, and most common, variations are disturbances of intermodal and integrative learning. Psychology must develop a conceptual framework that distinguishes these cognitive disturbances from normal; this is the basis for understanding the learning processes that result in dyslexia. Theoretical models would enhance development of methodologies for educational remediation, as well as for diagnostic and psychotherapeutic procedures.

Diagnosis of childhood dyslexia is not dependent on direct elicitation of organic manifestations of brain dysfunciton. Although assumed, these dysfunctions might be manifested only indirectly—through disturbed processes of cognition. Examination of cognitive abilities is the primary responsibility of the psychologist. Using psychological techniques he must determine the intactness of these processes verbally and nonverbally. He must ascertain the modality systems through which the child learns most effectively, and the success with which one type of information is being converted into the equivalent of another. The level of function must be determined for auditory-to-auditory, visual-to-visual, auditory-to-visual, visual-to-auditory, as well as for processes involved in attainment of meaning. Moreover, examination of ability to symbolize, verbally and nonverbally, is critical, with special emphasis on ability to symbolize read leanguage. Also, this examination should ascertain the intactness of storage and retrieval processes. Only such studies can reveal the presence of childhood dyslexia.

On the basis of his findings, the psychologist is obligated to assist special educators in outlining a program for fostering the child's learning to read. Unfortunately, often the teacher is alone, left to her own resources, at this critical juncture in meeting the needs of dyslexic children.

Language pathology is an area of professional specialization which includes study of cognitive processes in relation to all forms of language disorders: spoken, read, and written. These functions are investigated according to inner, receptive, and expressive processes. A major role of the language pathologist is assessment of auditory language and the extent to which deficiencies in this language form are related to disabilities in reading (McGrady, 1964, 1968; Zigmond, 1966; Duff, 1968). Moreover, this specialist carries responsibility for program planning, often serving as the principle language therapist.

The *special education* services most necessary relative to childhood dyslexia are usually performed by speech and language pathologists, teachers of learning disabilities and remedial reading, and counselors. However, unfortunately sometimes none of these special educators have advanced training in dyslexia, perhaps because there is an extreme limitation of the necessary graduate courses offered by universities and colleges. Although many do offer specialized degrees in reading disabilities, rarely do these programs include the area of dyslexia.

Dyslexic children require specialized curricula and flexibility within their school program if they are not to sustain difficulties in adjustment as a result of continuous failure. Wood (1976) outlines steps to be followed if dyslexic children are to be successful in learning to read. Vernon (1971) stresses the role of reading readiness, its correlation with intelligence, and the importance of social and emotional needs. Nonverbal functions must be included, as shown by Denburg (1977), who found that pictures provide cues that enhance learning. She states, "Pictures were introduced, not to supplant print, but to provide an additional source of information from which the beginner can sample as he reads. Increasing the amount of available information through the medium of pictures was shown to have a strong facilitative effect on word learning" (p. 176).

Rawson (1968) has demonstrated the importance of specialized educational procedures in teaching dyslexic children. She reports on 56 dyslexics who had specialized remediation as children, and on their successful adjustment vocationally in adult life. With further clarification of the nature and incidence of dyslexia in children, it will be incumbent on special education to further develop instructional programs designed specifically to foster learning in this group of children.

Myklebust and Johnson (1962) and Johnson and Myklebust (1967) have suggested methods and procedures for classroom teachers. To illustrate the types of remediation found to be successful with dyslexic children, from ages 7 to 17, a few of these suggestions are reviewed. These methods are based on the model discussed in this chapter. Therefore, auditory language is considered primary, so deficits at this level are given priority. Throughout, a task analysis, or modality systems approach, is used—making it possible to identify and recognize the types of deficits, the "breaks" in the systems which must be alleviated for success in reading.

The clinical teaching construct follows principles; fundamentals serve as a basis for assessing deficiencies and for planning remediation. These principles encompass (a) individualizing the problem, (b) input precedes output, (c) meaning must be taught, (d) initially the process is phoneme to grapheme, (e) encoding does not always result in attainment of meaning, and (f) the brain is prestructured to process information in systematic manners—so teaching materials and methods must be patterned on the hierarchies that ensue; meaning results from symbolization which assumes relating symbols to what has been learned previously.

Other fundamentals concern the ways in which information is presented. Teaching to the intact systems is useful but must be controlled. Moreover, unless interneurosensory systems are intact, approaching the child's problem through his integrities might be futile. Teaching to the deficient systems must be done in a way that does not cause overloading, irritation, or even debilitation. The remediation plan should include procedures for intraneurosensory, interneurosensory, and integrative learning. In addition, attention must be given to storage and retrieval processes because memory is essential for all learning.

The educational plan for any given child depends upon the precise nature of the dyslexia present. Nevertheless, usually it is beneficial to teach the names of letters and the sounds the letters make. After the child has learned the letter sounds, it has proved unusually helpful to teach syllabication. Perhaps all children first learn to read by associating sounds with letters, syllable by syllable. Both within-modality and cross-modal teaching often is necessary.

The psychoneurology of learning in dyslexic children has not been well established, but basic aspects have been ascertained. A major facet concerns poor integrative abilities; auditory and visual, verbal and nonverbal learning might be achieved within normal limits but each of these types is not integrated with the other. We conducted an investigation in which a large group of learning-disability children were matched with normal children (mental age, classroom, and sex). The Draw-A-Man test was administered to both groups. Although mean test scores for both groups fell within normal limits, the degree to which this score correlated with educational achievement was radically different. Of 17 measures of educational achievement, all correlated significantly with school learning for the normal children but none of these correlations were significant for the learning-disability children. These results indicate that the psychology by which dyslexic and other learning-disability children learn varies substantially. Different assumptions must be made when planning remedial programs for dyslexic children.

All aspects of the questions and issues involved in childhood dyslexia present challenges that not only are of great interest—they are of intense consequence to many children. The role of the dyslexiologist is to pursue resolution of these issues. Only when such resolutions are forthcoming will dyslexic children have the opportunities to which they are entitled.

REFERENCES

Bakker, D. Hemispheric specialization and stages in the Learning-to-Read process. *Bulletin Orton Society,* 1973, 23: 15–24.

Berger, M, Yule, W., and Rutter, M. Attainment and adjustment in two geographical areas: the prevalance of specific reading retardation. *British Journal of Psychiatry,* 1975, 126: 510–519.

Birch, H., and Belmont, L. Auditory-visual integration, intelligence and reading disability in school children. *Perceptual Motor Skills,* 1965, 20: 295–305.

Blank, M., and Bridger, W. Perceptual abilities and conceptual deficiencies in retarded readers. *In* J. Zubin and G. Jervis, eds., *Psychopathology of Mental Development.* New York: Grune & Stratton, 1967.

Blair, F. A study of the visual memory of deaf and hearing children. *American Annals of the Deaf,* 1957, 102: 254.

Boder, E. Developmental dyslexia: prevailing diagnostic concepts and a new diagnostic approach. *In* H. Myklebust, ed., *Progress in Learning Disabilities,* Vol. II. New York: Grune & Stratton, 1971.

Boder, E. Developmental dyslexia. *Developmental Medicine and Child Neurology,* 1973, 15: 663–687.

Broca, P. Perte de la parole. *Bulletin Society Anthropology,* April 1861.

Bryant, P. Cross-modal development and reading. *In* D. Duane and M. Rawson, eds., *Reading, Perception and Language.* Baltimore: York Press, 1975.

Calfee, R. Memory and cognitive skills in reading acquisition. *In* D. Duane and M. Rawson, eds., *Reading, Perception and Language.* Baltimore: York Press, 1975.

Connolly, C. Social and emotional factors in learning disabilities. *In* H. Myklebust, ed., *Progress in Learning Disabilities, Vol. II.* New York: Grune & Stratton, 1971.

Connors, K. Cortical visual evoked response in children with learning disorders. *Psychophysiology,* 1970, 7: 418–428.

Conrad, R. An association between memory errors and errors due to acoustic masking of speech. *Nature,* 1962, 196: 1314–1315.

Conrad, R. Acoustic confusions in immediate memory. *British Journal of Psychology,* 1964, 55: 75–84.

Conrad, R. Speech and reading. *In* J. Kavanagh and I. Mattingly, eds., *Language by Ear and by Eye.* Cambridge: MIT Press, 1972.

Costello, M. A study of speechreading as a developing language process in deaf and in hard of hearing children. Unpublished doctoral dissertation, Northwestern University, 1957.

Crowder, R. Visual and auditory memory. *In* J. Kavanagh and I. Mattingly, eds., *Language by Ear and by Eye.* Cambridge: MIT Press, 1972.

Denburg, S. The interaction of picture and print in reading instruction. *Reading Research Quarterly,* 1977, 12: 176–179.

Denny, D. Relationship of cognitive style to reading disabilities. *Journal of Educational Psychology,* 1974, 66, 5: 702–709.

Diringer, D. *Writing.* New York: Prager, 1962.

Drachman, D. Memory and cognitive function in man. *Neurology,* 1977, 8, 27: 783–793.

Duane, D. Developmental dyslexia: etiologic theories and therapeutic implications. *Psychiatric Annals,* 1977, 7, 9: 37–47.

Duff, M. Language functions in children with learning disabilities. Unpublished doctoral dissertation, Northwestern University, 1968.

Dyer, J. The role of the ophthalmologist in evaluation and treatment of dyslexia. *Psychiatric Annals,* 1977, 7, 9: 52–54.

Eisenberg, L. Psychiatric aspects of language disability. *In* D. Duane and M. Rawson, eds., *Reading, Perception and Language,* Baltimore: York Press, 1975.

Eisenberg, L. Developmental dyslexia. *Psychiatric Annals,* 1977, 7, 9:460–461.

Ferguson, E. The mind's eye: nonverbal thought in technology. *Science,* 1977, 197, 4306: 827–836.

Forster, F. Reading epilepsy, musicogenic epilepsy and related disorders. *In* H. Mykelbust, ed., *Progress in Learning Disabilities, Vol. III.* New York: Grune & Stratton, 1975.

Freud, S. *On Aphasia.* New York: International University Press, 1953.

Fries, C. *Linguistics and Reading.* New York: Holt, Rinehart and Winston, 1962.

Frisina, D. R. A psychological study of the mentally retarded child. Unpublished doctoral dissertation, Northwestern University, 1955.

Fuller, C. A study of the growth and organization of certain mental abilities in young deaf children. Unpublished doctoral dissertation, Northwestern University, 1959.

Gabrys, J. Methylphenidate effect on attentional and cognitive behavior in six-through twelve-year-old males. *Perceptual Motor Skills,* 1977, 45: 1143–1149.

Gagné, R. *The Conditions of Learning.* New York: Holt, Rinehart and Winston, 1965.

Galaburda, A., LeMay, M., Kemper, T., and Geschwind, N. Right-left assymetries in the brain. *Science,* 1978, 199:4331.

Gates, A. *The Improvement of Reading.* New York: Macmillan, 1950.

Gelb, I. *A Study of Writing.* Chicago: University of Chicago Press, 1963.

Geschwind, N. Language and the brain. *Scientific American,* April 1972, 76–83.

Geschwind, N. The apraxias: neural mechanism of disorders of learned movement. *American Scientist,* 1975, 63:188–195.

Gibson, E. Learning to read. *Science,* 1965, 148:1066–1072.

Gibson, E., and Levin, H. *The Psychology of Reading.* Cambridge: MIT Press, 1975.

Goldstein, K. *Language and Language Disturbances,* New York: Grune & Stratton, 1948.

Golinkoff, R. A comparison of reading comprehension processes in good and poor readers. *Reading Research Quarterly,* 1975–1976, XI, 4:623–659.

Guilford, J. *The Nature of Human Intelligence.* New York: McGraw-Hill, 1967.

Guthrie, J. Models of reading and reading disability. *Journal Educational Psychology,* 1973, 65:9–18.

Guthrie, J., ed. *Aspects of Reading Acquisition.* Baltimore: Johns Hopkins Press, 1976.

Hallgren, G. Specific dyslexia ("congenital word blindness"): a clinical and genetic study. *Acta Psychiatry and Neurology,* Suppl. 65, 1950, 1–287.

Hardy, M., Smythe, P., Stennett, R., and Wilson, H. Developmental patterns in elementary reading skills. *Journal of Educational Psychology,* 1972, 63, 5: 433–436.

Harris, A. *How to Increase Reading Ability.* New York: David Mckay, 1970.

Hebb, D. The semi-autonomous process. *American Psychologist,* 1963, 18:16–27.

Hécaen, H. Aphasic, apraxic and agnostic syndromes in right-left hemisphere lesions. *In* P. Vinken and G. Bruyn, eds., *Handbook of Clinical Neurology,* Vol. 4. Amsterdam: North-Holland, 1969.

Hinshelwood, J. *Congenital Word-Blindness.* London: Lewis, 1917.

Hughes, J. Electroencephalography and learning. *In* H. Myklebust, ed., *Progress in Learning Disabilities, Vol. I.* New York: Grune & Stratton, 1968.

Hughes, J. Electroencephalography and learning disabilities. *In* H. Myklebust, ed., *Progress in Learning Disabilities, Vol. II.* New York: Grune & Stratton, 1971.

Ilg, F., and Ames, L. *School Readiness.* New York: Harper &. Row, 1965.

Jeffrey, W., and Samuels, S. Effect of method of reading training on initial learning and transfer. *Journal Verbal Learning and Verbal Behavior,* 1967, 6:354–358.

John, E. R. Switchboard versus statistical theories of learning and memory. *Science,* 1972, 177:850–864.

John E. R. *Functional Neuroscience, Vol. II.* New York: Halsted Press, 1977.

John, E. R., Karmel B., Corning W., et al. Neurometrics. *Science,* 1977, 196, 4297:1393–1410.

Johnson, D., and Myklebust, H. Dyslexia in children. *Exceptional Children,* 1962, 29: 1: 14–25.

Johnson, D., and Myklebust, H. *Learning Disabilities: Educational Practices and Principles.* New York: Grune & Stratton, 1967.

Jonas, G. Clues to behavior from a divided brain. *Time-Life Science Annual,* 1978, 64–75.

Kasamatsu, T., and Pettigrew, J. Depletion of brain catecholamines: failure of ocular dominance shift after monocular occlusion in kittens. *Science,* 1976, 194:4261.

Kavanagh, J., and Mattingly, I., eds. *Language By Ear and By Eye.* Cambridge: MIT press, 1972.

Killen, J. A learning systems approach to intervention. *In* H. Myklebust, ed., *Progress in Learning Disabilities, Vol. III.* New York: Grune & Stratton, 1975.

Kinsbourne, M. Cerebral dominance, learning and cognition. *In* H. Myklebust, ed., *Progress in Learning Disabilities, Vol. III.* New York: Grune & Stratton, 1975.

Kinsbourne, M. Looking and listening strategies in beginning reading. *In* J. Guthrie, ed., *Aspects of Reading Acquisition.* Baltimore: Johns Hopkins, 1976.

Kinsbourne, M., and Smith, W. eds., *Hemispheric Disconnection and Cerebral Function.* Springfield, Ill.: Thomas, 1974.

LaBerge, D. Beyond auditory coding. *In* J. Kavanagh and I. Mattingly, eds., *Language by Ear and by Eye.* Cambridge: MIT Press, 1972.

LaBerge, D., and Samuels, S. Toward a theory of automatic information processing in reading. *Cognitive Psychology,* 1974, 6:293–323.

Langer, S. *Philosophy in a New Key.* Cambridge: Harvard University Press, 1957.

Langer, S. *Mind: An Essay on Human Feeling, Vol. II.* Baltimore: Johns Hopkins, 1972.

Levin, J., Divine-Hawkins, P., Kerst, S., and Guttman, J. Individual difference in learning from pictures and words. *Journal of Educational Psychology,* 1974, 66, 3:296–303.

Levy, J., and Reid, M. Variations in writing posture and cerebral organization. *Science,* 1976, 194, 4262:337–339.

Luria, A. *The Neuropsychology of Memory.* New York: Halsted Press, 1976.

MacKay, D. *Information, Mechanism and Meaning.* Cambridge: MIT Press, 1969.

Marsh, G., Desberg, P., and Farwell, L. Stimulus and response variables in children's learning of grapheme-phoneme correspondences. *Journal of Educational Psychology,* 1974, 1:112–116.

Mattingly, I. Reading, the linguistic process and linguistic awareness. *In* J. Kavanagh and I. Mattingly, eds., *Language by Ear and by Eye.* Cambridge: MIT Press, 1972.

McGrady, H. Verbal and nonverbal functions in school children with speech and language disorders. Unpublished doctoral dissertation, Northwestern University, 1964.

McGrady, H. Language and language pathology. *In* H. Myklebust, ed., *Progress in Learning Disabilities, Vol. I.* New York: Grune & Stratton, 1968.

McKeachie, W. Psychology in America's Bicentennial year. *American Psychologist,* 1976, 31, 12:819–833.

Menyuk, P. Relations between acquisition of phonology and reading. *In* J. Guthrie, ed., *Aspects of Reading Acquisition.* Baltimore: Johns Hopkins, 1976.

Morrison, F., Giordani, B., and Nagy, J. Reading Disability: an information-processing analysis. *Science,* 1977, 196, 4285:77–79.

Mowrer, O. *Learning Theory and the Symbolic Processes.* New York: Wiley, 1960.

Myklebust, H. *Auditory Disorders in Children: A Manual for differential Diagnosis.* New York: Grune & Stratton, 1954.

Myklebust, H. Babbling and echolalia in language theory. *Journal of Speech and Hearing Disorders,* 1957, 22, 3:356–360.

Myklebust, H. *The Psychology of Deafness* (2nd ed.). New York: Grune & Stratton, 1964.

Myklebust, H. *Development and Disorders of Written Language, Vol. I.* The Picture Story Language Test. New York: Grune & Stratton, 1965.

Myklebust, H. Learning disabilities in psychoneurologically disturbed children: behavioral correlates of brain dysfunction. *In* J. Zubin and G. Gervis, eds., *Psychopathology of Mental Development.* New York: Grune & Stratton, 1967.

Myklebust, H. ed., *Progress in Learning Disabilities, Vol. I.* New York: Grune & Stratton, 1968.

Myklebust, H., ed., *Progress in Learning Disabilities, Vol. II.* New York: Grune & Stratton, 1971.

Myklebust, H. Childhood aphasia: an evolving concept. Childhood aphasia: identification, diagnosis and re-mediation. *In* L. Travis, ed., *Handbook of Speech Pathology and Audiology,* chap. 46 & 47. New York: Appleton-Century-Crofts, 1971.(a)

Myklebust, H. *Development and Disorders of Written Language, Vol. II: Studies of Normal and Exceptional Children.* New York: Grune & Stratton, 1973.

Myklebust, H. Identification and diagnosis of children with learning disabilities. *In* S. Walzer and P. Wolff, eds., *Minimal Cerebral Dysfunctions in Children.* New York: Grune & Stratton, 1973.(a)

Myklebust, H. Nonverbal learning disabilities: assessment and intervention. *In* H. Myklebust, ed., *Progress in Learning Disabilities, Vol. III.* New York: Grune & Stratton, 1975.

Myklebust, H., and Johnson, D. Dyslexia in children. *Exceptional Children.* 1962, 29:1.

Myklebust, H., Bannochie, M., and Killen, J. Learning disabilities and cognitive processes. *In* H. Myklebust, ed., *Progress in Learning Disabilities, Vol. II.* New York: Grune & Stratton, 1971.

Neisser, U. *Cognitive Psychology.* New York: Appleton-Century-Crofts, 1967.

Norman, D. The role of memory in the understanding of language. *In* J. Kavanagh and I. Mattingly, eds., *Language by Ear and by Eye.* Cambridge: MIT Press, 1972.

Paivio, A. *Imagery and Verbal Processes.* New York: Holt, Rinehart and Winston, 1971.

Penfield, W., and Roberts, L. *Speech and Brain Mechanisms.* Princeton: Princeton University Press, 1959.

Petrides, M., and Iversen, S. Cross-modal matching and the primate frontal cortex. *Science,* 1976, 192, 4243:1023–1024.

Preston, M., Guthrie, J., and Childs, B. Visual evoked responses in normal and disabled readers. *Psychophysiology,* 1974, 11, 4:452–457.

Rawson, M. *Developmental Language Disability.* Baltimore: Johns Hopkins, 1968.

Robbins, K., and McAdam, D. Interhemispheric alpha assymetry and imagery mode. *Brain and Language,* 1974:189–193.

Rumelhart, D. *Human Information Processing.* New York: Wiley, 1977.

Samuels, S. Hierarchical sub-skills in the reading acquisition process. *In* J. Guthrie, ed., *Aspects of Reading Acquisition.* Baltimore: Johns Hopkins, 1976.

Satz, P., and Sparrow, S. Specific developmental dyslexia: a theoretical formulation. *In* D. Bakker and P. Satz, ed., *Specific Reading Disability–Advances in Theory and Method.* Netherlands: Rotterdam University Press, 1970.

Savin, H. What the child knows about speech when he learns to read. *In* J. Kavanagh and I. Mattingly, eds., *Language by Ear and by Eye.* Cambridge: MIT press, 1972.

Schilder, P. Congenital alexia and its relation to optic perception. *Journal of Genetic Psychology,* 1944, 65:67–88.

Schmitt, F., Dev, P., and Smith, B. Electronic processing of information by brain cells. *Science,* 1976, 193, 424:114–120.

Shankweiler, D., and Liberman, I. Misreading: a search for causes. *In* J. Kavanagh and I. Mattingly, eds., *Language by Ear and by Eye.* Cambridge: MIT Press, 1972.

Silver, A. Dyslexia: a symptom not a disease. *Hospital Tribune,* 1970.

Swanson, J., and Kinsbourne, M. Stimulant-related state-dependent learning in hyperactive children. *Science,* 1976, 192, 4246:1354–1357.

Taylor, I. *The Alphabet.* London: 1883.

Taylor, H., Satz, P., and Friel, J. Developmental dyslexia in relation to other childhood reading disorders: significance and clinical utility. Prepublication draft, University of Florida, 1977.

Teyler, T., Raemer, R., Harrison, T., and Thompson, R. Human scalp-recorded evoked-potential correlates of linguistic stimuli. *Bulletin Psychonomic Society,* 1973, 1:333–334.

Thatcher, R., and John, E. R. *Functional Neuroscience, Vol. 1.* New York: Halsted Press, 1977.

Travis, L., ed. *Handbook of Speech Pathology and Audiology.* New York: Appleton-Century-Crofts, 1971.

Underwood, B. Attributes of memory. *Psychological Review,* 1969, 76:559–573.

Vellutino, F., Steger, J., and Kandel, G. Reading disability: an investigation of the perceptual deficit hypothesis. *Cortex,* 1972, 8:106–118.

Vellutino, F., Smith, H., and Steger, J. Reading disability: age differences and the perceptual deficit hypothesis. *Child Development,* 1975, 46, 2:487–493.

Vellutino, F., Bentley, W., DeSetto, L., and Phillips, F. Inter vs intrahemispheric learning in dyslexic and normal readers. Prepublication draft, State University of N.Y. at Albany and Albany Medical College, 1977.

Vernon, M. *Reading and its Difficulties.* Cambridge University Press, 1971.

Vogel, S. An investigation of syntactical abilities in normal and dyslexic children. Unpublished doctoral dissertation, Northwestern University, 1972.

Vuckovich, D. M. Pediatric neurology and learning disabilities. *In* H. Myklebust, ed., *Progress in Learning Disabilities, Vol. I,* New York: Grune & Stratton, 1968.

Vygotsky, L. *Thought and Language*. Cambridge: MIT Press, 1962.

Wada, J., Clark, R., and Hamm, A. Cerebral hemispheric asymetry in humans. *Archives Neurology,* 1975, 32:239–246.

Weimer, W., and Palermo, D., eds. *Cognition and the Symbolic Processes*. New York: Wiley, 1974.

Wepman, J., and Jones, L. Five Aphasias. *In* D. McK. Rioch and E. Weinstein, eds., *Disorders of Communication*. Baltimore: Willaims & Wilkins, 1964.

Witelson, S. Sex and the single hemisphere. *Science,* 1976, 193, 4251:425–426.

Witelson, S. Developmental dyslexia: two right hemispheres and none left. *Science,* 1977, 195:309–311.

Witelson, S., and Pallie, W. Left hemisphere specialization for language in the newborn. *Brain,* 1973, 96:641–646.

Wood, H. The dyslexic child in the general classroom. *Bulletin of Orton Society,* 1976, 26:34–48.

World Federation of Neurology. *Bulletin of Orton Society,* 1968, 18:22.

Zigmond, N. Intrasensory and intersensory processes in normal and dyslexic children. Unpublished doctoral dissertation, Northwestern University, 1966.

II. Genetic Considerations in Dyslexia

JOAN M. FINUCCI

The years 1896 to 1917 mark the period of initial recognition and description of dyslexia. The condition was then generally referred to as congenital word-blindness and was recognized as an inability to learn to read easily which was developmental in nature, bore some of the characteristics of acquired reading disorders, and was distinct from developmental disorders of reading which were a result of or related to low intelligence, physical disability, indadequate schooling, or other exogenous factors. It was early in this period that the familial nature of dyslexia was noted and an hereditary basis for its occurrence postulated.

W. Pringle Morgan (1896) is credited with giving the first detailed description of a case, that of a 14-year-old boy. Earlier in the same year, however, in a long essay on school hygiene prepared for the Royal Statistical Society, a school medical officer, James Kerr (1896, 1897), mentioned a case of word-blindness in his list of unusual school problems. Stephenson (1904) reviewed 14 cased reported to that date and described 2 further cases. These early descriptions appeared primarily in medical journals and were made chiefly by British ophthalmologists and neurologists, but the condition was also being brought to the attention of school authorities. Thomas (1905) noted that as a result of a directive to head teachers of schools under the London County Council, nearly 100 cases of the condition were noted in the case books at special schools, and he estimated ''that 1 in 2000 of all London Elementary School children may be expected to show word-blindness to a considerable degree.'' Among early accounts, that of Nettleship (1901) is noteworthy for his insight with respect to the difficulty of diagnosis of word-blindness in children from disadvantageous environments, for his recognition of the need to differentiate between generally ''backward'' children and those ''whose only or principal difficulty is real inability to learn to read,'' and for his recognition of the disproportionate number of males among those affected.

In 1905, two separate accounts were made of more than one case occurring within a family. The first, by Thomas, described seven cases of word-blindness. Two of the cases were brothers and a third had a sister and mother who were similarly affected, although ample opportunity to learn to read had been provided. Thomas noted that ''it frequently assumes a family type . . . that there is a tendency to family character.'' The second description, by Fisher (1905), was of a girl whose maternal uncle had a similar problem. Fisher states, ''I think we may fairly take this as evidence of a family tendency to imperfection in development of the visual memory centre for words in the cortex of the left angular gyrus . . . such hereditary tendency seems not improbable.'' These reports were followed by a report by Hinshelwood (1907) of 4 affected sons in a sibship of 11 and a report by Stephenson (1907) of six affected members in three generations. (Several reviews have stated that Stephenson proposed a recessive mode of inheritance for dyslexia, but this is incorrect.) Four years later, Hinshelwood (1911) reported that a niece and nephew of the four brothers in his earlier paper were also affected. In the latter paper, he expressed the view that the evidence for the frequency of hereditary tendency of word-blindness would rapidly increase if observers of cases made careful inquiries into the family histories of present and previous generations.

This work was supported in part by NIH grant, HD 00486

41

In 1917, Hinshelwood published a monograph summarizing his many communications on the subject of congenital word-blindness. By this date, cases were also beginning to be reported in the United States (McCready, 1909–1910). In the 20 years after Morgan's publication of the first case, many of the characteristics of the condition had already been described, particularly the familial nature of the disorder and the increased incidence in males. Furthermore, largely as a result of speculation by Hinshelwood based on an analogy to acquired word-blindness in adults, congenital word-blindness was taken to be a developmental defect in the region of the left angular gyrus. To that time, however, specific principles for diagnosis were wanting. Hinshelwood listed gravity of defect and purity of symptoms as essential criteria for congenital word-blindness, but that the field of psychological and educational testing was just evolving in the period was reflected in the lack of standardized procedures for diagnosis. Likewise, beyond suggesting an hereditary tendency, no large pedigrees were studied nor were specific modes of transmission postulated.

Since 1917, several observations of multiple cases of congenital word-blindness or dyslexia within families have been reported and theories as to the role of the genes proposed. The aims of this chapter are (a) to consider the purposes of genetic studies of dyslexia (b) to compare and contrast various approaches used in family and genetic studies of dyslexia, and (c) to make suggestions for future research.

WHY STUDY THE GENETICS OF DYSLEXIA?

With few exceptions, most family and genetic studies of dyslexia continue to be published in journals of medicine or allied fields. This probably reflects a perception on the part of educators that genetic studies have limited usefulness with respect to efforts toward the remediation of dyslexia, yet there are several ways in which genetic studies can bring about greater understanding of dyslexia and thereby provide insight into the diagnosis and treatment of the condition.

There is an analogy with mental retardation. Consider, for example, the contribution of genetic and family studies to its diagnosis and treatment. Mental retardation is heterogeneous in nature with many different causes; some conditions are manifestations of genetic disorders, some are the result of environmental factors, and others are due to a combination of genetic and environmental factors. Family studies have helped to elucidate this heterogeneity and have contributed to the detection of characteristics of specific syndromes (Penrose, 1965; Roberts, 1952–1953). In a recent compendium, the wide variety of etiologies, states of severity, physical features, and prognoses were described for 173 disorders associated with mental retardation (Holmes, Moser, Halldorsson, et al., 1972). In some of these disorders—for example, the autosomal recessive condition, phenylketonuria (PKU)—recognition of the metabolic defect has led to early diagnosis and to the development of dietary treatment which, when well controlled, prevents severe intellectual impairment. For other disorders, such as Down's syndrome, recognition of the condition as a chromosomal abnormality has not led to treatment, but has led to prenatal diagnosis. For milder and more common cases of mental retardation, it has been shown through family studies that frequently several members of a family are affected, occurring in such a way that no Mendelian pattern of transmission could explain the familial aggregation. Penrose and Roberts attribute these cases to a combination of genetic and environmental factors. It is in such cases that improvement of environmental conditions—better nutrition, removal of toxic agents such as lead, increased stimulation during development—may prevent retardation.

Like mental retardation, dyslexia is probably heterogeneous, and many attempts have been made to identify characteristics which define subtypes (Ingram, Mason, and Blackburn, 1970; Boder, 1971, 1973; Mattis, French, and Rapin, 1975). But none of these has involved demonstration of the validity of characteristics as descriptive of a subtype by looking for within-family homogeneity—that is, finding that dyslexics within the same family have characteristics of the same subtype lends support to a biological basis for the subtype. The differentiation of validated subtypes within the total dyslexic population should serve as a starting point for tailoring remediation programs to the characteristics of individual children. Furthermore, while prognoses for dyslexics in general are now difficult to make, it is likely that the idenification of subtypes and monitoring of their response to remediation will provide valuable prognostic information in the future. The issue of subtypes of dyslexia will be elaborated on in a later section.

It is also to be hoped that understanding the nature and cause of dyslexia would lead to greater understanding of the child with the condition. As early as 1900, Hinshelwood stated, ''The recognition of the true character of the difficulty will lead the parents and teachers of these children to deal with them in the proper way, not by harsh and severe treatment, but by attempting to overcome the difficulty by patient and persistent training.'' The evidence that greater tolerance of the child's difficulties and more reasonable expectations for the child will result from understanding the cause is not at hand. However, it would seem that a realization that in many cases the child's difficulties stem not from a lack of motivation or intractability, but rather have a biological basis, should do much toward providing an environment more conducive to learning and toward preventing reactive emotional problems.

Dyslexia has a major impact on the life of an individual with the condition. Limitations that it places on the individual with respect to academic achievement are well documented and easily understood. Limitations on occupational satisfaction are less well understood. Perlo and Rak (1971) reported on 50 adults with reading disability, 15 of whom were nonreaders. Efforts to teach these individuals as adults resulted in only moderate success. A follow-up study by Rawson (1968) showed that dyslexic boys who had the advantage of a well-planned school program had fared reasonably well in later educational and occupational endeavors although marked spelling difficulties remained. Connolly (1971) notes that there is conflicting evidence with respect to the relationship between emotional disorder and reading disability, but that dyslexics as a group ''encounter serious obstacles to adjustment and all are endangered by the ramifications of school failure'' (p. 157). Determination that some cases of dyslexia, possibly the majority, have a genetic basis and elucidation of the mode of transmission involved can lead to early identification of individuals at risk and early efforts to help the dyslexic cope with his disability. Some genetic subgroups may in fact be characterized by their ability to adapt. Such a determination would be valuable for prognosis.

FAMILY AND GENETIC STUDIES OF DYSLEXIA

A number of family and genetic studies that have been carried out since the publication of Hinshelwood's monograph will be reviewed and evaluated in this section. The studies have been grouped according to their approaches and aims. While the aims of a study frequently dictate the approach to be used, some approaches limit the types of questions that might be asked and the conclusions that might be drawn. These limitations will be dealt with in the review.

Twin Studies

All behavioral characteristics are influenced by both the genetic make-up of the individual (his genotype) and the environment in which the individual is raised and lives. For some characters one gene might have an overriding effect on their development, for others an environmental factor might be of major importance, and for others there may be many genes or many environmental factors which determine their appearance. The primary purpose of twin studies is to estimate the relative contribution of the genes and of the environment in the development of a trait. Such studies take advantage of the fact that identical, or monozygotic (MZ), twins which develop from the division of a fertilized ovum have the same genotype, while fraternal, or dizygotic (DZ), twins which develop from two fertilized ova have no higher probability of being genetically alike than any two sibs.

One method used in twin studies is that of comparing rate of concordance for a trait among MZ twins and among DZ twins. Two twins are said to be concordant for a trait if both possess the trait; they are said to be discordant if only one possesses the trait. Since MZ twins share the same genotype and are exposed to more or less similar environments, a higher concordance rate for a trait among MZ twins than among DZ twins suggests that there is a large genetic component in the determination of the trait.

Zerbin-Rudin (1967) summarized data from eight reports made on the concordance rates of dyslexia in twins. Of 17 MZ twin pairs, all were concordant for dyslexia, while of 34 DZ twin pairs, only 12 showed concordance for the trait. Although these data are suggestive of a greater role of heredity than environment in the occurrence of dyslexia, one difficulty with that interpretation stems from the method of ascertainment of subjects. These cases were all members of a clinic population, and it is not known whether there might be a greater propensity for referral of twins when both manifest a trait. Bakwin (1973) conducted a study which obviated this criticism. In his investigation, 96 MZ male pairs, 100 MZ female pairs, 152 DZ male pairs, and 58 DZ female pairs, all between the ages of 8 and 18, were ascertained through organizaions for twins. Determination of reading disability was based on data gathered through interviews with parents, supplemented by telephone and mail questionnaires. Thirty-one of the MZ pairs and 31 of the DZ pairs were reported to have at least one twin with reading disability, but while 26 (84%) of the 31 MZ pairs showed concordance for the trait, only 9 (29%) of the 31 DZ pairs showed concordance. While this study eliminated some of the bias in ascertainment, it suffers from a vague definition of reading disability. Reading disability was defined as a reading level below the expectation derived from the child's performance in other school subjects. How expectation for each child was determined and whether parental opinion rather than test scores were relied upon to make classification decisions is not known. Thus, the evidence from twin studies is only suggestive of genetic factors as important determinants in dyslexia.

In some investigations of behavioral traits, the analysis of twin data has been taken one step further through the calculation of an index of heritability which is an estimate of the proportion of variance in a trait attributable to heredity. Heritability coefficients may be calculated from concordance rates in MZ twins and DZ twins for dichotomous measures, such as the presence or absence of reading disability, or from between- and within-pair variances for quantitative measures such as scores on a reading test. Vandenberg

(1967) calculated a heritability estimate of 0.49 from test scores of high-school-age twins on the Gray Oral Reading paragraphs, suggesting that performance on this test reflects a significant genetic contribution. It should be realized, however, that this estimate gives information about the factors contributing to a normally distributed trait such as reading ability and gives no information about the origin of significant outliers such as dyslexic individuals.

In summary, twin data and heritability estimates point to a genetic influence on normal reading ability as well as on the etiology of significant deviation from normal (dyslexia). Such studies are preliminary in nature and should be followed by others that address the issue of mode of inheritance.

Closely allied with twin studies with respect to their aims are adoption studies. By comparing the resemblance of adopted children to their foster and biological parents on a trait such as intelligence (Munsinger, 1975) or the presence or absence of schizophrenia in the biological and adoptive relatives of schizophrenics adopted early in life (Kety, Rosenthal, Wender, et al., 1975), it is possible to ascertain contribution of heredity to the character. No adoption study of dyslexia has been carried out, but such studies would serve essentially the same purpose as have twin studies.

Family Studies

Several studies of dyslexic children have included the familial history of reading disability as one of several factors under investigation. Among those studies are investigations by Eustis (1947), Symmes and Rapoport (1972), Ingram, Mason, and Blackburn (1970), and Rutter and Yule (1975), all of which found a high incidence of reported reading disability in the family. One study by Naidoo (1972) attempted to look at the relationship of familial history to other features of dyslexia.

Naidoo studied two groups of dyslexic boys between the ages of 8 years and 12 years 11 months who were seen in the Word Blind Centre of London. Fifty-six boys were identified as Reading Retardates through scores at least 2 years below chronological age on the Neale Analysis of Reading Ability Accuracy or on Schonell's Graded Word Reading Test. The second group of 42 included boys who were identified as Spelling Retardates through scores at least 2 years below chronological age on Schonell's Graded Spelling Test A. All of those in the second group also had some degree of reading difficulty, but it was less severe than that manifested by the first group. All subjects had a WISC Full-Scale IQ of at least 90, were physically and grossly neurologically normal on examination, had had no major absences from school and no evidence of severe emotional disturbance on a psychologist's examination. There were also two control groups matched to the Reading Retardates and Spelling Retardates, respectively, on age and type of school, state or private.

The purpose of the study was to examine several features of dyslexic children to determine if different types of dyslexia exist and to determine if the features of a subgroup might suggest etiology. Among the features studied were prenatal status, laterality, intelligence, reading, speech and language, social adjustment, and familial factors of reading or spelling difficulties or left-handedness. Although no clear clusters or subgroups based on several features emerged, there appeared to be two distinct groups of boys, one with a family history of reading or spelling difficulty and one with features suggestive of neurologic dysfunction, but with a negative family history. Furthermore, it is suggested by the author that within the group having a positive family history there appeared to be one type showing language and speech delays and another type with atypical laterality patterns.

All of these studies which reported a high incidence of reading disability in the families of dyslexics relied on interview data for the making of a diagnosis. Frequently one family member made the report for other members of the family, and no tests of other family members were carried out. Thus, these studies, like the Bakwin twin study, provide only suggestive evidence for a large familial component in dyslexia. Little confidence can be placed in the diagnosis unless one standard is applied uniformly in all families, which is unlikely to have been the case without measurement of each individual's reading and spelling performance.

Three family studies have been conducted which did include measurement of reading or spelling or both for all subjects in the study. Walker and Cole (1965) conducted a study to determine if familial aggregation of specific reading disability is nonrandom. The subjects consisted of 75 sibships with three children only in grades 2 through 12 in a middle-class suburban public school system. Sibs with an IQ below 90 were omitted. The authors considered spelling performance on the Stanford spelling tests to be indicative of specific reading disability if it was 6 months or more below grade level for children in grade 2, 1 year or more below grade level for children in grades 3 through 6, or 2 years or more below grade level for children in grades 7 through 12. Any subject with scores below these standards or who had been selected by the school earlier for remedial help was defined for the purposes of the study as a disabled reader. Of the 225 children examined, 25.3% met the criteria for being affected and were aggregated in only 32 of the 75 families. The number of families with no affected children and the number of families with more than one affected child differed significantly from the number of such families expected if the cases were distributed randomly in the families at the rate of 25.3%.

Owen, Adams, Forrest, et al. (1971) studied 76 quartets of children and their parents in an attempt to identify and describe the characteristics of academically handicapped children and to clarify the familial patterns of learning disorders. The subjects, from a middle- to upper-middle-class population, were 76 educationally handicapped (EH) children and their same-sex siblings (EHS) and 76 academically successful children (SA) and their same-sex siblings (SAS). The EH and SA groups were matched on grade, sex, and intelligence; and the EHS and SAS groups were matched on grade and sex. Criteria for selection into the EH group were a WISC Full-Scale IQ of at least 90 and school achievement in either reading or spelling or both, 1.5 to 2 years below grade level expectancy.

The siblings of the EH children were on average almost at grade level in reading, but approximately 1 year retarded in spelling, while the siblings of the SA children were approximately a year above grade level in reading and less than 3 months retarded in spelling. In a comparison of the parents of the two groups, the fathers of the EH group were found to have significantly poorer ($p < .05$) scores on WRAT Reading than the fathers of the SA children, and both the fathers and mothers of the EH group had significantly poorer grades in high school English courses than did the fathers and mothers of the SA children ($p < .02$ for both comparisons). These results showing poor achievement in language areas for both the parents and sibs of EH children suggest a strong familial factor in such underachievement. However, no attempt was made to determine the number of individuals affected within families or the degree of impairment within families. Also, in some of the families a number of other factors may have contributed to poor achievement in reading, and these factors were the subject of further analysis.

An attempt was made to assign the 76 EH children to one of five categories: (a) relatively high incidence of medical-neurologic findings; (b) positive performance-verbal discrepancy on the WISC of at least 15 points; (c) social deviancy; (d) relatively high full-scale IQ (117–154); and (e) relatively low full-scale IQ (90–99). Fifty-six children were assigned to one or more of the five groups. The authors concluded that the children in group b represented the most "pure" dyslexic group and that the siblings of this group of children gave evidence of many similarities of impairment. Also, the mothers of this group showed a significant language-learning handicap.

Foch, DeFries, McClearn, et al. (1977) studied 58 reading disabled children (probands), their parents, and one or two of their siblings, and 58 normal readers, matched to the probands on the basis of sex, age, grade, school environment, and home neighborhood, and their parents and one or two of their siblings. The probands and controls were between the ages of 7.5 and 12 years, scored at least 90 on a standardized IQ test, lived with both biological parents, had no apparent psychiatric or neurologic complications and no uncorrected visual or auditory defects. The probands were reading at one-half or less of grade-level expectancy, and the normal readers were reading at or above grade-level expectancy as measured by a standardized reading test. There were 13 female probands and 45 male probands. The purpose of the study was to identify familial patterns of impairment in cognitive abilities.

All subjects were administered a variety of achievement and ability tests including tests of reading, spelling, intelligence, auditory discrimination, perceptual speed, auditory and visual memory, and spatial reasoning. Probands and some of their male relatives manifested deficits in reading, spelling, auditory memory, perceptual speed, and verbal reasoning, while some of the mothers and sisters of the probands were less severely affected.

Considering the wealth of information gathered, it is unfortunate that the investigators made no attempt to study at least all members of the child's immediate family nor to classify each individual as either dyslexic or nondyslexic. The value of the Owen and Foch studies lies in the use of standardized tests for assessing reading and spelling abilities and the use of control families. Both studies demonstrate significant differences between reading and spelling performance of family members ascertained through disabled readers and that of those ascertained through normal readers when environmental differences in the families are minimized. Thus, the results are suggestive of a genetic influence on the presence of reading problems. These studies, however, are not informative with respect to the nature of the genetic influence since the level of analysis was at the group level rather than the individual level. Assessment of individuals in the immediate families of a proband and evaluation of transmission patterns within families is the goal of pedigree studies.

Pedigree Studies

The general conclusion of twin studies and family studies of dyslexia has been that there is a strong genetic influence involved in the etiology of dyslexia. Before proceeding with a discussion of pedigree studies, we will examine the meaning and scope of such a conclusion in order to clarify why pedigree studies of dyslexia are needed. We will begin by reviewing some basic genetics.

Basic genetic principles. The usual complement of genetic material for humans is 23 pairs of chromosomes contained in the nuclei of each somatic cell. Twenty-two pairs are called autosomes, and the remaining two chromosomes, which determine the sex of the individual, are called sex chromosomes. There are two different sex chromosomes, designated X and Y; a female has two X chromosomes, a male has an X chromosome and a Y chromosome. One of each pair of an individual's chromosomes is received from the mother, and one of each pair is received from the father. The one chromosome of each pair which a parent transmits to each offspring is randomly determined. The part of the chromosomes in which the genetic information is coded is deoxyribonucleic acid (DNA), and subunits of DNA which have fixed locations in the chromosomes and specific functions are referred to as genes. Alternative forms of genes at the same locus are called alleles. At some genetic loci, especially in the blood group systems, several alleles have been identified. An individual who has the same allele at a particular locus on both chromosomes of a pair is said to be homozygous for that locus; an individual who has different alleles at that locus on the two chromosomes is said to be heterozygous for that locus.

A genetic trait is said to be dominant if an individual expresses it whether he is homozygous or heterozygous for the allele which codes for that trait. A parent who is heterozygous for a fully expressed dominant trait will express that trait, and such a parent will on average transmit the allele to one-half of his/her offspring. A trait is said to be recessive when an individual expresses it only if he is homozygous for the allele which codes for it. If two parents are both heterozygous for a recessive trait, neither will express the trait, but on average one-fourth of their offspring will be homozygous for the recessive allele and will express the trait. For some traits, one gene locus has an overriding influence on their determination. These are referred to as single gene or Mendelian traits. For others, referred to as quantitative traits, a number of genetic loci contribute to their determination. For both Mendelian and quantitative traits, environmental factors may influence the degree to which the effects of the genes are manifested.

With this background, then, we might proceed with an analysis of the statement that there is a strong genetic influence involved in the etiology of a condition. For some conditions, such a conclusion would be close to understatement. This would be the case for any single gene disorder, such as PKU, most of the cases of dwarfism, color-blindness, and hemophilia. It would also be the case for disorders that result from an abnormal number of chromosomes, such as Down's syndrome, most of which cases have an extra chromosome, and Turner's syndrome in which there is only one sex chromosome, an X. If twin studies were to be done with single-gene disorders, the concordance rate among MZ twins would be 1.0 while that for DZ twins would depend on the transmission frequency. If family studies were done with single-gene traits, a greater incidence of the condition would be found among families ascertained through affected individuals than in families ascertained through unaffected individuals. But neither twin studies nor studies that selectively omit family members from examination are likely to suggest whether the condition is multifactorial, single-gene, or chromosomal. Nor for single-gene disorders would they suggest the mode of transmission.

The purpose of pedigree studies is to examine *at least* the immediate members of the proband's family for the presence of absence of the condition under study. For those conditions that are accounted for by genes at a single locus, typical patterns of transmission will emerge. We will examine here the methods and conclusions of several pedigree studies that have been conducted.

Single-family pedigrees.   Marshall and Ferguson (1939) reported on a 19-year-old male college student who had a history of reading and spelling difficulties since the early school grades and had considerable residual difficulties when seen at age 19. Both the mother and maternal grandmother of the subject had a history of spelling and reading difficulty, but the subject's two sibs, maternal and paternal uncles, and the other grandparents were said to read normally. The authors suggest that the disability is an hereditary form of congenital word-blindness, but they do not speculate concerning the mode of transmission.

Drew (1956) reported on the cases of a 16-year-old boy, his paternal half-brother, and his father, all of whom were diagnosed as dyslexic on the basis of reading and spelling test scores and educational history. Family history of three other generations of the family revealed only one other family member, the paternal grandfather, to be similarly affected. On the basis of test findings showing a complex of symptoms, including defective writing, poor spatial orientation, and poor figure-ground recognition, the author suggested that for this family there is a common defect which might be viewed as a disturbance in Gestalt function which is inherited as a dominant trait.

Hof and Guldenpfennig (1972) gave a report of one family pedigree ascertained through an adult male. The proband and five (1 boy and 4 girls) of his six children were given a diagnostic reading test, the Illinois Test of Psycholinguistic Abilities, eye and hearing tests, an auditory discrimination test, and a neurologic examination. All of those tested were given a diagnosis of specific reading disability. In addition, a history of severe reading and spelling disabilities was given for the proband's father, 2 of his 6 paternal uncles, and his paternal grandmother. The authors concluded, probably on the basis of observed or reported occurrence of reading disability in a direct line for four generations, that specific reading disability follows a dominant mode of inheritance.

In each of these case reports an attempt was made to give a diagnosis either through testing or by history of all members in at least three generations of single families. All of the families showed patterns of affected members which were consistent with a dominant mode of inheritance and, in the latter two reports, the authors suggest this to be the case. None of these case reports provides conclusive evidence, however. First of all, all three of them relied on historical data for the classification of most of the individuals in the pedigree. Secondly, although the pedigrees might be accounted for by a dominant mode of inheritance, there is no basis for rejecting a multigenic hypothesis. Reports of single pedigrees serve little purpose other than to *suggest* a mode of inheritance when dealing with a condition as common as dyslexia. It may be that each of these three reports was made because of the occurrence of more than one affected member in the family. The good pedigree study would include several families, each ascertained through a disabled reader, independent of the status of other family members.

Multiple-pedigree studies.   Probably the best known and largest study of the genetics of dyslexia was that conducted by Hallgren (1950) in Stockholm. Hallgren studied 112 families ascertained through 116 probands: 73 were identified through a secondary school which offered special instruction to dyslexics; 37 were identified through a child guidance clinic which saw referrals for dyslexia; and 6 were identified through both sources. The advantage of studying a large number of pedigrees is that it makes makes possible statistical tests of specific genetic hypotheses.

Hallgren listed the following as his criteria for a positive diagnosis of specific dyslexia: (a) difficulties in learning to read and write; (b) proficiency in reading and writing during the first years of school definitely below the average of the class the child attended; (c) a definite discrepancy between proficiency in reading and writing and in other school subjects; and (d) a definite discrepancy between proficiency in reading and writing and the child's general intelligence. Judgments as to whether children in the families met these criteria were based on reading, writing, spelling, and intelligence tests; histories from parents and teachers; and school records. In the case of adults, diagnoses were made primarily from interview data with limited use of test data. Hallgren indicated that he placed more reliance on history than on test results. "Thus, in every case where the results of the tests indicated reading and writing disabilities, I required a positive history for diagnosis of specific dyslexia. In certain cases, the diagnosis was made on the basis of history alone. Therefore, this was taken as the most important diagnostic criterion" (p. 37). Apparently only 205 of the parents (96 affected and 109 unaffected) were actually interviewed or examined, but a diagnosis was made for all 224 of them. On the basis of these diagnoses, the 112 families were divided into four groups: group I (3 families), families with secondary cases and both parents affected;[1] group II (90 families), families with secondary cases and one parent affected; group III (7 families), families with both parents unaffected and cases of specific dyslexia among the sibs, aunts, uncles, or grand-parents of the probands; and group IV (12 families), solitary cases.

Of the 116 probands, 89 were boys and 27 were girls, giving a ratio of 3.3 affected males to 1 affected female. Because the sex ratio among probands may reflect biases in selection, the sex ratio among affected sibs and affected parents of probands is generally taken as a more valid estimate of the true sex ratio. In Hallgren's series, 39 of the 83 brothers (47%) and 32 of the 91 sisters (35%) are affected, and among the parents, 52 of the 112 fathers (47%) and 43 of the 112 mothers (38%) are affected. These differences, when tested separately for sibs and parents, are not significant ($p > .05$); but when the sex ratios for the two groups are combined, the difference in the proportion of affected males and affected females (47% vs. 37%) is significant ($p > .05$); but when the sex ratios for the two groups are combined, the difference in the proportion of affected males and affected females (47% vs. 37%) is significant ($.01 < p < .05$). Even so, Hallgren concluded that it is probable that the sex distribution of specific dyslexia in the normal population does not differ appreciably from the normal sex distribution. The possibility of a sex-linked mode of inheritance was ruled out because of transmission from father to both son and daughter and from mother to both son and daughter. Despite his conclusion of no differences, he suggested that the somewhat higher incidence of dyslexia in males than in females may be due to sex-controlled inheritance or factors extraneous to those of genetically determined dyslexia. By sex-control, Hallgren meant that there was an autosomal mode of inheritance but a loss of manifestation in females.

The recessive hypothesis was rejected on the basis of the large number of families (93 out of 112) with at least one parent affected and the frequency with which dyslexia occurred in three generations.

Using the data for the parents (affected × unaffected) and offspring in the 90 families in group II, Hallgren calculated Mendelian ratios in a test of the hypothesis that specific dyslexia follows an autosomal dominant mode of inheritance. The Mendelian ratios, which consist of the observed proportions of affected persons among all offspring, were in good agreement with those expected. Hallgren concluded that "the Mendelian analysis of the families in Group II thus shows that, with a high degree of probability, specific

---

[1]The expression "secondary case" is sometimes used to refer to a disabled reader whose reading deficiencies are the result of another primary condition. Hallgren used the expression to refer to a dyslexic in the family other than the proband.

dyslexia follows a monohybrid autosomal dominant mode of inheritance with practically complete manifestations'' (p. 209).

Hallgren's conclusions have been quoted widely for more than 25 years with a minimum of criticism. The work must be acknowledged as an enormous task, for he gathered information, mainly through personal examination, on the physical and neurologic status, vision, hearing, speech, and intelligence of the probands, and information on factors influencing the family environment of the probands; and having made his diagnosis, his subsequent analyses were detailed and careful. The conclusions of his study, however, must be viewed in light of his method of diagnosis. For instance, in addition to relying primarily on history rather than test results to make his diagnoses, he used the very subject of his investigation, heredity, to rule out other etiological factors as primary factors in dyslexia. In discussing the presence of nervous disorders in some probands, he stated, ''The fact that specific dyslexia can be shown to be hereditary in the overwhelming majority of families in which the proband has some nervous disorder is a strong argument *a posteriori* against the hypothesis that specific dyslexia is secondary to the nervous disorders in these cases'' (p.109). Likewise, he rejected factors in the child's home environment as being of causal significance for dyslexia when other dyslexic cases were found in the family. He appeared to discard the idea that common environment might be a causative factor for the multiple cases in the family.

Secondly, although Hallgren recognized that there may be ''different biotypes of specific dyslexia which follow different modes of inheritance but have the same clinical manifestations'' (p. 212), he made no attempt to segregate out various subtypes in analyzing his data. Thus, his segregation analysis might be likened to a segregation analysis of families of a heterogeneous group of cases of mental retardation. Unless the group of families is clinically homogeneous, a number of modes of inheritance might be represented within the group.

Despite these very serious shortcomings, Hallgren must be credited with keeping alive the study of the genetics of dyslexia. He also must be acknowledged fo his recognition that dyslexia should not be studied as an isolated condition, but that other characteristics of the individuals should be considered. Even allowing for a number of misclassifications of his subtests, he has undoubtedly demonstrated a high degree of familial aggregation in the families, and his detailed description of many of them leave little doubt that there is a biological transmission of the condition.

No pedigree study since Hallgren's has investigated as many families as were included in his. One study which did include a segregation analysis was that reported by Zahálková, Vrzal, and Kloboutová (1972). They studied a sample of 65 dyslexics randomly selected from those who visited a counseling unit for dyslexics. Among this group were 29 children for whom there was reported a familial incidence of dyslexia. This group of 29 and any of their parents who were affected were taken as probands so that a total of 49 families was used for a determination of the proportion of dyslexics among sibships of the proband. The authors found a greater incidence of manifested dyslexia for fathers (22/49) and brothers (22/46) of probands than for mothers (11/49) and sisters (9/40) of probands. After segregation analysis, the authors concluded, in close agreement with Hallgren, that ''the hereditary form of dyslexia is inherited as an autosomal dominant influenced by sex.''

There are several criticisms that may be made of the procedures used in this study. First, the method of diagnosis used is not stated. It might be assumed that for the probands who visited the clinic, some sort of standardized testing was done, but there is no indication of which tests were used or what criteria were set for a diagnosis of dyslexia. It might also be assumed that diagnoses of parents, sibs, and grandparents were based on interview data. Thus, diagnostic procedures were open to question. Second a presumption of being affected was made for any adult who, although not manifesting dyslexia, had both a parent and child who were affected. Since the purpose of the study was to investigate the genetics of dyslexia, to assume that dyslexia is genetically transmitted from grandparent to child through the child's parent is to prejudge the role of the genes in dyslexia. Third, the inclusion of affected parents of probands as probands themselves provided a total group of 49 probands who were not independently ascertained. Thus, the conclusions of the authors concerning the mode of inheritance are suspect.

Finucci, Guthrie, Childs, et al. (1976) studied 20 family pedigrees ascertained through 15 boys and 5 girls attending one of three schools with special programs for dyslexic children. Subjects (probands, parents, and sibs) were given a battery of reading, spelling, and intelligence tests. Unique to the study was a set of tests, referred to as tolerance tests, which was administered only to adults. The tests, all of which required oral reading, were designed to detect adults who may have compensated for a reading disability which was more clearly manifested at a younger age. The tests required oral reading of (a) text which was presented upside-down, in mirror image, or backwards; (b) nonsense text; or (c) text presented at a rapid rate of speed. The object of their use was to make ineffectual mechanisms on which the compensated adult might rely, such as word shape cues, an extensive sight vocabulary, or a slowed rate of reading. With few exceptions, classification of each family member as affected or unaffected was made. The classification procedure used a well-specified set of standards based on the discrepancy between standard test performance and educational attainment and for adults an additional assessment of tolerance test performance relative to that of a comparison group. A discriminant analysis was carried out to determine how well a combination of test scores would discriminate between 17 normal readers and 19 disabled readers who had graduated from high school. A linear discriminant function which included eight variables discriminated between the two groups without overlap ($D = 12.98$, $F^{8,37} = 11.57$, $p < .001$).

In the 20 families, a disproportionate number of males were classified as affected. For the parents, 11 of the 18 fathers (61%) and 6 of the 18 mothers (33%) who were classified were listed as affected. For the sibs, 11 of the 22 brothers (50%) and 6 of the 18 sisters (33%) who were classified were said to be affected. When the parent and sib data are pooled, the hypothesis that there is no difference in the sex distribution of affected individuals among first-degree relatives was rejected ($\chi^2 df = 4.85$, $p < .05$).

The major results of the study are confirmation that dyslexia is not randomly distributed in the population, but aggregates within families and strong suggestion that it is unlikely that one mode of inheritance will account for the variety of familial patterns of aggregation. Thirty-four of 75 first-degree relatives were classified as dyslexic. In the 16 families in which both parents were classified, three had both parents affected, 10 had only one parent affected, and 3 had neither parent affected. In only 3 of the 20 families was the proband the sole identified case of dyslexia, and in 2 of these, only one of the parents was unclassified. Because of the small number of families in the study, no segregation analyses were carried out. The lack of uniform pedigree patterns suggests genetic heterogeneity, referred to by Hallgren as different "biotypes." Thus, as stated previously, the family patterns in this study support the contention that homogeneous subgroups of families of sizable number should be identified before tests of other genetic hypotheses are carried out.

Carter (1977) studied 13 families of dyslexic children in an effort to characterize patterns of cerebral asymmetry of both dyslexic and nondyslexic family members. Twelve of the families were ascertained through students attending a school for dyslexic children and the 13th was the family of an uncle of one of the probands. Members of the families were carefully diagnosed using a battery of intelligence, reading, and spelling tests.

If the oldest affected child in the 13th family and the oldest affected child in a family ascertained through two children are designated the probands in their respective families, there are eight male and five female probands. A tabulation of other affected members within families reveals (a) 2 families with both parents affected, 4 with one parent affected, and 7 with neither parent affected; (b) 4 fathers and 4 mothers affected; (c) 10 of 19 brothers affected and 5 of 17 sisters affected; and (d) 4 of the 13 families with no case other than the proband affected. As with the study of Finucci et al. (1976), no pattern of transmission could adequately explain the patterns of transmission within all families. Within these families, Carter also found more individuals than in normal reading samples of Sadick (1975) who demonstrated either ambilaterality (no difference between hemispheres for either dichotic listening or visual hemifield tasks) or unilaterality (high performance by one hemisphere for both linguistic and nonlinguistic dichotic listening and visual hemifield tasks). These characteristics might serve as one means for isolating homogeneous subgroups in which to test genetic hypotheses.

Smith, Kimberling, and Lubs (1977) observed 15 families from 8 kindreds. The purpose of the study was to look for genetic linkage between dyslexia and any of 40 genotypic and chromosomal markers, rather than to determine the degree of familial aggregation. This purpose dictated the method of ascertainment of the families requiring that each proband have a parent and grandparent affected—that is, families that were selected had dyslexia transmitted in an autosomal dominant fashion. Diagnoses of individuals were made using an extensive battery of reading and spelling tests and history of early significant reading problems, although no measure of intelligence was used. The reading deficit in the probands ranged from 3 to 8 years below grade level with a mean of 4.5 years below. In their affected sibs and cousins, the mean was 3.1 years behind. For the 18 adults who were diagnosed as affected, the mean reading grade level was 7.65 and the mean spelling grade level was 7.50. A linear discriminant function of test scores alone was sufficient to discriminate, with little overlap, normal readers from disabled readers, and when discriminant analyses were carried out with males only or children only, discrimination between normals and dyslexics was complete.

All of the probands are male, but if they are eliminated from the calculation, the sex ratio of affected family members is 1.4:1. The authors conclude that the sex ratio close to 1:1, the pattern of transmission within families, their similar phenotypes (no gross neurologic abnormalities, dysphonetic spelling errors, and less severely affected females), and a suggestion of linkage to one chromosome, point toward there being a homogeneous subgroup for whom there is a dominant form of dyslexia.

Summary of Conclusions of Previous Studies

Studies to date have been concerned mainly with demonstrating the familial nature of dyslexia in samples chosen to minimize the etiological importance of environmental factors. Three results in particular—(a) nonrandom familial aggregation of dyslexia (e.g., Walker and Cole); (b) lower reading and spelling ability in the members of immediate families of disabled readers than in the members of immediate families of normal readers (e.g., Owen, et al. and Foch, et al.); and (c) higher concordance rates for MZ than for D Z twins (e.g., Bakwin, Zerbin-Rudin)—all point toward the importance of genetic factors, but these studies have not attempted to examine the pattern of transmission. The few studies that have attempted to examine the mode of inheritance have not been conclusive because of uncertain diagnostic procedures, small samples, biased or nonindependent ascertainment or probands, or heterogeneous samples of families. The remainder of the chapter will deal with some guidelines that should aid in designing studies investigating the role of genes in dyslexia.

GUIDELINES FOR FUTURE STUDIES

Diagnosis, Selection, and Classification of Subjects

Selection of probands. The essential ingredient of any genetic study is careful diagnosis of probands. Despite much confusion as to the definition of dyslexia, the minimum criterion for selection of probands should be evidence of difficulty in learning to read which is severe enough to be outside the range which a subject's intelligence and level of schooling might predict. With the ready availability of standardized measures of intelligence, reading, and spelling, there is little reason not to employ such measures in characterizing a subject. There are, however, no well-specified procedures that have gained universal acceptance in the diagnosis of dyslexia and the decision as to which tests to use and how to employ their scores diagnostically are decisions left to the investigator.

There does seem to be general agreement that a number of characteristics of potential subjects for a dyslexic research sample should serve as exclusionary factors (Critchley, 1970; Symmes and Rapoport, 1972; Naidoo, 1972). These include primary emotional disturbance, uncorrected sensory defects, inadequate schooling, below-average intelligence, and severe CNS dysfunction. Exclusion of subjects because of the presence of any of these factors does not imply that those subjects might not also have dyslexia, but rather that if anything is to be learned about the nature of the condition, it might best be learned when the sample under study includes only well-defined cases.

The reading and/or spelling tests which an investigator uses in the selection of probands are dependent on his view of dyslexia. One view of dyslexia is that it is a condition that first manifests itself during the period when a child is in the acquisition stages of reading. The skills acquired by most children during this stage—visual discrimination of letters and words, decoding of letters and syllables to sounds, blending of sounds into words, and automatic word recognition—are basic to fluent oral reading. The holder of this view might deem an oral reading test and/or a test of spelling measuring related skills as appropriate for detecting dyslexics.

Another view of dyslexia is that it is a condition characterized by the inability to comprehend written material, to get meaning from text. The holder of this view would place more emphasis on measuring the product rather than the process of reading and might deem a silent reading comprehension test appropriate for detecting dyslexics.

The problem that exists in test selection is illustrated in Figure 1. Assuming for the moment that a suitable cut-off has been chosen between the "good" and "poor" designation, there is little doubt as to the characterization of individuals who would fall into cell 1 or cell 4. Those in cell 1 who show no reading deficits would be called normal readers, and those in cell 4, if not eliminated because of any of the exclusionary factors mentioned, would be called dyslexic. Individuals in cells 2 and 3, however, differ from those in cell 4 by reason of showing only one form of deficit. With respect to those in cell 2, Wiener and Cromer (1967) state that

READING COMPREHENSION SKILLS

	GOOD	POOR
GOOD	Good Reader 1	Good Oral Reader Poor Comprehender 2
POOR	Poor Oral Reader Good Comprehender 3	Poor Reader 4

ORAL READING/ SPELLING SKILLS

Fig. 1. CHARACTERIZATION OF SUBJECTS ACCORDING TO READING SKILLS.

The inability to demonstrate comprehension . . . may be a function of restricted language, restricted experience, limited intelligence, or combinations of these, rather than a function of reading difficulty. If comprehension is used as the critical behavior of reading, then these other possible antecedents of noncomprehension must be ruled out before the problem can be called "a reading difficulty." (p. 620)

It is proposed here that characterization of individuals in cell 2 as a subtype of dyslexics is only proper when it can be demonstrated that their oral language comprehension is adequate. With respect to individuals in cell 3, it is proposed that this group might be characterized as a subtype of dyslexics who are able to skirt the usual (visual form) −> (sound) −> (meaning) route to comprehension and progress from (visual form) −> (meaning) with little dependence on analytic skills.

Having decided on the qualities to be measured in the process of subject selection, the investigator must decide on how the scores from these measures will be used for diagnosis. Probably the most common approach used is that of specifying as dyslexic a child who performs on standardized tests of reading or spelling a specific number of grades below his present grade level. Some investigators use the same standard, for instance two grade levels below for all subjects, without regard to the age or present grade level of the subject. Others, recognizing the fact that a deficit of 2 years represents a more severe disability in the younger child than in the older child, have used a sliding scale. Thus, Foch, et al. (1977) selected probands who were reading at one-half or less of grade-level expectancy, Walker and Cole (1965) classified 3rd through 6th graders as dyslexic if the deficit was at least 1 year and 7th through 12th graders as dyslexic if the deficit was at least 2 years, and Finucci, et al. (1976) classified 3rd and 4th graders as dyslexic if the deficit was at least 1½ years and 10th through 12th graders as dyslexic if the deficit was at least 3 years. Other than setting a minimum IQ test score as a criterion for selection as a proband, these three studies did not express the requisite deficit in reading as a function of IQ. Symmes and Rapoport (1972) did take into account the IQ of their potential probands by requiring that, in addition to having an IQ score grater than 100, the Wide Range Achievement Test (WRAT) Reading score be at least one standard deviation below the WISC Full-Scale IQ. Use of the WRAT facilitated this procedure because of the availability of normalized scores, but not all standardized tests provide such scores.

Two techniques that provide a means for classifying a subject which take into account his age, grade, and/or IQ make use of a quotient or a regression procedure. Some quotients are based on the principle that a child's reading achievement should be considered in comparison to an expected achievement. Thus, Myklebust (1968) made use of a Learning Quotient (LQ): LQ = Test age ÷ Expectancy age, where Test Age is an age equivalent score on a test measuring the skill under study (such as reading, spelling, or arithmetic) and the Expectancy Age = (Mental Age + Life Age + Grade Age)/3. Mental Age, derived from a standardized IQ test, is included as a reflection of the child's mental maturity; Life Age, or chronological age, is included as a reflection of the child's physiologic maturity; and Grade Age is included as an indicator of the child's school experience. When this quotient was derived for a population of 932 public school children in grades 3 and 4 who were administered the Gates Advanced Primary reading Tests, Myklebust found that 14.5% of the group had LQs below .90, which he considered to be indicative of high risk for underachievement. Of the 14.5%, 25% after further pediatric, neurologic, electroencephalographic, ophthalmologic, psychological, and educational examination were classified as having a neurogenic type of learning disability.

We have calculated two quotients, one for Gray Oral Reading Test scores and one for WRAT Spelling Test scores, using the Myklebust formula and then calculated the average so as to give a single score. One of the values of quotients lies in their use as a quantitative measure enabling examination of where in a distribution relatives of probands lie. This is illustrated in Figure 2, which depicts the distribution of the average quotients for four groups of children. Group I includes all 44 consecutively tested children with WISC-R IQ $\geq$ 95 who are attending one of three schools with special programs for reading-disabled children. Group II includes their 58 school-age sibs with IQ $\geq$ 95. Group III includes 15 children with IQ $\geq$ 95 from a regular school selected because their scores on the California Test of Basic Skills reading were at or above grade level, and Group IV includes their 23 school-age sibs. The distributions indicate that the bulk of the sibs of disabled readers are reading below expectation, with many falling in the dyslexic range while the majority of the sibs of normal readers are reading at or above expectation. Two of the three subjects with quotients <.80 in group IV are themselves sibs.

Yule, Rutter, Berger, et al. (1974) used a regression procedure to identify underachievers in reading. Using randomly selected control groups, they developed equations for the prediction of scores on the Neale Analysis of Reading Ability from the sum of four scaled scores on a short form of the WISC. Separate equations were derived for different age groups. Children whose actual scores on the reading test were two standard errors of prediction from the predicted scores were considered to have gross underachievement in reading. If such differences were normally distributed, 2.28% of such differences should fall into this category; yet they found that in three large populations from the Isle of Wight and London the percentage falling into this category varied from 3% to 9%. They suggested that this significant deviation from normality can best be explained by a group with "a specific reading retardation" not explainable by factors contributing to a normal distribution of reading disability.

The distributions of any of these measures, whether a deviation from grade level, a standard score difference between IQ and reading, a learning quotient, or a deviation of observed scores from that predicted from a regression equation, reveal no point that unambiguously discriminates between normal readers and dyslexics. Thus, although these measures facilitate classification, there is no magic procedure for determining how deviant a score must be for someone to be classified as dyslexic. This classification problem is not

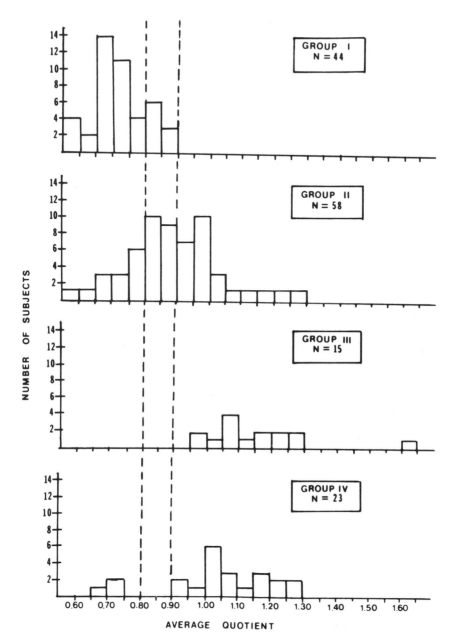

Fig. 2. DISTRIBUTIONS OF AVERAGE LEARNING QUOTIENTS ON THE GRAY ORAL READING TEST AND WRAT SPELLING TEST. GROUP I, CHILDREN IN SPECIAL READING PROGRAMS; GROUP II, SIBS OF CHILDREN IN GROUP I; GROUP III, NORMAL READING CHILDREN; GROUP IV, SIBS OF CHILDREN IN GROUP III.

unique to the field of reading. Similar problems exist in the diagnosis of such common disorders as hypertension, diabetes, and gout, in which measures of blood pressure, blood sugar, and uric acid are continuously distributed and show no bimodality. There are ranges in all of these distributions in which there is little doubt that scores indicate being affected or unaffected. But all also include a range of ambiguity.

In our recent studies, we have chosen average quotients of .80 or less on the Gray Oral Reading Test and WRAT Spelling Test as designating dyslexia. Probands with average quotients between .80 and .90 are designated as borderline cases. Of particular interest to us will be whether the latter will be shown to have the same degree of familial aggregation as do more severe cases. This consideration, which will be discussed later, is important to the resolution of whether there is a large subgroup of multigenic cases of dyslexics. Rutter and Yule (1975) separated cases in a similar fashion, designating subjects whose difference between predicted and observed scores were at least two standard errors of prediction as "specifically reading retarded" and those for whom such differences were less, but who were still reading several months below grade level, as "reading backward."

Classification of relatives.   A major difference between a family study and a study which compared normal readers and dyslexics is that in the latter the investigator has the luxury of omitting from study subjects whose classification is ambiguous. In a family study, however, in addition to subjects *selected* as probands, there are subjects to be *classified* who are considered because they are related to a proband. Thus, procedures must be developed for classifying subjects in several age groups, including adults. These should include tests that detect adults who have compensated for dyslexia which was more clearly manifested in childhood.

The methods used for classifying children are not as easily applied to adults. For instance, the use of grade-equivalent scores and standard scores are not as reliable at the upper end of a test scale as the ones in the middle of the test scale. Furthermore, the use of a quotient procedure for adults that is similar to that used for children is precluded by the plateauing of mental age near adulthood and the lack of reliable and valid grade-equivalent scores for adults on many tests. A more suitable procedure for classifying adults makes use of regression equations using such variables as sex, education, and intelligence as predictors for reading test scores. Using this procedure, actual test performance which is a specified number of standard errors poorer than that predicted is designated as characteristic of dyslexics. No such equations have been developed on a large representative sample of adults in the United States.

Who Should be Studied?

Immediate family members.   If anything new is to be learned about transmission of dyslexia within families, at a minimum *all* first-degree relatives—that is, parents and sibs of a proband—should be included for study. That there is a greater proportion of dyslexics or a greater degree of poor reading ability among the relatives of dyslexics than among the relatives of normal readers has been amply demonstrated. Not only does segregation analysis depend upon complete families, but without complete families no progress can be made in the elucidation of subtypes, since the latter depends upon showing within-family homogeneity of expression and between-family differences.

Second- and third-degree relatives.   There are a number of reasons why extended family pedigrees should be studied. First, the suggestion of a particular pattern of transmission in several nuclear families is given further support if their second- and third-degree relatives (aunts, uncles, grandparents, cousins) are affected according to a pattern consistent with that hypothesized. Thus, if there are several nuclear families in which children are affected, but neither parent is affected, the observation that aunts and uncles are not affected, suggests a recessive mode of inheritance for that group of families. Or, if nuclear families presented a dominant pattern of inheritance, this mode of inheritance is supported by the observation of affected grandparents, aunts, or uncles.

The study by Smith, et al. (1977) necessitated the investigation of at least three generations of the families because they were testing the hypothesis of genetic linkage of dyslexia to known genetic loci, a procedure that demands the inclusion of relatives outside the nuclear family. Although they selected only those families that showed a dominant pattern in a direct line for three generations, their diagnosis of additional affected members—aunts, uncles, and cousins—consistent with a dominant pattern of transmission gave added support to that hypothesis.

Second, the study of uncles, aunts, and cousins might also aid in a test of the multifactorial hypothesis. Multifactorial conditions may be the result of alleles at many genetic loci which act in concert with factors in the environment. For either a single gene or a multifactorial condition, the likelihood of being affected drops off as the relationship to the proband becomes more distant. With dominant inheritance, the expected proportion of affected third-degree relatives is half that for second-degree relatives, which is half that for first-degree relatives; but for multifactorial conditions, a much sharper drop in the proportion affected is expected as the relationship declines (Carter, 1969). Such tests can be carried out only if second-degree and third-degree relatives are examined.

Third, a further test of the multifactorial hypothesis involves observations of the proportion of affected relatives as a function of the severity of the proband, providing that a quantitative measure of severity is available. If severity is related to the number of genes involved, then since the more severely affected probands should have the greater number of alleles determining the condition, their relatives should be at higher risk.

Female probands.   None of the family studies reviewed here had as many female probands as males, undoubtedly because of the sex differential between the number of males and females affected, but also possibly reflecting a differential in referral rate to school programs for dyslexics. Special effort should be made, however, to study a large number of families of female probands (a) to determine whether affected females are more severely affected than males, (b) to determine whether there is a difference in patterns of transmission depending upon the sex of the proband, and (c) as a test of the hypothesis that there is a multigenic threshold which is a function of sex. Carter (1961) has demonstrated that for congenital pyloric stenosis, which has a M/F sex ratio of 5:1, the risk for being affected among the relatives of female probands is three times greater than that for relatives of male probands. This suggests that the threshold for being affected is higher in females than in males.

A Search for Subtypes

Throughout this chapter it has been suggested that dyslexia is not a unitary syndrome, but is heterogeneous in nature. This conjecture is based on clinical observation by many researchers (Boder, 1971, 1973; Mattis, French, and Rapin, 1976; Doehring, 1968; Denckla and Rudel, 1976; and Naidoo, 1972) and on the observation of no consistent pattern of transmission within families (Finucci, et al., 1976). But that subtypes of dyslexia exist has not yet been satisfactorily demonstrated. Two procedures that could be used for the validation of subtypes are (a) demonstration that subtypes respond differentially to treatment or remedial efforts or (b) demonstration that there is within-family homogeneity and between-family heterogeneity—that is, that although different subtypes occur in different families, within a family all members are of the same subtype.

These procedures could be applied to the putative subtypes already proposed. For instance, Boder (1971, 1973) suggests that there are three subtypes of dyslexics who may be identified through their reading-spelling patterns: (a) dysphonetic dyslexics evidence a primary defect in grapheme-phoneme integration (they read words globally rather than analytically, and their spelling reflects an inability to syllabicate or phonetically analyze a spoken word); (b) dyseidetic dyslexics evidence a primary deficit in perceiving words as visual Gestalts (they read analytically and spell phonetically); (c) mixed dysphonetic-dyseidetic dyslexics evidence both defects and are the most severely handicapped. In a single sentence in a paper describing the diagnostic procedure, Boder (1971) stated that all but two sets of dyslexic sibs in a group of 39 from 16 families fall into the same reading-spelling pattern group. Unfortunately, no quantitative scoring system was given for allocating dyslexics to each category. Nor do we know whether designation of each sib is made without knowing that of the other.

In addition to using measures of reading and spelling behavior, nonreading measures should be used to further characterize subtypes already identified or to identify additional subtypes. For instance, Mattis, et al. (1975) describe three subgroups: (a) a language-disorder subgroup with anomia, speech-sound discrimination problems, and spoken-language-comprehension problems; (b) a group with speech-articulation problems; and (c) a group with visuospatial-perception problems. Each of these subgroups was identified through tests of functions other than reading and spelling. A question that should be investigated is whether any of these latter subtypes might be congruent with those of Boder or might any of them be subtypes within the subgroups of Boder.

Another characteristic that should be further investigated as a potential descriptor of a subtype is the evoked response. Conners (1970) noted similar patterns of attenuated waveforms for four disabled readers in the same family when the measures were made at a left parietal electrode in response to light flashes. Group differences have been found between normal and disabled readers, both adults and children, in response to linguistic stimuli presented visually (Preston, Guthrie, and Childs, 1974; Preston, Guthrie, Kirsch, et al., 1977; Symann-Louett, Gascon, Matsumiya, et al., 1977). For adults the differences are most pronounced on the left parietal electrode for the component of the waveform referred to as P300 or the late positive component. When the group differences are probed, it is found that about 20% of disabled readers fall outside the range of that for normal readers, suggesting that there is a subgroup of disabled readers who exhibit an abnormal visual evoked response (Preston, 1978).

Other measures that might be used to characterize subtypes are measures of cerebellar-vestibular dysfunction (Frank and Levinson, 1973), hemispheric asymmetries of cognitive processing (Whitelson, 1977; Carter, 1977), and verbal/performance discrepancies (Kinsbourne and Warrington, 1963), or subtest patterns (Huelsman, 1970) on Wechsler IQ tests. While each of these measures has been used separately for distinguishing between dyslexics, any comprehensive study of the issue of subtypes should test all members of subject families on several of these characteristics. The use of many measures will lead to a more complete description of a subtype in terms of both behavioral and physiologic characteristics. The validity of a subtype would be demonstrated by finding several families in which dyslexics are identified by the same cluster of characteristics.

SUMMARY

This review has considered several twin, family, and pedigree studies which convincingly demonstrate the familial nature of dyslexia, even when environmental influences on reading ability are controlled. This finding, together with the demonstration by Yule, et al. (1974) that there are more dyslexics than can be accounted for by factors contributing to a normal distribution of reading ability and numerous demonstrations of a disproportionate sex ratio among dyslexics, points toward a genetic basis for dyslexia in a large number of cases. When familial patterns of dyslexia are examined, however, no single mode of transmission, either multigenic or monogenic, will explain all patterns. It is proposed that future research should be directed at the identification of subtypes of dyslexia which show homogeneity within families. Tests of specific genetic hypotheses should proceed only on families of dyslexics demonstrating a similar cluster of characteristics. While identification of subtypes furthers the study of the genetics of dyslexia, the validity of subtypes would be substantiated by finding within-family homogeneity for the defining characteristics of a subtype.

REFERENCES

Bakwin, H. Reading disability in twins. *Developmental Medicine and Child Neurology,* 1973, 15:184–187.

Boder, E. Developmental dyslexia: prevailing diagnostic concepts and a new diagnostic approach. *In* H. Myklebust, ed., *Progress in Learning Disabilities,* Vol. 2. New York: Grune & Stratton, 1971, 292–321.

Boder, E. Developmental dyslexia: a diagnostic approach based on three atypical reading-spelling patterns. *Developmental Medicine and Child Neurology,* 1973, 15:663–687.

Carter, B. Patterns of cerebral asymmetry in families affected by specific developmental dyslexia. Unpublished doctoral dissertation, University of Connecticut, 1977.

Carter, C. The inheritance of congenital pyloric stenosis. *British Medical Bulletin,* 1961, 17:251–254.

Carter, C. Genetics of common disorders. *British Medical Bulletin,* 1969, 25:52–57.

Conners, C. Cortical evoked response in children with learning disorders. *Psychophysiology,* 1970, 7:418–428.

Connolly, C. Social and emotional factors in learning disabilities. *In* H. Myklebust, ed., *Progress in Learning Disabilities,* Vol. 2. New York: Grune & Stratton, 1971, 151–178.

Critchley, M. *The Dyslexic Child.* Springfield, Ill.: Thomas, 1970.

Denckla, M., and Rudel, R. Rapid automatized naming (R.A.N.): Dyslexia differentiated from other learning disabilities. *Neuropsychologia,* 1976, 14:471–479.

Doehring, D. *Patterns of Impairment in Specific Reading Disability.* Bloomington: Indiana University Press, 1968.

Drew, A. A neurological appraisal of familial congenital word-blindness. *Brain,* 1956, 79:440–460.

Eustis, R. Specific reading disability. *New England Journal of Medicine,* 1947, 237:243–249.

Finucci, J., Guthrie, J., Childs, A., Abbey, H., and Childs, B. The genetics of specific reading disability. *Annals of Human Genetics,* 1976, 40:1–23.

Fisher, J. Case of congenital word-blindness (inability to learn to read). *Ophthalmic Review,* 1905, 24:315–318.

Foch, T., DeFries, J., McClearn, G., and Singer, S. Familial patterns of impairment in reading disability. *Journal of Educational Psychology,* 1977, 69:316–329.

Frank, J., and Levinson, H. Dysmetric dyslexia and dyspraxia. *Journal of Child Psychiatry,* 1973, 12:690–701.

Hallgren, B. Specific dyslexia: a clinical and genetic study. *Acta Psychiatrica et Neurologica,* 1950, Suppl. 65.

Hinshelwood, J. Four cases of congenital word-blindness occurring in the same family. *British Medical Journal,* 1907, 2:1229–1232.

Hinshelwood, J. Two cases of hereditary word-blindness. *British Medical Journal,* 1911, 1:608–609.

Hinshelwood, J. *Congenital Word-Blindness.* London: H. K. Lewis, 1917.

Hof, J., and Guldenpfennig, W. Dominant inheritance of specific reading disability. *South African Medical Journal*, 1972, 46:737–738.

Holmes, L., Moser, H., Halldorsson, S., Mack, C., Pant, S., and Matzilevich, B. *Mental Retardation: An Atlas of Diseases with Associated Physical Abnormalities*. New York: MacMillan, 1972.

Huelsman, C. The WISC subtest syndrome for disabled readers. *Perceptual and Motor Skills*, 1970, 30:535–550.

Ingram, T., Mason, A., and Lackburn, I. A retrospective study of 82 children with reading disability. *Developmental Medicine and Child Neurology*, 1970, 12:271–281.

Kerr, J. School hygiene, in its mental, moral, and physical aspects. *Journal of the Royal Statistical Society*, 1897, 60:613–680. (Howard Medal Prize Essay, June 1896).

Kety, S., Rosenthal, D., Wender, P., Schulsinger, F., and Jacobsen, B. Mental illness in the biological and adoptive families of adopted individuals who have become schizophrenic: a preliminary report based on psychiatric interviews. *In* R. Fieve, D. Rosenthal, and H. Brill, eds., *Genetic Research in Psychiatry*. Baltimore: Johns Hopkins University Press, 1975, 147–165.

Kinsbourne, M., and Warrington, D. Developmental factors in reading and writing backwardness. *British Journal of Psychiatry*, 1963, 54:145–156.

Marshall, W., and Ferguson, J. Hereditary word-blindness as a defect of selective association. *Journal of Nervous and Mental Disease*, 1939, 89:164–173.

Mattis, S., French, J., and Rapin, I. Dyslexia in children and young adults: three independent neuropsychological syndromes. *Developmental Medicine and Child Neurology*, 1975, 17:150–163.

McCready, E. Congenital word-blindness as a cause of backwardness in school children: Report of a case associated with stuttering. *Pennsylvania Medical Journal*, 1909–1910, 13:278–284.

Morgan, W. A case of congenital word-blindness. *British Medical Journal*, 1896, 2:1378.

Munsinger, H. Children's resemblance to their biological and adoptive parents in two ethnic groups. *Behavior Genetics*, 1975, 5:239–254.

Myklebust, H. Learning disabilities: definition and overview. *In* H. Myklebust, ed., *Progress in Learning Disabilities*, Vol. 1. New York: Grune & Stratton, 1968, 1–15.

Naidoo, S. Specific Dyslexia. New York: Halstad, 1972.

Nettleship, E. Cases of congenital word-blindness (inability to learn to read), *Ophthalmic Review*, 1901, 20:61–67.

Owen, F., Adams, P., Forrest, T., Stolz, L., and Fisher, S. Learning disorders in children: sibling studies. *Mongraphs of the Society for Research in Child Development*, 1971, 36: No. 4.

Penrose, L. *The Biology of Mental Defect*. New York: Grune & Stratton, 1965.

Perlo, V., and Rak, E. Developmental dyslexia in adults. *Neurology*, 1971, 21:1231–1235.

Preston, M. Personal communication, 1978.

Preston, M., Guthrie, J., and Childs, B. Visual evoked responses (VERs) in normal and disabled readers. *Psychophysiology*, 1974, 11:452–457.

Preston, M., Guthrie, J., Kirsch, I., Gertman, D., and Childs, B. VERs in normal and disabled adult readers. *Psychophysiology*, 1977, 14:8–14.

Rawson, M. *Developmental Language Disability*. Baltimore: Johns Hopkins University Press, 1968.

Roberts, J. The genetics of mental deficiency. *The Eugenics Review*, 1952–1953, 44:71–83.

Rutter, M., and Yule, W. The concept of specific reading retardation. *Journal of Child Psychology and Psychiatry and Applied Disciplines*, 1975, 16:181–197.

Sadick, T. Language laterality and handedness in relation to reading acquisition: A developmental study. Unpublished doctoral dissertation, University of Connecticut, 1975.

Smith, S., Kimberling, W., and Lubs, H. Family studies in specific dyslexia. Presented at the twenty-eighth annual meeting of the American Society of Human Genetics, San Diego, October 19–22, 1977.

Stephenson, S. Congenital word-blindness. *The Lancet*, 1904, 2:827–828.

Stephenson, S. Six cases of congenital word-blindness affecting three generations of one family. *The Ophthalmoscope*, 1907, 5:482–484.

Symann-Louett, N., Gascon, G., Matsumiya, Y., and Lombroso, C. Waveform difference in visual evoked responses between normal and reading disabled children. *Neurology*, 1977, 27:156–159.

Symmes, J., and Rapoport, J. Unexpected reading failure. *American Journal of Orthopsychiatry*, 1972, 42:82–91.

Thomas, C. Congenital word-blindness and its treatment. *Ophthalmoscope*, 1905, 3:380–385.

Vandenberg, S. Heredity and dyslexia. *Bulletin of the Orton Society*, 1967, 17:54–56.

Walker, L., and Cole, E. Familial patterns of expression of specific reading disability in a population sample. *Bulletin of the Orton Society*, 1965, 15:12–24.

Wiener, M., and Cromer, W. Reading and reading difficulty: a conceptual analysis. *Harvard Educational Review,* 1967, 37:620–643.

Witelson, S. Neural and cognitive correlates of developmental dyslexia: age and sex differences. *In* S. Gershon and C. Shagass, eds., *Psychopathology and Brain Dysfunction.* New York: Raven Press, 1977.

Yule, W., Rutter, M., Berger, M., and Thompson, J. Over- and underachievement in reading: distribution in the general population. *British Journal of Educational Psychology,* 1974, 44:1–12.

Zahálková, M., Vrzal, V., and Klobouková, E. Genetical investigation in dyslexia. *Journal of Medical Genetics,* 1972, 9:48–52.

Zerbin-Rudin, E. Congenital word-blindness. *Bulletin of the Orton Society,* 1967, 17:47–54.

III. Reading Disabilities: An Epidemiologic Approach

JANE SCHULMAN
ALAN LEVITON

Two major problems pervade the literature on reading disabilities. First, no common definition of reading disability exists, so subjects are selected according to each investigator's set of criteria. This implies that the results of any one study tend not to be comparable to those of any other study because different populations of children have been evaluated. Second, most studies have evaluated the association of only one risk factor of reading handicap without considering the confounding effect of other risk factors. This is especially important because of the complex interrelationships among factors thought to be associated with reading disability (e.g., low socioeconomic class, inadequate educational opportunities, suboptimal prenatal care, malnutrition, infection, exposure to lead). Thus, much of the literature about the risk factors of reading handicap may have less value than has been claimed for it.

Definition
A definition of a reading disability useful for epidemiologic purposes should not imply causation, and, in addition, should provide an objective means of accurately identifying those children who cannot read. Any definition of reading handicap that implies causation and is thus based on one putative etiologic factor, or group of factors, gives rise to an underestimate of the number of children who have the disorder. Implicit in the second prerequisite is the assumption that those children are identified who are not reading at the level expected of them. A definition of reading disability, therefore, must include some quantitive measure of the discrepancy between the child's actual and expected reading levels. Problems arise in trying to define such a measure. For example, what are the proper criteria to use in the measurement of the child's "expected" reading level? Also, how much of a discrepancy between actual and expected levels is needed before a child has a reading disability?

A reading disability is often defined as a discrepancy of at least 2 years between a child's actual reading level and expected grade level based on chronological age. Inherent in this definition is the assumption that all chidren should be reading at their grade level regardless of the school they attend, where they live, and/or how intelligent they are. Moreover, a 2-year deficiency at grade 3 is not equivalent to a 2-year deficiency at grade 9 (Applebee, 1971). If available, local norms may be used as the standard with which to compare a child's actual reading level. Nevertheless, a child who reads at a level comparable to his peers but beneath the level of which he is capable would be misclassified as not being retarded in reading.

Some investigators have the child serve as his own standard and assume that the child should be reading on the same level as his performance in subject areas that are influenced minimally by variations in reading capability. Another approach is to compare the child's reading score to his score on a performance IQ test. The problem here is similar to the problem of a set discrepancy between reading level and grade level. A child whose PIQ is 100 and RA is 70 (discrepancy of 30 points) would be considered to have the same amount

65

of disability as a child whose PIQ is 150 and RA is 120 (difference of 30 points). Also, subtracting a child's reading age from his mental age makes very intelligent children appear to be underachieving while very dull children seem to be overachieving because of the effects of regression toward the mean (Yule, 1976).

The use of a ratio score (achievement divided by expectancy) has been suggested by Myklebust (1968), although it too may have a regression effect (Yule, Rutter, and Berger, 1974). The learning quotient that Myklebust proposed is the achievement (in any area of learning) expressed as an age score divided by an expectancy age defined as the mean of mental age (the higher of the verbal and nonverbal tests), chronologic age, and grade age. For one study he defined a severe learning disability as a learning quotient of 84 or less and a moderate disability as 85 to 90 (Myklebust, 1973).

Yule, et al. (1974) proposed using a regression equation based on nonverbal IQ scores for defining underachievement and overachievement in reading. By using this method one can predict reading levels in any sample of children (assuming the statistical requirements of the method, for example, linearity, are met). Subsequently, these expected reading levels can be compared to those observed. A lack of documented correlation between nonverbal IQ and reading scores may be the main reason this is rarely used.

One issue that may be dealt with, regardless of how reading disability is defined, is where to draw the line between disabled readers and normal readers. If interest is confined to the most severe cases of reading disability, the criterion will be more stringent than if the investigator wants to include every child who has trouble reading. This decision is often complicated by such practical considerations as the quantity and quality of data that are available and/or by how willing the investigator is to discard data.

From an epidemiologic viewpoint, spurious results arise because of bias in (a) selection of cases, and/or controls, (b) the ascertainment of exposure, (c) classification of outcome, and/or (d) the analysis due to uncontrolled variables. Each of these sources of bias will be discussed; however, bias due to misclassification of outcome is widespread and is mentioned here. This bias, to a large extent, reflects the common view that the reading-disabled population is homogeneous with respect to both underlying causes and the nature of the problems that these children experience. Although the heterogeneity in this population has been recognized by various investigators (Applebee, 1971; Myklebust, 1968; Kinsbourne and Warrington, 1963; Weiner and Cromer, 1967), we are aware of only a few studies (Owen, et al., 1971; Kucera, Matejcek, and Langmeier, 1963; Rutter and Yule, 1975) which have directly addressed this issue.

HEREDITY

The problems of evaluating the genetic contribution to occurrence of reading handicaps center around the nature-nuture issue and, therefore, are similar to those that plague the genetics and IQ controversy (Layzer, 1974; Thompson, 1975; Jackson, 1975). Generally, the studies in this area can be classified into two categories: familial histories and twin studies.

Family Histories

The validity of these studies has been questioned on the grounds that data are often obtained retrospectively by interviewing the child's parent(s). The late ascertainment of past events suffers from the fact that people, whether consciously or not, selectively censor certain types of information, and/or experience changes in perspective about past familial events (Wenar, 1963; Wenar and Coulter, 1962; Chess, Thomas and Birch, 1966; Yarrow, Campbell, and Burton, 1970; Chamberlain and Johnstone, 1975).

In Hallgren's (1950) famous study of the familial aggregation of reading disability, congenital dyslexia was defined only in terms of its symptoms—that is by (a) difficulty in learning to read or write, (b) reading and writing below class average during the first years at school, (c) a discrepancy between proficiency in reading and proficiency in other subject areas, and (d) a discrepancy between general intelligence and proficiency in reading. On the basis of these criteria, Hallgren found that approximately 10% of a normal population of secondary school children was dyslexic.

The 116 dyslexic subjects were drawn from the Stockholm Child Guidance Clinic (73 cases), and from the three youngest classes of the Stockholm Secondary School (43 cases). The diagnosis of dyslexia was inferred for the clinic patients from referral histories, and for the school children from teachers' reports.

The dyslexics, their sibs and parents and the controls were interviewed. Of the 116 dyslexic subjects, there were three in whom both parents were affected and 94 in whom one parent was affected. Thus, 83.6% of the probands had at least one parent who was dyslexic. Seven of the 19 dyslexic children who did not have a dyslexic parent (or 6% of 116), had a dyslexic sibling, uncle, aunt, or grandparent. Only 12 of the 116 children (10.3%) had no close relatives who were dyslexic.

This study would have been more helpful if (a) two-thirds of the children were not drawn from a highly biased child guidance clinic, (b) the evidence for dyslexia in relatives was either measured objectively or collected prior to the families' recognition of the probands' handicaps, and (c) comparison data were provided (i.e., if the rate of dyslexia was ascertained in the close relatives of children who were not dyslexic).

Precisely this kind of comparison data were provided by Hunter and Johnson (1971). They sent behavioral and developmental questionnaires to the parents of 20 boys who had been recommended for a summer remedial reading clinic and to the parents of 20 boys who had not been recommended for this program. The two groups were matched for age, grade, race, intelligence level, and socioeconomic status. The mean ages of the reading disabled and control groups were 9¾ years and 9 11/12 years, respectively. The reading-disabled group was retarded in reading proficiency on the WRAT by a mean of 2.4 years, and the control group was accelerated in reading by a mean of 1.9 years (i.e., after allowing for actual age-grade placement at time of testing).

The results from the questionnaires revealed 22 incidents of reading problems in the immediate families of the reading-disabled group but only two were noted in the immediate families of the control group. Of these 24, 2 occurred in fathers, 2 in mothers, 7 in sisters, and 13 in brothers. The authors also tallied the total number of spelling errors made by the mothers on the questionnaires. A total of 14 errors were made by mothers of controls, whereas 30 errors were made by mothers of reading-disabled boys.

Walker and Cole (1965) studied all of the families having three children in one suburban public school. The population located in a high-income suburb was relatively homogeneous. Specific reading disability (SRD) was defined on the basis of spelling scores obtained on the Stanford spelling tests. A rating on the Stanford scale was considered indicative of SRD if it was at least 6 months below grade norm at grade 2 (age 7 years); at least 1 year below grade norm at grades 3 to 6 (age 8 to 11 years); or at least 2 years below grade norm at grades 7 to 12 (age 12 to 17 years). Children with an IQ less than 90 were excluded from study.

On the basis of these criteria, 25.3% of the population studied was found to have

SRD. This estimate is high in comparison to Hallgren's estimate of 10%. Hallgren, however, did not include poor spelling as a criterion of dyslexia, whereas Walker and Cole did. This may account for part of the difference between the two estimates.

The numbers of affected sibs were analyzed under the assumption that the occurrence of familial SRD should be random and normally distributed. A comparison was made between the observed and expected number of families with 0, 1, and either 2 or 3 affected children using the rate of 25.3% to calculate expected frequencies. It was expected that 31.2 of the 75 families would have one child affected, and the remaining 12 families would have either two or three children who were affected. However, the observed members of families in these categories were 43, 16, and 16, respectively. The familial concentration of affected children was found to be highly significant ($p < .005$) using the Chi-Square Test. On this basis, it was conluded that SRD is associated with hereditary factors.

The study of Owen, et al. (1971) was confined to a middle- and upper-middle-class population. A child was considered educationally handicapped if he was 1.5 to 2 years below grade level in spelling and/or reading given that his full WISC was at least 90. A group of academically successfully children were identified and matched for sex, grade, and IQ with the educationally handicapped children. Same sex siblings were also chosen for each group, and these two groups of siblings were matched on grade and sex. Thus, comparisons could be made between educationally handicapped and academically successful children, between educationally handicapped children and siblings of academically successful children. Altogether, 304 elementary and junior high school children were included in the study, 244 of whom were boys. The mean age of the children in each of the four groups was approximately 10 years.

A significant discrepancy was noted between verbal and performance WISC IQs for the educationally handicapped children. The magnitude of this discrepancy was found to be significantly greater than that noted for academically successful controls. Compared to their respective controls, the educationally handicapped children and their siblings were significantly impaired on information, arithmetic, digit span, and coding subtests. However, this pattern was reversed for the picture-completion subtest.

On the WRAT, educationally handicapped children were 1 year retarded in reading and 1.8 years retarded in spelling. Their siblings read almost at grade level but were approximately 1 year retarded in spelling. Academically successful children and their siblings scored almost 1 year above grade level in reading, and less than 3 months below grade level in spelling. Further, the reading and spelling discrepancies of the educationally handicapped group increased with age and grade level. According to their teachers, educationally handicapped children and their siblings were noted to be significantly poorer in school adjustment and behavior compared to the academically successful children and their siblings.

Parents of educationally handicapped children were also found to have had, and still to be having, learning disabilities. Fathers of these children scored significantly lower than fathers of controls on the WRAT reading test. Mothers and fathers of educationally handicapped children had significantly poorer English grades when they were in high school than did parents of controls. Unfortunately, the authors do not state whether these results reflect an overall depressed performance by the siblings and parents of educationally handicapped children, or a poor performance by a small subgroup of these relatives.

The 76 children in the educationally handicapped group were divided into five categories to see if any forms of disability were familial. They were (a) medical-neurologic group (17/76), (b) high performance discrepancy group, including those whose performance IQ was at least 15 points superior to his verbal IQ (20/75), (c) low IQ group, including children with IQs between 90 and 99 (18/76), (d) high full IQ group, including children with full-scale IQs ranging from 117 to 154 (17/76), and (e) social deviants (11/76). Because these categories are not mutually exclusive, the number of children per subgroup total to more than 76.

Although one may find fault with these groupings, the only group that showed significant familial aggregation of learning handicaps was the high performance discrepancy group. Kucera, et al. (1963) also reported evidence of hereditary factors in dyslexia in children with high performance-low verbal discrepancies in IQ. Their sample of subjects included 91 Czechoslovakian children between the ages of 7 and 13½ years reading at or below the 2nd grade level. The authors classified 19 of these 91 children (or 21%) into the "heredity" subgroup. This percentage closely approximates the 22% (17/76) reported by Owen, et al. (1971). Thus, much of the familial aggregation seen in both samples of educationally handicapped children was contributed by a relatively small subsample.

Twin Studies

Twins are concordant for reading handicaps if both are reading disabled. If genetic features influence the frequency of reading handicap, then monozygous twins should have a higher concordance rate for reading handicap than do dizygous twins. There are three well-known studies concerned with reading disability in twins. In 1954, Norrie (Zerbin-Rüdin, 1967) studied nine pairs of monozygotic twins, all of whom are concordant for reading disability. Of the 30 pairs of dizygous twins, however, concordance was noted in only 10. In 1959, Hermann studied 45 sets of twins. At least one twin per pair was reading disabled. All 12 pairs of monozygotic twins were concordant for reading handicap. Again, only 33% of the dizygotic twins were found to be concordant for reading disability. Twins were included in Hallgren's study in 1950. All three pairs of monozygotic twins and one of the three sets of dizygotic twins were concordant for reading disability. Thus, in each of these three studies, concordance was found in 100% of monozygotic and 33% of dizygotic twins.

More recently, Bakwin (1973) studied 388 pairs of like-sex twins from a middle-class population. The twins were obtained through organizations for mothers of twins in the New York area. Zygosity was determined objectively (i.e., by blood type). Data were obtained through interviews and questionnaires. A child was considered reading disabled if he was reading at a level below the expectation derived from his performance in other school subjects. However, the specific criterion used for the identification of reading-disabled subjects was not stated by the author. Ninety-seven of the 676 children (14.5%) were found to be reading disabled. No overall difference in frequency of reading disability was seen between the monozygotic and dizygotic twins. However, when a pairwise analysis was performed, it was found that 84% of the monozygotic and 29% of the dizygotic twins were concordant for reading disability.

The familial aggregation of reading handicaps demonstrated by Hallgren (1950), Walker and Cole (1965), and Owen, et al. (1971), cannot separate environmental from genetic effects. The much greater concordance for reading handicap in monozygotic twins than in the same-sex dizygotic twins is the most substantial evidence available that the genetic contribution to the occurrence of reading handicap is a large one. It can be expressed quantitatively with an estimate of heritability, called the *H* value (Harvald and Hague, 1965):

$$H = \frac{\text{Concordance in monozygotic twins} - \text{concordance in dizygotic twins}}{1 - \text{concordance in dizygotic twins}}$$

Using Bakwin's (1973) data; the H value for reading handicaps is .78, a very impressive value indeed.

Matheny and Dolan (1974) used a different approach to the question of whether reading handicap is influenced by hereditary factors. They individually administered the California Reading Achievement test to 70 pairs of same sex twins, aged 9 to 12 years, enrolled in the Louisville Twin Study. Their goal was to study hereditary influences, if any, on reading ability in preadolescent twins. On the basis of blood type, 44 of the 70 pairs of twins were classified monozygotic and the remaining 26 pairs as dizygotic.

Intraclass (i.e., within-pair) correlations of scores were calculated for monozygotic and dizygotic pairs of twins based on the results from the reading test. The observed correlations for monozygotic twins were 0.84, 0.85, and 0.89 for reading vocabulary, reading comprehension, and total reading, respectively. However, the comparable correlation values for dizygotic twins were found to be significantly lower—that is, they were only 0.65, 0.52, and 0.61. The amount of variability within pairs of scores was significantly greater for dizygotic than for monozygotic twins. The authors concluded that monozygotic twins are more similar than dizygotic twins in their reading capabilities, and these results clearly implicate an hereditary component in reading achievement.

SOCIAL CLASS

Several problems face the investigator who wants to evaluate the relationship between social class and reading handicap. First, no universal definition of social class exists. Thus, the investigator must decide whether socioeconomic status is to be defined on the basis of income, educational level, employment status, residential area, or some combination of these. Second, the investigator also needs to be able to differentiate between the risk factors for reading disability that are closely associated with social class. The two groups of covariates of social class that appear to be the most relevant are the biological risk factors, encompassing heredity, poor prenatal care, poor nutrition, prematurity, increased risk of central nervous system infection, head trauma, lead, and poor general health care (Walzer and Richmond, 1973; Rider, Taback, and Knoblock, 1955; Chase and Byrnes, 1970; Hanshaw, et al., 1976), and the educational risk factors, which include lack of early stimulation, excessive absenteeism, and lower quality instruction and educational facilities (Eisenberg, 1966). We appreciate that reducing the confounding effect of social class covariates is extremely difficult.

A few investigators have tried to evaluate the independent effects of social class covariates by sampling from a homogeneous population with respect to social class. For example, Kappleman, et al. (1972) compared a group of learning-disabled children to a matched group of controls performing successfully in the same "disadvantaged" socioeconomic and educational environment. The learning-disabled group of children consisted of children within the Baltimore school area referred to a clinic by their teachers due to serious learning and behavior problems. Any child whose diagnosis of learning disability was confirmed by the clinic was included in the study, regardless of the nature of his problem. The control group consisted of a randomly selected group of children, each of whom was matched to a learning-disabled child on age, sex, and neighborhood. A total of 125 matched pairs of children were studied, and their ages ranged from 5 to 14 years, with a median age of 6 years.

Interviews with all the families were conducted to obtain information on family history, prenatal history, birth weight, pregnancy and delivery complications, and developmental problems. Medical records were also obtained from all the institutions and private facilities that had cared for and were caring for each mother and child. Significantly more family histories of mental retardation, behavior, psychiatric, speech, visual, and auditory problems were noted in the clinic population than in the control group. The only factor that differentiated between groups in terms of prenatal history was the incidence of preeclampsia, an unusual rise in blood pressure during the second and third trimester. Forty clinic mothers had experienced this problem at least one time, whereas only 15 control mothers did so. Birth weights of less than 2012 g were noted four times as frequently in the histories of the clinic children compared to the controls. Finally, 10 clinic children were breach births but only one control was. This was the only birth complication that distinguished between groups.

Twenty-two clinic mothers compared to 10 control mothers had terminated their education before grade 9. On the other hand, 48 clinic mothers compared to 63 control mothers completed high school. Nineteen clinic children and five controls came from homes where there were at least nine children either in residence or having been in residence for the child's lifetime. Seventy-seven control and 46 clinic children were living with both natural parents. Thirteen clinic children compared to two controls were living with their mother and an unrelated male. Finally, 18 clinic children versus five controls were living in a house without their natural mother.

These data emphasize the importance of distinguishing between the independent effects of covariates of social class and social class standing, per se, when studying the possible association between learning disabilities and socioeconomic status. This follows because, although all these children came from families of low social class standing, significant differences were found between the learning-disabled and control groups in terms of their prenatal, birth, and family histories, as well as in terms of their living situations. Thus, these children's learning problems probably can be attributed, at least in part, to the above factors and not to their social class standing per se. Unfortunately, this must remain a tentative conclusion since the authors do not state exactly what kinds of problems the children had.

Eisenberg (1966) studied data from two groups of people, both of whom lived in the same county. One group was composed of white exurbanite white collar workers and the second group consisted of poor, rural Blacks. He noted that 12% of the white children and 36% of the Black children were reading at least 2 years below their expected grade level. Within each group, the proportion of reading-disabled boys was higher than the proportion of reading-disabled girls—that is, 16.8% of the white boys versus 7.1% of white girls were reading disabled, and 42% of Black boys versus 26% of Black girls were reading disabled. These results were attributed to differences in social class standing between the groups because only 7% of the white families as compared to 62% of the Black families were found to be in the lowest social class (social class V). Unfortunately, in this study the effect of social class covariates was not explored.

During the spring of 1970, a national survey was conducted by the U. S. Office of Education (Silverman and Metz, 1970), in which principals were asked to complete a questionnaire concerning the number of pupils with specific learning disability (SLD). SLD was defined as a disorder in at least one of the basic psychological processes involved in understanding or using spoken and written language. Any child who had problems with listening, thinking, talking, reading, writing, and/or spelling was considered to have an SLD. Children were excluded if they had been culturally disadvantaged, or if they had physical and/or emotional problems. Each principal was asked to estimate the minimum and the maximum number of children with SLD. The minimum estimate reflected only those children who were already enrolled in special classes. The latter estimate included both the number of children who were attending special classes and the number who were in need of remedial help but were not receiving it due to space and/or teaching limitations. Responses were obtained from 85% of the schools asked to participate. The sample included approximately 2000 schools and was believed to be representative of the total population of the 31,000 schools in the United States in districts with at least 300 pupils.

Results showed that enrollment size did not affect rates of SLD. Schools in large cities located in low-income areas reported rates two and three times higher than schools in large cities not located in low-income areas. Secondary schools in low-income areas reported higher rates than did the elementary schools. This pattern, however, was reversed in all other income areas. These data appear to support the hypothesis that an association exists between low social class and reading and/or learning disabilities. However, because SLD was defined in a general manner, it is unclear whether each principal identified problem children in the same way. Thus, the children who were included in the sample probably constituted a heterogeneous population with regard to the kinds of problems that they had.

Kerdel-Vegas (1968) tested 1035 children in the 2nd through 6th grades in Caracas, Venezuela, for the presence or absence of strephosymbolia—reversal of letters. Each subject was shown a series of cards with individual letters and asked to read aloud. If the subject missed a letter, he was shown a series of cards with words and asked to copy them. The subject was considered to have the disorder if he inverted more than two symbols in any phase of the test.

More than 300 children were chosen from each of three schools. School A was located in a low socioeconomic area, school B was in a middle socioeconomic area, and school C in a high socioeconomic area. The percentages of children with the disorder were found to be 35.6, 12.77, and 10.56 for schools A, B, and C, respectively. The difference between schools A and B was found to be significant, but the difference between schools B and C was not.

Kerdel-Vegas concluded that these results probably reflected variation in quality of education among social classes. The validity of this generalization can be questioned, however, on the basis that the author did not indicate whether or not the three groups were comparable with respect to any potential confounders (e.g., the children's past and/or present health statuses, their mothers' prenatal histories, or cultural expectations).

Miller, Margolin, and Yolles (1957) tried to assess the percentage of reading-disabled children in a county adjacent to Washington, D. C. This county includes urban, suburban, and rural areas, and all children in the county are given standardized reading tests five times a year. Subjects included all 3rd- (6150) and 5th- (3953) grade children. Nineteen percent of the 3rd graders were found to be reading at or beneath the 1st-grade level, and 16% percent of the 5th graders were reading at or beneath the 2nd-grade level. IQ did not account for these differences. Compared to schools with the lower reading levels, schools with higher reading levels tended to be rated at least one quartile higher in regard to quality of housing, and one quartile lower in regard to population density, rate of social assistance, and juvenile court cases.

Results similar to those of Miller, Margolin, and Yolles (1957) were observed by Dinitz, et al. (1958) in their study of 717 6th-grade pupils enrolled in 11 schools in Columbus, Ohio. These schools were chosen to insure equal representation of all census tracts. The children who were living in the more desirable tract areas scored significantly lower on delinquency indices as measured by the California Personality Inventory and significantly higher on IQ and school achievement measures. (The authors do not state which IQ and achievement tests were used.) Further, a graded decrease in IQ, reading, and arithmetic scores was observed as the "quality" of census tract decreased.

Potential confounding due to educational variables was somewhat minimized in the study of Miller, et al. (1957) but not in the work of Dinitz, et al. (1958), since only one board of education supervised teaching methods, curricula, and materials for the entire county adjacent to Washington, D. C. We conclude from these data that the covariates of social class and the risk of reading handicap vary inversely with social class, per se.

Sheldon and Carrillo (1952) published data obtained from a population of 868 elementary, junior, and senior high school students in eight schools in central New York State. These children constituted the highest and lowest 5% of readers in their classrooms according to their teachers' judgments and on the basis of IQ and reading achievement tests administered prior to selection. The authors then gave the Progressive Reading Test to 844 of the 868 children, using the appropriate form of the test for the child's grade level. According to this test, 51% were good readers, reading at least one grade level above their present grade level; 24% were average readers, reading on their appropriate grade level; and the remaining 25% were poor readers, reading at least one grade below their present grade level. A questionnaire developed by the Reading Laboratory at Syracuse University was then sent to the parents of the children; 537 of 868 were returned for a response rate of 62%.

The results of these questionnaires showed that as the size of the family increased, the percentage of good readers decreased. For example, 62% of the children in families with three or four members compared to 20% of the children in families with nine or more members were good readers. Further, as the ordinal position of the child increased from 1 to 5, the percentage of good readers decreased from 72 to 20 and the percentage of poor readers increased from 9 to 60. Similar trends were noted with regard to the number of books in the home. With respect to parents' educational level, 35%, 5%, and 7% of the parents of good, average, and poor readers, respectively, reported having completed college.

The data on fathers' occupations were classified according to the Dictionary of Occupational Titles and showed that children who were good readers had fathers in professional and managerial positions 55% of the time. However, children who were average and poor readers had fathers in these positions only 25% and 27% of the time, respectively. Further, of the parents who were in agricultural, fishery, and forestry professions, 23% had children who were poor readers and 8% had children who were good or average readers. Only 5% of the good readers came from families where the father was employed as a semiskilled or unskilled laborer, but 25% of the average and 16% of the poor readers came from such homes.

In 1972, Farrar and Leigh published follow-up results of a survey done in northern Tasmania. All state schools and all but two independent schools had participated in the initial study. The data concerned those children born between 1956 and 1962. In 1970, scores on the Schonell's Word Recognition Test were obtained from the schools for 1067 of the original 1198 children. Of these children, 144 (13%) were considered to have failed the test, reading at least 2 years below their chronological age. A significantly higher rate of reading failure was observed for those children who came from the two lowest classes compared to the other socioeconomic classes. Of the children who failed, 61% were enrolled in rural schools and 39% attended urban schools. This trend was almost exactly reversed for the 132 best readers.

Weinberg, et al. (1974) studied 360 Caucasian boys, aged 8 to 9½ years, from St. Louis, Missouri. The children were drawn from the total population of children in this age group in three St. Louis city and four St. Louis county schools. These particular schools were chosen for study because the children who attend them come from different socioeconomic and ethnic backgrounds. Socioeconomic status was estimated for each subject using the Hollingshead-Redlich Two Factor Index. The scale is based on the number of years of education completed by the natural father and on his occupation. Class I represents professional men and high level executives whose minimum level of education is a college degree. Class V is composed of semiskilled and unskilled workers with little formal schooling. Each class was equally represented in the sample.

Each child was given the vocabulary, similarities, and block design subtest of the WISC, the reading section of the WRAT, and the Peabody Picture Vocabulary Test (PPVT). Measurements of head circumference, height, weight, and skeletal age were also taken. No statistically significant social class differences were noted for chronological age, weight, or skeletal age. However, children from classes I, II, and III were significantly taller and had significantly larger head sizes than children from classes IV and V.

Socioeconomic status alone was the most predictive measure of psychometric scores, and it accounted for 29 to 38% of the variance in these scores. Further, all psychometric test scores differentiated between the upper (I and II), middle (III), and lower (IV and V) classes. For example, the class I mean score was 28.8 points higher on the WISC, 26.7 points higher on the PPVT, and 24.8 points higher on the WRAT than the class V mean score. On the WRAT, significant differences were seen when classes I, II, and III were compared to classes IV and V; and on both the WISC and PPVT, significant differences were found between classes I and III, III and IV, and IV and V. Thus, it appears from these data that the higher the social class (as measured by education and occupation of the child's father), the greater the IQ, reading age, head circumference, and height of the child.

Chandler (1966) published California Reading Achievement test scores obtained from 346 6th-grade children of different socioeconomic backgrounds in Berkeley, California. The city of Berkeley is built in such a way that the "flats" are lowest in topography and in cost of housing, next are the "foothills," and the "hills" are at the top. The mean reading test scores for the hills, foothills, and flats were 106, 92, and 73, respectively. When the scores were analyzed according to the fathers' occupation, it was seen that approximately 90% of the children of executives, professionals, and self-employed merchants were reading on their appropriate grade levels. However, 84% and 65% of the children of upper and lower white-collar employees, respectively, were reading at this level. Finally, only 30 to 40% of the children whose fathers were skilled, semiskilled, or unskilled manual workers scored on their grade levels.

Also, the children of professional parents in the hills had better test scores than did the children of professionals in the foothills, and the children of manual workers in the foothills did better than their peers in the flats whose parents were manual workers. Thus, confounding due to covariates of social class standing (as measured by parental occupational level) may account for the difference among the hills, foothills, and flats.

Davie, Butler, and Galdstein (1972) reported follow-up data at age 7 years on a cohort of 15,468 children who were born during the week of March 3 to 9, 1958, in England, Scotland, and Wales. Information was obtained from the children's schools and parents and from the school health services. Reading ability was assessed using (a) scores on the Southgate Reading Test, (b) the stage of reading reached by the child in school, and (c) teachers' ratings of reading ability on a five-point scale. Social class standing was measured via the fathers' occupational status according to the Registrar General; Class I (high professionals), II (other professional and technical), and IIIa (nonmanual) were considered to represent the middle class and classes IIIb (skilled manual), IV (semiskilled manual), and V (unskilled manual) were classified as the working class.

Family size was defined by the number of children in the home under 21 years of age. Middle-class families tended to be smaller than working-class families. Also, when allowance was made for social class difference, families in Scotland were found to be larger than those in England and Wales. Children in a one- or two- child family read at a level 12 months higher than children in a family with five or more children. The difference in reading age between first and fourth or later-born children was equivalent to 16 months of reading age.

Twelve percent of the parents in social class I left school at the minimum age compared to 87% in social class V. A higher level of parental education was associated with a gain of approximately 6 months in reading age when class, family size, and sex of child were controlled. The group of children living in a family situation without both natural parents, in an atypical family situation, contained more poor readers (score of 0 to 20 on Southgate) than did the normal group. Also, more working-class children than middle-class children were living in these atypical situations. But, within social class groups, the children from middle class or skilled manual working class families (classes I to IIIb) who had atypical living conditions were still found to be at a disadvantage in reading compared to their peers from normal family situations. No differences in reading performance were noted, though, in classes IV and V between children from typical and atypical home situations.

Overcrowding (more than 1.5 persons per room) was seen to be associated with 2 or 3 months' retardation in reading. Absence or sharing of amenities (hot water, bathroom, indoor lavatory) was associated with approximately 9 months' backwardness in reading. These results were obtained when social class, sex, country, and type of accommodation (whole house, flat, room) were taken into account. A class V child was six times more likely than a class I child to be a poor reader —that is, 8% of class I children were poor readers, but 15, 14, 30, 37, and 48% of classes II, IIIa, IIIb, IV, and V, respectively, scored this poorly on the test.

Davie, Butler and Goldstein (1972) demonstrated that when sex, social class, maternal height and age, mother's smoking during pregnancy, length of pregnancy, birth order, and number of younger sibs in the house were all accounted for, every kilogram reduction in birth weight was associated with a 4 months' reduction in reading age at age 7 years. Similarly, when allowance was made for all other factors mentioned above, children of mothers who had regularly smoked at least 10 cigarettes a day during their pregnancies had a 4-month lower reading age than did children of nonsmokers.

PRE-, PERI-, AND EARLY POSTNATAL FACTORS

The results from studies of the relationship between reading disability and adverse pregnancy, labor, and delivery experiences have not been entirely consistent. Differences in (a) characteristics of the sample populations—socioeconomic status, (b) sources of data used—hospital records or direct interviews with mothers, (c) definitions of terms—anoxia, prematurity, pregnancy complications, and (d) methods of controlling confounding factors in the analyses, may account for some of these discrepancies.

Corah, et al, (1965) published a study which was concerned with the hypothesized relationship between anoxia at birth and the child's subsequent overall development. Anoxia was defined according to clinical signs and/or postnatal apnea. The clinical signs presumed to contribute to and/or represent anoxia included maternal conditions such as diabetes, anemia, poor reproductive history, bleeding during pregnancy, prolonged labor, and eclampsia; newborn conditions such as sleepiness, respiratory delay, and delayed or absent cry; and signs of CNS damage, such as somnolence, weak or absent sucking, poor feeding, convulsions, and bloody spinal fluid. Ratings of anoxia were weighted scores derived from the number and intensity of these signs. Infants were excluded if they were premature, had a congenital anomaly, or central nervous system maldevelopment. Controls were matched for sex, date, and place of birth.

Tests of cognitive, personality, perceptual, and neurologic development were administered to 275/666 children at age 7 years. The final sample included 101 anoxics and 134 controls. Losses to follow-up were evenly distributed between the group of anoxics and the group of controls.

Results from the 7-year evaluations showed that the control children read better than the anoxic children based on the Gilmore Oral Reading Test for accuracy, comprehension, and reading rate. However, the difference between the groups was not statistically significant; the t values for accuracy, comprehension, and reading rate were 1.91, 1.07, and 0.73, respectively. The data were then analyzed separately for pre-, peri-, and postnatal anoxia. The accuracy and reading rate scores for the postnatal subgroup were significantly lower than were those of the controls.

This study by Corah, et al. (1965) has limitations. The reading test results are based on scores obtained from only a subsample of the children, 103 normals and 70 anoxics. Also, many of the children in both the anoxic and control groups (29.3 and 22.6%, respectively) were not able to read at all, but the difference in percentage of nonreaders per group did not reach statistical significance. The group labeled as anoxic may be so heterogeneous that only a small proportion of them had anoxia. In addition, newborns who display the clinical abnormalities thought to represent anoxia may do so because of preexisting brain dysfunction (Drage, et al., 1966; Gottfried, 1973).

Kawi and Pasamanick (1958) evaluated the relationship of pregnancy factors to reading disability without interposing the construct of anoxia. Reading-disabled subjects were identified through the active case registers of reading clinics in the Department of Education in Baltimore city. The study population was restricted to white males between the ages of 10 and 14, with Binet IQs greater than, or equal to, 85. All of the boys had been studied through the reading analysis program and were found to be at least 2 years retarded in reading. Birth certificates were obtained for these subjects. As a control series, the next birth reported from the same place of birth, matched for race, sex, and mother's age, was selected. Information on birth and pregnancy was obtained from hospital records and birth certificates. Complete information was obtained for only 205 cases (55% of 372).

One hundred and four pregnancy complications were noted for mothers of reading-disabled children compared to 50 for mothers of controls ($p \leq .05$). The percentage of mothers with at least one complication was 37.6 for the reading-disabled group versus 21.5 for the normal group ($p \leq .05$). Mother's age or number of previous pregnancies did not account for these results. Further, 16.6% of the reading-disabled children versus 1.5% of the normal children had been exposed to at least two complications. Preeclampsia, hypertension, and vaginal bleeding were the most frequently noted complications in the histories of children with reading disability.

Prematurity, defined as birth weight less than 5.5 lbs (2.5 kg), was noted significantly more often in the reading-disabled children (11.5%) than in the normal children (4.6%). Duration of labor and types of operative procedures did not differ between the two groups. Finally, abnormalities of the pre- and paranatal periods involving either the mother or child were noted in 45.4% of the reading-disabled group compared to 28.2% of the normal group ($p = .05$).

Subsequently, Kawi and Pasamanick (1959) analyzed the data from the same two groups of subjects according to the distributions of duration of labor, and socioeconomic status. Mothers of 66.5% of the cases and 64.5% of the controls were found to have been in labor from 2 to 24 hours. The mothers of controls were slightly more likely to be found in the under-2-hour category (3.4%) than were mothers of cases (.9%). On the other hand, 8.1% of mothers of cases had been in labor for more than 24 hours compared to 4.8% of mothers of controls. The distribution of economic levels also differed between the two groups. Families of 67.2% of the cases were in the lower half of the economic scale but only 56.3% of the controls' families fell into this category. Further there were significantly more cases than controls in the third lowest income group.

The study of Kawi and Pasamanick remains one of the better studies of its kind. It suffers from examining a heterogeneous group of reading handicaps, the potential selection bias that might result from a loss of 45% of the sample, and from an analysis that handles confounding factors (e.g., socioeconomic level) less well than desired.

The work by Douglas (1960) and Robinson and Robinson (1965) gives evidence for the need to control socioeconomic level in studies of this kind. The former study compared the school performance at ages 8 and 11 years of 675 prematurely born children, birth weight less than or equal to 5.5 lbs (2.5 kg), to that of 675 children who were not born prematurely. Both samples of children were born during the first week of March 1946.

These two groups were matched in terms of social group and degree of crowding in the home, as well as for such factors as legitimacy, having a single birth, sex, ordinal position in family, and mother's age. The premature children scored lower on all the achievement tests and were rated more poorly by their teachers in comparison to their matched controls. However, the author found that the families of the two groups were not comparable with respect to fathers' occupational status, amount of unemployment, ability to manage the children, cleanliness of home and child, and parental interest in the child's schooling. Families of controls were consistently and significantly rated superior by the health visitor and by the children's teachers on all these measures as compared to families of children who were born prematurely. When the children's test scores were reanalyzed by taking into account all of the sociological information, it was found that the prematures who came from "disadvantaged" homes performed significantly worse than their matched controls. But those prematures who did not have poor family histories performed as well or better than their matched controls.

Robinson and Robinson (1965) obtained similar results in their follow-up study at 8 to 10 years of age of children who were born in Wake County, North Carolina, between October 1, 1948, and October 31, 1951. Their sample consisted of 90 children who had birth weights greater than 2.5 kg and 124 children who weighed less than or equal to 2.5

kg at birth. The two groups were matched via their birth certificates for single or multiple birth, race, sex, place of birth, father's occupation, marital status of mother, age and parity of mother, and attendant at birth. Children who had major physical defects were excluded from study. History and birth data were obtained through direct interviews with families.

For the analysis, the group of 124 low-birth-weight children was subdivided into two groups: those 99 children who had birth weights between 1.5 and 2.5 kg and those 25 children who had birth weights less than 1.5 kg. No significant differences were noted between the three birth weight groups on the Stanford Binet IQ test, the Goodenough-Harris test, the Jastak Reading Achievement test, or the children's school behavior. However, when the data were analyzed according to the families' social class standing, using Warner's Index of Social Characteristics (Warner, 1960), it was found that children whose birth weights were less than 1.5 kg came from significantly poorer homes than did the other children, and significant differences favoring the upper classes became apparent on all of the IQ, achievement, and behavior variables. Thus, the authors concluded, as did Douglas (1960), that the groups of low-birth-weight infants did not perform any worse than expected on the basis of their social class standing. Although these two studies emphasize the need to control for socioeconomic factors, both sets of authors failed to control for other important factors—for example, history of prenatal care and gestational age. This last fact may account for the observed lack of significant differences on the psychometric tests between low-birth-weight groups and controls.

In 1970, Lyle published a study of the relationship between reading disability and antenatal, perinatal, and developmental factors. One hundred eight boys, one-half of whom were reading disabled, were selected from six primary school grades in Sydney State Schools. Only boys between the ages of 6 and 12, with IQs of at least 90 on either the verbal or performance section of the WISC, were included in the sample. All were from middle-class English-speaking homes.

Reading disability was defined as a discrepancy between grade norms and reading age. Reading age was assessed using Schonell's Graded Word Reading Test. As grade level increased, a progressively greater amount of discrepancy was required in order for the child to be classified as reading disabled. Only children who had failed to master the "basic elements of reading" were included as reading-handicapped subjects. None of these children had a RA greater than 7.5 years, and approximately 2 years difference in reading age existed between the normal and disabled groups. The difference between the two groups in IQ scores was approximately six points; mean full WISC scores were 100.85 and 106.53 for the retarded and normal groups, respectively.

Questionnaires were sent to the mothers of all children, requesting information concerning (a) antenatal variables, (b) perinatal variables—length of labor and condition of child at birth, and (c) developmental variables—delays and/or anomalies of locomotion and speech. These women were then interviewed. Multiple regression techniques were applied to the data from the questionnaires in order to predict factor scores on each of two previously defined factors and membership in either the reading-disabled group or normal group. Factor 1 was defined by perceptual and perceptual-motor distortions, whereas factor 2 included verbal problems. The authors found that the birth variables predicted factor 1, and the developmental variables predicted factor 2. Toxemias, low birth weight, and threatened miscarriages were not found to be predictive.

The results of this study provide support for the hypothesis that reading disabilities are associated with prenatal and birth factors. The discrepancy between these results and the results observed by Kawi and Pasamanick (1958, 1959) can have several explanations. Only middle-class subjects were used in this study. Thus, the prenatal care which these mothers experienced might have been of better quality and of more homogeneous distribution than the care to the mothers in the Kawi and Pasamanick studies. Second, the way that reading disability was defined differed between the two studies. Finally, the data in this study were obtained solely from mothers' reports which are highly subjective and, therefore, potentially biased. Kawi and Pasamanick, however, relied on hospital records and birth certificates which are unbiased data sources because exposure was ascertained years before reading ability was assessed.

Colligan (1974) studied the possible relationship between psychometric test scores and "perinatal stress" in 386 7-year-old Minnesota children (205 boys, 181 girls), who were enrolled in the Collaborative Perinatal Project (Medelson, 1967). This population was chosen for study because a detailed, uniform, prospective history was available for each child. Children who, at age 7, had abnormal or suspect ratings on their neurologic examinations were excluded from study, as were children whose mothers had less than five contacts with the obstetrician before delivery.

A simple count of potentially stressful experiences recorded in the histories of the mother and child was used as the index of perinatal stress. The 386 children were then divided evenly into three groups—the least-stressed group, the suspected-stress group, and the presumed-stress group. However, the criteria used to classify a child into one of these groups were not stated. Also, the "stressful" symptoms abstracted from the histories ranged from minor problems, as cold with sore throat, to potentially serious complications, as breech presentation or convulsions.

The data obtained at age 7 revealed that the estimate of perinatal stress did not separate the three groups on any of the variables under study, including a behavior checklist, Jastak Wide Range Achievement test, WISC, Draw-a-Man test, ITPA, Bender Gestalt, and the Tactile Finger Recognition test. Similarly, no significant differences were noted between groups for data obtained at age 4 years (Stanford-Binet IQ, Graham Ernhart block sorting test, gross and fine motor coordination), 1 year (neurologic examination), 8 months (Bayley Scale of Mental and Motor Development), or at 4 months (pediatric examination).

The author concluded that the failure of these results to provide support for a relationship between perinatal stress and subsequent performance on psychometric tests can be attributed to (a) the fact that the perinatal stress score did not increase systematically with evidence of neurologic problems, and (b) the possibility that the perinatal score contained too many items of little or no predictive value (colds) which masked those items which were important (birth weight and gestational age).

Support for this last conclusion comes from a study of the educational sequelae of prematurity (Rubin, Rosenblatt, and Balow, 1973), which also drew its sample from the Minnesota branch of the Collaborative Perinatal Project population (Mendelson, 1967). These children were born between 1960 and 1964 and were registered in the Educational Follow-Up Project as well as in the Collaborative Perinatal Project. The group of premature children included all the Educational Follow-Up subjects with birth weights less than or equal to 2.5 kg and those of full-birth-weight whose gestational ages were less than or equal to 37 weeks. Controls were randomly chosen from the remainder of the Educational Follow-Up population and weighed more than 2.5 kg at birth, and had gestational ages longer than 37 weeks. The two groups were matched on age within 1 year. The children were then divided into four groups on the basis of their birth weights and gestational ages;

low-birth-weight and preterm ($N = 32$), low-birth-weight and full-term or small-for-dates ($N = 46$), full-birth-weight and preterm ($N = 78$), and the controls, who were full-birth-weight and full term ($N = 85$).

Significant differences were found favoring the high-birth-weight over low-birth-weight groups on the Stanford-Binet at age 4 years and the WISC at age 7 years, the ITPA and Metropolitan Readiness test administered at age 5 years, and the WRAT given at age 7 years. The mean WRAT reading scores, expressed in grade levels, for the low-birth-weight groups were 1.6 and 1.5 for the preterm and full-term children, respectively. However, the comparable scores for the full-birth-weight preterm and full-term groups were 1.8 and 2.0, respectively. Similar trends were noted in spelling and in arithmetic. Further, it was found that low-birth-weight preterm males and small-for-dates of both sexes constituted a particularly high-risk population in terms of eventual impairment of school functioning, as two-thirds of the former group and more than one-half of the latter group manifested problems severe enough to warrant special-education placement or special services in elementary school.

Wiener (1970) also studied the relationship of birth weight and length of gestation to subsequent intellectual development. The WISC, WRAT, and Bender Gestalt tests were given to 417 low-birth-weight (< 2.5 kg) and 405 full-birth-weight (≥ 2.5 kg) children between 8 and 10 years old who were enrolled in the Johns Hopkins Study of Premature Infants. The two samples were matched on race, season of birth, parity, hospital of birth, and socioeconomic status according to census tract data. All children were single-born. Subjects were excluded if they had IQs less than 60, if they attended special schools, and if they had impairing sensory or motor problems.

The mean IQ of the full-birth-weight group, 95.9, was found to be significantly higher than that of the low-birth-weight group, 90.9. Within the low-birth-weight group, length of gestation was not found to be differentially related to future problems on any of the three tests given. However, within the full-birth-weight group, longer gestational age, > 40 weeks, was associated with higher IQ and with better performance on the Bender Gestalt, speech maturity as rated by psychologists, and WRAT reading and spelling tests. These findings were obtained when race and socioeconomic status were controlled.

Douglas and Gear (1976) followed 163 children who weighed ≤ 2 kg at birth and 163 matched control children whose birth weights were > 2 kg. All children were born during one week of March 1946. Sex, birth order, home circumstances, mother's age, father's occupation, and geography were also controlled in the matching. At age 15, 53/163 pairs of these children were also given reading, verbal, nonverbal, and arithmetic tests (Pidgeon, 1964). The mean scores for the low-birth-weight children were almost identical to those of their controls' on all four indices. However, when the low-birth-weight group was divided into two subgroups—that is, light-for-dates and others, it was seen that the light-for-dates scored significantly worse than their matched controls whereas the other low-birth-weight children scored approximately the same as their controls. Unfortunately the data are not presented separately for each test, but when the four test scores were aggregated into one score, the 15 light-for-dates scored 6.7 points below their controls while the others scored .3 points above their controls ($.05 < p < .1$). Long hospital stay after birth did not account for these differences.

It appears from all these data that some association exists between reading disability and pre-, peri-, and postnatal factors. The exact nature of the relationship is yet to be fully understood but at least three simple models can be hypothesized (Fig. 1).

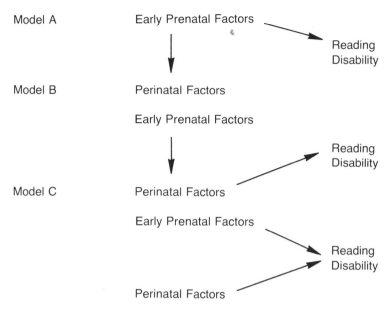

Fig. 1. READING DISABILITY AND PRE-, PERI-, AND POSTNATAL FACTORS: THREE MODELS.

Currently, it is unknown which of these three models is the most tenable and/or if the true relationship incorporates some combination of them. Thus, further research in this area is definitely in order.

The public health consequence of Model A is that major improvements in the management of labor, routine availability of fetal heart monitoring capability, may be expected to have relatively little effect on the risk of reading handicaps. Support for this viewpoint has come from the work of British obstetricians (Chalmers, 1976), who reported no "striking advantage or disadvantage to the foetus of differences in obstetric practice" based on data from a survey of all women delivered in Cardiff since 1965. Included in this survey were hospital and home deliveries as well as births to women who resided in Cardiff but delivered elsewhere.

MALNUTRITION AND READING DISABILITIES

Much has been written about the sequelae of infant and childhood malnutrition. Most of the studies present follow-up data on growth and development collected approximately 5 years after the onset of the acute attack of malnutrition. A few studies are concerned with the relationship of malnutrition to global deficits of cognition, (Birch, 1972; Chase and Martin, 1970; Champakan, et al., 1968; Hertzig, et al., 1972), but to our knowledge only one (Klein, Forbes, and Nader, 1975) has specifically addressed the question of whether any association exists between malnutrition and reading disability. We review here only two studies relating malnutrition to school performance.

Malnutrition may only be a marker of high risk of reading disability rather than being a risk factor itself. This follows because malnutrition, whether intrauterine or postnatal, is clearly linked to low socioeconomic status (Mauer, 1975; Lowe et al., 1973). Low socioeconomic status is, in turn, closely related to increased risk of infection, lead exposure, head trauma, poor prenatal care, suboptimal educational opportunity, decreased expectation of school performance, and so on.

Malnutrition and School Performance

Richardson, Birch, and Hertzig (1973) examined the school performance of Jamaican children who were severely malnourished during the first 2 years of life. They were interested in studying the association between performance level and age at onset of malnutrition. Seventy-four boys who had been hospitalized for malnutrition during their first 2 years were included in the study as index cases. The average hospital stay had been approximately 8 weeks. Follow-up was conducted for all 74 children until the age of 5. At the time of the study, the subjects' ages ranged from 5 years 10 months to 10 years.

Six of the index subjects did not attend school and were, therefore, excluded. Two classmate or yardmate comparisons matched for sex and age were identified for each case. Same-sex sibs without a history of malnutrition and between the ages of 6 and 12 years were also subjects of this study. Controls were chosen for the sibs in the same manner as they were identified for the index children. The final sample was composed of 62 index subjects, 31 siblings, 31 sibling comparisons, and 68 index comparisons.

WRAT scores and teacher questionnaires were obtained for all subjects. The results from the WRAT showed that (a) the malnutrition cases performed significantly worse than their classmate comparisons in reading, spelling, and arithmetic, (b) the sibs performed significantly worse in all three areas than did the controls, (c) the malnutrition cases and their sibs had lower scores than their respective controls across the entire distribution of scores, (d) no significant difference existed between the malnutrition cases and their sibs or between the two sets of controls, and (e) reading was the only area in which sibs performed significantly worse than their controls.

Only pairs of children who were judged by the same teacher were included in the analysis of the teacher questionnaire data. Twenty-four percent of the index subjects compared to 8% of their comparisons were noted to be in the lowest category of school work. The index subjects also had lower median grades and more special problem areas than their classmates. Finally, no differences were seen between the sibs and their comparisons. No relation was noted between the age of malnutrition and level of school functioning or between time of hospitalization and test scores.

The authors concluded that the common elements in the backgrounds of the malnutrition cases and their sibs led to their lowered levels of cognitive function. The acute attack of malnutrition was viewed as an additional risk factor of suboptimal school performance. The malnutrition cases were the only subjects of the study who were hospitalized. Douglas (1975) has reported that one admission to hospital of more than a week's duration between the ages of 6 months and 4 years is associated with increased risk of behavior disturbance and poor reading in adolescence. Thus, the possibility exists that factors related to hospitalization, not malnutrition, accounted for the deficits of the malnourished children.

Winick, Meyer, and Harris (1975) studied a population of Korean children who had been malnourished before the age of 2, but who had subsequently been adopted by U.S. middle-class parents. The goal was to eliminate the confounding effects of such covariates of malnutrition as decreased home stimulation, lowered parental expectation of school performance, and suboptimal educational opportunities. Information on height, weight, and date of birth was available for 908 subjects who had been admitted to one adoption service in Korea between 1958 and 1967. Only females who had been full term at birth and who had no evidence of physical defects were eligible for inclusion into the study. Further, all subjects had to have been followed for at least 6 years after adoption and they had to be enrolled in a U.S. elementary school at the time of the study.

Two-hundred-twenty-nine of the 908 possible subjects were chosen at random and placed in one of three groups on the basis of how their height and weight at time of admission to the Service related to the reference standard of normal Korean children of comparable ages. Group 1 included the "malnourished" children, those below the third percentile for height and weight. Group 2 was composed of the "moderately mal-nourished" children, those between the 3rd and 24th percentile for height and weight. Group 3 was the control group of "well fed" children, or those whose height and weight were above the 25th percentile.

Information for 141 of the 299 (61%) subjects was obtained from questionnaires sent to parents concerning health, growth, nutrition, and socioeconomic level, and the chil-dren's elementary schools, which provided their scores on standard IQ and achievement tests. With regard to growth, it was found that all the adopted children surpassed the expected mean, 50th percentile, for normal Korean children of comparable ages for height and weight, group-1 children were significantly shorter than group-3 children, and all the adopted children were below the 50th percentile when compared to American standards of height and weight. The mean IQs for groups 1, 2, and 3 were 102, 106, and 112, respectively. The difference in mean IQ between groups 1 and 3 was found to be statisti-cally significant, and the mean IQs of all three groups were noted to be above the American mean IQ of 100. The Korean children's achievement test scores were at least at the mean for U.S. children of the same age. Finally, achievement scores of group 1 were significantly lower than those of both groups 2 and 3.

The authors concluded that the absence of serious problems in this sample of children could probably be attributed to their improved environments. However, it is conceivable that a depression in IQ would have been noted for the Korean children if the mean IQ of middle-class American children had been used as the standard for comparison. Because all these children were reared in middle-class homes, using middle-class norms (which are higher than national norms) would probably have been more appropriate. Unfortunately, the authors failed to discuss the observed differences between groups in IQ and achieve-ment test scores. These differences may represent one manifestation of problems that result from early exposure to malnutrition. Also, the various achievement test results were not analyzed separately, and thus it is unclear whether any of these children had specific problem areas in school.

Klein, Forbes, and Nader (1975) studied the effects of starvation in infancy due to pyloric stenosis on subsequent learning ability in 44 boys and 6 girls. Congenital hyper-trophic pyloric stenosis is a "naturally occurring type of malnutrition" in early infancy (birth to 3 months) and does not seem to be associated with low social class. None of the children included had evidence of prenatal and antenatal rubella, convulsive disorders, or head injury. All birth weights were between 2.3 kg and 4.3 kg. Mean age at the time of testing was 9 years 2 months.

Two groups of controls were used: sibling controls and matched controls. The mean age of the 44 sibling controls was 10 years 1 month. The 50 matched controls were drawn from a random sample of the population who lived in the same area as did the index cases and were chosen on the basis of their age, sex, and father's occupation. The degree of starvation to which the index cases had been exposed was assessed by expressing the observed weight deficit as a percentage of the expected weight for age (extrapolated from Heimindinger, 1964). A deficit of 0 to 10% was defined as mild starvation, 11 to 20% as moderate starvation, and 21 to 42% as severe starvation.

The WRAT reading test was used to assess reading ability for all subjects. There was no difference between the scores of the siblings and those of the matched controls. The index cases, however, performed significantly worse than both groups of controls. The *t*-value comparing mild index cases and their matched controls was −1.86 (*p* < .05; one-tailed test). The *t*-value comparing moderate index cases and their sibs was −2.26. Finally, the *t*-value for severe index cases versus their matched controls was −2.01. Thus, these data imply that malnutrition and reading handicap are positively associated even when social class is controlled.

CENTRAL NERVOUS SYSTEM INFECTION

Meningitis and Encephalitis

Most studies of the persistent complications of meningitis and encephalitis have emphasized such severe neurologic sequelae as mental retardation, spasticity, and seizures (e.g., Earnest, et al., 1971). These problems are most frequent and severe in those children who become ill before 1 year of age, and in those children whose episode of meningitis or encephalitis is most severe at the time of onset. Some studies in this area, though, do concern themselves with the subgroup of postinfection children who did not develop severe neurologic problems. The dependent variable in most of these studies include IQ and psychometric test scores. A few have also used WRAT scores and/or expected grade level based on chronological age as the outcome variables of interest.

Certain methodologic problems in this group of studies deserve comment. First, the number of years between the time the child contracted the disease and the time the follow-up evaluations were performed varies a great deal both within and between studies. Second, test results are often reported for an entire group of children between the ages of 2 and 15 years without giving adequate considerations to the possibility that scores obtained at age 2 may not be comparable to those obtained at age 15. Third, some studies do not account for such important variables as age at onset or degree of severity of the disease. Fourth, appropriate reference data are often available because the study design did not call for a (matched) group of control children. In such studies, scores obtained from postinfection children are compared to nationally standardized group norms. When controls have been selected, they tend not to have been hospitalized (see Douglas, 1975). Finally, potential bias exists in these studies because losses to follow-up are high.

Kresky, Buchbinder, and Greenberg (1962) analyzed the physical, neurologic, mental, and emotional status of 80 children who had been hospitalized with bacterial meningitis at Meadowbrook Hospital in Nassau County, New York, between the years 1951 and 1955. Follow-up evaluations took place 3 to 5 years after the children were released from the hospital. During these years, a total of 129 children were discharged from this hospital with a diagnosis of bacterial meningitis. In 1959, they were asked to return to the Pediatric Neurology Clinic for evaluation. The age distribution, etiology, and clinical course of meningitis did not differ significantly between the 80 children available for follow-up and 49 who were not. Forty-nine of the 80 children who returned were boys, all were white, and most had been infected before the age of 5 years. The average hospital stay was 2 to 3 weeks. All were considered by their parents to be physically and mentally normal prior to the episode of meningitis. All had been discharged from the hospital as improved without obvious neurologic sequelae.

Growth, development, and maturation levels were within normal limits and the interval incidence of illness, communicable disease, and respiratory infection was similar to that seen in a nonselected group of children of comparable ages and socioeconomic status. A total of 43 defects were found among 28 of these 80 children. Thus, 34% (28/80) of the children had at least one neurologic problem. The exact distribution of neurologic defects was as follows: 6 defects were visual; 14 involved retarded language development; 9 were auditory; 14 were classified as "other" and included convulsions (5), poor coordination, slowness, difficulty with fine motor function (5), facial paresis (2), hyperactivity (1), and dysmetria (1).

The distribution of IQ was found to be similar to that in the Nassau County schools. Of the 73 children of school age, 61 (81%) were attending school in their expected grades. Nine of the 73 were in grades below what was expected based on their chronological ages. Six of these 9 children had IQs above 100, but were either neurologically handicapped or showed evidence of disturbed behavior. The three children who were severely handicapped were unable to attend school due to deafness, visual deficits, convulsive disorders, behavior problems, or anxiety.

Several important questions remain unanswered by these data. First, we do not know how these children would have scored on their IQ tests in comparison with a matched group of controls. Second, we have inadequate information about the problems that were experienced by those children who repeated a grade (or grades). Third, it is unclear if the nine who were attending school but below grade level were younger at the time of ictus or had more severe infection than their peers. Fourth, we do not know whether those children who were in their "expected" grades had any problems at all, and, if so, what the nature of these problems was.

Mathews, Chun, Granbow, et al. (1968) studied the psychological sequelae resulting from California arbovirus encephalitis in 25 boys and 8 girls who had been hospitalized in Wisconsin between 1960 and 1965. Mean age at the time of encephalitis was 5.88 years. The mean number of years since the attack was 2.85 and ranged from 1 to 6 years. At the time of testing, the children ranged in age from 2 to 15 years, but the mean age was 8.73 years. Each child was first given either the WISC or the WAIS, the Stanford Binet Short Form L-M, or the Cattell Infant Intelligence Test. The following tests were then administered to all the children: Porteus Maze, Raven Progressive Matrices, WRAT, finger tappings, grooved pegboard, behavior rating scale based on parent interviews, and a follow-up neurologic examination.

Only two children scored below average on the tests of full IQ and overall achievement. The mean WISC score was 106.66, and not much discrepancy was noted between the children's verbal and performance scores. The mean discrepancy scores on the WRAT were +0.86 in reading, +0.53 in spelling, and −0.12 in arithmetic. Each of these discrepancy scores represents the difference between scores that were observed and those that were expected on the basis of the child's age and grade. No differences were seen between these children's scores and scores expected based on standardization data for the maze coordination, grooved pegboard, or category test (Halstead, 1947). The finger tapping test was the only test in which significant differences were noted between observed and expected scores, and the postinfection children performed significantly better than expected (t-test; $p < 0.05$).

The behavior ratings for all 33 children were then compared to those of a matched group of controls drawn from a population of 300 similar children who had previously been rated on this scale. The only difference seen between these two groups of children was that the postencephalitis children were less independent. It appears from these data that California arbovirus encephalitis did not adversely affect these children. However, the authors acknowledge that this conclusion should be viewed with caution since standardization data and grade-level expectations were used as control data for comparison purposes. Stronger support for this conclusion would have been provided if similar results had been obtained using a matched group of controls.

In 1972, Sell, et al. reported on their follow-up study concerned with the long-term sequelae of hemophilus (H-) influenza meningitis. Fifty-six of the 88 survivors (63.6%) returned for examination. At the time of testing, all children were of school age and the majority were less than 10 years old. WISC IQs ranged from less than 20 to 140, with a mean of 84. The correlation of IQ with age at onset of illness, interval between onset and therapy, or complications in hospital was not statistically significant.

Reliable data were available for the 56 children who were examined and for 19 children who responded to the questionnaire. Of these 75 children, 49.3% were considered free of detectable defects; they had IQs of at least 90, no school problems, no physical, sensory, or neurologic abnormalities, and no history of convulsions or behavior problems. Sixteen percent had "possible" defects which included an IQ between 70 and 89, mild hearing loss and/or speech difficulty, failure in school with other activities reported normal, or behavior problems. Significant defects, an IQ between 50 and 69, seizures requiring medication, hearing loss greater than 30 db, paresis or paralysis, partial blindness, and failure in school, were noted in 29.3% of these children. The remaining 5.3% had IQs less than 50, were unable to attend school, and/or were institutionalized. According to the questionnaires, 6 of the 19 children (31.6%) were failing in school but we do not know what kinds of problems these children had. The IQs of nine children in the group with no detectable problems were later compared to the IQs of their nearest-age siblings. Two of the nine children were found to have full IQs more than 15 points (one standard deviation) lower than their controls. This result serves to reemphasize the need for matched controls in studies of this kind.

Sells, Carpenter, and Ray (1975) reported on a controlled follow-up study of 19 children who had been hospitalized between August 1, 1966, and May 1, 1972, with confirmed enterovirus infection of the central nervous system. Of these 19 children, 9 had aseptic meningitis, 9 had meningoencephalitis, and 1 had acute cerebellar ataxia. These children were all between the ages of 2½ and 8 years at time of follow-up and all had been hospitalized at least 1 year prior to the start of the study. The median age at time of illness was 7 months, and ranged from 1 to 64 months. The interval between illness and follow-up ranged from 17 to 67 months and averaged 38.2 months.

Controls were matched for age, sex, and social class according to the three-point scale of socioeconomic status of Hollingshead. They were drawn from well child clinics or day care centers. All were given complete physical and neurologic examinations, psychologic evaluations which included the Standford Binet, WISC, WPPSI, and Bayley Scale of Infant Development, speech and language evaluations, and audiologic evaluations. Three of the 19 (16%) children who had enterovirus infection had severe problems, including seizure disorders (in 2), spastic quadriplegia (in 1), and delayed speech and language (in all 3). Five children (26%) were considered to have possible impairment, IQs between 70 and 89, delayed speech, or behavior problems even though their IQs were greater than 90. The remaining eleven (58%) were free of detectable anomalies. Most of the children had normal results on their physical and neurologic examinations. Mean head circumference of the total group of post EVI children was comparable to the mean head circumference of the controls. However, the mean head circumference for the subgroup of children who had been ill during their first year of life was significantly less than that of their matched controls. The postinfection children scored significantly lower than the controls on the psychological tests, and this was found to be a result of extremely low scores obtained by those children who had been ill before they were 1 year old. The range of IQs for controls was 89 and 145 compared to 38 to 136 for postenterovirus children. Thirteen of the children who had been ill were functioning below their matched controls. In 10 of these 13, illness onset had been before 1 year of age.

The children who had had enterovirus infection scored significantly lower than controls on all language and speech measures. This result was also due to the scores of children whose illness began on or before their first birthday. No significant correlations were seen between IQ, speech, language development, or head circumference and clinical diagnosis, severity of clinical illness, presence of coma, duration of coma, severity of fever, length of hospital stay, or etiologic agents. The mean IQ of children who experienced their infection during the first year of life was 97, a value that may be considered normal. Their controls, however, had a mean IQ of 115. The observed discrepancy emphasizes the need for controls rather than relying on historical norms or standards. This is underscored by the observation that the subgroup of postinfection children whose onset of illness took place after the first year of life had a mean IQ identical to their controls: the observed values were 118.5 and 119.3, respectively.

Pate, et al. (1974) compared the neurologic, psychologic, and school development of 25 survivors of meningitis to that of 25 matched control children. The postmeningitic children were identified through the records of local hospitals and practicing pediatricians in the Nashville area. All of the postmeningitic children had survived an acute attack of bacterial meningitis prior to age 4 years, were judged free of sequelae, and were currently enrolled in regular primary grades in school. Fifteen of these 25 children had suffered from H-influenza, 5 from meningococcus, and 5 from pneumococcus. Controls were matched to the postmeningitic children by age, sex, classroom membership, and social class standing according to Hollingshead. Mean ages at time of testing were 7 years 10 months (± 11 months) for the meningitis group, and 7 years 8 months ($\pm$ 12 months) for the control group.

All subjects were taken to the Vanderbilt University Center for psychiatric, pediatric, and neurologic examinations. Tests for school adjustment were administered in a mobile laboratory at the respective schools. Finally, family interviews were conducted in the children's homes. The data were analyzed by comparing the number of postmeningitic children who performed poorer than their matched controls to the number of control children who performed poorer than their matched postmeningitic counterparts. Sixteen of the 25 postmeningitic (64%) children scored lower than their controls on the Durrell Analysis of Reading Difficulty test, whereas only 3 of the 25 control (12%) subjects performed poorer than their matched counterparts on this same test ($\chi^2 = 8.8$). Significant differences in the same direction were also noted on the ITPA, the Frostig P.Q. (a developmental test of visual perception), the Peabody Picture Vocabulary test, and on tests of gross motor coordination. According to their teachers, postmeningitic children tended to lack motivation and self-confidence as compared to the control children. These authors concluded from these data that, in comparison to controls, children who had had meningitis seem to have trouble grasping and responding to the verbal world and lack the necessary skills for portraying the role of an interested, alert, and popular student due to their lack of self-confidence, poor motivation, and poor motor coordination.

Sell, et al. (1972) reported very similar results to those of Pate, et al. (1974). Twenty-five postmeningitic subjects were identified from hospital records and pediatrician reports; 15 had H-influenza, 5 had meningococcus, and 5 had pneumonococcus. All appeared free from sequelae at discharge and were attending one of the first three grades in public school. Each index case was matched to a classroom control for age, sex, and social class. Mean age at time of testing for the index cases was 7.1 ± .9 years, and 7.8 ± 1.0 years for the controls. Sixteen of the 25 subjects in each group were male. The mean score on the ITPA was 225.48 for the index cases versus 327 for the controls ($p = .004$). The cases also performed worse than the controls on the Frostig Developmental Test of Visual Perception—that is, the mean score for the former was 92.36 versus 101.84 for the controls. Finally, mean scores for the Peabody Picture Vocabulary Tests were 90.96 for the cases and 102.6 for the controls ($p = .035$).

Congenital Infections

The association between exposure to rubella during pregnancy and subsequent congenital defects in the newborn was first noted by Gregg in 1941 (Witte, et al., 1969). These neonates often show evidence of deafness, heart disease, and/or cataracts (Dodrill, MacFarlane, and Boyd, 1975; Menger, Dods, and Harley, 1967; Ames, et al., 1970, Chess, 1971). The fetus is most obviously affected when the maternal infection occurred during the first trimester of pregnancy, but the amount of damage seems to bear little relationship to the severity of the disease in the mother (Chess, 1971).

It can reasonably be hypothesized that these children are at high risk of developing reading and/or learning handicap. The first and most obvious reason for this is that so many physical problems are either present at birth, or develop as the child grows, which might interfere with his subsequent level of intellectual functioning (Dodrill, MacFarlane and Boyd, 1975; Weinberger, et al., 1970). Second, many other physical problems frequently associated with suboptimal school performance (low birth weight, small head circumference, delayed neonatal growth, and psychomotor retardation) also seem to be related to congenital rubella (Chess, 1971; Weinberger, et al., 1970; Cooper, 1968; Lejarraga and Pickham, 1974). Third, there is evidence for a high rate of psychologic and psychiatric problems in these children including autism, reactive behavior disorders, separation anxiety, sleeping, eating and dressing abnormalities, and inability to enter into social relationships due to hitting, kicking, and biting (Chess, 1971). Finally, many investigators have noted retarded language development and poor intellectual performance in older children who were exposed to rubella in utero (Weinberger, et al., 1970; Feldman, et al., 1971; Hardy, 1973).

Although much attention has been devoted to elucidating the exact nature of the sequelae of congenital rubella, we are not aware of many studies which directly address the question of whether an association exists between congenital rubella and reading disability. An explanation for this is that it is extremely difficult to efficiently deal with the large number of correlates of congenital rubella that are also associated with reading disability—for example, low birth weight, retarded growth, delayed language, deafness, and psychosocial problems.

We are familiar with only one study that compared the school performance of "normal" rubella children to that of a control group. Lundstrom and Ahnsjö (1962) performed a follow-up study of children with histories of maternal rubella who had (a) been born during or shortly after the rubella epidemic of 1951, and (b) had already been evaluated with regard to their condition at birth and thereafter. The population used in this study included all single births whose mothers had rubella in one of the first 5 months of pregnancy. The controls were drawn from Lundstrom's original series. The 725 children exposed to rubella during the first half of pregnancy were compared to 836 children not exposed to rubella.

School maturity test scores were available for 449 rubella children and 403 controls (Lindahl, 1951; Levin, 1960; Wigforss, 1953). Data were classified by month of maternal infection and each rubella subgroup was compared to the other subgroups and to the controls. Second-month rubella children showed a higher incidence of unreadiness for school than did controls (26% versus 13%). A higher incidence of postponement was observed in the second- and third-month rubella children (13% and 11%, respectively), compared with the controls (3%). This was attributed to lack of school maturity as verified by school maturity tests. Of those who started school at the correct age, more of the second-month rubella children (30%) were assigned to the bottom third of the class than were controls (21%). No differences were seen among the first-, fourth-, and fifth-month rubella children. The findings were not appreciably influenced by differences between rubella children and controls with regard to social group, maternal age, and place of residence (urban or rural).

More information is needed before definitive statements can be made about the existence of a relationship between congenital rubella and reading and/or learning disabilities. A more complete school follow-up of all these children, including individual tests for reading, spelling, and arithmetic, would be useful in determining if any other differences exist between rubella children and controls. Differences might become manifest only as the children grow older and the demands for academic achievement increase.

LEAD

Only a portion of the vast amount of literature concerned with sequelae of lead poisoning in children is addressed to the possible association between lead and reading and/or learning disabilities. There are at least two good reasons for hypothesizing that such an association exists. First, lead exposure severe enough to require hospitalization and/or treatment often leads to such problems as mental retardation, cerebral palsy, recurrent seizures, and optic atropy (Perlstein and Attala, 1966). Second, excess amounts of lead are especially prevalent in areas that are at high risk for learning disabilities. The high rates of elevated blood and tooth lead levels in school-age children in some communities (Lin-Fu, 1972) indicate the potential public health importance of lead exposure.

Byers and Lord (1943) were the first authors to recognize the possible association between lead poisoning and poor school achievement. They reviewed all the records of the Children's Hospital in Boston, Massachusetts, for the years 1930 to 1940, and identified a total of 128 cases of infantile lead poisoning. The medical records of the 71 children (38 boys) who lived near enough to Boston to be available were then reviewed. Of this group, 12 (9 boys) showed gross evidence of cerebral damage at the time of discharge from the hospital and were not further considered. Of the remaining 59 discharged as cured, 20 had entered school by the time of the study, and were the subjects of this report.

None of these children showed striking evidence of encephalopathy (stupor, coma, seizures) during primary admission to hospital. Lead poisoning had been diagnosed radiographically; all had evidence of bands of increased density at the ends of long bones. With two possible exceptions, all of these children were failing in school. Such problems as short attention span and poor motivation were common. The usual correlation between IQ and ability to learn in school did not hold for these children; for example, the second-most successful child in school had an IQ of 82, while several children with above-average IQs were unable to do their school work. Finally, sensorimotor defects (problems with shape, direction, and/or space and projected imagery) were noted in those children who had average IQs but were failing in school. These data provide support for the hypothesis that an association exists between poor school achievement and lead poisoning. However, they also emphasize the need for further research in this area so the exact nature of the observed learning disabilities may be elucidated.

In 1966, Perlstein and Attala reported on a follow-up study of 214 boys and 211 girls who had lead intoxication; 389 of the 425 children were diagnosed at the Children's Neurologic Clinic of Cook County Hospital and the remaining 36 were identified through the private practice of the authors. Eighty-four percent of these subjects were black and culturally deprived. Period of follow-up ranged from 6 months to 10 years. At time of hospital admission, the children's ages ranged from 9 months to 8 years, and the median was 2 years. The mortality rate of chidlren who did not have lead encephalopathy was negligible, but sequelae were seen in 30%. Sequelae were seen in 10 to 20% of the children whose onset of poisoning was "asymptomatic"—that is, with fever only.

Of all these children, 61% (257/425) showed complete recovery. Mental retardation was the most common sequel, occurring in 22% of the total series. The only sign of impaired learning in some of those children whose brain damage was minimal was a "learning block," usually of a visual perceptual type. It is possible that the 257 children who were considered free of sequelae did indeed develop other, less severe, problems but no data were provided for evaluation of this possibility.

The two studies mentioned above dealt with sequelae resulting from lead poisoning which was severe enough to require hospitalization. Research in this area has also been concerned with possible sequelae of subclinical lead poisoning. As yet, the nature and extent of the effects of chronic subclinical lead exposure are unclear. One reason for this is that investigators who wish to study the latter, more subtle, question face two methodologic problems. The first is how to deal efficiently with confounding factors such as pica, social class, and hyperactivity. The second is one of finding a way to measure objectively the extent of the exposure so that the dose response relationship can be understood.

Until recently, blood lead was the only method available for quantitating the extent of exposure. However, blood lead levels are a measure of current exposure only, and do not reflect the accumulated effects of past exposure (Needleman, Tuncay, and Shapiro, 1972). The determination of the "normal" range of blood lead has posed many problems. Depending on the particular study, the cutoff point between "normal" and "elevated" blood lead has been set at 80, 60, 40, or 20 μg/100 ml whole blood. In fact, many people assume that the upper limit of normal is synonymous with the lowest indicative of poisoning. However, a level that does not reflect overt poisoning may be indicative of problems that were never before associated with lead because no one knew what the symptoms were (Lin-Fu, 1972).

In the past few years, a method for analyzing tooth lead has been developed (Needleman, Tuncay, and Shapiro, 1972; Needleman, et al., 1974). Because tooth lead is relatively permanently stored in the calcified tissue and is dose-related, the investigator can accurately assess the extent of past exposure using this technique. Presently, 200 μg/g of tooth lead is used as the upper cutoff point for "normal" (Burde and Choate, 1975). Most of the studies concerned with the sequelae of subclinical lead used IQ and developmental test scores as outcome variables (Landigran, et al., 1975; Perino and Ernhart, 1974). The results from these studies are confusing and inconclusive for two reasons: First, exposure status was determined by blood levels of lead. Second, the samples studied were drawn from very high risk populations—for example, Black preschoolers in Queens,

New York, or children whose families reside in highly industrialized towns. Thus, baseline data from normal children are not available.

Landsdown, et al. (1974) investigated the relationship between place of residence in terms of distance from a smelting works and blood lead levels, intelligence, reading ability, and behavior disturbances for a "relatively homogeneous" population in the east end of London. They performed a house-to-house search for all children up to and including the age of 16 years who lived within 500 m of the factory. Blood was obtained for all of the 119 preschool children and for 105 of their mothers. The WISC or WAIS IQ test and the Burt Graded Word Reading Test were administered to the school children. Teachers were asked to complete questionnaires concerning each child's ability to function in school.

A significant difference was found between the distributions of blood lead levels of preschool children living within 400 m of the factory ($\chi^2 < .05$). However, address only accounted for less than 4% of the variance in lead levels for school-age children. No relationship was noted between IQ and behavior problems when current lead level was used. Nor was any association seen between reading ability and current lead level with age held constant. Contrary to expectation, the children who moved into the area after they were 2 years old were found to be significantly less intelligent, more overactive, and more disturbed than those who had lived in the area since birth.

The authors concluded that (a) other factors besides proximity to factory influenced blood lead levels, (b) mild exposure to lead did not appear to exert adverse effects, (c) social factors seemed more important in determining mental development than did actual physical exposure to lead, and (d) no relationships were observed between lead and mental development. The reliability of using distance to evaluate the extent of lead exposure may be questioned, especially since it only accounted for less than 4% of the variance in lead levels for the school-age children. Finally, all these children were exposed to lead for most, if not all, of their lives and so any relationship between length of exposure to lead and mental development might have been obscured. This follows because the amount of total exposure may have been similar for all the children even though differences were noted between them in terms of current blood lead levels.

Two studies concerned with investigating the latent sequelae of lead exposure were conducted by de la Burde and Choate (1972, 1975). The same two groups of children were included in both studies but the first one compared them with respect to development at age 4 and the second compared their levels of school performance at age 7. The sample of subjects was drawn from the Collaborative Perinatal Project population (Mendelson, 1967) and included 67 subjects who had histories of eating paint and plaster between 1 and 3 years of age, and 70 subjects without such histories. None of the children in the former group had clinical symptoms of poisoning, but all had positive urine coproporhyrine tests and elevated blood lead levels and/or evidence of lead burden on X-rays of long bones or abdominal flat plate. None of the control children had positive results on the urine tests. Because blood and radiologic tests were not available for the controls, they were carefully chosen by living conditions to exclude paint and plaster intake. Most of the children were Black, approximately one-half were boys, and the socioeconomic index for both groups was 3.2 based on U.S. Bureau of Census criteria.

Behavior problems such as negativism, distractibility, and need for constant attention were noted approximately three times more often in the exposed group than in the control group. The mean IQs for the exposed and nonexposed groups were 89 and 94, respectively. It was also found that 89% of the nonexposed children compared to 75% of the exposed children failed Grooved Pegboard and Porteus Maze tests twice as often as did the nonexposed children. Five children (3 exposed and 2 nonexposed) had to be excluded from the evaluations performed at age 7 due to CNS damage which had occurred between 4 and 7 years. However, the two groups were still comparable with respect to age, sex, race, and socioeconomic variables.

Pediatric neurologic examinations were performed for all subjects at 7 years and repeated at 8 years for 58 subjects in each group. To control for confounding due to educational variables, only the children who attended the Richmond Public Schools were included in the analysis of school data. School evaluations were obtained for 54 of the 64 exposed children, and 49 of the 68 nonexposed children. Teeth readings were obtained for 29 exposed and 32 nonexposed children to insure that the two groups did, in fact, differ with respect to exposure status. Mean tooth lead was 202.1 μg/g ($\pm$ 34.6) for the exposed group, and 111.6 μg/g ($\pm$ 13.3) for the nonexposed group. Forty-five percent of the exposed group had values which exceeded 200 μg/g, whereas only 9.3% of the nonexposed group had values in this range.

More than twice as many exposed children as controls had deficits on the neurologic examination at 7 years when suspect and abnormal ratings were combined. These diagnoses were based on the experimenter's judgment of various combinations of neurologic signs (e.g., clumsiness on gross motor tests, difficulties with fine motor performance, hyperactivity) in accordance with prescribed procedures, which were regularly monitored by quality control trials for the entire Collaborative Project. More deficits were recorded for the exposed group than for the nonexposed group at 8 years.

The majority of children in both groups had average IQs. The mean full IQ was 86.6 ($\pm$ 10.4) for exposed children and 90.1 ($\pm$ 7.7) for nonexposed children. However, the number of children in the borderline and defective range was significantly larger in the exposed group. No differences were noted between the two groups on the WRAT, but significantly more exposed children received abnormal or suspect ratings on the Bender Gestalt and the ITPA. The behavior of children during the test session was coded suspect or abnormal eight times more frequently in the exposed than in the nonexposed children. More specifically, the exposed children were considered to lack self-confidence, to need attention, and to be fearful in comparison to the nonexposed children. Behavior problems at home were more often noted for the exposed children than for the nonexposed children—that is, 22% of the exposed children versus 9% of the nonexposed were found to have problems with lying, stealing, running away, and fire-setting.

No differences were seen between the two groups with regard to amount of absenteeism from school, but 28% of the exposed compared to 4% of the nonexposed were making poor academic progress and 26% of the exposed compared to 6% of the nonexposed repeated at least one grade in school. It appeared that the difficulties which the exposed children were experiencing in school could be attributed to their behavior problems. The authors concluded that the behavior problems noted in the exposed children at age 4 were aggravated by a school environment and that these problems were probably due to the children's experiences with lead. The latter part of this conclusion was supported by the fact that no differences between groups were noted on developmental test scores obtained at 8 months. The observed differences between the two groups can, in part, be attributed to differences in lead exposure. It also seems likely that subclinical lead exposure may not increase the risk of any one perceptual handicap, but rather results in reading retardation via the lead influenced attention and behavior problems.

Pihl and Parkes (1977) compared the lead content in hair of 31 learning-disabled children to that of 22 normal controls. The learning-disabled children were selected from a sample of 1030 regular third and fourth grade students, all of whom had a Pupil Rating Scale (Myklebust, 1971) completed by their teachers. This scale includes ratings for auditory comprehension, spoken language, orientation, behavior, and motor skills. The 220 children who received scores less than 67 on this scale were then given the Peabody Picture Vocabulary test, and the reading, spelling, math computation and math problem-solving subtests of the Metropolitan Achievement test. A learning-disabled child was defined as one who had an average or above-average IQ but who failed at least one subtest of the achievement test. Controls were chosen from the original group of 1030 children on the basis of Pupil Rating Scores of 68 or higher. The two groups were matched for school, class, sex, and socioeconomic status according to parental occupation.

The mean content of lead in hair was 23 ppm for the learning-disabled group and 4 ppm for the control group ($p < .001$). This indicates that lead exposure may, in fact, be more common in learning-disabled children than in normal children. It should be noted, however, that hair outside the scalp has significant interaction with environment and only freshly grown hair can be expected to reflect internal tissue trace-element levels (Maher, 1976). This means that hair lead may reflect present exposure levels only and may not serve as an accurate measurement of cumulative exposure. Also, because learning disability was defined in such a general way, it is unfortunate that the IQ and achievement test results were not presented. Finally, it would have been desirable to administer the tests to the control children so that a comparison of specific problems could be made in light of the hair-analyses results.

REFERENCES

Ames, M., Plotkin, S., Winchester, R., and Atkins, T. Central auditory imperception: a significant factor in congenital rubella deafness. *Journal of the American Medical Association*, 1970, 213(3):419–421.

Applebee, A. Research in reading retardation: two critical problems. *Journal of Child Psychology and Psychiatry*, 1971, 12:19–113.

Bakwin, H. Reading disability in twins. *Developmental Medicine and Child Neurology*, 1973, 15:184–187.

Birch, H. Malnutrition, learning, and intelligence. *American Journal of Public Health*, 1972, 62(6):773–784.

Burdé, B. de la, and Choate, M. Does asymptomatic lead exposure in children have latent sequelae? *Journal of Pediatrics*, 1972, 81(6):1088–1091.

Burdé, B. de la, and Choate, M. Early asymptomatic lead exposure and development at school age. *Journal of Pediatrics* 1975, 87(4):638–642.

Byers, R., and Lord, E. Late effects of lead poisoning on mental development. *American Journal of Diseases of Children*, 1943, 66(5):471–494.

Chalmer, I. Obstetric delivery today. *Lancet*, 1976, 1:1125.

Chamberlain, G., and Johnstone, F. Reliability of the history. *Lancet*, 1975, 1:103.

Champakam, S., Srikantia, S., and Goplan, C. Kwashiorkor and mental development. *American Journal of Clinical Nutrition*, 1968, 21(8):844–852.

Chandler, T. Reading disability and socioeconomic status. *Journal of Reading*, 1966, 10(1):5–21.

Chase, H., and Byrnes, M. Trends in prematurity: United States 1950–1967. *American Journal of Public Health*, 1970, 60:1967–1983.

Chase, H., and Martin, H. Undernutrition and child development. *New England Journal of Medicine*, 1970, 282(17):933–939.

Chess, S. *Psychiatric Disorders of Children with Congenital Rubella*. New York: Bruner/Mazel, 1971.

Chess, S., Thomas, A. and Birch, H. Distortions in developmental reporting made by parents of behaviorally disturbed children. *Journal of the American Academy of Child Psychiatry*, 1966, 5:226–234.

Colligan, R. Psychometric deficits related to perinatal stress. *Journal of Learning Disabilities*, 1974, 7(3):154–160.

Cooper, L. Rubella: a preventable cause of birth defects. *In* D. Bergsma, ed., *Birth Defects: Original Article Series*. The National Foundation, 1968, Vol. 4, No. 7.

Corah, N., Anthony, E., Painter, P., Stern, J., and Thurston, D. Effects of perinatal anoxia after seven years. *Psychological Monogram*, 1965, 79(3), Whole No. 596.

Davie, R., Butler, N., and Goldstein, H. *From Birth to Seven*. London: Longman, 1972.

Dinitz, S., Kay, B., and Reckless, W. Group gradients in delinquency potential and achievement scores of sixth graders. *American Journal of Orthopsychiatry*, 1958, 28:598–605.

Dodrill, C., MacFarlane, D., and Boyd, R. Effects of intrauterine rubella infection and its consequent physical symptoms on intellectual abilities. *Journal of Consulting and Clinical Psychology*, 1974, 42(2):251–255.

Douglas, J. "Premature" children at primary schools. *British Medical Journal*, 1960, 1:1008–1013.

Douglas, J. Early hospital admissions and later disturbances of behavior and learning. *Developmental Medicine and Child Neurology*, 1975, 17:456–480.

Douglas, J., and Gear, R. Children of low birthweight in the 1946 national cohort. *Archives Diseases Children*, 1976, 51:820–827.

Drage, J., Kennedy, C., Berendes, H., Schwartz, B., and Weiss, W. The Apgar score as an index of infant morbidity. *Developmental Medicine and Child Neurology*, 1966, 8:141–148.

Earnest, M., Goolishian, H., Calverley, J., Hayes, R., and Hill, H., Neurologic, intellectual and psychologic sequelae following western encephalitis. *Neurology*, 1971, 21(9):969–974.

Eisenberg, L. The epidemiology of reading retardation and a program for preventive intervention. *In* J. Money, ed., *The Disabled Reader*. Baltimore: Johns Hopkins Press, 1966.

Farrar, J., and Leigh, J. Factors associated with reading failure. *Social Science and Medicine*, 1972, 6:241–251.

Feldman, R., Lajoie, R., Mendelson, J., and Pinsky, L. Congenital rubella and language disorders. *Lancet*, 1971, 2:978.

Gottfried, A., Intellectual consequences of perinatal anoxia. *Psychological Bulletin*, 1973, 80(3):231–242.

Graham, F., Ernhart, C., Thurston, D., et al. Development 3 years after perinatal anoxia and other potentially damaging newborn experiences. *Psychological Monogram*, 1962, 76:522.

Hallgren, G. Specific dyslexia ("congenital word blindness"): a clinical and genetic study. *Acta Psychiatry and Neurology Suppl.*, 1950, 65:1–287.

Halstead, W. *Brain and Intelligence: A Quantitative Study of the Frontal Lobes*. Chicago: University of Chicago Press, 1947.

Hanshaw, J., Scheiner, A., Moxley, A., Gaev, L., Abel, V., and Scheiner, B. School failure and deafness after "silent" congenital cytomegalovirus infection. *New England Journal of Medicine*, 1976, 295(9):468–470.

Hardy, J. Clinical and developmental aspects of congenital rubella. *Archives of Otolaryngology*, 1973, 98:230–236.

Harvald, B., and Hauge, M. Hereditary factors elucidated by twin studies. In J. V. Neel, M. W. Shaw, and W. J. Schull, eds., *Genetics and the Epidemiology of Chronic Diseases*. PHS Publication #1163, Washington, D.C.: U.S. Government Printing Office, 1965.

Heimendinger, J. Gemischt longitudinal messungen von koperlange, gewicht, oberen segment, thoraxumfang und kopfumsfang bei 1–24 monate alten sauglingen. *Helv Paediatr Acta*, 1964, 19:406.

Hermann, K. *Reading Disability: A Medical Study of Word Blindness and Related Handicaps*. Springfield, Ill.: Thomas, 1959.

Hertzig, M., Birch, H., Richardson, S., and Tizard, J. Intellectual levels of school children severely malnourished during the first two years of life. *Pediatrics*, 1972, 49(6):814–824.

Hunter, E., and Johnson, L. Developmental and psychological differences between readers and nonreaders. *Journal of Learning Disabilities*, 1971, 4(10):33–38.

Jackson, D. Intelligence and ideology. *Science*, 1975, 189:1078–1080.

Kappelman, M., Rosenstein, A., and Ganter, R. Comparison of disadvantaged children with learning disabilities and their successful peer group. *American Journal of Diseases of Children*, 1972, 124:875–879.

Kawi, A., and Pasamanick, B. Association of factors of pregnancy with reading disorders in childhood. *Journal of the American Medical Association*, 1958, 166(12):1420–1423.

Kawi, A., and Pasamanick, B. Prenatal and paranatal factors in the development of childhood reading disorders. *Monographs of the Society for Research in Child Development*, 1959, 24(4), Ser. #73.

Kerdel-Vegas, O. Strephosymbolia: incidence in the school sectors of Caracas. *Diseases of the Nervous System*, 1968, 29:548–549.

Kinsbourne, M., and Warrington, E. Developmental factors in reading and writing backwardness. *British Journal of Psychology*, 1963, 54(2):145–156.

Klein, P, Forbes, G., and Nader, P. Effects of starvation in infancy (puloric stenosis) on subsequent learning abilities. *Journal of Pediatrics*, 1975, 87:8–15.

Kresky, B., Buchbinder, S., and Greenberg. I. The incidence of neurologic residua in children after recovery from bacterial meningitis. *Archives of Pediatrics,* 1962, 79:63–71.

Kucera, O., Matejcek, Z., and Langmeier, J. Some observations on dyslexia in children in Czechoslovakia. *American Journal of Orthopsychiatry,* 1963 3:448–456.

Landrigan, P., Baloh, R., Barthel, W., Whitworth, R., Staehling, N., and Rosenblum, B., Neuropsychological dysfunction in children with chronic low level lead absorption. *Lancet,* 1975, 1:708–712.

Lansdown, R., Shepherd, J., Clayton, B., Graham, P., Delves, H., and Turner, W. Blood lead levels, behavior and intelligence—a population study. *Lancet,* 1974, 1, 538–541.

Layzer, D. Heritability analyses of IQ scores: science or numerology. *Science,* 1974, 183:1259–1266.

Lejarraga, H., and Peckham, C. Birthweight and subsequent growth of children exposed to rubella inutero. *Archives of Diseases of Children,* 1974, 49:50–54.

Levin, G. *Uppsalaundersoleningen av hyborjare. Anvisningar.* Uppsala: Levins Skolforlag, 1960.

Lindahl, R. Skolemodenhedsproblemer. H-H nyborjartest. *Psyck. Paediat. Bibl.* 1951, 13:154.

Lin-Fu, J. Undue absorption of lead among children—a new look at an old problem. *New England Journal of Medicine,* 1972, 286:702–710.

Lowe, C., Forbes, G., Garn, S., Owen, G., Smith, N., and Weil, W. The ten state nutrition survey: a pediatric perspective. *Pediatrics,* 1973, 51(6):1095–1099.

Lundstrom, R., and Ahnsjo, S. Mental development following maternal rubella: a follow up study of children born in 1951–1952. *Acta Paediatrica Suppl.,* 1962, 135:153–159.

Lyle, J. Certain antenatal, perinatal, and developmental variables and reading retardation in middle class boys. *Child Development,* 1970, 41:481–491.

Maher, C. Factor influencing hair trace-element. Unpublished doctoral dissertation, University of Michigan, 1976.

Matheny, A., and Dolan. A. A twin study of genetic influences in reading achievement. *Journal of Learning Disabilities,* 1974, 7(2):43–46.

Matthews, C., Chun, R., Grabow, J., and Thompson, W. Psychological sequelae in children following California arbovirus encephalitis. *Neurology,* 1968, 18:1023–1030.

Mauer, A. Malnutrition—still a common problem for children in the United States. *Clinical Pediatrics,* 1975, 14(1):23–24.

Mendelson, M. Interdisciplinary approach to the study of the exceptional infant: A large research probject. *In* J. Hellmuth, ed., *Exceptional Infant, Vol. 1.* Seattle: Special Child Publications, 1967.

Menser, M., Dods, L., and Harley, J. A twenty-five year follow up of congenital rubella. *Lancet,* 1967, 2:1347–1350.

Miller, A., Margolin, J., and Yolles, S. Epidemiology of reading disabilities: some methodologic considerations and early findings. *American Journal of Public Health,* 1957, 47:1250–1256.

Muller, A., Margolin, J., and Yolles, S. Epidemiology of reading disabilities: some methodologic considerations and early findings. *American Journal of Public Health,* 1957, 47:1250–1256.

Myklebust, H. *The Pupil Rating Scale.* New York: Grune & Stratton, 1971.

Myklebust, H. Learning disabilities: Definition and Overview. *In* H. Myklebust, ed., *Progress in Learning Disabilities, Vol. 1.* New York: Grune & Stratton, 1968.

Myklebust, H. Identification and diagnosis of children with learning disabilities: An interdisciplinary study of criteria. *In* S. Walzer and P. Wolff, eds., *Minimal Cerebral Dysfunction in Children.* New York: Grune & Stratton, 1973.

Needleman, H., Tuncay, O., and Shapiro, I. Lead levels in deciduous teeth or urban and suburban American children. *Nature,* 1972, 235:111–112.

Needleman, H., Davidson, I., Sewell, E., and Shapiro, I. Subclinical lead exposure in Philadelphia school children. *New England Journal of Medicine,* 1974, 290(5):245–248.

Owen, F., Adams, P., Forrest, T., Stolz, L., and Fisher, S. Learning disorders in children: sibling studies. *Monographs of the Society for Research in Child Development,* 1971, 36(4):1–74.

Pate, J., Webb, W., Sell, S., and Gaskins, F. The school adjustment of postmeningitic children. *Journal of Learning Disabilities,* 1974, 7(1):30–34.

Peckham, C. Clinical and laboratory study of children exposed in utero to maternal rubella. *Archives of Diseases of Children,* 1972, 47:571–577.

Perino, J., and Ernhart, C. The relation of subclinical lead level to cognitive and sensorimotor impairment in black preschoolers. *Journal of Learning Disabilities,* 1974, 7:26–30.

Perlstein, M., and Attala, R. Neurologic sequelae of plumbism in children. *Clinical Pediatrics,* 1966, 5(5):292–298.

Pidgeon, D. Tests used in 1954 and 1957 surveys. *In* J. Douglas, ed., *The Home and the School.* London: McGibbon and Kee, 1964.

Pihl, R., and Parkes, M. Hair element content in learning disabled children. *Science,* 1977, 198:204–206.

Richardson, S., Birch, H., and Hertzig, M., School performance of children who were severely malnourished in infancy. *American Journal of Mental Deficiency,* 1973, 77(5):623–632.

Rider, R., Taback, M., and Knobloch, H. Associations between premature birth and socioeconomic status. *American Journal of Public Health,* 1955, 45:1022–1028.

Robinson, N., and Robinson, H., A follow up study of children of low birth weight and control children at school age. *Pediatrics,* 1965, 35:425–433.

Rubin, R., Rosenblatt, C., and Balow, B. Psychological and educational sequelae of prematurity. *Pediatrics,* 1973, 52:352–363.

Rutter, M., and Yule, W. The concept of specific reading retardation. *Journal of Child Psychology Psychiatry,* 1975, 16:181–197.

Sell, S., Merrill, R., Doyne, E., and Zirnsky, E. Long term sequelae of hemophilus influenzae meningitis. *Pediatrics,* 1972, 49(2):206–211.

Sell, S., Webb, W., Pate, J., et al. Psychological sequelae to bacterial meningitis. *Pediatrics,* 1972, 49:212–217.

Sells, C., Carpenter, R., and Ray, C. Sequelae of central nervous system enterovirus infections. *New England Journal of Medicine,* 1975, 293(1):1–4.

Sheldon, W., and Carrillo, L. Relation of parents, home, and certain developmental characteristics to children's reading ability. *Elementary School Journal,* 1952, 52:262–270.

Silverman, L., and Metz, A. Numbers of pupils with specific learning disabilities in local public schools in the United States. Spring, 1970. *Annals of the New York Academy of Science,* 1973, 205:146–157.

Thompson, W. Heritability of IQ: methodologic questions. *Science,* 1975, 188:1125–1126.

Walker, L., and Cole, E. Familial patterns of expression of specific reading disability in a population sample. *Bulletin of the Orton Society,* 1965, 15:12–24.

Walzer, S., and Richmond, J. The epidemiology of learning disorders. *Pediatric Clinics of North America,* 1973, 20(3):549–565.

Warner, W. *Social Class in America.* New York: Harper, 1960.

Weinberg, W., Dietz, S., Penick, E., and McAlister, W., Intelligence, reading achievement, physical size, and social class. *Journal of Pediatrics,* 1974, 85(4):482–489.

Weinberger, M., Masland, M., Asbed, R., and Sever, J. Congenital rubella presenting as retarded language development. *American Journal of Diseases of Children,* 1970, 120:125–128.

Wenar, C., and Coulter, J. A reliability study of developmental histories. *Child Development,* 1962, 33:453–462.

Wiener, G. The relationship of birthweight and length of gestation to intellectual development at ages 8 to 10 years. *Journal of Pediatrics,* 1970, 76(5):694–699.

Wiener, M., and Cromer, W. Reading and reading difficulty: a conceptual analysis. *Harvard Educational Review,* 1967, 37:620–643.

Wigforss, F. *Ar barnet skolmoget? Anvisnigar for lareren med tabellbilaga.* Stockholm: Almqvist and Wiksell, 1953.

Winick, M., Meyer, K., and Harris, R. Malnutrition and environmental enrichment by early adoption. *Science,* 1975, 190(4220):1173–1175.

Witte, J., Karchmer, A., Case, G., Herrmann, K , Abrutyn, E., Kasanoff, I., and Neill, J. Epidemiology of rubella. *American Journal of Diseases of Children,* 1969, 118:107–111.

Yarrow, M., Campbell, J., and Burton, R. Recollections of childhood: a study of the retrospective method. *Monographs of the Society for Research in Child Development,* 1970, 35(5):1–83.

Yule, W., Rutter, M., Berger, M., and Thompson, J. Over-and under-achievement in reading: distribution in the general population. *British Journal of Educational Psychology,* 1974, 44(1):1–12.

Yule, W. Dyslexia. Psychological Monographs, 1976, 6:165–167.

Zerbin-Rüdin, E. Congenital word blindness. *Bulletin of the Orton Society,* 1967, 17:47–54.

IV. Reading, Spelling, Arithmetic Disabilities: A Neuropsychologic Perspective

BYRON P. ROURKE

The purpose of this chapter is to review studies done in our laboratory which have focused upon the neuropsychological aspects of reading, spelling, and arithmetic disorders in children. The material has been divided into three sections: (a) studies of children with undifferentiated learning disabilities, (b) studies of "specific" learning disabilities, and (c) future directions.

Except where specifically noted to the contrary, the subjects employed met a fairly standard definition for children with learning disabilities (Rourke, 1975). That is, these children (a) were markedly deficient in at least one school subject area, (b) obtained Full Scale IQs on the WISC within the roughly normal range, (c) were free of primary emotional disturbance, (d) had adequate visual and auditory acuity, (e) lived in homes and communities where socioeconomic deprivation was not a factor, (f) had experienced only the usual childhood illnesses, (g) had attended school regularly since the age of 5½ or 6 years, and (h) spoke English as their native language. Some investigations are discussed which involved subjects chosen in terms of criteria for neurologic impairment or mental subnormality. In all other cases, the subjects were as described above.

A related issue of crucial importance for the interpretation of the investigations is the manner in which the data have been collected. For the most part, the learning-disabled children were referred to the Neuropsychology Laboratory at Windsor Western Hospital Centre by school boards or family physicians because they were doing poorly in one or more subjects at school. In virtually all cases, the child's teacher had exhausted her catalogue of techniques for teaching the child how to read, spell, or do arithmetic. In addition, clinical or prescriptive teachers, school psychologists, and other special education personnel had intervened in an attempt to remedy the child's problem. For the most part, it was after these interventions had met with less than expected success that the child was referred for a neuropsychological assessment. Thus, it should be clear that the "typical" learning-disability child who is contained in the bulk of these studies is one who is doing poorly in one or several school subjects, and whose difficulties in these areas have shown themselves to be quite refractory to a wide variety of educational intervention techniques.

It is necessary to accentuate the care that has been taken in the choice of subjects for these investigations, principally because any generalizations made on the basis of the data generated must be evaluated in light of these selection constraints. Failure to do so may simply add to the confusion which appears to haunt the study of learning disabilities in children even to this day.

Finally, it is important to note that most of the data for these studies was gathered as part of a routine administration of a standard battery of neuropsychologic and other tests administered in the recommended manner by psychometrists specifically trained for that

Some of the research reported herein was supported under a grant from the Ontario Mental Health Foundation and by grants from the Ontario Ministry of Education Grants-in-aid of Educational Research and Development Programme. Funds were also provided by Windsor Western Hospital Centre.

purpose. The tests typically included the following: the Halstead Neuropsychological Test Battery for Children, the Reitan-Indiana Neuropsychological Test Battery for Children, the Kløve-Matthews Motor Steadiness Battery, the Reitan-Kløve Sensory-Perceptual, Lateral Dominance, and Form Recognition Tests, the Halstead-Wepman Aphasia Screening Tests, the Trail Making Test for Children (all of these test batteries and procedures are described in Reitan and Davison, 1974), and a number of other tests involving more specific auditory-perceptual and visual-perceptual abilities. In addition, the Wechsler Intelligence Scale for Children (WISC; Wechsler, 1949), the Wide Range Achievement Test (WRAT; Jastak and Jastak, 1965), and the Peabody Picture Vocabulary Test (Dunn, 1965) were administered.

It should be clear that this test battery is designed to be weighted heavily in favour of measures of sensory-perceptual, motor, psychomotor, linguistic, and higher-order concept-formation abilities. Our reasons for this have been outlined elsewhere (Rourke, 1976a, 1976b). The battery of tests employed is fairly extensive for the express purpose of attempting to do justice to the wide range of abilities which are subserved by the human brain. As Reitan (1966, 1974a) has argued impressively, failure to do so may eventuate in the generating of conclusions regarding the relationships between the brain and behavior in this and other areas of neuropsychologic investigation which are limited if not erroneous. Be that as it may, the interested reader may refer to a recent article dealing with these matters of concern (Rourke, 1976b) wherein issues relating to the aims of this type of assessment, test interpretation, and the rendering and implementation of educational and other recommendations are discussed.

With these remarks regarding definition, subjects typically employed, and the types of tests routinely administered in mind, we are in position to review the results and implications of the studies. In the first section of the review, an outline of some of our findings with respect to children who exhibit learning disabilities of an undifferentiated sort are presented.

STUDIES OF CHILDREN WITH LEARNING DISABILITIES (GENERAL)

The respective histories of the neuropsychologic investigation of human adults with well-documented cerebral lesions and the neuropsychologic investigation of children with learning disabilities have several things in common. One of these similarities is the nature of the initial questions for which answers were sought in both fields. In the case of adults with brain lesions, investigators such as Halstead and Reitan attempted to determine whether and to what extent brain-damaged and normal persons differ in their performance on psychological tests—that is, would persons who are equated for other relevant variables (such as sex, age, and level of education), but who differ with respect to the integrity of the cerebral hemispheres, perform in a reliably and validly differentiatable fashion on selected psychological tests? In the area of the neuropsychology of learning disorders, an analogous question needed to be answered—that is, is it the case that the performances of learning-disabled and normal children differ in a reliable and valid fashion on tests known to be sensitive to the integrity of the cerebral hemispheres in children? A review of our attempts to answer the latter question has been presented recently (Rourke, 1975). The purpose of that which follows is to bring this review up to date and to focus particularly on the extent to which this question has been answered.

Level-of-Performance Studies

The most basic and traditional method for providing an answer to this question has been to conduct studies that utilize the "level-of-performance" approach. Within this context, one is concerned with constructing a test having specific properties, performance on which will differentiate between learning-disability and normal children. One example of this approach is that involved in our construction and validation of the Children's Word-Finding Test (CWFT; Pajurkova, Orr, Rourke et al., 1976; Rourke and Fisk, 1977). The Pajurkova, et al. (1976) study includes a description of the construction of this test, which is essentially a downward extension of a measure originally developed by Reitan (1972) for use with brain-damaged patients. We thought that a children's version of this test would be particularly useful for our purposes because the task includes a linguistic component as well as a problem-solving component. The latter feature is especially important because most verbal and language-related tasks which are typically used in the assessment of brain-damaged and learning-disabled children do not require verbal processing or verbal expression of a problem-solving nature. (For example, the Vocabulary and Digit Span subtests of the WISC and the Peabody Picture Vocabulary Test seem virtually bereft of a novel problem-solving component.) The importance of this component in the assessment of children with learning disabilities seems to be related to the well-known principle that tests that involve a novel and/or problem-solving component are those that are most sensitive to impairment at the level of the cerebral hemispheres (Reitan, 1966). Indeed, it was because adults with chronic lesions of the left cerebral hemisphere did not exhibit the extensive verbal and language-related deficits which characterize patients suffering from acute lesions within the left hemisphere that motivated Reitan (1972) to develop the adult version of this test.

Be that as it may, in our study, the CWFT was administered to 9- and 10-year-old learning-disabled and normal children. The results indicated that performance differed markedly for the learning-disabled and normal children. This separation was evident in spite of the fact that the two groups were equated for WISC Full Scale IQ, Verbal IQ, and Performance IQ. In addition, the separation of the groups was remarkable with respect to overlap: the cutoff point which successfully "classified" the normal children eventuated in only 25% misclassification of the learning-disabled children. Subsequently, we shortened this 20-item test with no loss in classifactory accuracy (Rourke and Fisk, 1977).

These clear-cut results are not entirely common in either the brain-damaged adult literature or in studies done on learning-disabled children where such factors as age and level of psychometric intelligence have been controlled. In this sense, the results of this study are encouraging. However, it should be borne in mind that the results of this and similar level-of-performance studies do little to clarify the etiological and habilitational issues of principal concern. For example, these results do not speak to the issue of whether and to what extent brain dysfunction may be a limiting factor in the behaviour of learning-disabled children. Also, there is little, if anything, in the way of habilitational or treatment information which can be gleaned from these results. Finally—and this is a criticism that can be leveled against all of the investigations in this section—the inclusion of a heterogeneous group of learning-disabled children in this study renders impossible the generating of inferences regarding the relationship between CWFT performance and different types of reading, spelling, and arithmetic retardation.

Nevertheless, the fact remains that the performances of learning-disabled and normal children differed markedly on a downward extension of a test which was specifically designed to be sensitive to impairment at the level of the cerebral hemispheres in adults. As such, these results are at least consistent with the view that cerebral dysfunction is an important limiting feature in the behavioural repertoire of children with learning disabilities.

Studies of Pathognomonic Signs, Clinical Symptoms, and Clinical Tests

Another approach to the assessment of the neuropsychologic significance of learning disabilities in children is one that attempts to exploit the "pathognomonic sign" approach. Here, the emphasis is upon the determination of signs that are present if the pathology in question (i.e., a learning disability) is present. As such, it is an approach that has much in common with the so-called "medical model."

Our research in this area has focused on the pathognomonic significance of attentional deficits (as symptoms) and has involved the use of brain-damaged subjects (e.g., Czudner and Rourke, 1970, 1972; Rourke and Czudner, 1972) and learning-disability children (Pulvermacher, 1973). We have also attempted to expand this type of inquiry into related areas such as platelet seratonin levels in hyperactive children (Goldman, Thibert, and Rourke, 1978).

However, within the current context, the investigation of clinical tests (which, like symptoms, we can consider to be similar to pathognomonic signs in that they are evaluated from the point of view of the extent to which they mirror the presence of pathology) has been our main focus of concern. Of the studies carried out in this area, one (MacDonald and Rourke, 1975) will be described at some length.

We performed this investigation because we were particularly interested in determining the relationship between the rate of habituation of the cortical arousal response (i.e., alpha blocking) and the integrity of various adaptive abilities in learning-disabled children. The experimental hypothesis was quite simple: namely, that on tests known to be sensitive to the integrity of the cerebral hemispheres, the performances of children who habituate in a normal fashion would be superior to those of children who did so in an abnormal fashion.

The results failed to offer support for this hypothesis. However, a closer inspection of the data indicated that there was a subgroup of children who habituated in a normal fashion, but who did not exhibit alpha blocking on the first two presentations of the stimulus. The results for this "no-blocking" (NB) group as well as those for the normal-habituating (HB) group and a group that exhibited fairly consistent blocking (CB) throughout the testing session on nine of the dependent measures are contained in Figure 1. These results are plotted in terms of standardized T scores, and are arranged in such a way that good performance is represented in one direction (above 50) and poor performance in the opposite direction (below 50). A T score of 50 represents the performance of normal control subjects on these measures. As reflected in Figure 1, the performances of group HB were virtually the same as those of the normal control group, and superior to those of groups CB and NB on eight of the nine dependent measures. The exception to this general trend was in the case of performance on the Tactual Performance Test (TPT). In this instance, the performances of groups CB and HB did not differ significantly from each other or from normals, but were superior to that of group NB.

It is of interest that the task requirements for the TPT involve placing six blocks in the Seguin-Goddard formboard (first with the dominant hand, then with the nondominant hand, and finally with both hands together) *while blindfolded*. Presumably, the performance of the CB group "becomes normal" under such conditions, whereas that of the NB group does not. In other words, limiting the level of environmental stimulation (by

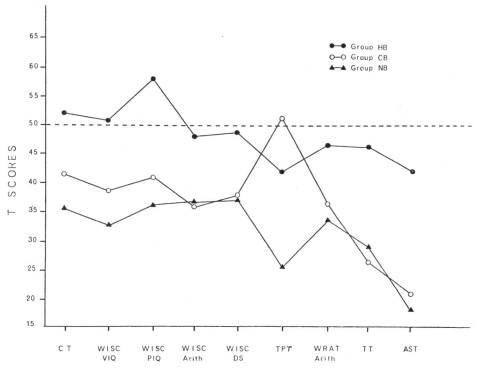

Fig. 1. Performance of three groups of children (HB,CB,NB) on tests sensitive to the integrity of the cerebral hemispheres. (CT: Halstead Category Test; V: Verbal; P: Performance; Arith: Arithmetic; DS: Digit Span; TPT: Tactual Performance Test; TT: Target Test; AST: Aphasia Screening Test.)

preventing input through the visual modality) has opposite effects on the performance of these two groups of children. More specifically, the children in group CB (who appear to be hyperaroused in the sense that they do not exhibit habituation of alpha blocking) seemed to benefit from reduction in level of environmental stimulation, whereas the children in group NB (who exhibit a kind of hypoarousal, at least to the first two presentations of the stimulus) do more poorly under reduced levels of environmental stimulation.

If confirmed by cross-validation, these findings suggest the following: (a) that children who are doing poorly in school, but who exhibit normal patterns of habituation of the cortical arousal response, can be expected to exhibit essentially normal performances on neuropsychologic measures; (b) that children who exhibit particular patterns of EEG hypo- or hyperarousal can be expected, in general, to do poorly on such measures; (c) that children who exhibit a pattern of hyperarousal may benefit from a decrement in environmental stimulation; and (d) that children who exhibit a pattern of hypoarousal may need *more* rather than *less* environmental stimulation and pattern salience in order to affect a normalization of their learning efficiency.

The importance of the method of approach used in this study should be emphasized. Had we confined our observations to an analysis of differences in *levels* of habituation, we would have generated essentially negative results. It was only when *qualitative* differences were used to form the groups for study that meaningful differences emerged. Had this not been done, the NB group would not have been separated from the other "habituators," and potentially meaningful neuropsychologic relationships would have been overlooked. As it now stands, it would seem reasonable to infer that further study of the relationships between various types of EEG alpha blocking patterns and adaptive performances in learning-disabled children should be heuristic with respect to elucidating brain-behaviour relationships.

Differential-Score Studies

Yet another manner in which the question posed at the onset of this section can be answered is through application of the "differential-score," "configurational," or "pattern-analysis" approach. The aim of this approach is to determine the neuro-psychologic significance of *patterns* of scores (i.e., various relationships and differences between them) rather than that of absolute *levels* of performance. For example, one can attempt to determine the concurrent or predictive validity of WISC Verbal IQ alone (which is, essentially, a level-of-performance consideration) or one can investigate the significance of WISC Verbal IQ in relationship to WISC Performance IQ (i.e., various patterns of WISC Verbal IQ—Performance IQ discrepancies).

We have carried out some studies that speak to this issue (Rourke, Dietrich, and Young, 1973; Rourke and Finlayson, 1978; Rourke and Orr, 1977; Rourke, Young, and Flewelling, 1971), the results of which can be summarized as follows: (a) WISC VIQ considered in isolation is a rather poor indicator of either current or future levels of reading and spelling; (b) a pattern of high Verbal IQ—low Performance IQ is most often associated in older (10- to 14-year-old) children with reading and spelling performances which are superior relative to arithmetic proficiency; and (c) a pattern of low Verbal IQ—high Performance IQ is most often associated with uniformly deficient reading and spelling performances.

These differences between reading, spelling, and arithmetic achievement levels will not be expanded upon because they serve as the focus for the next section, which deals with more "specific" learning disabilities. The principal point of interest within the present context is the determination of the relative concurrent or predictive validity of a specific level of performance (e.g., WISC Verbal IQ) versus that which obtains when the pattern generated by various relationships between this level of performance and that on another measure (e.g., WISC Performance IQ) are compared. The results of our studies of learning-disabled children appear to confirm the notion that, within fairly broad limits, much more valid inferences can be drawn from pattern analysis than from absolute levels of performance. In fact, it can be the case that conclusions based upon absolute levels of performance do more to becloud than illuminate the issues in question. An example of the latter will be illustrated in the next section when the results of the Rourke and Finlayson (1978) and Rourke and Strang (1978) studies are dealt with in greater detail.

Furthermore, it should be pointed out that the efficacy of the configurational or pattern-analysis approach in this field is not confined to patterns of performance on the WISC or to academic achievement levels. For example, when older children with learning disabilities are grouped according to patterns of performance on the Trail Making Test that are similar to those exhibited by adults with well-documented cerebral lesions (Rourke and Finlayson, 1975), it is found that the children who exhibit these various patterns perform in ways that are similar to those that would be predicted (on the basis of the results of the adult studies) were they to be suffering the adverse effects of cerebral dysfunction of the left or the right or both cerebral hemispheres. In each of these instances, it is the *pattern* of performance on the Trail Making Test that yields classificatory accuracy with respect to "membership" in one of the three groups.

More generally, it appears that the results of these pattern-analysis studies not only support the view that cerebral dysfunction can be a limiting feature in the academic performances of learning-disabled children but that there are different subgroups of learning-disabled children which can be differentiated on the basis of patterns of brain-related abilities. However, more of this later.

Comparisons of Performance on the Two Sides of the Body

Another type of configurational or differential score analysis is one based upon the contralateral patterns of motor and sensory projections in the brain—namely, conparisons of performance on the two sides of the body. So far, we have virtually confined our study of this particular type of pattern analysis to investigations of the neuropsychologic significance of patterns of psychomotor performances with the upper extremities.

In an early study, where we were concerned with the investigation of a number of psychomotor abilities in learning-disability children (Rourke and Telegdy, 1971), we found that older children with learning disabilities who exhibited a pattern of low Verbal IQ—high Performance IQ on the WISC did much better with both hands on the Grooved Pegboard Test (GPT; Kløve, 1963) than did those who exhibited a pattern of high Verbal IQ—low Performance IQ; a group of learning-disability children who exhibited a pattern of Verbal IQ = Performance IQ performed at a level intermediate to that of the other two groups on this test. The results for the GPT (which requires eye-hand coordination under speeded conditions) yielded the most clearcut differences between the three groups in this study. In general, the results of this investigation were felt to be compatible with the view that patterns of WISC Verbal IQ—Performance IQ discrepancies in older children with learning disabilities are reflective of the differential functional integrity of the two cerebral hemispheres in these children. As such, these results said more about the validity of the WISC than about comparisons of performance on the two sides of the body.

This being the case, it was necessary to carry out a study wherein differing patterns of psychomotor performance constituted the criteria for group selection. In this study (Rourke, Yanni, MacDonald, et al., 1973), we compared the performances of two groups of children with learning disabilities who exhibited lateralized deficits on the GPT and two groups of children who did not. We found that the differences between these groups of learning-disabled children with and without lateralized motor deficits were strikingly similar to the differences between analogous groups of adults with well-documented cerebral lesions as reported in previous research (e.g., Reed and Reitan, 1963). In addition, as was found in the Rourke and Telegdy (1971) study, the overall GPT performance of the two groups who exhibited a pattern of low Verbal IQ—high Performance IQ on the WISC was superior to that of the two groups who exhibited the opposite WISC pattern. In spite of this, the differences between the ''lateralized'' and the ''non-lateralized'' groups were, in general, in the expected direction.

In addition to providing additional support for the contention that learning-disabled children exhibit patterns of behaviour that are consistent with the view that cerebral dysfunction plays a role in their learning deficiencies, these data also illustrate the futility of slavish dependence upon a ''level-of-performance'' approach in attempts to elucidate brain-behaviour relationships in this clinical population. For example, on a number of psycholinguistic measures, the group that exhibited completely *normal* right- and left-hand performances on the GPT performed at a level *intermediate* to that of a group characterized by normal right-hand and impaired left-hand GPT performance and another group chosen solely on the basis of impaired right-hand and normal left-hand GPT performance. Furthermore, this ''normal'' GPT group performed in reading and spelling at levels *identical* to that of a group with uniformly impaired right- and left-hand GPT performances. That these relationships obtain as a result of the analysis of differential configurations or patterns of scores rather than simple levels of performance is, by no means, a surprising finding in neuropsychologic investigations of clinical disorders. In fact, there is a distinct tendency for this to be the case in such investigations (Reitan and Davison, 1974). Unfortunately, the level of complexity involved in the interpretation of this data also tends to pose a problem for commentators who have little familiarity with such nuances [see, for example, Ross (1976) for his evaluation of this particular study].

Developmental Studies

Another "method" which we have attempted to exploit in this area is the developmental approach. To this end, we have undertaken one longitudinal study and several cross-sectional investigations of learning-disabled children. The importance of a developmental mode of approach to the study of brain-behaviour relationships in children with learning disabilities cannot be overemphasized. At the very least, a review of the results of these studies should demonstrate that facile generalizations regarding the supposed behavioral and other characteristics of learning-disabled children which do not take into account the age and stage of development of the children in question must, almost by definition, be seriously limited, if not completely erroneous. The following brief review of the results of our studies in this area is designed to speak to this issue in particular.

In one series of studies dealing with the attentional skills of brain-damaged and normal children at two different age levels (Czudner and Rourke, 1970, 1972; Rourke and Czudner, 1972), we found that differences between these two groups of children in reaction-time performance were in evidence only at the younger (i.e., 6 to 8 years) age level. Within the limitations imposed by the absence of longitudinal data regarding this issue, it appeared that older (i.e., 10 to 14 years) brain-damaged children had adapted to and/or recovered from their presumed deficiencies in readiness to respond in both the visual and the auditory modalities. This being the case, it should be clear that the question of whether brain-damaged children do or do not exhibit a deficit in attention has two answers, each of which is valid only within a suitable developmental context. Our cross-sectional studies of learning-disabled children have yielded analogous conclusions.

For example, in one study of 6- to 8-year-old children (Rourke, Dietrich, and Young, 1973), we found that patterns of performance related to WISC Verbal IQ—Performance IQ discrepancies which were evident among 10- to 14-year-old children (Rourke and Telegdy, 1971; Rourke, Young, and Flewelling, 1971) were either not present at all or that the salience of these patterns was greatly reduced. An analogous situation obtained in another study (Sweeney and Rourke, 1978) where we compared the performances of normal, phonetically accurate, and phonetically inaccurate spellers—that is, patterns of differences evident in a clear and fairly robust fashion at the older (13-year-old) age level were absent or considerably attentuated at the younger (9-year-old) age level.

Other interesting findings emerged when the performances of groups of normal, learning-disabled, and mentally retarded children at different age levels were compared (Fisk and Rourke, 1978). In this study, we were particularly concerned in determining whether and to what extent developmental "lag" or "deficit" interpretations (Rourke, 1976c) would be compatible with the performances exhibited by learning-disabled and mentally retarded children. One conclusion was that the developmental lag interpretation seemed to fit the performance patterns of the mentally retarded children quite well, whereas a deficit interpretation was more compatible with the performance patterns of the learning-disabled children. A fuller treatment of the implications of the developmental lag vs. deficit positions will be offered in a subsequent section dealing with the Rourke (1976c) study. In addition, because our other cross-sectional and longitudinal investigations dealt specifically with retarded readers, these will be discussed in a subsequent section devoted to that issue.

In conclusion, the results of the studies reviewed in this section constitute support for the proposition enunciated at its outset—namely, that data from developmental studies are absolutely crucial if we are to formulate reliable and valid inferences regarding the brain-related abilities and deficits of learning-disabled children. A corollary of this proposition is that statements regarding the presence or absence of such abilities or deficits should not be made until the performances in question are tested across the age span of interest. Unfortunately, far too many investigators in the area of children's learning disabilities seem all too ready to overgeneralize conclusions based upon the results of studies that do not take such factors into account. For example, their studies may involve only one restricted age level (with consequent restrictions on the generalizability of the conclusions based upon such data), or they may cover such a wide range of ages that specific abilities and deficiencies operative among children at different age levels will effectively cancel each other. It should be clear that the univariate study of one restricted age range would encourage both type-I and type-II errors, and that a similar study of an overly inclusive age range would increase substantially the probability of type-II error.

STUDIES OF CHILDREN WITH PARTICULAR LEARNING DISABILITIES

In this section, our investigations of children who were chosen for study on the basis of their particular pattern of disabilities in the areas of reading, spelling, or arithmetic are discussed. Unlike the studies focused upon in the previous section, where subjects "qualified" for inclusion on the basis of any number of heterogeneous learning problems, the investigations herein discussed were designed to speak to more specific issues regarding the neuropsychology of learning disorders. In this sense, the historical development of the series of studies dealt with in these two sections mirrors that evident in the neuropsychologic investigation of adults with documented brain-lesions—that is, there is a progression from the investigation of heterogeneous learning disabilities (substitute: heterogeneous brain lesions in the adult literature) to the determination of the special characteristics of specific learning disorders (substitute: particular neurologic disease syndromes in the adult literature).

This section is divided into three parts which deal, in turn, with our focus on reading, spelling, and arithmetic disorders. However, it would be well to bear in mind that these divisions are somewhat arbitrary in that they are based solely upon the criteria used for subject selection. As should become clear as we proceed, there is little that is "specific" (in the sense of an *isolated* disability within the context of an otherwise normal ability structure) about particular learning disabilities. Consequently, even in attempting to deal with more specific learning disorders, we are still faced with the necessity of dealing with more general issues and effects.

Studies of Reading Retardation

In this section the results of five investigations will be reviewed. The first two are cross-sectional in nature, another two deal with empirical and theoretical issues within a longitudinal framework, and the final one has to do with the specification of subtypes of retarded readers. They have in common an attempt to clarify one or several aspects of brain-behaviour relationships in children known to be afflicted with a reading disability.

In the first study in this series (Young and Rourke, 1975), we were particularly interested in determining the relative importance of auditory and visual sequencing deficiencies in reading retardates. In order to do this, we employed 32 second-grade and

32 sixth-grade subjects (half of whom were good readers and half of whom were poor readers) who were matched for age and WISC prorated Performance IQ. The subjects were presented with equivalent verbal sequences, which varied in complexity, through the visual and auditory channels. Half of the subjects received the visual task first and the auditory task 2 days later, and the other half received the auditory task first and the visual task second. The results indicated that all subjects performed faster on the auditory task than on the visual task, regardless of order of presentation or level of complexity. The results also indicated that the younger poor readers made more errors than did the younger good readers on both tasks, but particularly on the auditory task; the performances of older poor and good readers, in general, did not differ.

This investigation is important for a variety of reasons. Within the present context, however, it is particularly relevant because it speaks to the same issue in the case of retarded readers as did our previous studies of attentional deficits in brain-damaged children (Czudner and Rourke, 1970; 1972; Rourke and Czudner, 1972)—that is, the question of whether and to what extent retarded readers exhibit relative deficiencies in auditory and/or visual sequencing is amenable to vastly different answers depending upon the particular developmental context within which it is asked.

Another cross-sectional study of retarded readers was carried out for far different reasons. Because of recent speculations regarding sex differences in cerebral organization and specialization among school-aged children (see Witelson, 1976, 1977), we compared the performances of younger (6½- to 8½-year-old) and older (10½- to 12½-year-old) male and female retarded readers on a number of measures which have been shown to be sensitive to the integrity of the cerebral hemispheres. We found virtually no sex differences on these measures of perceptual, visual-motor, linguistic, and concept-formation abilities at either age level. Thus, these data are not consistent with the view that there are sex differences in cerebral organizaton and specialization among retarded readers. Furthermore, these results argue against provision of remedial intervention strategies which are tailored differently for retarded-reading boys than for retarded-reading girls.

The next two studies to be discussed were based upon data derived from our longitudinal investigation of normal and retarded readers. In order to appreciate the implications of the results of these studies, it is necessary to describe in some detail the 4-year investigation upon which they are based. In the initial phase of this investigation (study 1), there were 30 subjects in the normal-reading (NR) group and 29 subjects in the retarded-reading (RR) group. The subjects were drawn from a population of grade-1 and grade-2 male students from seven schools in a school system in Windsor, Ontario. The schools were selected because of their geographic proximity and relatively homogeneous socioeconomic makeup (lower-middle to middle-middle class).

Normal readers were selected on the basis of the following criteria: a centile score of 50 or above on the Reading subtest of the Metropolitan Achievement Test (MAT) and a score of 60 or above on either the Word Knowledge or the Word Discrimination subtest of the MAT. Subjects in the RR group all had a centile score of 20 or below on the Reading subtest of the MAT and 35 or below on either the Word Knowledge or the Word Discrimination subtest. All subjects in both groups obtained a Full Scale IQ of between 91 and 117 on the WISC. The exclusion of subjects who fell outside of this roughly normal range was considered desirable for two reasons: (a) it would be reasonable to assume that "dull" and "bright" children, quite apart from differences in reading ability, would differ markedly on a large number of the dependent variables employed in this study; and (b) the results of this investigation were intended to apply to groups of "average" children at the age levels in question, not to subjects for whom special class placement was being considered. In study 1, the groups were matched for age: the age range for subjects in the NR groups was 88 to 100 months ($\bar{x} = 92.87$); for those in the RR group, 87 to 100 months ($\bar{x} = 92.10$). The groups were also tested at intervals of 2 years (study 2), 3 years (study 3), and 4 years (study 4) after this initial examination.

In study 4, 24 NR subjects and 20 RR subjects from the original groups were still in the school system and available for retesting. In this study, the age range for subjects in the NR group was 133 to 148 months ($\bar{x} = 139.07$), and for subjects in the RR group it was 133 to 146 months ($\bar{x} = 139.28$); the WISC Full Scale IQ scores ranged from 101 to 125 for subjects in the NR group and from 82 to 120 for subjects in the RR group.

The tests administered in studies 1, 2, 3, and 4 covered a wide range of adaptive abilities, ranging from simple sensory and motor skills through those of a psychomotor and psycholinguistic variety, up to and including higher-order concept-formation abilities. In all, 114 measures were available for analysis. The results of this investigation can be summarized as follows.

In spite of the fact that several subjects initially classified as retarded readers made significant advances in reading performance over the 4-year period, the overall performance of the retarded readers at the time of the fourth testing was more inferior to that of the normal readers than it was at the time of the initial examination. Most of the normal readers made more than 4 years of progress in reading over the 4-year period, whereas a majority of the retarded readers made less than 2 years of progress over the same time span. Of special interest were those variables that differentiated between the subjects initially classified as retarded readers who made significant progress in reading and those who made very little, if any, progress; these results will be discussed in the context of the Rourke and Orr (1977) study.

Hypotheses relating to the likelihood that cerebral dysfunction plays a role in reading retardation (Doehring, 1968) received some support from the data, as did some hypotheses relating to the changing nature of the deficits responsible for reading retardation with advancing age (Satz, Friel, and Rudegeair, 1974). In this latter connection, the data offered some support for Satz's notion that visual-motor integration is relatively more important in the early stages of learning to read, whereas language and formal operational thought become increasingly more relevant at more advanced stages of reading development. For example, performance on the Grooved Pegboard Test (a measure of relatively fine visual-motor coordination which was discussed above) significantly differentiated between the normal and retarded readers initially, but these differences were not as pronounced at the time of the fourth testing. On the other hand, whereas performance on the children's version of the Halstead Category Test (a measure of problem solving, hypothesis testing, and abstract reasoning) did not differentiate between the groups initially, differences on this test were significant in the 4-year follow-up. Throughout the age period studied, measures of auditory-verbal and language-related abilities consistently differentiated between the groups.

It is important that the retarded readers exhibited deficits in a large number of abilities, some of which do not seem, at first blush, to be related in any very direct way to reading. Thus, as pointed out by Doehring (1968) and Reitan (1964), the notion that reading retardation is a specific deficit (i.e., not associated with deficits in other areas of psychologic functioning) is not a supportable position.

Finally, from a methodologic point of view, at least one feature of this investigation should be emphasized—namely, that it allowed for the utilization of all of the approaches to the analysis of neuropsychologic test data explained above: level-of-performance, pathognomonic sign, differential score, comparisons of performance on the two sides of the body, and developmental analysis. Although we have yet to finish our analysis of these data in terms of all of these approaches, the next two studies to be discussed have been completed, and they provide a fairly representative "flavour" of the types of questions that can be addressed within this framework.

One important issue with which this investigation was concerned was to determine the relative merits of the "developmental lag" position and "deficit" position vis-à-vis the explanation of reading retardation in children. To this end, seven developmental lag-deficit paradigms were constructed which would allow for just such a determination, and the results of the Satz, et al. (1974) study and our own longitudinal investigation were compared in the light of these paradigms (Rourke, 1976c).

The conclusions arrived at on the basis of these comparisons were as follows. In general, the developmental lag position seemed tenable in the case of fairly simple, early-emerging abilities. The specific developmental lag position that was examined in this investigation—that is, the one espoused by Satz and Van Nostrand (1973)—postulates a particular lag in the development of the left cerebral hemisphere. We found that the results of our investigation and that of Satz, et al. (1974) lent support to the notion that dysfunction of the left cerebral hemisphere is particularly involved in the genesis of reading retardation. However, we did not find that retarded readers, as a group, eventually "caught up" in those abilities thought to subserve the reading function—nor, for that matter did they "catch up" in reading ability itself. Thus, the weight of the evidence in the Rourke (1976c) study favors a deficit rather than a developmental lag position.

That some children initially classified as "retarded readers" in our longitudinal investigation did make fairly substantial gains in reading (an analysis of which forms a basis of the study to be described next) lends support to the developmental lag position. However, the results of the groupwise comparisons in the Rourke (1976c) investigation indicated that at least some, if not most, of the retarded readers studied suffered from a deficit or deficits in at least some of those abilities ordinarily thought to be subserved primarily by the left cerebral hemisphere. And, although this group of retarded readers exhibited marginal advances in those skills crucial for reading and in reading ability itself over the years, there was little or no reason to predict, on the basis of the data analyzed in this study, that they would ever either catch up to or even closely approximate the performance of their normal reading agemates in these particular abilities.

To recapitulate, our longitudinal investigation of retarded and normal readers as described to this point had several aims, including (a) description of the neuropsychologic correlates of normal and retarded reading through the early grade-school years (b) a determination of the relative merits of the developmental lag and deficit positions; and (c) the prediction of long-term reading and spelling retardation (i.e., the identification of "high-risk" children).

With respect to aim (a), our results are consistent with those of other studies in this field (e.g., Doehring, 1968; Reed, 1968; Satz, et al., 1974) in that we have found reading retardation to be a multifaceted problem—that is, it can be related to a host of verbal, visual-perceptual, auditory-perceptual, visual-motor, and cognitive deficiencies. With respect to aim (b), there was evidence that supports both a particular developmental lag position and a deficit position, although the weight of the evidence favours the latter point of view.

It became evident during the course of this investigation that a child who is retarded in reading in grades one or two will probably still be retarded in reading in grades five or six. However, it was also clear that a rather small percentage of children, initially classified as retarded readers, did show significant improvement by the time of the middle grade-school years, to the point where they became able to read and spell at normal or near-normal levels. These two subgroups of children initially classified as retarded readers (i.e., those who improved signficiantly and those who did not), consistent with aim (c) mentioned above, were the principal focus of the next study to be described.

The purpose of this investigation (Rourke and Orr, 1977) was to determine the relative predictive accuracy for reading and spelling performances of a number of measures (reading, spelling, psychometric intelligence, the Underlining Test) administered during the first phase (study 1) of our longitudinal investigation. The criterion measures were the Word Knowledge and Reading subtests of the MAT and the Reading and Spelling subtests of the WRAT, all of which were administered in study 4. Three sets of stepwise regression analyses were carried out for each of the four criterion measures: one for the normal readers, one for the retarded readers, and one for the two groups combined. The results indicated that there were some accurate predictive measures of reading and spelling achievement levels over the 4-year age span studied, and that the relative accuracy of these measures differed markedly for normal and retarded readers. Especially in the case of retarded readers, performance on the Underlining Test (Doehring, 1968; Rourke and Petrauskas, 1977) was shown to be a much more accurate predictor of eventual achievement levels in reading and spelling than were the tests of reading, spelling, or psychometric intelligence which were employed.

Those subtests of the Underlining Test which appeared in the best regression models most often (i.e., numbers 8 and 4) involved target and distractor items which were nonverbal: sequences of geometric forms (number 8) and gestalt figures (number 4). The fact that these subtests contained only "nonverbal" items, however, does not necessarily imply that verbal mediation was not important for performances on them. In fact, it may be the case that those subjects who were most adept at employing a strategy involving verbal labeling of the fairly complex nonverbal configuration involved in subtests 4 and 8 were those who performed best on them.

The results of this study offered some support for the developmental lag view of Satz and his colleagues (e.g., Satz, et al., 1974) in that "younger" (ages 7–8) retarded readers exhibited particularly poor performance as compared to age-matched normal readers on tasks that seem to require primarily visual-perceptual and visual-motor abilities (e.g., the Underlining Test). However, it should be noted that, at the time of study 1, the normal and retarded reading groups did not differ significantly on the WISC Performance IQ measure (which is composed primarily of tests heavily weighted in terms of visual-spatial and visual-motor components). In addition, as was pointed out above, it may be the case that verbal labeling of the complex visual forms of the Underlining Test was one of the crucial elements responsible for success on them.

Finally, the fact that the accurate predictive antecedents at ages 7 to 8 of reading and spelling levels at ages 11 to 12 for the retarded readers differed markedly from those for the normal readers could be construed as evidence in support of either the developmental-lag or the deficit position. However, it should be emphasized that only 5 of the 19 subjects originally classified as "retarded readers" made fairly substantial (and, on the basis of the results of this study, predictable) gains in reading achievement (i.e., more than 20 centile points on the MAT Reading subtest), whereas approximately three-quarters of this group made little, if any, progress. This being the case, it may be that a developmental lag model would be appropriate for those few who made significant advances, whereas a deficit interpretation would be appropriate for those who did not.

In summary, if confirmed by cross-validation (a study of which is currently underway in our laboratory), the results of this investigation suggest that performance on the Underlining Test is a far more potent means of identifying retarded readers who are "at risk" (at ages 7–8) with respect to deficiencies in eventual reading and spelling achievement (at ages 11–12) than are the measures of psychometric intelligence, reading, or spelling which were employed. However, interpretations of the relative predictive accuracy of the various measures used must be viewed in the light of the restricted range of the WISC Full Scale IQ and the truncated and restricted distributions of initial MAT subtest scores which were employed in this study. For these and other reasons, the drawing of clinical inferences (including prognoses) in individual cases of children who are retarded in reading on the basis of this type of test data must be approached with considerable caution [see Rourke (1976b) for an elaboration of this issue]. This is especially important in this particualr study when one considers the limitations imposed on such inferences by reason of the restricted age span and fairly small number of measures chosen for comparison.

The final study to be discussed in this section constitutes our first attempt to identify subgroups of retarded readers. As has been pointed out in recent reviews of the neuropsychologic literature in this area (e.g., Benton, 1975; Rourke, 1978b), there is abundant evidence to indicate that reading retardates comprise a heterogeneous rather than a homogeneous population. A number of research "models" have been presented recently which have identified subgroups within the general population of reading retardates (e.g., Boder, 1973; Johnson and Myklebust, 1967; Mattis, French, and Rapin, 1975). Studies such as these have provided useful clinical insights for potential remedial approaches and prognostic outcomes (e.g., Boder, 1973; Tallal, 1976), as well as some information regarding etiological considerations (Rourke and Finlayson, 1978).

In view of the encouraging results reported in these earlier studies, our investigation (Petrauskas and Rourke, 1978) was designed to identify subgroups of retarded readers by using a multivariate classification procedure (Q-type factor analysis) similar to that employed by Doehring and Hoschko (1977). For this purpose, 160 subjects between the ages of 84 and 107 months were selected. The sample was comprised of 133 poor readers (110 males, 23 females) chosen from a clinic sample and 27 normal readers (all males) who were tested in the longitudinal investigation described above. Subjects were screened for evidence of sensory deficits, primary emotional disturbance, linguistic and cultural deprivation, and mental retardation. Only right-handed subjects with WISC FSIQ scores between 80 and 120 were included. All subjects had received our standard battery of neuropsychologic tests.

Test measures were divided into six skill areas based on categorizations suggested by Reitan (1974b). Test scores were converted into T scores in terms of normative data. A Pearson product-moment correlational analysis (employing all data from the 160 subjects) was carried out to determine the degree of relatedness between test measures. From a total of 44 test measures, 20 were selected for further analysis based on the following criteria: (a) variables in particular skill areas that exhibited lowest correlations with one another; (b) similar densities of variables in differenct skill areas; and (c) clinical explanatory potential of the variables when taken together.

The total sample was then randomly subdivided into two subsamples of 80 subjects (group A and group B). The only control that was introduced was to insure that a similar number of normal readers was included in each subsample. The data matrix of each subsample was transposed, and Pearson product-moment correlation analyses for subjects were determined. The resultant matrices of intercorrelations were factored for each subsample (using an iterated principal-axis solution); emerging factors that yielded eigenvalues of 4.00 or greater were retained and rotated orthogonally to Varimax criterion. The analyses yielded six factors for each subgroup. (Of the six factors derived for group A, one was excluded from consideration because few subjects loaded highly on it, and those that did so demonstrated both positive and negative loadings.) Subjects with single-factor loadings equal to or greater than .50 were extracted for each factor, and T score means for the test scores were plotted. These graphs represented profiles for those subjects who loaded highly on single factors.

In addition, the same factoring and subject extraction procedures were carried out for the two subsamples (groups A and B) combined; this analysis also yielded six factors. Once again, subjects with single factor loadings equal to or greater than .50 were extracted for each factor, and T score means for the test scores were plotted. Composite graphs were plotted for the factors for groups A, B, and A and B which appeared most similar. These groupings constituted the "types" of retarded readers.

What follows is a description of the salient features of the most reliable subgroups that were extracted by this procedure.

Type 1. The test performances of type 1 could be characterized as follows: (a) relatively well-developed visual-spatial and eye-hand coordination skills; (b) average or near-average performances on measures of tactile-kinesthetic abilities, abstract reasoning, and nonverbal concept formation (although performance on one test of concept formation which involves substantial verbal coding was mildly impaired); (c) near-average performances on word definitions; mildly impaired word blending, immediate memory for digits, and store of general information; moderately to severely impaired verbal fluency and sentence memory.

Type 2. The test performances of type 2 could be characterized as follows: (a) average or near-average kinesthetic, psychomotor, visual-spatial constructional and word-definition abilities, and nonverbal problem-solving and abstract reasoning skills within a context that provides immediate positive and negative feedback; (b) borderline to mildly impaired immediate memory for digits and other "sequencing" skills, store of general information, souund blending, verbal fluency, and concept formation when substantial verbal coding is required and/or when no positive and negative feedback is provided; (c) moderately to severely impaired finger recognition, immediate visual-spatial memory, and memory for sentences.

Type 3. The test performances of type 3 could be characterized as follows: (a) average or near-average finger recognition (left hand), kinesthetic, visuo-spatial constructional, vocabulary and sound-blending abilities, and nonverbal concept formation within a context of immediate positive and negative feedback; (b) borderline to mildly impaired finger recognition (right hand), immediate memory for digits, eye-hand coordination under speeded conditions, store of general information, and nonverbal abstraction and the shifting of set without the benefit of positive and negative feedback; (c) mildly to moderately impaired verbal fluency, sentence memory, and immediate visual-spatial memory; (d) moderately to severely impaired concept formation which involves substantial verbal coding.

Type 4   The performances of type 4 could be characterized as follows: average or above-average finger recognition, kinesthetic, sequencing, eye-hand coordination, visuo-spatial constructional, visual memory, auditory-verbal receptive, and concept-formation abilities.

Type 5.   Although the reliability of this retarded reader type was rather low, the test performances could be characterized as follows: (a) average to high-average finger recognition and kinesthetic skills, visuo-spatial contructional, vocabulary, and sound-blending abilities; (b) near-average immediate memory for digits, eye-hand coordination skills, store of general information and nonverbal abstract reasoning and concept forma-tion when positive and negative feedback are provided; (c) mildly to moderately impaired verbal fluency, sentence memory, and immediate visual-spatial memory.

It should be noted that it was the normal readers included in the study who loaded on type 4, and that type 5 is of somewhat questionable reliability because of some discrepan-cies between groups A and B on this factor. Thus, at this stage in our examination of this issue of subtypes of reading retardation, it would appear that we have isolated at least three (i.e., types 1, 2, and 3) of retarded readers at the 7- to 8-year age level. The next step in this series of investigations is to determine if similar or different types are in evidence at older and younger age levels.

Studies of Spelling Retardation

The results of three studies will be discussed in this section, all of which have to do with our attempts to analyze spelling errors from the point of view of their degree of phonetic accuracy. Although the space available here does not allow a complete exposi-tion of our rationale for focusing on this particular aspect of spelling, our point of departure should at least be mentioned. And, as in so many other areas of the neuro-psychologic investigation of learning disorders, the ''idea'' emerged from clinical practice with such children and research evidence derived from studies of adults with well-documented cerebral lesions (e.g., Kinsbourne and Warrington, 1964). [See Rourke (1976a) for an extended treatment of this issue.] In a word, we were impressed by the relative ''intactness'' (from a neuropsychologic point of view) of children who (say) rendered ''nacher'' for the word, ''nature'' (i.e., whose misspelling was essentially accurate from a phonetic point of view), as compared to children whose rendering of the same word was ''diltum'' or ''qpwo'' (i.e., whose misspelling was phonetically inaccu-rate). At the same time, it was abundantly clear that adults with well-documented lesions of the so-called ''language areas'' of the left cerebral hemisphere exhibited a tendency to spell in a phonetically inaccurate fashion. It was for these reasons that we decided to study these two ''types'' of retarded spellers.

In our first study (Burgher and Rourke, 1978), we examined the spelling produc-tions of the subjects in our longitudinal investigation of reading retardation. The produc-tions of these subjects were rated for degree of phonetic accuracy, and it was found that the retarded readers had significantly fewer phonetically accurate spelling errors than did the normal readers, even though the normal readers' (whose *level* of achievement in spelling was far superior to that of the retarded readers) spelling errors occurred on more difficult words. Finally, the degree of phonetic accuracy of the misspellings of the re-tarded readers tended to ''level off'' after the second year of testing (i.e., at ages 9–10 years). This finding would seem to be consistent with the ''deficit'' or ''difference'' position with respect to retarded reading which has been alluded to earlier (Rourke, 1976c;

Usprich, 1976). There were other interesting results of this study, but to go into them at this point would take us too far afield.

The next investigation which we carried out in this area (Sweeney and Rourke, 1978) was cross-sectional in nature and was inspired by two groups of studies: (a) those of Newcombe (1969) and Nelson and Warrington (1974) wherein a positive relationship between spelling retardation characterized by phonetically inaccurate errors and a general impairment in language functioning was demonstrated; and (b) those of Boder (1973), which demonstrated a positive relationship between spelling performances characterized by an excess of phonetic accuracy and poor memory for what words look like (similar to the pattern which Myklebust (1965, 1973) has referred to as "visual dyslexia").

We expected that the results of this study would reflect a generalized impairment in language functioning for phonetically inaccurate spelling retardates (referred to as PIs). In addition, the investigation was designed to examine the development of very specific verbal abilities (e.g., speech-sounds perception, short-term auditory-verbal memory, and auditory-closure) in these children. We also predicted that, just as phonetically accurate spelling retardates (referred to as PAs) do not seem to be able to conjure up accurate visualizations of the written word in response to the spoken word, they would also have difficulty in conjuring up visualizations on the basis of pictorial clues in order to prompt an accurate verbal response. Finally, we thought that any deficiencies in language functioning experienced by PIs and PAs would tend to increase with age, being more pronounced at older age levels.

The subjects for this cross-sectional study were at age levels corresponding to grades 4 and 8. The groups at each age level were equated for age and WISC Performance IQ. Retardation in spelling was defined operationally as a centile score of 20 or below on the Spelling subtest of the WRAT. Normal spellers (Ns) were selected on the basis of a centile score of 50 or above on the Spelling subtest of the WRAT.

There were one control group and two experimental groups at each age level. Each of the six groups consisted of eight subjects (5 males and 3 females). One younger and one older experimental group were composed of retarded spellers who rendered 40% or less of their misspelled syllables on the WRAT Spelling subtest in a phonetically accurate manner (PIs). One younger and one older experimental group were composed of retarded spellers who rendered at least 60% of their misspelled syllables on the WRAT Spelling subtest in a phonetically accurate manner (PAs). There was no statistically significant difference in *level* of retardation in spelling between PIs and PAs. Also, the differences in degree of phonetic accuracy of misspelled syllables between Ns and PAs at each age level were not statistically significant. A syllable-by-syllable analysis of the misspellings was carried out in terms of a procedure designed specifically for this study [see Sweeney and Rourke (1978) for a fuller explanation of this method].

A number of tests involving auditory discrimination, psycholinguistic abilities, and visual closure were administered to all subjects. The results indicated that the PIs were inferior to the PAs and the normal spellers on most measures of psycholinguistic abilities, but only at the older (grade 8) age level. Differences between PIs and the other two groups were all but absent at the younger (grade 4) age level.

The performance of the older PAs in this study was particularly interesting. They were as inferior to normal spellers as were the PIs only on tests that involved the response requirement of generating a word string involving information not deducible from the information given in the question—that is, on tests very much akin to the question-and-answer type of situation which is common to most elementary school classrooms. This deficiency, coupled with their very inadequate level of spelling performance, may serve to mask their other abilities in the eyes of teachers and parents. This seems to be particularly unfortunate because the PAs are clearly possessed of many more well-developed neuropsychologic abilities than are their PI agemates.

The fact that one of the two differences evident among the three groups at the younger age levels was on the WRAT Arithmetic subtest suggested to us that one important deficiency operative in the PIs at this age level might be in their ability to benefit from formal instruction in the use of rules and, consequently, in logical-grammatical reasoning. Thus, in a second study of these subjects at the grade-4 level (Sweeney, McCabe, and Rourke, 1978), we compared their performances on the Logico-Grammatical Sentence Comprehension Test (Wiig and Semel, 1974). This test samples logical-grammatical reasoning in five areas of relationships: comparative, temporal, passive, familial, and spatial.

The results of this study indicated that the PIs were significantly inferior to the normal spellers in performance on this test, whereas PAs were not. This finding suggests at least two not-mutually-exclusive possibilities: (a) that younger PIs are deficient in the ability to benefit from formal instruction in rules by which different forms of symbolic information are processed, and (b) that they have difficulty in processing language that could be viewed as somewhat more complex than "everyday" discourse.

There are a number of other interesting findings that emerged in these studies which would be too complex to examine within the present context. However, there are some general observations which should be mentioned. First, it is clear that a qualitative analysis of the spelling errors of children is a heuristic path to follow if the nature of the underlying deficiencies of spelling retardates are to be explicated. This use of a kind of "pathognomonic sign" approach (i.e., attempting to demonstrate that phonetically inaccurate spelling is "diagnostic" of a general psycholinguistic deficiency) yielded striking differences between groups of spellers who had been *equated for level of retarded performance* in spelling. Furthermore, it should be noted that *equating for level of phonetic accuracy* of misspellings (as was the case for the normals and the PAs) was also no guarantee of similarity of performance on many of the dependent measures employed. Secondly, it is clear that the age at which the children were tested was a very important consideration with respect to the relationship between degree of phonetic accuracy of misspellings and performance on the dependent variables. For example, had only the grade-4 group been utilized in the Sweeney and Rourke (1978) study, there would have been little reason to expect that this particular dimension of spelling was a fruitful one to examine. Finally, there is good reason to anticipate that forms of educational intervention which would be effective for PAs and PIs would have to differ considerably as a function of their different ability structures. A series of studies has just begun in our laboratory to determine if such is the case.

Studies of Arithmetic Retardation

When compared to the number of investigations of retarded reading and spelling which have been conducted over the past two decades, the number of studies of arithmetic disability is miniscule. As one attempt to correct this disparity, three studies dealing with arithmetic disability which have been conducted in our laboratory will be described. The first involved the use of a now-popular variation on the "comparisons of performances on the two sides of the body" approach; the other two were attempts to exploit the "differential score approach."

In the first investigation (Roach and Rourke, 1976) two studies employing the divided visual field technique were conducted to determine if there was any evidence of "hemispheric dominance" for the process of calculation. In study 1, right-handed boys between the ages of 9 and 11 years who were performing in reading and arithmetic at an age-appropriate level were employed. The results of this study indicated a right visual-field superiority (or, as inferred, a left-hemisphere superiority) for the type of arithmetic processing under investigation. In study 2, right-handed boys ranging in age from 9 to 11 years who were reading at their expected grade level but who were deficient in arithmetic skills were employed. The subjects in study 2 did not exhibit any evidence of visual-field superiority for calculation.

The results of these two studies—specifically, an apparent degree of hemispheric specialization exhibited by subjects who are performing normally with respect to a specific academic skill, and an absence of this specialization exhibited by subjects who are deficient in the skill—were analogous to the findings of others who have investigated patterns of hemispheric dominance in good and poor readers (e.g., Marcel and Rajan, 1975). The results of this study served to alert us to the notion that the investigation of various degrees and patterns of impaired performance in arithmetic might be fruitful. As a first approximation to this aim, the next two investigations were conducted.

The Rourke and Finlayson (1978) study was an attempt to determine if children who exhibited arithmetic retardation within the context of differing patterns of reading and spelling performances would also exhibit differing patterns of brain-related abilities. In this study, children between the ages of 9 and 14 years who fit the general definition of "learning disabilities" adopted for this series of investigations were divided into three groups on the basis of their patterns of performance in reading and spelling tasks relative to their level of performance in arithmetic. The subjects in group 1 were uniformly deficient in reading, spelling, and arithmetic. Group 2 was composed of subjects whose arithmetic performance, although clearly below age-expectation, was significantly better than their performances in reading and spelling. The subjects in group 3 exhibited normal reading and spelling and markedly impaired arithmetic performance. Although all three groups performed well below age-expectation in arithmetic, the performances of groups 2 and 3 were superior to that of group 1; groups 2 and 3 did not differ from one another in their arithmetic performance. The three groups were equated for age and Full Scale IQ on the WISC. The three groups' performances on 16 dependent measures were compared, and the results can be summarized as follows: (a) the performances of groups 1 and 2 were superior to that of group 3 on measures of visual-perceptual and visual-spatial abilities; and (b) group 3 performed at a superior level to that of groups 1 and 2 on measures of verbal and auditory-perceptual abilities.

These results were interpreted as being consistent with the view that the subjects in group 3 may have a relatively dysfunctional right cerebral hemisphere, and that the subjects in groups 1 and 2 were suffering from the adverse effects of a relatively dysfunctional left cerebral hemisphere. This inference was felt to be reasonable because the subjects in group 3 did particularly poorly only on those tasks ordinarily thought to be subserved primarily by the right cerebral hemisphere, whereas the subjects in groups 1 and 2 were particularly deficient only in those skills ordinarily thought to be subserved primarily by the left cerebral hemisphere. Of particular concern within the present context was the fact that two groups of subjects who had been equated for deficient arithmetic performance (i.e., groups 2 and 3) exhibited vastly different performances on verbal and visual-spatial tasks. These differences were clearly related to their *patterns* of reading, spelling, and arithmetic rather than to their *levels of performance* in arithmetic per se.

Be that as it may, the fact remained that the performances of groups 1 and 2 in the

Rourke and Finlayson (1978) study were quite similar to one another. Furthermore, if inferences regarding differential hemispheric integrity among these three groups were to be subjected to additional scrutiny, one way to do so would be to determine if these groups of subjects would exhibit patterns of performance on motor, psychomotor, and tactile-perceptual tasks that would be consistent with that view. It was for these reasons that the Rourke and Strang (1978) investigation was carried out.

In this study, the subjects in groups 1, 2, and 3 referred to above were administered a number of motor, psychomotor, and tactile-perceptual tests that would allow for comparisons of overall level of performance on such measures, as well as comparisons of performance on the two sides of the body. The results can be summarized as follows: (a) there were no significant differences evident on the simple motor measures; (b) the group with an outstanding deficiency in arithmetic (i.e., group 3) performed in a markedly impaired fashion on the more complex psychomotor measures and on a composite tactile-perceptual measure; and (3) there was some evidence that would be consistent with the view that the group 3 subjects were suffering from the adverse effects of a relatively dysfunctional right cerebral hemisphere within the context of satisfactory left hemisphere functioning, whereas the group that performed better in arithmetic than in reading and spelling (i.e.; group 2) exhibited some indications that would be consistent with the opposite pattern of hemispheric integrity. Furthermore, it should be noted that the absence of statistically significant differences on the simple "motor" measures within the context of the clearly significant differences evident on the complex "psychomotor" measures would serve to reinforce the view held by many (e.g.; Reitan, 1966; Rourke, 1975, 1976b) that performances on heterogeneous (i.e.; complex) tests are much more likely than are performances on homogeneous (i.e.; simple) tests to reflect meaningful aspects of brain-behavior relationships among clinical groups such as those employed in this study.

Of particular importance from a psychoeducational standpoint is the pattern of results that emerged in these two studies in the case of the group with outstanding or "specific" deficiencies in arithmetic (i.e.; group 3). It is clear that these children exhibited a number of adaptive deficiencies which should render them the focus of more serious concern than is ordinarily the case. It is quite probable that they are not seen as in need of "help" early in their scholastic career because they read and spell at normal levels and, possibly, because "specific" deficiencies in arithmetic are thought by many to result from socio-emotional disturbances, genetic predispositions, or motivational shortcomings, the adverse effects of which will either pass in time or over which teachers and clinicians have little or no control. Such may very well be the case in some instances. However, it is also clear that at least a subset of such children would appear to have a number of significant brain-related deficiencies which can and should be recognized and dealt with early.

Finally, the striking differences evident between the two groups which were *equated for level of performance* in arithmetic calculation (i.e., groups 2 and 3) should serve as a note of caution to those inclined to compose groups of learning-disabled children for study solely on the basis of such a consideration. Had subjects from group 2 and group 3 been combined to form a group "retarded in arithmetic" for the purpose of comparisons with normal control or other learning-disabled children, it is clear that the differences evident between these two groups would simply have been cancelled in the process. More generally, the important conclusion that emerges from this type of analysis is that it is no longer acceptable within the field of developmental or learning disabilities to constitute groups of children for study solely on the basis of their levels of performance on academic tasks: one must at least be prepared to designate qualitatively distinct types of (say) reading or arithmetic disabilities, if such exist, before launching into a measurement of the supposed correlates of these problems. Failure to do so may not only pose severe and unnecessary limitations on the conclusions that can be drawn from such studies, it may also increase the probability that blatantly false "findings" will be generated and propagated.

FUTURE DIRECTIONS

It should be clear that the research program herein described has only begun to deal with the crucial issues within the field of the neuropsychology of learning disorders. However, we have been encouraged by the results of our efforts to this point, and we feel that there is more than ample justification to continue to proceed along these lines. At the same time, we feel that we are now in a position to begin to approach the problems of remediation in a systematic fashion.

Until recently it has not been possible to deal in a systematic way with the educational and other therapeutic implications of this research. There have been some attempts to delineate the important issues involved in the neuropsychologic assessment of learning-disabled children (Rourke, 1976b), comparisons with other modes of assessment (Fox, Orr, and Rourke, 1975), comments on the necessity of diagnosis in related areas (Rourke, 1978a), and evaluations of alternative models (Rourke, 1977). We have also carried out a systematic study of differential interaction patterns within the families of reading-retarded boys (McDermott and Rourke, 1978). However, although we plan to continue this type of study in the future, it is obvious that such investigations do not come to grips with the evaluation of educational and other therapeutic programs that are designed to deal with the problems in adaptation of learning-disabled children.

It is for this reason that we plan to begin a series of studies which will have as their goal the matching of remediation programs with "types" of reading, spelling, and arithmetic retardation delineated above. It is felt that this particular strategy will be fruitful because programs can be designed to deal constructively with the patterns of brain-related abilities and deficits which we have already demonstrated to exist within this rather heterogeneous group of disorders. In retrospect, it would seem likely that previous attempts to do this have been largely unsuccessful because children with (say) a reading disorder have been treated, for the most part, as though they were members of a homogeneous group. Although there have been some encouraging examples of an approach more in line with that which is advocated here (see Johnson and Myklebust, 1967), systematic attempts to evaluate such modes of intervention in terms of commonly accepted criteria of scientific verification have been lacking. This being the case, the future direction of our research program will be in terms of greater specification of the brain-related abilities of various subtypes of learning-disabled children across the 5- to 15-year age span, with the concomitant systematic design and evaluation of programs for their remediation.

REFERENCES

Benton, A. Developmental dyslexia: neurological aspects. *In* W. Friendlander, ed., *Advances in Neurology,* Vol. 7. New York: Raven, 1975.

Boder, E. Developmental dyslexia: a diagnostic approach based on three atypical reading-spelling patterns. *Developmental Medicine and Child Neurology,* 1973, 15:663–687.

Burgher, P., and Rourke, B. A comparison of the phonetic accuracy of spelling errors of normal and retarded readers. Prepublication manuscript, 1978.

Czudner, G., and Rourke, B. Simple reaction time in "brain-damaged" and normal children under regular and irregular preparatory interval conditions. *Perceptual and Motor Skills,* 1970, 31:767–773.

Czudner, G., and Rourke, B. Age differences in visual reaction time of "brain-damaged" and normal children under regular and irregular preparatory interval conditions. *Journal of Experimental Child Psychology,* 1972, 13:516–526.

Doehring, D. *Patterns of Impairment in Specific Reading Disability.* Bloomington: Indiana University Press, 1968.

Doehring, D., and Hoschko, I. Classification of reading problems by the Q-technique of factor analysis. *Cortex,* 1977, 13:281–294.

Dunn, L. *Expanded Manual for the Peabody Picture Vocabulary Test.* Minneapolis: American Guidance Service, 1965.

Fisk, J., and Rourke, B. Mental retardation and learning disabilities: A neurodevelopmental perspective. Paper presented at the meeting of the International Neuropsychological Society, Minneapolis, February 1978.

Fox, F., Orr, R., and Rourke, B. Shortcomings of the standard optometric visual analysis for the diagnosis of reading problems. *Canadian Journal of Optometry,* 1975, 37, 57–61.

Goldman, J., Thibert, R., and Rourke, B. Platelet seratonin levels in hyperactive children. Prepublication manuscript, 1978.

Jastak, J., and Jastak, S. *The Wide Range Achievement Test.* Wilmington, Del.: Guidance Associates, 1965.

Johnson, D., and Myklebust, H. *Learning Disabilities.* New York: Grune & Stratton, 1967.

Kinsbourne, M., and Warrington, E. Disorders of spelling. *Journal of Neurology, Neurosurgery, and Psychiatry,* 1964, 27:224–228.

Kløve, H. Clinical neuropsychology. *In* F. Forster, ed., *The Medical Clinics of North America.* New York: Saunders, 1963.

MacDonald, G., and Rourke, B. Neuropsychological abilities of children with learning disabilities who differ in EEG alpha blocking patterns. Paper presented at the meeting of the International Neuropsychological Society, Tampa, February 1975.

Marcel, T., and Rajan, P. Lateral specialization for recognition of words and faces in good and poor readers. *Neuropsychologia,* 1975, 13:489–497.

Mattis, S., French, J., and Rapin, I. Dyslexia in children and young adults: Three independent neuropsychological syndromes. *Developmental Medicine and Child Neurology,* 1975, 17:150–163.

McDermott, W., and Rourke, B. Differential interaction patterns within the families of reading-problem boys. Prepublication manuscript, 1978.

Myklebust, H. Development and disorders of written language, Vols. 1 & 2. New York: Grune & Stratton, 1965, 1973.

Nelson, H. and Warrington, E. Developmental spelling retardation and its relation to other cognitive abilities. *British Journal of Psychology,* 1974, 65:265–274.

Newcombe, F. *Missile Wounds to the Brain.* London: Oxford University Press, 1969.

Pajurkova, E., Orr, R., Rourke, B., and Finlayson, M. Children's word-finding test: a verbal problem-solving task. *Perceptual and Motor Skills,* 1976, 42:851–858.

Petrauskas, R., and Rourke, B. Identification of subgroups of retarded readers: a neuropsychological multivariate approach. Paper presented at the meeting of the International Neuropsychological Society, Minneapolis, February 1978.

Pulvermacher, G. The effect of positive reinforcement on the reaction time of young brain-damaged and normal children. Unpublished doctoral dissertation, University of Windsor, 1973.

Reed, H., and Reitan, R. Intelligence test performances of brain damaged subjects with lateralized motor deficits. *Journal of Consulting Psychology,* 1963, 27:102–106.

Reed, J. The ability deficits of good and poor readers. *Journal of Learning Disabilities,* 1968, 2:134–139.

Reitan, R. Relationships between neurological and psychological variables and their implications for reading instruction. *In* H. Robinson, ed., *Meeting Individual Differences in Reading.* Chicago: University of Chicago Press, 1964.

Reitan, R. A research program on the psychological effects of brain lesions in human beings. *In* N. Ellis, ed., *International Review of Research in Mental Retardation,* Vol. 1. New York: Academic Press, 1966.

Reitan, R. Verbal problem solving as related to cerebral damage. *Perceptual and Motor Skills, 1972, 34:515–524.*

Reitan, R. Methodological problems in clinical neuropsychology. *In* R. Reitan and L. Davison, eds., *Clinical Neuropsychology: Current Status and Applications.* Washington, D.C.: V. H. Winston & Sons, 1974a.

Reitan, R. Psychological effects of cerebral lesions in children of early school age. *In* R. Reitan and L. Davison, eds., *Clinical Neuropsychology: Current Status and Applications.* Washington, D.C.: V. H. Winston and Sons, 1974b.

Reitan, R., and Davison, L. *Clinical Neuropsychology: Current Status and Applications.* Washington, D.C.: V. H. Winston and Sons, 1974.

Roach, P., and Rourke, B. Evidence for hemispheric dominance in children's arithmetic calculation performance. Paper presented at the meeting of the Canadian Psychological Association, Toronto, June 1976.

Ross, A. *Psychological Aspects of Learning Disabilities and Reading Disorders.* New York: McGraw-Hill, 1976.

Rourke B. Brain-behaviour relationships in children with learning disabilities: a research program. *American Psychologist,* 1975, 30:911–920.

Rourke, B. Interactions between research and assessment. *Journal of Pediatric Psychology,* 1976, 1:7–11.

Rourke, B. Issues in the neuropsychological assessment of children with learning disabilities. *Canadian Psychological Review,* 1976b. 17:89–102.

Rourke, B. Reading retardation in chidren: developmental lag or deficit? *In* R. Knights and D. Bakker, eds., *Neuropsychology of Learning Disorders: Theoretical Approaches.* Baltimore: University Park Press, 1976c.

Rourke, B. Neuropsychological models of cognitive developmental disabilities: review, evaluation, synthesis. Paper presented at the meeting of the International Society for the Study of Behavioral Development, Pavia, Italy, September 1977.

Rourke, B. Minimal brain dysfunction: is diagnosis necessary? *Journal of Learning Disabilities,* 1978a, in press.

Rourke, B. Neuropsychological research in reading retardation: a review. *In* A. Benton and D. Pearl, eds., *Dyslexia: An Appraisal of Current Knowledge.* London: Oxford University Press, 1978. (b)

Rourke, B., and Czudner, G. Age differences in auditory reaction time of "brain-damaged" and normal children under regular and irregular preparatory interval conditions. *Journal of Experimental Child Psychology,* 1972, 14:372–378.

Rourke, B., Dietrich, D., and Young, G. Significance of WISC verbal-performance discrepancies for younger children with learning disabilities. *Perceptual and Motor Skills,* 1973, 36:275–282.

Rourke, B., and Finlayson, M. Neuropsychological significance of variations in patterns of performance on the Trail Making Test for older children with learning disabilities. *Journal of Abnormal Psychology,* 1975, 84:412–421.

Rourke, B., and Finlayson, M. Neuropsychological significance of variations in patterns of academic performance: verbal and visual-spatial abilities. *Journal of Abnormal Child Psychology,* 1978, 6:121–133.

Rourke, B., and Fisk, J. *Children's Word-Finding Test (revd).* Unpublished, 1977 (available from author).

Rourke, B., and Orr, R. Prediction of the reading and spelling performances of normal and retarded readers: a four-year follow-up. *Journal of Abnormal Child Psychology,* 1977, 5:9–20.

Rourke, B., and Petrauskas, R. *Underlining Test: Revised form.* Unpublished, 1977 (available from author).

Rourke, B., and Strang, J. Neuropsychological significance of variations in patterns of academic performance: motor, psychomotor, and tactile-perceptual abilities. *Journal of Pediatric Psychology,* 1978, 3, in press.

Rourke, B., and Telegdy, G. Lateralizing significance of WISC verbal-performance discrepancies for older children with learning disabilities. *Perceptual and Motor Skills,* 1971, 33:875–883.

Rourke, B., Yanni, D., MacDonald, G., and Young, G. Neuropsychological significance of lateralized deficits on the Grooved Pegboard Test for older children with learning disabilities. *Journal of Consulting and Clinical Psychology,* 1973, 41:128–134.

Rourke, B., Young, G., and Flewelling, R. The relationships between WISC verbal-performance discrepancies and selected verbal, auditory-perceptual, visual-perceptual, and problem-solving abilities in children with learning disabilities. *Journal of Clinical Psychology,* 1971, 27:475–479.

Satz, P., Friel, J., and Rudegeair, F. Differential changes in the acquisition of developmental skills in children who later became dyslexic: a three-year follow-up. *In* D. Stein, J. Rosen, and N. Butters, eds., *Plasticity and Recovery of Function in the Central Nervous System.* New York: Academic Press, 1974.

Satz, P., and Van Nostrand, G. Developmental dyslexia: an evaluation of a theory. *In* P. Satz and J. Ross, eds., *The Disabled Learner: Early Detection and Intervention.* Rotterdam, The Netherlands: Rotterdam University Press, 1973.

Sweeney, J., McCabe, A., and Rourke, B. Logical-grammatical abilities of retarded spellers. Prepublication manuscript, 1978.

Sweeney, J., and Rourke, B. Neuropsychological significance of phonetically accurate and phonetically inaccurate spelling errors in younger and older retarded spellers. *Brain and Language,* 1978, in press.

Tallal, P. Auditory perceptual factors in language and learning disabilities. *In* R. Knights and D. Bakker, eds., *Neuropsychology of Learning Disorders: Theoretical Approaches*. Baltimore: University Park Press, 1976.

Usprich, C. The study of dyslexia: two nascent trends and a neuropsychological model. *Bulletin of the Orton Society*, 1976, 25:34–48.

Wechsler, D. *Wechsler Intelligence Scale for Children*. New York: Psychological Corp., 1949.

Wiig, E., and Semel, E. Development of comprehension of logicogrammatical sentences by grade school children. *Perceptual and Motor Skills*, 1974, 38:171–176.

Witelson, S. Sex and the single hemisphere: right hemisphere specialization for spatial processing. *Science*, 1976, 193:425–427.

Witelson, S. Developmental dyslexia: two right hemispheres and none left. *Science*, 1977, 195:309–311.

Young, G., and Rourke, B. A comparison of visual and auditory sequencing in good and poor readers in grades two and six. Paper presented at the meeting of Canadian Psychological Association, Quebec, June 1975.

V.   Brain Event Related Potentials: Contributions to Research in Learning Disabilities

LEE ELLIOTT, ROY HALLIDAY, ENOCH CALLAWAY

In studies of childhood learning disabilities, measures of brain electrical potentials hold two sorts of promises. The first is the promise of advances in basic understanding and the second is the promise of advances in clinical practice. In what follows we hope to show that the first promise has already been partially fulfilled. In addition, we will look at some barriers against keeping the second of the two promises.

We will consider two types of event related potential studies. One deals with averages of responses to repeated, more or less identical, events—in this case flashes of light. Here the sequence of brain responses to simple stimuli permits one to study the finer structure of attention. The other approach deals with ongoing patterns of brain potentials associated with ongoing mental operations. These ongoing operations are of a less time-locked nature and do not lend themselves to averaging. Here global patterns of hemispheric engagement can be seen and suggest general strategies of cortical organization. We will return to the details of these two different measures later, but let us start first with considering their common ground.

The brain is involved in generating behavior and in carrying out cognitive processes that support behavior. The brain is also involved in generating some of the electrical activity that we can record at the scalp. Since both mental activity and electrical activity can arise from the brain, it seems logical to search for a relationship between these two brain products. This position is reinforced by the finding of relationships between conventional observable behavior and these brain electrical potentials. The final step (some might say ''leap'') is to use these brain electrical potentials to make inferences about mental processes when those processes are not so clearly indicated by observable behavior. In short, since mind and brain electrical potentials both come from the brain, brain electrical potentials can provide a window on the mind. But will that electrical window have any advantages over other ways of looking in on mental processes? The question is, of course, rhetorical.

The two event-related potential studies of children carried out recently at Langley Porter Institute deal with two different psychological processes that pose some problems for conventional behavioral measures and that also may have some relevance for understanding reading disabilities. In one study we used averaged evoked potentials to assess an early ''channel-selection'' aspect of attention in hyperkinetic children. In the other, we used a measure of ongoing electrical patterns to assess strategies of short-term memory relevant to reading disorders.

Dr. Elliott's research was supported by a National Institute of Mental Health National Research Service Award for Individual Fellows, Mr. Halliday's was supported by the National Institute of Mental Health and by the Ciba Pharmaceutical Co. This research also was supported by the Office of Naval Research.

METHYLPHENIDATE DOSAGE EFFECTS ON THE AVERAGE EVOKED POTENTIAL

Minimal brain dysfunction (MBD) is a broad diagnostic category that includes dysfunctions in perception, fine and gross motor control, difficulties in acquiring symbolic codes, such as writing, and certain kinds of behavioral disorders. Some MBD children show dysfunctions in many of these areas while others show specific deficits.

There is almost universal agreement that the MBD category is composed of a number of subgroups. One of these subgroups, hyperactive children, has been of particular interest because of the dramatic behavioral changes that often follow treatment with stimulant drugs. We and others have suggested that isolation of particular patterns of brain electrical responses associated with treatment outcome might provide a model for understanding the nature of the core symptoms and their response to these drugs. Having had some modest success along these lines, we decided to examine the effects of methylphenidate dosage on evoked potential and clinical outcome measures. The rationale for this approach was that by examining the effects of a variable known to influence clinical outcome (Werry and Sprague, 1974) on the evoked potential we would be in a better position to relate changes in underlying brain responses with dosage-specific improvements in behavior. While we are still continuing along these general lines, it now appears that different behavioral and physiologic systems may show quite different dose-response curves. For example, Sprague and Sleator (1977) have shown that teachers' ratings tend to improve directly with dosage while performance on cognitive tasks degrades at higher dosage levels.

In this section we report preliminary results detailing some of the effects that methylphenidate dosage exerts on concurrent measures of the evoked potential and cardiac and behavioral activity in hyperactive children. These findings suggest that each of these systems has a somewhat different dose-response relationship and that some of the components of these systems, themselves, have unique dose signatures.

Subjects

The subjects in this experiment were 8 hyperactive boys referred to us by the Learning Disabilities Clinic, Kaiser Permanente Medical Center, Oakland, California. Diagnostic criteria are similar to a previous series of children (Halliday, Rosenthal, Naylor, et al., 1976). In addition, however, each child in the experiment was rated by his teacher on the Conners Teacher Rating Scale at least two standard deviations above current norms.

Parents of the children were referred to our project if the pediatrician felt that a clinical trial of methylphenidate (Ritalin) was indicated. The project was then explained to the parents and voluntary consent obtained. Treatment was not contingent on participation in the project. Preliminary to actual acceptance, the pediatrician administered 5, 10, and 20 mg of Ritalin to test for possible allergic or other deviant responses. Two children were eliminated because of atypical responses. A third was subsequently eliminated when he developed an allergic reaction during the clinical phase of the design.

Evoked Potential Procedures

A psychologic battery, which included concurrent measures of visual evoked potential (VEP) activity, heartrate, and reaction time during the attended portions of the experiment were administered to each child on four different sessions. A placebo capsule was always administered on session 1. In the remaining sessions the child took three different dosages of Ritalin 45 to 60 min before the start of a run. The capsules were individually compounded for each child. The active dosages were 0.16, 0.33, and 0.66 mg Ritalin/kg body weight (mg/kg). For an 80-lb. (36-kg) youngster, this dosage would be 5, 10, and 20 mg of Ritalin. Order of drug administration was randomly assigned to one of three possible sequences.

The entire experiment was controlled by a small laboratory computer (NOVA 1220). VEPs were recorded from a single gold vertex electrode referred to linked ears. Eye-movement and cardiac activity were monitored by Beckman electrodes. The EEG was amplified by a special fixed-gain amplifier with filters set at 1 and 35 Hz. The trial sequence was initiated by the R wave of the cardiac cycle which triggered a brief pulse to the computer. A 50-msec flash of light followed 150 msec after this initializing pulse. This delay prevented the R wave from contaminating the VEP activity. The next trial was randomly initiated after the second, third, or fourth R waves. The interbeat intervals between R waves on each trial were stored and the means and standard deviations printed out at the termination of the experimental condition. The EEG was sampled every 4 msec beginning 50 msec prestimulus and continued over a 1000-msec interval. Individual trials and the averaged VEP were stored on the computer floppy disk system for subsequent analysis. Reaction time and response accuracy in the attending tasks were also stored.

The within-sessions conditions consisted of an active-attention task (ATT) and a passive-observing task (PAS). The tasks were repeated such that an entire experimental sequence consisted of ATT, PAS, PAS, ATT (replications). For the ATT task the child was asked to press a microswitch whenever he detected a dim flash (signal) embedded in a series of brighter flashes (nonsignals). Signal events occurred in 10% of the trials, and each correct detection earned a 10¢ reward. Heartrate and VEP data for approximately 100 nonsignals were collected in each attending sequence. In the PAS task the child was requested to simply observe the flashes. A special eye-movement algorithm continuously computed activity from the eye electrodes and tagged records that exceeded preset levels. These records were excluded from the computation of the averaged VEP. Intertrial interval was approximately 2 to 3 sec. Each attentional run took approximately 5 to 7 min. Thus, each session with appropriate rest periods required 30 to 45 min to complete.

The child was seated in a comfortable chair in a sound-attenuated, electrically shielded room. Signal and nonsignal stimuli were delivered by a small box located 153 cm from the child. Before the start of each session the child was given sufficient practice to ensure that he understood the procedures. He was encouraged to sit quietly during the run and cautioned against irregular breathing or looking around the room.

Results

Three different sets of data derived from the psychophysiologic battery will be described: (a) changes in the VEP for nonsignal (bright) flashes due to dosage and attentional variables, (b) changes in mean heartrate, and (c) reaction time differences.

Dosage Effects of the Evoked Potential. The VEP consists of a series of voltage changes which result in a series of peaks, or components, that occur at reliable time points with respect to the onset of the stimulus. Time to the various peaks is measured in milliseconds (msec) and the size of the component given in microvolts (μV). Figure 1 shows VEPs obtained from two children in this experiment. We avoid the term "typical" waveform, because young children show considerable individual variation in waveform configuration. These individual differences are, however, remarkably constant over repeated testings of the same child. This presents several methodological problems in

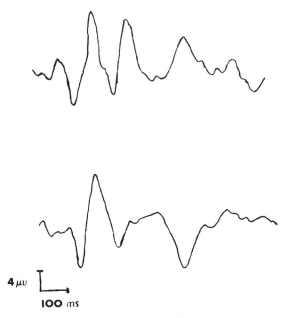

Fig. 1. VEPS OBTAINED FROM TWO HYPERACTIVE CHILDREN.

measuring the different peaks. To circumvent these difficulties we quantified the VEP in two ways. For the first analysis we visually identified two peaks which were consistently observed across children. These peaks consist of a negative deflection that occurs at approximately 150 msec (N150) followed by a positive component (P220) at 220 msec. Secondly, we factor-analyzed the entire AEP waveform. This technique provides an objective means of identifying and quantifying AEP components for subsequent statistical analysis.

Repeated measure analyses of variance (ANOVA) were applied to the amplitude and latency measures obtained in each replication × attention × drug dosage condition. These analyses showed that only the N150 amplitude was significantly affected by any of the experimental treatments. Figure 2 shows that both dosage and task affected the amplitude of the N150 component ($p < .05$). Further analysis revealed that this interaction had a significant quadratic component ($p < .05$). In the attending conditions, N150 was generally larger and increased with increasing dose more rapidly than in the passive-observing condition up to the next highest dose. However, at high dosages of Ritalin the N150 amplitude in the active task decreased to placebo levels while in the passive task amplitude continued to increase.

Factor analysis was performed to assess the effects of our experimental manipulations on the late components of the VEP. Essentially, the 16 VEPS for each individual were normalized with respect to his grand average VEP. These normalized averages were then factor-analyzed by principle components, and nine factors accounting for 81% of the VEP waveform variance rotated to a varimax solution. Normalized weights were obtained and used to describe the influence of the experimental manipulations on each of the nine factors. In effect this procedure results in a series of components that are mathematically independent of each other. The process of normalization removes individual differences in the typology of the waveform so that the changes that take place in the various components can be compared across subjects. The rotated factors, along with the place or time

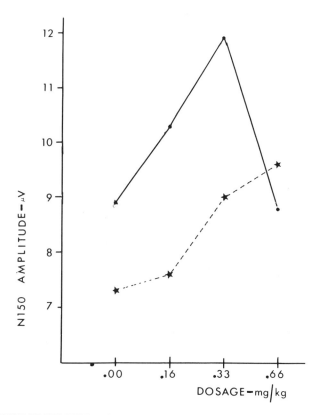

Fig. 2. THE EFFECT OF METHYLPHENIDATE DOSAGE ON THE N150 AMPLITUDE OF NONSIG-
NAL STIMULI. ———— =ACTIVE ATTENTION TASK; —————— = PASSIVE OBSERVING TASK

in the VEP waveform where they exerted their maximal loadings effect, are shown in
Table 1.

Factor scores for the dosage × attention × replication conditions were then analyzed
by repeated measures ANOVA. The effects of attention significantly changed factors 1
and 9, but drug dosage had no effect on these VEP components. Factor 5, a late component between 704 and 800 msec, was affected by replication but showed no other significant effects. Factor 6 showed a significant dosage × attention condition effect. This
latter factor appears similar to the visually identified N150 component. Factor 7 was
influenced by dosage, attention, and replication. Finally, factors 2, 3, 4, and 8 were not
significantly changed by any of the experimental treatments.

In summary, while different portions of the VEP are affected by attention, they were
not necessarily affected by dosage. Dosage effects were primarily restricted to the 100 to
200 msec portions of the VEP.

Heartrate. The mean interbeat interval was averaged over the four cardiac cycles.
Dosage significantly increased heartrate and the trend was entirely linear ($p < .05$). Thus,
methylphenidate increased heartbeat in proportion to dosage.

Reaction Time. Reaction times to signals (dim flashes) in the attend condition
(ATT) were averaged within a run and analyzed by ANOVA in which replications and

Table 1

TIME DOMAIN, PERCENT VARIANCE, AND EXPERIMENTAL VARIABLES THAT AFFECTED AEP
FACTOR

Factor Number	Latency of Maximal Loadings (msec)*	Percent Variance	Variables that Affected Factor
1	288–320	29	Attention
2	352–384	11	None
3	560–592	10	None
4	64–96	6	None
5	768–800	7	Replication
6	128–161	5	Drug × Attention
7	672–704	5	Drug × Attention × Replication
8	208–240	5	None
9	432–464	4	Attention

*Maximal loadings were the two latency points in the normalized averaged evoked potential between which the largest factor loadings occurred.

dosage were the principle factors. These RTs decreased with increasing dosage up to the medium dose, after which they increased. However, the differences were not significant for this sample size.

Discussion

Several studies (Satterfield, Cantwell, and Satterfield, 1974; Dykman, Ackerman, Clements, et al., 1971) have suggested that hyperactive children have an arousal deficit which blocks inhibitory centers and results in impulsive and distractible behavior. Stimulants in this context are viewed as acting to increase general arousal primarily by facilitating activity in the reticular brainstem system. The finding that heartrate increased linearly with dosage is consistent with this hypothesis. The VEP data, on the other hand, argue for a more restricted version of this formulation. Late portions of the VEP were, as expected, modified by the entire attentional task. However, there was little evidence that these components were influenced by drugs.

The N150 component, identified both by visual inspection and objectively by principal component analysis, was affected by both Ritalin dosage and attention. This component increased in both active and passive-attention conditions up to 0.33 mg/kg. Further dosage increases enhanced the amplitude of N150 in the passive condition but markedly reduced it in the active task.

The results of this study suggest that both task and methylphenidate dosage act to increase some selective form of arousal. The dissociation in N150 between the active and passive tasks at higher dosages could be explained by an inverted U-shape function relating N150 to this hypothetical attention-arousal system. When task requirements are low, as in the case of the passive-observing task, arousal is primarily a function of dosage. When dosage is increased to 0.66 mg/kg, N150 increases, because the increment is still within the ascending portion of the curve. However, when further stimulation is added by increasing the task requirements, the total arousal level exceeds the theoretical maximum, and N150 begins to decline. Task requirements then become of central importance in determining whether a particular dosage will enhance or depress performance. The interaction of these two factors has also been pointed out by Sprague and Sleater (1977). They reported that performance on a short-term memory task was depressed by high dosages of Ritalin (1.0 mg/kg), with the greatest depression occurring when the informational load was largest. They also found, as we did, that larger doses of methylphenidate significantly increased heartrate. Porges (1976) has reported that coherence measures between heartrate and respiration, which index autonomic changes accompanying attention, also decrease at high dosages of methylphenidate.

Although the vigilance paradigm used in the present experiment may on the surface seem to be relatively easy, the results of several studies reviewed by Sroufe (1975) indicate that hyperactive children have great difficulty in sustaining their attention during these tasks. The finding that reaction times were not significantly affected by dosage, although they tended to decrease at the high dosage, is not totally surprising and highlights the sensitivity of the evoked-potential measures.

The present data are consistent with behavioral and other neurophysiologic studies in that they demonstrate that low and moderate doses of methylphenidate increase certain measures of attention and memory in hyperactive children. Higher doses, on the other hand, appear to decrease these measures. The evoked-potential data also suggest that one of the effects of stimulant medication is to increase the deployment of attentional resources early in the temporal course of information processing. This may not be the sole effect of these drugs, since a recent study by Klorman (Personal Communication) has shown enhancement of late component activity in a paradigm which is known to maximize the occurrence of P300.

HEMISPHERIC ASYMMETRY AND SHORT-TERM MEMORY

Different disciplines have independently suggested that consciousness is not a unitary phenomena. Cognitive psychologists have proposed that imaginal-visual and auditory-verbal short-term memory is mediated by dual memory storage systems. Neurophysiologists have proposed that the two halves of the brain sense, perceive and conceptualize differently. The left hemisphere excels at speech, writing, and mathematical calculation, while the right hemisphere best performs tasks involving spatial relationships and musical patterns. Furthermore, the corpus callosum, which connects the two hemispheres, appears to be largely nonfunctional at birth and has a prolonged period of myelination which continues to develop until late childhood. Developmental psychologists, such as Piaget, have shown that cognitive development takes place in reliable, generalized stages.

A broad sense of commonality pervades all of these theoretical formulations, yet there have been few attempts to interrelate the findings obtained from cognitive, developmental, and neurophysiologic research. The following review is addressed to the parallel trends among these disciplines. Behavioral data derived through short-term memory experiments and Piaget's research permit a theoretical description of human cognitive functioning which can stand independently on any physiologic substrate. Nevertheless, cognition is a function of the brain—a biologic organism. Therefore, theoretical inferences derived from psychology could be extended by direct measurement of brain activity. Electroencephalography (EEG) can provide one such measure. The research described herein represents an attempt to integrate and unify the methodologies of short-term memory psychology and the EEG into a single empirical design so that the results may be justifiably compared. This research has indicated developmental differences in hemispheric specialization so that at one time a child may be superior in auditory-verbal memory and superior in imaginal-visual memory at another point in time. Alternatively, the child may maintain superiority in one modality throughout life. *The following theoret-*

ical framework and research, related as it is to the neurologic correlates of auditory-verbal and visual-imaginal memory, may have particular relevance as a basis for specifying cognitive deficits associated with auditory and visual dyslexia.

The Dual Memory Systems and Encoding Hypotheses

Current theoretical speculation in the psychology of memory has centered on the notion of distinct imaginal-visual and auditory-verbal short-term memory (STM) systems. Visual images, or pictorial stimuli, are functionally related to visual perception, whereas verbal stimuli are related to the auditory-motor-speech system. Thus, a functional distinction in the nature of the representational mechanisms underlying these two types of symbolic systems is proposed. Because the representational mechanisms, imaginal-pictorial and verbal stimuli, differ, it is reasonable to assume that these are stored in separate and distinct STM systems.

Paivio (1971) has proposed two distinct yet richly interconnected encoding systems: a verbal system specialized for serial processing of sequential information, and an imaginal system specialized for encoding and processing of spatial information. Linguistic stimuli are always subject to verbal encoding processes, but abstract words have only a verbal code, whereas concrete words may also have an imaginal code. Pictorial stimuli are always subject to imaginal processing, but verbal processing may occur in addition, particularly when the pictures are readily named. Finally, imaginal encoding is assumed to result in a more durable memory representation than verbal encoding (Paivio and Csapo, 1969).

The existence of dual STM systems and the dual-encoding hypothesis has received support from a number of sources. One line of research has provided evidence for the existence of separate visual and acoustic storage of individual letters, depending on the original presentation modality (Posner, 1967; Posner and Keele, 1967; Kroll, Bee, and Gurski, 1973; Kroll, Parkinson, and Parks, 1972). Another has used tasks requiring items and position recall from a visually presented matrix of labelable objects (Murray and Newman, 1973; den Heyer and Barrett, 1971) In a third line of research, superior recall and recognition of pictorial materials, as well as the positive effects of imagery strategies (Bower, 1971; Paivio, 1971), have been interpreted as support for the dual-encoding hypothesis.

An additional body of evidence, providing support for both hypotheses, is based on research involving selective interference of verbal or pictorial information as a function of the nature of the intervening task (den Heyer and Barrett, 1971; Meudell, 1972; Salthouse, 1975; Elliott, 1973; Elliott and Strawhorn, 1976; Pellegrino, Siegel, and Dhawan, 1975). The rationale behind this line of research assumes that if words and pictures are encoded into separate visual and verbal short-term stores, these should be differentially amenable to interference by tasks of a visual and verbal nature. For example, Elliott (1973) employed the Peterson and Peterson (1959) technique under conditions where two independent groups of subjects were instructed to learn words of high and low imagery value either by creating images or by rote repetition. It was assumed that the instructed mental imagery condition would place the items in the imaginal memory store, whereas the rote repetition condition would place them in the auditory stores. Interference activity, consisting of a visual language task and an auditory numerical task, provided differential and maximal interference under imaginal and rote repetition conditions, respectively. It was concluded that the facilitative effect of mental imagery depends on the simultaneous storage of a verbal and visual representation. Similarly, Pellegrino, Siegel, and Dhawan (1975) contrasted the effects of an auditory numerical task, a visual (Hidden Figures) task and a combination of the two on retention of pictures over words as a function of auditory numerical distraction. However, superior retention of words over pictures resulted from the visual-numerical combination task. The results are interpreted as support for separate visual and acoustic storage systems, as well as the dual encoding of pictures.

Hemispheric Lateralization Studies

The impetus for the recent research in lateralization of cerebral function was provided by studies on commissurized patients being treated for epilepsy ((Sperry, 1964; Bogen and Gazzaniga, 1965; Gazzaniga, 1970; Levy, Trevarthen and Sperry, 1972; Sperry, 1974).Thus, the communication channels between the two hemispheres had been severed in these patients. Such "split-brain" persons manifested two separate streams of consciousness indicative of two independently functioning hemispheres. Thus, it was possible to explore the capabilities and limitations of each hemisphere. Extensive study indicates that specialized neural mechanisms required for the processing and generation of speech and arithmetic are lateralized in the dominant hemisphere (usually the left in right-handed people). On the other hand, visual-imaginal, spatial, and musical processing are lateralized in the subdominant hemisphere.

Electroencephalography

EEG hemispheric lateralization research has also focused on the possiblity that the two hemispheres of the brain may be functionally specialized for different types of cognitive procession (Callaway and Harris, 1974; Galin and Ornstein, 1972; McKee, Humphrey and McAdam, 1973; Morell and Salamy, 1971; Butler and Glass, 1974). These studies have measured EEG activity while a person is alert and engaged in a cognitive task. In contrast, the clinical EEG is recorded while the patient is relaxed with eyes closed.

One EEG technique used in the study of cognition is based on the observation that power in the alpha band (8–12 Hz) decreases with cognitive activity (Smyk and Darway, 1972). Hence, the ratio of the alpha powers from homologous leads can serve as a measure of relative activity of the two hemispheres. Using the ratio of alpha band power from each hemisphere, Butler and Glass (1974) found the left, but not the right, hemisphere active in mental arithmetic. Recording from the temporal and parietal regions, Galin and Ornstein (1972, 1973) found relatively higher alpha amplitude (a measure of idling) over the right hemisphere during verbal tasks and relatively more alpha over the left hemisphere during spatial tasks.

Callaway and Harris (1974) developed another technique, "cortical coupling," to show that if two areas of the brain increase their functional communication, the EEGs from these two areas should show increased coupling. Cognitive processing should alter this functional communication and be reflected in changes in cortical coupling. Using a verbal (left hemisphere) task and a spatial (right hemisphere) task they found that the processing of verbal stimuli increased coupling between the central and parietal areas of the left hemisphere, whereas the processing of visual stimuli increased coupling on the right. Thus, it was concluded that the cortical coupling measure is influenced by cognitive processing.

Although the idea that specialized structures for processing verbal stimuli are located in the left hemisphere, it is generally accepted that there are some discrepant results which give rise to alternative explanations. Kinsbourne (1970, 1973) argues that lateralization effects are in large part a function of the relative level of activation of the cerebral hemispheres. In support of their position, Bruce and Kinsbourne (1974) report an experiment in which subjects were asked to remember complex visual forms. When done as a direct recognition task, left-visual-field/right-hemisphere performance was slightly superior. However, when subjects had to perform the figure recognition task while retaining a list of words in memory, right-visual-field/left-hemisphere performance was superior. They argue that the added requirement of retaining verbal material in memory raised the level of activation of the left hemisphere, thus producing a superior left hemisphere performance on a visual-spatial task.

Another explanation is advanced by Hardyck, Tzeng, and Wang (1978). These authors used reaction time as the measure of lateralization and varied the number of stimuli and trials from few to many in six experiments. Their results suggest that lateralization effects, as often reported, are not a function of ongoing cognitive processing in specialized cortical areas but do reflect differences in memory storage locations. In other words, hemispheric lateralization effects may be a function of memory demands other than ongoing task activity.

Implications for Piaget's Theory of Cognitive Development

Piaget and Inhelder have described in detail the development of thinking in children. Although they write, "We have little detailed knowledge about maturation, and we know next to nothing about the conditions that permit the foundation of the general operatory structures," they nevertheless believed that cognitive development can be meaningfully considered only as an extension of certain fundamental biological characteristics (1969, p. 155). In other words, inherited biological structures condition what we may directly perceive, and it is through functioning that the succession of structures are constituted.

The fundamental characteristics of intellectual functioning which are invariant over the whole developmental span, are (a) organization, (b) adaptation (comprising two related but conceptually distinct processes, assimilation and accommodation), and (c) equilibration. Piaget (1952) sums up his belief that bilogical substrates underlie cognitive development in this way:

> If there truly is a functional nucleus of intellectual organization, it comes from biological organization. It is apparent that this invariant will orient the whole of successive structures which the mind will then work out in its contact with reality (p. 2–3).

Piaget sees the ontogeny of cognitive activity as being characterized by qualitatively different periods:

1. *Sensory-motor period* (0–2 years). The child moves from a reflex level of self-world undifferentiation to a coherent organization of sensorimotor actions vis-à-vis his immediate environment.
2. *Preoperational thought* (2–7 years). The child comes to grips with the world of symbols.
3. *Concrete operations period* (7–11 years). The period is characterized by the beginning of logical thought and the ability to categorize and coordinate things in a series.
4. *Formal operations period* (11–15 years). Cognitive development achieves maturation as manifested by logical and abstract thinking.

Since, according to Piaget, biological organization is the nucleus of cognitive functioning, it is conceivable that hemispheric lateralization research may provide a basis for identifying and verifying these cognitive stages. Such an endeavor would make it possible to construct veridical models of cognition.

Neurophysiology

The various brain commissures, including the corpus callosum, are among the last structures to develop and become myelinated. Myelination of the brain continues through puberty (Conel, 1941; Yakovlev and Lecours, 1967). Gazzaniga (1974) suggests that the young child is essentially a "split brain" individual. in that interhemispheric communication is poorly developed. He presents evidence from lesion studies suggesting that the young child lays down engrams in both hemispheres until age 8. From ages 8 to 10, hemispheric lateralization for language begins and becomes firmly established between ages 11 to 14. Witelson and Rabinovitch (1972) concur that speech representation is bilateral in the early years of life, begins to lateralize in the preschool years and becomes permanently established during adolescence.

The development of concrete operational thought—that is, when the child begins to categorize—appears to parallel changes in brain hemisphere specialization (Galin, 1974). On the basis of their research, Ornstein and Galin (1976) state, "it is reasonable to suppose that the lateralization of cognitive function is still in flux in young children after the acquisition of speech and maturation of the child's cognitive power may be paralleled by, and perhaps even depend upon, increasing lateralization with a resulting decrease in interference between cognitive systems" (p. 65).

Several authors have suggested that right hemisphere dominance in infants (Turkewitz, Gordon, and Birch, 1965; Aronson and Rosenbloom, 1971; Seth, 1973) is related to the development of spatial abilities (Bower, 1971; Ambrose, 1961). In another vein, Marcel and Rajan (1975) found that good and poor readers did not differ in their ability to recognize faces (there was a clear right hemisphere superiority), but good readers showed greater left hemisphere processing.

Generally, the above research indicates a neurologic sequence moving from right hemisphere dominance, to bilaterality, to left hemisphere dominance. If we were to assume that these sequences were isomorphic with cognitive stages of development, then they would probably be represented as follows: sensorimotor functions would reflect right hemisphere dominance; preoperational thought would reflect bilaterality; concrete operational thought would represent the initiation of left hemisphere dominance; and formal operational thought would represent left hemisphere dominance. Further, if the EEG can provide an index of neurophysiologic changes in the form of differential right and left hemisphere activity, it would seem reasonable to begin investigating the uppermost borderline of the various periods.

Short-term Memory Assessment of Auditory and Visual Encoding

Elliott (1973) first examined the imagery phenomenon via the Peterson and Peterson (1959) technique. This is a method that allows one to assess short-term memory by interpolating various interference tasks between the presentation of the material and its subsequent recall. Elliott proposed that material learned under mental imagery and presumably encoded into an imaginal-visual memory store should be differentially interfered with by visual, as opposed to aural, interference tasks. The data supported this hypothesis. Elliott and Strawhorn (1976) found evidence that vocalization was the most potent dimension associated with the Peterson and Peterson classic interference task. Selective interference paradigms have since been used extensively to assess imaginal and auditory encoding. These paradigms are especially desirable as they incorporate ongoing interference activity with prior memory demands. This is imperative in view of the recent conjecture that hemispheric lateralization is a function of previous memory demands rather than ongoing cognitive task activity.

Experimental Objectives

Measures of hemispheric asymmetry acquired simultaneously with the acquisition of STM data might be a more sensitive way of assessing imaginal-visual and auditory-verbal encoding. The research reported here employs measures of hemispheric activity during the retention of pictures and words, utilizing the classic Peterson and Peterson technique for selective interference.

A primary objective of the experiment was to explore the developmental sequence in regard to imaginal-visual and auditory-verbal memory stores. Imposed mental imagery in the form of a dynamic pictorial interaction differentially facilitates learning for older and younger children Paivio (1970), Milgram (1967). The adult literature indicates that pictures are remembered better than words. However, this is not the case in research with children. Indeed, Elliott and Strawhorn (in press) noted that their youngest group (age 7–8) remembered words better than pictures, though not consistently across different interference tasks. The evidence on brain myelination leads us to expect EEG changes at the borderlines of Piagetian cognitive stages.

Specifically, the experiment was intended to examine the neurologic correlates of memory over the developmental stages during which verbal and/or visual symbolic representations prevail and are most effective. Hemispheric brain activity during memory for pictures or words was assessed via the cortical coupling technique. Three age groups of children (7–8, 10–11, 13–14) were used representing the Piagetian stages of preoperations, concrete operations, and formal operations, respectively. The youngest group also falls in the range where verbal versus pictorial memory changes have been noted. The oldest group falls in the stage where cognitive development has reached maturation and their memory performance should resemble that of adults (i.e., pictures are remembered better than words).

Overview of the Experiment

Triads consisting of pictures or words were presented to each of the three age groups, followed by three types of interference tasks. Two of the tasks involved selecting out words of a specified category from a larger group, and these were performed either silently or vocally. These two tasks were intended to produce greater interference with retention of words as opposed to pictures. The third task was a graphic task designed to interfere more with retention of pictures than words. The intent was to assess the relative potency of vocalized interference activity (in contrast to the other two tasks) on retention of pictures. Vocalization has already been shown to be a potent source of interference with retention of words. EEG measures of brain activity were recorded during the retention task interval.

STM Phase of the Experiment

Design. The two between-groups independent variables of presentation modality (words and pictures) and age (7–8, 10–11, 13–14) were combined factorially with the within-subject independent variable of interpolated task activity (graphic, silent-word, vocal-word). The dependent variable of retention was measured by the number of words or pictures correctly recalled after 30 sec of interference activity.

Interference tasks.   Interference activity consisted of three tasks which were performed during the 30-sec STM retention interval. For the graphic (G) task, the subject examined pairs of graphs with dots located in various blocks within the graph, placing a dot between those pairs that were alike. For the silent-word (SW) task, the subject was instructed to read silently a list of words, placing a dot after those words belonging to a specified conceptual category. For the vocal-word (VW) task, the subject was instructed to read aloud, again placing a dot after category members. Each task was presented eight times (randomized within blocks of 6) for a total of 24 trials. Nine practice trials were given (3 at each of the task conditions) in order to minimize the practice effect and allow proactive interference to aysmptote.

Subjects.   Thirty-six right-handed subjects from the Walnut Acres Elementary Public School participated in the experiment. Subjects were selected on the basis of average to above-average reading ability as measured by the Metropolitan Reading Achievement Test. Twelve subjects (6 males and 6 females) representing each of the three age groups were randomly assigned to the picture and word conditions.

Stimuli.   Thirty-three noun triads, consisting of nouns rated from moderate to high imagery value, were developed from the Elliott, Strawhorn, and Shook (1974) norms. Stimuli were projected through a translucent screen via two Kodak Carousel 800 slide projectors equipped with electronic shutters.

Procedure.   Following practice, subjects received 24 experimental trials. A trial consisted of the following sequence of events designated by separate slides: a READY slide for 5 sec; the picture or word trials for 2 sec; a signal for one of the three interference tasks for 30 sec; a ". . . ." slide symbolizing recall for 5 sec; a REST slide for 5 sec.

EEG Phase of the Experiment

The EEG cortical coupling measure was chosen for this research because it has been shown to be sensitive to changes in cognitive functioning (Callaway and Harris, 1974; Yagi, Bali, and Callaway, 1975; Yingling, 1977). It is also possible to implement this measure in psychological STM studies involving retention intervals as long as 30 sec. Prior research attempting to relate memory to EEG has been primarily confined to iconic memory storage (retention intervals up to 1 sec) due to the temporal nature of the evoked potential measure. The instantaneous temporal nature of the evoked potential measure precluded its use in view of the length of our retention interval.

Briefly, the cortical coupling technique consists of taking EEG recordings from two leads. The two EEGs can, at any instant, be classified on the basis of polarity and direction of change of potential (slope). Each channel from the various montage locations is sampled every 4 msec. Each of the two channels is classified as to whether its polarity is positive or negative and as to whether its voltage is greater or smaller than the preceding sample from the same channel. Each of the samples is thus classified in one of four categories (according to polarity and direction of change), and the contingencies (between the two channels) are tallied into a 4 × 4 table for a fixed number of samples. Once a contingency table is formed, a measure of contingency can be computed by comparing the actual cell frequencies with expected cell frequencies as calculated from marginal frequencies. We measured coupling by using the coefficientt of information transmission, or uncertainty reduction. A more complete explanation of this measure can be found in Shannon and Weaver (1949) and Garner (1972).

Cortical Coupling Procedure

For this study, electrodes were placed on left and right frontal (F3,F4), left and right temporal (T3, T4), left and right parietal (P3, P4) and midline occiput (Oz). The frontal, temporal, and parietal electrodes were referenced to ipsilateral ears. In addition, an eye-movement electrode was placed on the forehead about 2 cm above the right eyebrow, and a groundplate was placed on the left arm. Seven channels of EEG were amplified by a Grass Polygraph and digitized every 4 msec on-line with a NOVA 1220 computer. The computer program included an objective editing subroutine which deleted records with excessively large voltages. This procedure eliminated most of the records that contained eye- and large-movement artifact. The program also yielded power values (integrated mean square voltages) for each of the frontal, temporal, parietal, and occipital locations.

Cortical coupling was measured throughout the 30-sec task interval, during which time the subject was required to simultaneously retain the picture or word triad presented in the preceding 2-sec interval while (s)he performed the task. Since there were 24 trials consisting of 8 trials with each of the 3 tasks, this constituted a cortical coupling sample of 240 sec per task and 720 sec collapsed across task for each of the 36 subjects.

RESULTS AND DISCUSSION OF STM RECALL PERFORMANCE

The retention data showing the relationship between words (right panel) and pictures (left panel) for the three interference tasks at each of the three age groups are plotted in Figure 3. As can be noted, the vocal word task created the greatest amount of interference of the three tasks and also interfered more with retention of words than pictures.

The data were analyzed by means of a 3 (Age Groups) $\times$ 2 (Modality—words vs. pictures) $\times$ 3 (Interference Task) analysis of variance with repeated measures on the latter variable. The main effect of age, $F(2,30) = 21.01$, was statistically significant ($p < .01$). The modality main effect was not significant. Thus, superior retention of pictures over words (as noted in the adult literature) was not observed in this experiment. However, the Age $\times$ Modality interaction, $F(2,30) = 3.78$, was statistically significant ($p < .05$). Thus, collapsed across task, the youngest group tended to recall words better than pictures, whereas for the two older groups, retention of pictures was slightly better than or equal to retention of words.

The main effect of task, $F(2,60) = 59.92$, was statistically significant ($p < .001$). In addition, the Modality $\times$ Task interaction, $F(2,60) = 4.26$ ($p < .05$), attained statistical significance, indicating that tasks interfered differentially with pictures and words. There was no evidence of a triple interaction. A series of post hoc tests revealed that of the task comparisons between pictures and words only the vocalized task (i.e., vocal words under word presentation vs. vocal words under picture presentation), $F(1,60) = 7.15$ ($p < .01$), yielded significant differences. In other words, vocalization produced selective retroactive interference, depressing retention considerably more under the word condition than under the pictures condition.

Some component associated with pictorial representation renders it less susceptible than verbal representation to interference from vocalized activity. Elliott and Strawhorn (1976) emphasized the degree of complexity associated with transducing a stimulus to its

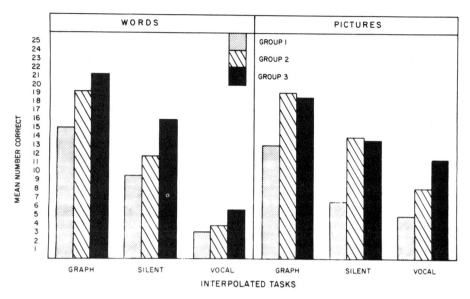

Fig. 3. MEAN NUMBER OF WORDS (LEFT PANEL) AND PICTURES (RIGHT PANEL) COR-
RECTLY RECALLED AS A FUNCTION OF GRAPH, SILENT WORD, AND VOCAL WORD ACTIVITY
FOR GROUP 1 (AGE 7–8), GROUP 2 (AGE 10–11), AND GROUP 3 (AGE 13–14).

auditory equivalent for oral recall. In view of that explanation, we might now infer that the
transduction of pictures to their auditory equivalent requires less information-processing
capacity than a similar transformation for words. This would be particularly true for the
stimuli in this experiment which represented highly familiar concrete objects probably
encountered early in the experience of each child. Visual experience with these objects,
therefore, preceded learning of their vocalized names. This is tantamount to what the
Russians refer to as the ''first signal system,'' the first basis of learning in the human being
(Stevenson, 1972). Subsequently, an association with the vocal and then the written word
was formed, and at this point the child comes under the control of what Soviet investigators call the ''second signal system.'' The second signal system involves higher order
activity of the nervous system and is referred to as higher order conditioning. The second
signal system must activate the first signal system to elicit the response. The transduction
of pictures to their auditory equivalent represents a forward association from the basic
reference point to the next higher order of learning. On the other hand, transforming
words to their auditory equivalent would represent a backward association through two
prior orders of learning.

The explanation of this phenomenon in terms of complexity associated with transduction relies on the assumption of separate memory stores for imaginal and auditory-verbal
stimuli (i.e., qualitatively different representations in memory). The fact that silent activity produced similar interference for words and pictures suggests that pictures may be
almost instantaneously encoded imaginally and semantically as suggested by Paivio

(1971). We are, however, emphasizing the hypothesis that there is greater facility in the transduction of pictures, as opposed to words, to their auditory equivalent. This is the factor primarily responsible for superior recall of pictures, as opposed to words, to their auditory equivalent. This is the factor primarily responsible for superior recall of pictures under the vocal condition.

The youngest group (age 7–8) generally remembered words better than pictures. Children in this group would fall on the borderline between the preoperations and concrete operations stages of cognitive development according to Piaget's theory. This period, ranging from ages 7 to 11, is marked by a transition to higher levels of cognitive functioning characterized as the beginning of logical thought and the ability to coordinate and classify things in a series. There is also some indication (Bower, 1971; Marcel and Rajar, 1975) that this period may represent a transition from right hemisphere to left hemisphere dominance. Witelson and Rabinovitch (1972) hypothesize that the lateralization of language starts in the preschool years and becomes increasingly established through adolescence. Prior to this, language representation is bilateral.

It might be theorized that 7- and 8-year-old children are in a stage of cognitive transition accompanied by a shift in hemispheric dominance. The cognitive transition would, of course, be represented by Piaget's demarcation of preoperational thought (age 2–7) from concrete operational thought (age 7–11). Thus, it may be that for this age group, words are represented bilaterally, having two qualitatively different memory representations. Whereas adults are able to encode words efficiently only into the auditory-verbal store, children of this age still tend to tag them with two representations. Words belong to the second signal system, and this age group lacks the experience to code them independently and efficiently.

Alternatively, but not excluding the above interpretation, perhaps the lateralization of verbal behavior represents the initiation of a developmental stage which prevails cognitively over imaginal memory functioning. This is analogous to a situation such as the acquisition of language which temporarily subsides when the developmental task of walking is initiated. Children ages 7 to 8 have only recently learned to read. Clearly, much of their attention and energy is narrowly focused on the acquisition of this new skill. In this study there was only a slight tendency toward superior retention of pictures over words in the two older groups, which can be viewed as a further manifestation of the theory suggested above. Perhaps the stimuli, geared as they were to the age span of all experimental groups, represented highly overlearned words for the oldest group. The usual effect of superior retention for pictures over words, as noted with adults, may have failed to emerge for this reason.

RESULTS AND DISCUSSION OF CORTICAL COUPLING DATA

Figures 4, 5, and 6 show the coupling scores for channel pairs as a function of memory for words (left panel) and pictures (right panel) for the three groups of children, ages 7 to 8, 10 to 11, and 13 to 14, respectively. These scores are collapsed across interference tasks in order to depict the contrast associated with modality. In general, cortical coupling scores increase as a function of increasing age. It can also be noted that left versus right hemisphere differences as a function of modality becomes most prominent in the oldest group. However, the direction of left versus right hemisphere differences is the same at all three age levels for channel pairs involving frontal-temporal and frontal-parietal areas. Since frontal leads are most likely to have eye-movement contamination, the parietal-temporal channel pairs represent the critical area. Here we see a complete reversal for left versus right hemisphere differences in magnitude of coupling score between the oldest and youngest group for both words and pictures. The direction of left versus right hemisphere scores for the middle age group conforms with the oldest group in regard to pictures and with the youngest group in regard to words.

The data were assessed by means of a variety of statistical analyses. The montage used resulted in a total of 21 coupling pairs and seven powers. Discarding nonhomologous interhemispheric pairs, we retained 15 couplings as being of potential interest. Four analyses of variance were performed. The first of these was a 2(Modality) × 3(Age) × 3(Task) × 15(Coupling Pairs) analyses of variance with repeated measures on the latter two variables. The main effects were significant for task, $F(2,60) = 8.07$, and coupling pairs, $F(14,420) = 22.04$ ($p < .01$). The statistically significant interactions were Task × Modality, $F(2,60) = 5.53$, ($p < .01$), Task × Modality × Age, $F(4,60) = 3.01$ ($p < .05$), Coupling Pairs × Modality, $F(14,420) = 1.77$ ($p < .05$), Coupling Pairs × Modality × Age, $F(28,420) = 2.04$ ($p < .05$), and Task × Coupling Pairs, $F(28,840) = 2.47$ ($p < .01$).

A second analysis of variance was performed on the power data. This was a 2(Modality) × 3(Age) × 3(Task) × 7(Power) design with repeated measures on the latter two variables. The main effects of task, $F(2,60) = 3.96$ ($p < .05$), and power, $F(6,180) = 3.63$ ($p < .01$), were statistically significant.

The parietal temporal areas were clearly the critical region, because they reflected gross physiologic age differences. We selected the two relevant coupling pairs—namely, P3-T3 and P4-T4—and four relevant powers—that is, T3, T4, P3, and P4—and submitted these to separate analyses of variance based on the following rationale:

1. These locations showed clear physiologic age differences.
2. The frontal area was most likely to be contaminated by eye-movement artifact.
3. There were too many variables for the N of 36 used in this experiment.
4. Any interpretation and inferences drawn are limited to this explanation of variable selection.

The third analysis of variance was performed using the two coupling pairs—that is, P3-T3 and P4-T4. This was a 2(Modality) × 3(Age) × 3(Task) × 2(Coupling Pairs) analysis with repeated measures on the latter two variables. It resulted in significant main effects for modality, $F(1,24) = 4.58$, and task $F(2,24) = 4.12$($p < .05$). The interaction effects of Task X Modality, $F(2,48) = 4.12$, and Coupling Pairs × Modality × Age, $F(2,24) = 4.77$ were significant ($p < .05$). A fourth analysis of variance involving the four powers, T3, T4, P3 and P4, resulted in a significant main effect for power, $F(3,72) = 4.12$ ($p < .01$), indicating that power varied independently of the other three variables.

As an exploratory procedure, knowing full well that the results would be only suggestive and would require replication on a larger sample, a multivariate discriminant analysis was performed. We contrasted the two youngest groups, one of which had been presented pictures and the other words, with the two oldest groups—namely, one presented with pictures and the other with words (each group representing an N of 6). The same two coupling pairs (P3-T3, P4-T4) and four powers (T3, T4, P3, and P4) were used as indicated above. Two factors emerged as statistically significant. Factor 1 accounted for 76% of the variance, $df = 8$, $p < .01$, and factor 2 accounted for 16% of the remaining variance, $df = 6$, $p < .05$. Factor 1 was clearly at P4-T4 (coupling pair) factor with a

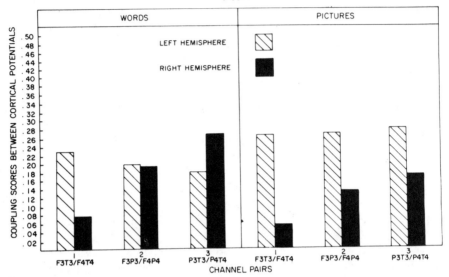

Fig. 4. COUPLING SCORES FOR CHANNEL PAIRS, OF CHILDREN AGE 7 TO 8, AS A FUNCTION OF MEMORY FOR WORDS AND PICTURES, COLLAPSED ACROSS INTERPOLATED TASKS.

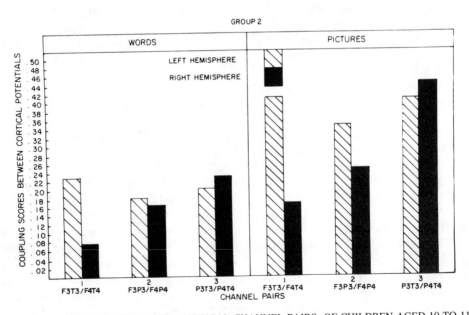

Fig. 5. COUPLING SCORES FOR CORTICAL CHANNEL PAIRS, OF CHILDREN AGED 10 TO 11, AS A FUNCTION OF MEMORY FOR WORDS AND PICTURES, COLLAPSED ACROSS INTERPO-LATED TASKS.

138

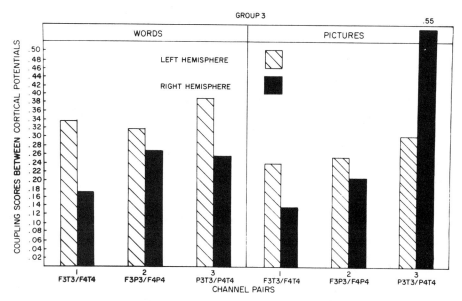

Fig. 6. COUPLING SCORES FOR CORTICAL CHANNEL PAIRS, OF CHILDREN AGED 13 TO 14, AS A FUNCTION OF MEMORY FOR WORDS AND PICTURES, COLLAPSED ACROSS INTERPOLATED TASKS.

correlation of $r = .81$. Factor 2 was negatively correlated with P3-T3 (coupling pair), $r = -.54$, and positively correlated with the power P3, $r = .54$. Factor 1 separated the oldest group who had received pictures from the other three groups (i.e., young-pictures, young-words, old-words). Factor 2 separated the young group who had received words from the other three groups. The negative-coupling and positive-power correlation associated with the second factor is interpreted as a relative suppression of P3-T3 coupling and increased power over the left hemisphere that occurs with words in the young group. It will be remembered that the young group, which was presented words, manifested higher coupling scores in the right hemisphere. One conjecture is that they were apparently not relying on left hemispheric memory storage for retention of words.

If picture recall performance in the middle group (age 10–11) is correlated against their score for the discriminant variable, P4–T4, the correlation $r = .43$ is in the predicted direction. In other words, high picture recall performance correlates well with their simultaneously attained coupling scores, and these are similar to the oldest group (age 13–14). However, word recall performance for the middle group versus their coupling scores for P3-T3 results in the correlation $r = -.66$. This is in the opposite direction with good word recall performance and the simultaneously attained coupling scores resembling coupling associated with the youngest group (age 7–8).

The best old—young discriminator is P3-T3 minus P4-T4 (P3T4 − P4T4). This separates the two groups without overlap if you consider pictures and words independently. Correlating picture recall performance of the middle group with their P3T3 − P4T4 score results in a correlation of $r = -.66$ in the predicted direction. However, word recall performance of middle age children versus P3T3 − P4T4 yields a correlation of $r = -.71$, which is in the opposite direction.

In other words, children in the age group of 10 to 11 years who process pictures like the oldest group (age 13–14) have better picture recall performance. On the other hand, children in this age group (age 10–11) have higher word recall performance scores if they process words like the youngest children (age 7–8).

Cortical coupling appears to reflect cognitive changes related to retention of words and pictures rather than the ongoing interference activity during which the measure was recorded. This is consistent with the Hardyck, et al. (1978) position which states that lateralization effects are not a function of ongoing cognitive processing in specialized cortical areas but do reflect differences in memory storage locations. These results are also in accord with Kinsbourne's (1973) findings wherein the added requirement of retaining verbal material in memory produced superior left hemisphere performance on a visuospatial task.

The coupling scores associated with types of task exhibited no consistent interpretable pattern. The only possible statement at this point concerning task differences is that vocalized activity produced the lowest coupling scores. Perhaps the movement associated with vocalizing caused the electrical potentials to become uncoupled. This precise disruption may also be the cause of memory disruption and hence be responsible for the potent interference effect attributed to the dimension of vocalization in the Peterson and Peterson (1959) task.

The complete reversal for left versus right hemisphere differences in magnitude of coupling score between the oldest and youngest group for both words and pictures presents a unique and unexpected finding. The oldest group demonstrates higher left hemisphere coupling scores for words and higher right hemisphere coupling scores for pictures. This is in the predicted direction, as the left hemisphere has long been associated with auditory-motor-verbal functions, whereas the right hemisphere is associated with visual-imaginal and spatial functions. However, the youngest group manifests a pattern of scores exactly opposite from the predicted direction. In addition, the middle group shows a slight tendency to produce a coupling pattern similar to the older group for pictures and similar to the younger group for words.

A consideration of the neurologic development of the brain, findings from short-term memory psychology, and the Piagetian stages of cognitive development provide a framework to which these findings might be addressed. The brain commissures, including the corpus callosum, are the last structures to develop and become myelinated. Lateralization for speech begins in the preschool years and becomes permanently established in adolescence.

Extending these concepts to our findings, for the youngest group (age 7–8) both aural words and pictures are represented bilaterally although specialization of function has begun. Due to its inherent superior visual processing capacity (Molfese, Freeman, and Palermo, 1975; Crowell, Jones, Kappuniai, et al., 1973), the right hemisphere is predominantly utilized during the early stages for acquisition of reading skills. The child at this stage has only recently learned to read. Utilization of the visual system is imperative to effect an association between the visual configuration and its internal representation. Hence, the right hemisphere is more effective in the early stages for acquisition of written words. Processing of pictures by the right hemisphere has subsided as a result of the imposition of this new developmental task (reading). This is analogous to the developmental trend wherein one skill becomes latent as a new skill emerges. Since pictures are represented bilaterally, reliance on the left hemisphere for their storage and retrieval emerges temporarily as a substitute. This description is suggestive of a borderline transition with functions being worked out through contact with requirements imposed by reading. For, as Piaget has stated, the functional nucleus of intellectual organization derived from biological organization will orient successive structures, the function of which will be worked out through contact with reality.

The middle group (age 10–11) falls on the borderline between concrete operational (i.e., the stage of logical thought, categorization, and sequencing ability) and formal operational (i.e., the stage of logical and abstract thinking) thought processes. This cognitive transition is perhaps made possible by the "now more complete" myelination of the corpus callosum. The brain is now capable of interhemispheric communication, and hemispheric lateralization is nearly established. With optimal interhemispheric communication, the left hemisphere can now take over the function of transforming the written word to its verbal equivalent, relying somewhat on the right hemisphere to process and communicate necessary visual cues. Although the child is neurologically mature enought to process the word in the verbal sequential mode, (s)he may still resort to his/her previous strategy while the new strategy is becoming conditioned or established. The processing of pictures, on the other hand, is not a new skill, and its functional lateralization in the right hemisphere is accomplished with facility. Some theorists (e.g., Paivio) claim that pictures may continue to be dually encoded into adulthood.

Cortical coupling scores associated with the middle group are consistent with this explanation. Children with high word recall performance manifested coupling scores similar to the younger children while those with high picture recall performance had coupling scores similar to the older children. An extension of this study to auditory and visual dyslexics is presently in progress.

CONCLUSION

As a result of the above research, there are some basic points on which we can be fairly certain. With respect to the effects of methylphenidate in minimal brain dysfunction, it seems quite clear that the drug exercises an effect on the early channel selection phase of attention. Effects on later aspects of attention would perhaps be expected since a defect in the early phase of attention should also be apparent in later cognitive operations. Furthermore, it appears that the effect of methylphenidate has a u-shaped function. Such a therapeutic window is a phenomenon common to other drugs which act on the arousal system. Finally, these points are consistent with data coming from other evoked-response laboratories and from investigations using more classical behavioral measures.

The advantage of the evoked-potential studies lies both in their sensitivity and in the fact that they supply convergent data. The interaction of event-related potentials and behavioral data needs emphasis. An increased N-1 amplitude is not the same as increased attention, but the fact that evoked potential data is not the same as behavioral data is one justification for evoked-potential investigations. If the evoked potential gave the same information as behavioral data, it would give no additional information, and one must be on guard against the temptation to equate an evoked-response phenomenon with a cognitive or behavioral phenomenon.

The issue of using the evoked-potential measure to determine the optimal dosage of methylphenidate is another question, and this requires a great deal more investigation. Although the studies reported here represent a third replication of this phenomenon, assertions of clinical utility require great caution.

The cortical coupling data is, in a sense, at once more surprising and more in need of replication. Muscle activity, eye-movement, and level of arousal can all influence the cortical-coupling measure in ways that are not entirely clear at present. Nevertheless, again both behavioral and electrophysiologic data provide convergent indications of dramatic changes in the strategies for short-term memory between ages 7 and 14. It is during these ages that reading skills are developed, and a better understanding of these rather dramatic changes in cortical organization should provide a better basis for understanding both normal and abnormal development of reading skills. There is already evidence that brain-event-related potentials of dyslexics differ from those of normals and that, within a group of dyslexics, ERPS of dyseidetics differ from those of dysphonetics. The use of cortical coupling to provide additional diagnostic information is a distinct possibility, but again one that is at present only a promise for the future.

REFERENCES

Ambrose, J. The development of the smiling response in early infancy. *In* B. Foss, ed., *Determinants of Infant Behavior*. New York: Wiley, 1961.

Aronson, E., and Rosenbloom, S. Space perception in early infancy: perception within a common auditory-visual space. *Science,* 1971, 173:1161–1163.

Bogen, J., and Gazzaniga, M. Cerebral comissurotomy in man: minor hemisphere dominance for certain visual-spatial functions. *Journal of Neurosurgery,* 1965, 23:394–399.

Bower, G. Analysis of a mnemonic device. *American Scientist*, 1971, 58:496–510.

Bower, T. The object in the world of the infant. *Scientific American*, 1971, 225:30–38.

Bruce, R., and Kinsbourne, M. Orientational model of perceptual asymmetry. Paper presented at the 15th annual convention of the Psychonomic Society, Boston, November, 1974.

Butler, S., and Glass, A. Asymmetries in the EEG associated with cerebral dominance. *EEG and Clinical Neurophysiology*, 1974, 36:481–491.

Callaway, E., and Harris, P. Coupling between potentials from different areas. *Science,* 1974, 183:873–875.

Conel, J. *The Postnatal Development of the Human Cerebral Cortex: Vol. II, The Cortex of the One Month Infant*. Cambridge: Harvard University Press, 1941.

Crowell, D., Jones, R., Kappuniai, L., and Nakagawa, J. Unilateral cortical activity in newborn humans: An early index of dominance? *Science*, 1973, 180:205–208.

den Heyer, K., and Barrett, B. Selective loss of visual and verbal information in STM means of visual and verbal interpolated tasks. *Psychonomic Science*, 1971, 25:100–102.

Dykman, R., Ackerman, P., Clements, S., and Peters, J. Specific learning disabilities: an attentional deficit syndrome. *In* H. Myklebust, ed., *Progress in Learning Disabilities*, Vol. II. New York: Grune & Stratton, 1971.

Elliott, L. Imagery versus repetition encoding in short- and long-term memory. *Journal of Experimental Psychology,* 1973, 100:270–276.

Elliott, L., and Strawhorn, R. Interference in short-term memory from vocalization; Aural versus visual modality differences. *Journal of Experimental Psychology: Human Learning and Memory 2,* 1976, 6:70–71.

Elliott, L., Strawhorn, R., and Wass, M. Vocalization interference in short-term retention of pictures and words across developmental stages. *Developmental Psychology,* in press.

Elliott, L., Strawhorn, R., and Shook, B. Imagery value of 974 nouns, from elementary reading series, scaled by children in grades 1 through 6. Unpublished manuscript, August 1974.

Galin, D. Implications for psychiatry of left and right cerebral specialization. *Archives of General Psychiatry,* 1974, 31:572–583.

Galin, D., and Ornstein, R. Lateral specialization of cognitive mode: an EEG study. *Psychophysiology,* 1972, 9:412–418.

Galin, D., and Ornstein, R. Hemispheric specialization and the duality of consciousness. *In* H. Widroe, ed., *Human Behavior and Brain Functioning*. Springfield, Ill.: Thomas, 1973.

Garner, W. *Uncertainty and Structure as Psychological Concepts*. New York: Wiley, 1972.

Gazzaniga, M. *The Bisected Brain*. New York: Appleton-Century-Crofts, 1970.

Gazzaniga, M. Cerebral dominance viewed as a decision system. *In* S. Diamond and J. Beaumont, eds., *Hemispheric Function in the Human Brain*. New York: Wiley, 1974.

Halliday, R., Rosenthal, J., Naylor, H., and Callaway, E. Averaged evoked potential predictors of clinical improvement in hyperactive children treated with methylphenidate: an initial study and replication. *Psychophysiology,* 1976, 13:429–440.

Hardyck, C., Tzeng, O., and Wang, W. Cerebral laterization of function and bilingual decision processes: Is thinking lateralized? *Brain and Language*, 1978, 5:56–71.

Kinsbourne, M. The cerebral basis of lateral asymmetries in attention. *Acta Psychologia*, 1970, 33:193–201.

Kinsbourne, M. The control of attention by interaction between the cerebral hemispheres. *In* S. Kornblum, ed., *Attention and Performance*, Vol. 4. New York: Academic Press, 1973.

Kroll, N., Parkinson, S., and Parks, T. Sensory and active storage of compound visual and auditory stimuli. *Journal of Experimental Psychology*, 1972, 95:32–38.

Kroll, N., Bee, J., and Gurski, G. Release of proactive interference as a result of changing presentation modality. *Journal of Experimental Psychology*, 1973, 98:131–137.

Levy, J., Trevarthen, C., and Sperry, R. Perception of bilateral chimeric figures following hemispheric deconnection. *Brain*, 1972, 95:61–78.

Marcel, T., and Rajan, P. Lateral specialization for recognition of words and faces in good and poor readers. *Neuropsychologia*, 1975, 13:489–497.

McKee, G., Humphrey, B., and McAdam, D. Scaled laterization of alpha activity during linguistic and musical tasks. *Psychophysiology*, 1973, 10:441–443.

Meudell, P. Short-term visual memory: comparative effects of two types of distraction on the recall of visually presented verbal and nonverbal material. *Journal of Experimental Psychology*, 1972, 94:244–247.

Milgram, N. Verbal context versus visual compound in paired associate learning by children. *Journal of Experimental Child Psychology*, 1967, 5:597–603.

Molfese, D., Freeman, R., and Palermo, D. The ontogeny of brain lateralization for speech and nonspeech stimuli. *Brain and Language*, 1975, 2:356–358.

Morell, L., and Salamy, J. Hemispheric asymmetry of electrocortical responses to speech stimuli. *Science*, 1971, 174:164–166.

Murray, L., and Newman, F. Visual and verbal coding in short-term memory. *Journal of Experimental Psychology*, 1973, 100:58–62.

Ornstein, R., and Galin, D. Physiological studies of consciousness. *In* P. Lee, R. Ornstein, D. Galin, A. Deikman, and C. Tart, eds., *Symposium on Consciousness*. New York: Viking Press, 1976.

Paivio, A. On the functional significance of imagery. *Psychological Bulletin*, 1970, 73:385–392.

Paivio, A. *Imagery and Verbal Processes*. New York: Holt, Rinehart, and Winston, 1971.

Paivio, A., and Csapo, K. Concrete image and verbal memory codes. *Journal of Experimental Psychology*, 1969, 80:279–285.

Pellegrino, J., Siegel, A., and Dhawan, M. Short-term retention of pictures and words: evidence for dual coding systems. *Journal of Experimental Psychology: Human Learning and Memory*. 1975, 104:95–102.

Peterson, L., and Peterson, M. Short-term retention of individual verbal items. *Journal of Experimental Psychology*, 1959, 58:193–198.

Piaget, J. *The Origins of Intelligence in Children*. New York: International University Press, 1952.

Piaget, J., and Inhelder, B. *The Psychology of the Child*. New York: Basic Books, 1969.

Porges, S. Peripheral and neurochemical parallels of psychopathology: a psychophysiological model relating autonomic imbalances to hyperactivity, psychopathy and autism. *Advances in Child Development and Behavior*, Vol. II. New York: Academic Press, 1976.

Posner, M. Characteristics of visual and kinesthetic memory codes. *Journal of Experimental Psychology*, 1967, 75:103–107.

Posner, M., and Keele, S. Decay of visual information from a single letter. *Science*, 1967, 158:137–139.

Salthouse, T. Simultaneous processing of verbal and spatial information. *Memory and Cognition*, 1975, 3, 221–225.

Satterfield, J., Cantwell, D., and Satterfield, B. Pathophysiology of the hyperactive child syndrome. *Archives of General Psychiatry*, 1974, 31:829–844.

Seth, G. Eye-hand coordination and handedness: a developmental study of visuo-motor behavior in infancy. *British Journal of Educational Psychology*, 1973, 43:35–49.

Shannon, E., and Weaver, W. *The Mathematical Theory of Communication*. Urbana: University of Illinois Press, 1949.

Smyk, K., and Darway, B. Dominance of a cerebral hemisphere in electroencephalographic records. *Acta Physiologica Polonica*, 1972, 23:407.

Sperry, R. The great cerebral commissure. *Scientific American*, 1964, 42:210.

Sperry, R. Lateral specialization in the surgically separated hemispheres. *In* F. Schmitt and F. Worden, eds., *The Neurosciences: Third Study Program*. Cambridge: MIT Press, 1974.

Sprague, R., and Sleater, E. Methylphenidate in hyperkinetic children: differences in dose effect on learning and social behavior. *Science, 1977, 198:1274–1276.*

Sroufe, L. Drug treatment of children with behavior problems. *In* F. Horowitz, ed., *Review of Child Development Research,* Vol. 4. Chicago: University of Chicago Press, 1975.

Stevenson, H. *Children's Learning.* New York: Appleton-Century-Crofts, 1972.

Turkewitz, G., Gordon, E., and Birch, H. Head turning in the human neonate: spontaneous patterns. *Journal of Genetic Psychology,* 1965, 107:143–158.

Werry, J. and Sprague, R. Methylphenidate in children—effect of dosage. *Australian and New Zealand Journal of Psychiatry,* 1974, 8:9–19.

Witelson, S., and Rabinovitch, M. Hemispheric speech lateralization in children with auditory-linguistic deficits. *Cortex,* 1972, 8:412–426.

Yagi, A., Bali, L., and Callaway, E. Optimum parameters for the measurement of cortical coupling. *Physiological Psychology,* 1975,   :   −   .

Yakolev, P., and Lecours, A. Myelogenetic cycles of regional maturation of the brain. *In* A. Minkowski, ed., *Symposium—Regional Development of the Brain in Early Life.* Oxford: Blackwell, 1967.

Yingling, C. Lateralization of cortical coupling during complex verbal and spatial behaviors. *In* J. Desmedt, ed., *Language and Hemispheric Specialization in Man: Cerebral ERPs. Progress In Clinical Neurophysiology,* Vol. 3. Basel: Karger, 1977.

VI. Tactile Learning and Reading Failure

HELEN SHANER SCHEVILL

Of the estimated 10% of school children in the United States with specific or potential reading disabilities, most have problems due to auditory or visual disorders. The prognosis for success in reading is limited when dysfunctions occur in one or both of these areas, but opportunities are increasing for aiding these children through combined therapeutic and curricular programs. These opporutnities recently have been furthered by federal and state legislative educational support, available particularly since the enactment of Public Law 94-142 (Education for All Handicapped Children Act of 1975).

The present research project was subsidized by a grant from the National Science Foundation in the RANN program (research applied to national needs). For the past 5 years we have been designing and using tactile instrumentation to measure letter decoding. During these years we have worked with over 300 children in public and private schools in the Philadelphia area. The objective was to help young children to improve basic skills in alphabet letter recognition, serial ordering, and other areas.

A few of the children were dysgraphic. Some had poor spatial orientation, did not know left from right, put their shoes on the wrong feet, and could not tie their laces. During the first dozen sessions in tactile training, they were unable to find their way from the classroom to the tactile testing room in the same school building. Other children in the study had adequate visuoconstructive skills but poor verbal recall. They would "forget" the name of the vehicle taking them to school (bus), and would misname letters and words in reading and spelling.

Our goal in working with these children was to develop appropriate curricula, based on a tactile approach, which would incorporate kinesthetic, auditory, and visual tasks and be available to larger groups of children. Some tactile tasks were constructed to facilitate learning distinctive features of pairs of letters. In later exercises they would categorize these letters in word patterns by sound and by shape. Multisensory analysis was used for the youngest group of children as a means of developing recognition of letter forms by tactile, visual, and ideomotor processing. Appropriate tasks in categorizing letter shapes would later be incorporated into spelling and reading exercises.

TACTILE DECODING BEHAVIOR

Because this was exploratory research, it was first necessary to evaluate the children's behavior in tactile decoding under a variety of conditions. We did not know how well the learning-disabled child could perceive features of letter shape, how proficient he was in tactile-verbal labeling, visual matching, and ideomotor imagery. We did not know how flexible the disabled reader's cognitive processes would be in successively shifting attention from the tactile to visual, written, or oral responses. Before methods of instruction could be developed, it was necessary to have indications of the skills on which certain

This work was supported by The National Science Foundation and by the Smith-Kettlewell Eye Research Foundation. My appreciation to members of the Philadelphia Public School System for their unlimited cooperation in providing students for testing, and to the principals and staff of two Philadelphia schools, Brookline and Germantown Academy, to Dr. Carolyn Hartsough for technical assistance in statistical analysis, for the testing and training assistance of the dozen psychologists, teachers and aides who worked in the project, and finally, for the cooperation of the children.

children performed better than others. These skills were to be the basis of a multisensory curricula. It was also relevant to have information about how children with a particular set of deficiencies process tactile information when compared to those with another set of deficiencies.

Tactile letter decoding essentially is a means whereby the child identifies letters by movement and by shape. He feels the letter form being drawn on his palm but does not see it. By using the tactile sense one moment and the visual sense the next, the child learns to develop a concept of letter form in more than one dimension. This kind of association is easier than making a connection with an abstract label. For the young potentially reading-disabled child who is unable to relate a visual form to a verbal label, it is a triumph to make a relationship between tactile and visual letters. It is also an achievement when he can decode the letters through tactile sensations on the back of his hand and recognize the letter forms through passive hand motion as the teacher steers his finger to draw the letters.

As school districts expand their learning-disabilities programs, more children between the ages of 5 and 7 years are being designated as potentially learning disabled or as being high risk for reading problems. One principle underlying the use of tactile training is that high-risk children should receive early intervention in intersensory training. In so doing, not only does the child learn the distinctive features of letter forms and movement tactilely but he also develops a more astute awareness in noting differences between letters in visual representation and in writing.

We recognized at the outset that in development of curricula using the tactile modality it is necessary to consider developmental factors regarding intersensory integration of letters for the nonreader between 5 and 7 years of age, and cognitive factors which would influence both young and old. In this study, the children between 5 and 7 years are referred to as "young," and those between 7 and 9 years as "old." The young high-risk child who recognized only the alphabet characters in his own first name had a different set of requirements than the slightly older child who was struggling with sound-symbol decoding of words. An older disabled reader who knew letter names and was able to read at first-grade level might have difficulty, however, in verbal recall of letters, in focusing attention on word endings, in left-to-right orientation in word recognition, and in classifying and identifying letters similar in construction (m-n; p-b-d; h-k; c-u).

We also recognized that not all children would learn equally well by this method. The child with deficiencies in spatial orientation or in visual imagery might be as deficient in tactile imagery and form as he is in visual imagery. He has different processing tendencies than the child with auditory deficits and intact visuospatial sense. Whereas the first child may be able to supply the phonetic equivalent for letter names, he can become confused in spelling and in tactile letter decoding. The second child may be able to recognize the conversion of a serial order of letters to a particular visual pattern. He may be able to copy the visual pattern successfully, even though he "forgets" how to supply the ending sound for the word *map* after having learned the word *mat* almost by rote. We recognized, then, that these two considerations, the age of the child and the nature of his particular disability in processing information, were factors in determining how the tactile mode could be used most effectively for letter decoding. Our primary objective was to investigate how intervention in the form of one specific kind of tactile practice could facilitate underlying cognitive processes in integrating the visual, kinesthetic, and spoken-language systems.

It is proposed here that a spatial factor is an important aspect of the cognitive process for the disabled reader in learning tactile letters. Three hypotheses were set forth.

The first was that the young disabled child readily learned to make intersensory associations within a spatial framework between the tactile, visual, and ideomotor systems. Tactile training would enhance skills in recognition of ideomotor and visual imagery of single letters for the child between 5 and 7 years of age. The second hypothesis was that a spatial factor, poor visual memory skills, would correlate significantly with poor tactile serial ordering performance. After training, the disabled reader with deficiencies in visual memory would not be as proficient in converting the serial succession of tactile letters to a visual representation as the reader with adequate visual memory. The third hypothesis was that the spatial factor either dominates integration with language or is too weak to contribute to the integration with language in tactile decoding. The disabled reader with adequate visual memory can use this cognitive strength, however, as a means of integrating the spatial and language elements in many of the tactile tasks. The pattern of intercorrelations among the tactile tasks would be different for him than for the disabled reader with deficient visual memory.

COGNITIVE POTENTIAL: ENHANCEMENT OF SPATIAL IMAGERY

The first hypothesis was that as the child would increase his proficiency in attending to the spatial dimensions of the tactile stimulus, he would be enhancing his ideomotor and visual imagery of letter movement and form. This intersensory enhancement would provide a broader basis for language associations, and pave the way for an easier transition to reading. Gibson (1971) states that the most relevant kind of training for letter discrimination is practice that provides experience in distinguishing the distinctive characteristics of one letter from another. By calling attention to the distinctive characteristics of specific pairs of letters perceived on the palm, it was anticipated and found that the young child would be sensitized to these features, recognize them on a visual array, and select an appropriate printed letter. He would also recognize the distincitve features of the letters in passive hand movement (when the teacher steered his hand in drawing the letter) and identify the letter name by his own hand movement, sight occluded.

Certain children in the young age group have disturbances in spatial ordering, and others have specific verbal-receptive or expressive disabilities, but are intact in spatial, visual, and tactile processes. Our theory was that young children, whether or not they had deficiencies in visual memory, would be trained to attend to distinctive spatial characteristics of the moving tactile letter forms in simple recognition tasks. The assumption was that the younger the child was when special training began, the more promise there would be for the development of intersensory processing that focuses on the spatial aspects of letters. This early training would serve as a precursor and a facilitation of concepts of notation. If the tasks were simple enough, tactile discrimination proficiency would be as possible for the child with poor visual imagery and spatial orientation as for the child with intact visuospatial skills. Thus, tactile training would be beneficial in developing a network of associations in ideomotor imagery, visual matching, and, indirectly, in verbal recall.

Visual, Kinesthetic, and Language Modalities

There is evidence that the visual and kinesthetic modalities have a strong bond, and that practice in one area reinforces imagery in the other area. Remediation work in special education has advocated finger tracing and copying exercises as means of establishing concepts of the relationship between visual form and hand movement (Fernald, 1943;

Monroe, 1932; Orton, 1937; Montessori, 1964). Rehabilitation work with patients with occipital brain damage has also emphasized the dependence of hand and eye movement on visual recognition and comprehension. Luria (1963) describes a procedure of helping a patient with occipital injury to recognize separate letters by tracing them. The patient could recognize the letters he was tracing, even though he was unable to recognize them by vision alone. Gradually the tracing method was replaced by scanning with the eyes until finally the patient could recognize the letters visually and identify them by name. This remedial procedure suggests that practice with hand and eye movement evoked an association with the language processes and was a temporary substitute for visual processing.

The relationship between the visual and the kinesthetic modalities has been ascertained by neurologic investigation. Konorski (1970) states that imagining a certain movement leads to its latent performance as manifested by the EMG record. The relationship has also been hypothesized in psychological constructs. James (1950) states that the image of a movement is an agent in eliciting the movement.

There is also evidence that the kinesthetic and language systems are linked. The premise that the motor systems of the kinesthetic and language processes are closely related can be substantiated in pragmatic evidence and observation of how children learn verbal skills and concepts. The blind child readily learns to read by the substitution of the tactile-kinesthetic senses for the visual. In this instance, the kinesthetic-tactile systems evoke a verbal assocation. The young child learns concepts of *up, down, in,* and *out* through sensorimotor activities and appropriate gestures in games. The combination of hand movement and language activities in the Kodaly method of music instruction (Sandor, 1966) teaches the young child to relate hand movements with specific sound intervals of the major scale. In working with 5- and 6-year-old high-risk children, we have often found that they are unable to name a specific letter until they draw it. The motion of the hand spontaneously evokes a verbal assocation, whereas the visual representation does not.

Tactile Intervention as a Reinforcing Factor

Our theory was that the tactile intervention could be introduced as a reinforcing factor. If the visual and kinesthetic modalities are closely related, it is conceivable that they would also be closely related to the tactile modality. By focusing attention on the tactile, the child could develop cross-modal assocaitions using visual imagery even when sight is omitted in the tactile processing.

It was anticipated that tactile practice would activate a chain of intersensory processes for the child between 5 and 7 years; the development of kinesthetic imagery would in turn evoke verbal association. Specific tactile training, using the surface of the palm, would develop a kinesthetic sense of how the movement could be programmed in the act of recognizing and even reproducing letter characters. As the young child follows the tactile sensations on the palm of his hand, he would be forming a mental image of drawing the letters. In a transfer task of passive (involuntary) finger movement while the teacher steered the child's hand, he would identify through his own hand motions the names of individual letters.

One premise for introducing tactile instruction is that this form of intervention would facilitate the underlying cognitive processes considered to be delayed in immature children. These children, it was hypothesized, would be able to learn, with the 10 hours of specific training, specific skills in cross-modal matching and verbal association, using the tactile mode. Training which emphasizes the spatial dimensions of letter formation would facilitate tactile and tactile-kinesthetic letter recognition and categorization skills.

Another premise for introducing tactile intervention for the high-risk child between 5 and 7 years is that the young child's brain is flexible enough to absorb and transcode tactile movement to the kinesthetic and visual modalities. He is ontogenetically "ready" for assimilating ideomotor images of letters. He readily learns in nursery games how concepts of space relate to body movement, touching, and seeing. Similarly he could readily learn in tactile practice how concepts of space and movement can be interpreted on the surface of his hand, and in other ways such as through hand motions and by printed letters on cards. For example, the young child feels on his palm three descending lines for the letter *m*. He counts "1," "2," "3." He then sees the letter and writes it. Another day he learns the letter *n* by spatial cues. He counts only two lines as they move on his palm and writes the letter. As he matches the tactile image to a visual representation, he is using verbal and spatial cues to facilitate the tactile, visual, and kinesthetic image of these and other letters. All of these sensory modalities are interacting and reinforcing each other.

It was anticipated that the young disabled reader would make a more successful transfer to passive hand tasks than the old disabled reader. The young child learns easily through kinesthetic imagery. The older child, already engrossed in beginning reading, and still hampered by limited cognitive processing skills, may be placing all of his attention on the visual and auditory aspects of the letters, and may be decreasing his attention on kinethetic imagery.

In sum, the first set of hypotheses viewed intersensory skills between the tactile, visual, and kinesthetic modes as a cognitive strength for young high-risk children. The specified tasks were as easy for those with deficiencies in visual memory as for those with adequate visual memory. Only single letters were used in the stimulus, and the tasks were considered easier than those with two or more letters in the stimulus. The data showing that most young high-risk children could perform the specified spatial recognition skills would provide a basis later on for incorporating a version of these skills into a reading-readiness curriculum design.

COGNITIVE LIMITATIONS IN TACTILE LEARNING: SERIAL ORDERING SKILLS AND POOR VISUAL MEMORY

The second set of assumptions considered tasks that would be especially difficult for disabled readers with a specific syndrome of poor visual memory and spatial orientation. The main premise was that children with poor visual memory skills would also be deficient in converting a serial order of tactile letters to a contiguous spatial arrangement. The tactile tasks in which two or more letters were presented in succession for stimulation were considered to be serial in nature. The response qualified whether the temporal succession of tactile letters had to be transposed to a spatial arrangement. If the response was verbal, the child ideally named the letters in the correct order of presentation, and did not have to imagine how the temporal order would be converted when written or read on the page. If the response was visual or written, however, the child converted the temporal succession to a spatial arrangement from left to right on the page. It was anticipated that this conversion would be significantly difficult for the disabled reader with poor visual memory skills.

It is now well-established that deficiencies in visuomotor skills and visual imagery may be symptomatic of a specific form of dyslexia sometimes called "visual dyslexia"

(Johnson and Myklebust, 1967) or "dyseidetic" dyslexia (Boder, 1971). One of the behavioral manifestations in this kind of dyslexia is poor spatial orientation.

A Review of the Literature

Kinsbourne (1975) describes a syndrome of behavior in reading-disabled children which includes dysfunction in figure copying as well as in spatial orientation and serial ordering of letter symbols. These children display poor motor planning in copying and in reproducing familiar forms from memory, although they have a normal history of early language development and normal scores in verbal areas of the WISC. These children, presumably with intact language functions, nevertheless have a dysfunction in serial-ordering skills.

Kinsbourne (1975) and Satz, Rardin, and Ross (1971) suggest that children with a syndrome of deficiencies in right-left orientation, serial-ordering skills, and copying ability may have a dysfunction of the left more than of the right hemisphere. If that particular syndrome reflects a left-hemisphere dysfunction, the behavioral pattern is different from another syndrome which also presumably reflects a left-hemisphere dysfunction but which includes characteristics of adequate copying skills and spatial orientation, and of inadequate auditory-verbal association and recall and expressive language.

Benton (1975) considers the empirical evidence ascribing a neurologic basis for specific reading disability as both circumstantial and inconsistent. He suggests that defining homogeneous subtypes of learning-disabled children with correlates of each subtype might elucidate the contradictory hypotheses and findings relating to developmental dyslexia. Boder's (1971) classification of "dysphonetic" and "dyseidetic" reading disabilities provides a dual basis for evaluating different types of reading disability and different patterns of strengths and weaknesses in intersensory integration skills.

Myklebust (1975) uses the term "intra- and interneurosensory processing" to describe the duality existing between the neurologic and psychologic functions subserving a particular learning systems model. In broad terms, this construct implies that the language functions in the left hemisphere and the visuospatial functions in the right hemisphere can be relatively strong or weak in different individuals and can influence the intra-and intersensory communications among the kinesthetic, tactile, visual, and auditory processes.

Spatial Deficiencies in Tactile Decoding

An operational interpretation of system processing might suggest how performance in poor copying is related to poor performance in serial-ordering in the conversion of letters from a temporal order to a spatial arrangement. In tasks that require such conversion, children who have poor spatial orientation can be distinguished from those who have adequate spatial orientation. The syndrome does not necessarily affect serial-ordering responses that are verbal and do not require adaptation to a left-to-right order.

While this study cannot presume to localize the specific cerebral source of a particular kind of syndrome in tactile letter decoding, it can, nevertheless, demonstrate how two behavioral elements (spatial reconstruction in serial ordering and visual memory) are closely related, and how these factors might interact in intersensory tactile learning, particularly in the conversion of a temporal order of tactile letter decoding to a spatial arrangement.

Spatial and Temporal Interaction

The concept of tactile letter movement subsumes an ability to deal with multipoints in space and time at various levels of conceptualization. One can consider the hand lengthwise from finger tip to wrist as two extremities in vertical space, and from little finger to forefinger as lateral space. In tactile letter decoding, one spatial point precedes another in lateral, vertical, or oblique motion. In respect to temporal succession, a letter segment will precede the next in time. Implicit in the mechanical multipoint tactile technique used in this study is ability cognitively to follow one dot after the other on the surface of the palm, and to convert these fragmented impulses into a gestalt image. This specific skill constitutes a form of tactile figure-ground imagery in its own right. There are also the built-in components of temporal-spatial synchronization in the formation of letters. For example, if the tactile stimulus is the letter *i,* the punctuated occurrence of the final dot to this letter can be as significant by its temporal as by its spatial occurrence. In fact, the concept of tactile movement implies interaction of spatial arrangement and temporal succession. At a higher level, the temporal order of pairs of letters used in timed succession can be a measure of assessing the child's ability to recall the temporal order of letter names verbally, or to match the temporal order to a spatial arrangement.

The synchronizing of temporal-spatial elements in letter perception is accentuated in tactile discrimination. Synchronizing is implicit on one level in regard to spatial and temporal elements of tactile movement. Synchronizing is also implicit at a higher level in regard to the recall of a chain of letter characters in time as they are converted to a spatial representation. At both these levels the same processes are involved—namely, the conceptualization of spatial arrangement as it interacts with temporal order.

Successful performance on the easiest tactile or tactile-kinesthetic tasks is hardly an indication of the reading-disabled child's normality in spatial analysis of tactile movement or in visual imagery. Only in conversion of a tactile succession of letter symbols to a visual-spatial representation could the child's deficiency show up in visuoconstructive performance. We anticipated, therefore, that levels of visual memory would correlate more with performance in the conversion of temporal order to a visuospatial arrangement than with a verbal or purely temporal response. Thus, it may be that the specific syndrome of poor tactile letter discrimination, serial-spatial ordering, and copying skills is related to an underlying general spatial impairment factor in certain reading-disabled children. This spatial impairment does not exist in reading-disabled children with adequate skills in copying patterns. They have better tactile letter discrimination and serial-spatial ordering skills.

Assessment of Visual Memory Skills

The criterion for assessing figure-copying skills was the Benton Revised Visual Retention Test, form C (1974). In this test the child copied a series of simple line drawings consisting of geometric patterns. The model was kept in view throughout. Error scores were adjusted according to critical scores established for chronological age. In the present investigation the disabled readers with poor visual retention constituted over 37% of the disabled population. There were no normal readers with deficient visual memory scores. It is noteworthy that such a large population of reading-disabled children were defective in visuoconstructive skills and placed in the lowest 10th percentile of performance; and that virtually none of the normal control group had a score performance in the lowest 10th percentile. Whatever facility the normal child has in sequential memory, verbal association, and other verbal-related skills, he also has adequate visual retention and copying skills of geometric patterns. This visuomotor ability must be a strong complementary factor to the language cognitive strengths in reading and writing skills.

THE TACTILE TASKS VIEWED AS A COGNITIVE PROCESSING MODEL

The third set of hypotheses presents new relationships among various tactile tasks and assumes that the reading-disabled child benefits from tactile training only within the limits of his own cognitive strengths. His cognitive strengths are limited partly because of the nature of the training instrument used and partly because he himself has limitations in integrating nonverbal and verbal information. We used a tactile training device that projected discontinuous impulses on the palm (DIP), emphasizing spatial analysis. Findings suggested that the reading-disabled child could benefit in the early stages of intersensory integration using nonverbal spatial memory, but that because of his poor verbal memory skills he was at a disadvantage when the spatial and verbal requirements of the stimulus became too demanding. Findings also suggested that when the disabled reader was too intent upon analyzing the spatial dimensions of the stimulus, as in the mechanized stimulation of the DIP, the weaker verbal associations became partly inhibited. The normal child, stronger in nonverbal and verbal integration, was able to combine at a higher level the language and visual memory processes needed in DIP tactile decoding.

Task and Group Comparison

In the present investigation it was anticipated and found that the reading-disabled child's strongest skill using the DIP mechanical instrument was in visual matching, and that his weakest skill was in naming letters. In addition, through analysis of the discontinuous tactile impulses on the palm, the disabled reader enhanced his sense of ideomotor imagery and tactile discrimination in the transfer task with other tactile strategies. He had greater facility in these transfer tasks than he did in naming letters with the DIP instrument itself. By contrast, the normal reader, once trained in the DIP mechanical system, became as competent in this medium as in the manual forms, and his scores in DIP letter-naming were even more accurate than they were in the transfer task of deciphering letters manually drawn on the back of the hand.

As stated earlier, the main assumption of the third hypothesis was that the disabled reader's cognitive strengths in tactile decoding are limited by the nature of the DIP training instrument and by the fact that the disabled child had limitations in integrating the nonverbal and verbal elements of the stimulus and response. One approach in proving this assumption was to compare subjects and tasks in a series of Group by Task by Sex analyses of variance. The findings gave evidence that normal subjects surpassed the disabled, and that the verbal naming response was the most difficult in tasks using the mechanical DIP stimulation.

Intercorrelation Measures

Another approach in assessing whether the disabled-reader has limitations in tactile skills is to compare through correlation measures the number of intercorrelations for normal and disabled readers.

Myklebust, Bannochie, and Killen (1971) had hypothesized that the cognitive structure underlying the reading process is mediated by both nonverbal and verbal systems.

Whereas the normal child is able to integrate these two systems in reading, the reading-disabled child may be deficient in either system. Guthrie (1973) suggests that the reading process requires the presence of component subskills which may be of different strengths but which are nevertheless interdependent. When subtest intercorrelations were computed in the Guthrie and Myklebust studies, the results indicated that the intercorrelations among subtests for normal readers were remarkably frequent, and that the intercorrelations for disabled readers were relatively infrequent.

Similarly, it was assumed in the present investigation that underlying the tactile decoding process the cognitive structure is ideally mediated by both nonverbal and verbal systems, and that a common factor, the integration of these two systems, would account for interfacilitation among the subtasks. It was hypothesized that if visual memory is a strong underlying cognitive component for disabled readers with intact visual memory skills this factor would facilitate integrating the nonverbal and verbal systems, and the level of significant intercorrelations would be numerous in tactile tasks. If, however, visual memory is not a strong underlying cognitive factor for the disabled reader with deficient visual memory skills, the number of intercorrelations among the tactile tasks would be relatively few. The visual memory processes in the latter instance would be too weak to be a prime factor in tactile decoding and to facilitate integration with the verbal systems.

THE TACTILE TESTS

General Description

The original purpose of assessing tactile discrimination in reading-disabled children was to evaluate how tactile learning could be incorporated into a curriculum. Methods employed to investigate tactile discrimination are diverse, and one kind of tactile stimulation may not produce the same findings as another. The investigation reported here deals with a precise and difficult set of tactile tasks that require figure-ground, spatial, directional, and visual imagery. Regardless of whether the child has been tactilely trained by the DIP technique, it is easier for him to recognize letters drawn on the back of the hand than to recognize a series of discontinuous impulses on the palm such as received in the DIP technique. It may also be easier for both the trained and untrained child to recognize letters by passive hand movement than by the DIP method.

The experimental design required an elaborate conceptual framework. More than one kind of tactile stimulation has to be used to study cognitive patterns in transfer and serial ordering. Core problems are the comparison of age, adequacy of copying ability, and amount of tactile training within the learning-disabled population. Other considerations are contingent on these variables, such as the complexity of the tactile stimulus, the fact that it might activate underlying processes in a transfer skill in the kinesthetic mode, the kinds of memory requirements involved, the presence or lack of timing requirements in the stimulus, and the nature of the response. Implicit in any investigation of the tactile mode, even when it is limited to lower-case alphabet letter discrimination, as in this study, is the assumption that the tactile sense does not act in isolation, or in the same way for comparable sets of tasks. Each tactile task is indicating how certain sensory mechanisms are being influenced and whether the task is within the scope of the child's capacities to use either spatial imagery or verbal cues or both in the decoding process.

Three Kinds of Tactile Stimulation

Three kinds of tactile stimulation were assessed as a basis of evaluating group differences on task performance and task differences for the various groups. The first type of tactile stimulation was used for the first time with any group of children. The system, designed by Schevill and Kwatney, consisted of a computerized keyboard and a tactile display. The tactile display produced a series of points or discontinuous impulses on the palm of the hand (DIP). The child placed his hand on the flat surface of the tactile matrix (a box 3 x 3½ in.) and felt a series of dots or points that touched his hand and formed a specific letter. The surface of the tactile box had a matrix of indentations (7 columns and 7 rows). When the tactile box was activated by a computerized stimulus generator, one-by-one, small lucite pegs protruded 1/16 of an inch beyond the surface of the box, touched the child's hand at an even predetermined rate, and formed the impressions of a letter. These impulses were converted in the child's mind to a sense of the spatial movement used to form lower-case alphabet letters.

The second type of stimulation was not purely tactile, but rather tactile-kinesthetic. The teacher steered the child's passive hand (PH), taking his forefinger and tracing specific forms of letters on a flat 4-in. surface of the desk. The child, sight-occluded, deduced the letters from his own involuntary finger action.

The third type of stimulation was manual "drawing" of letters on the back of the child's hand (BOH), which was done by lightly "drawing" with a stylus or blunted tip of a ballpoint pen specific lower-case letters on the back of the hand. The child, sight-occluded, deduced the letters from the tactile contact.

The entire group of tactile tests assessed a spatial and motoric concept of letter formation as well as ability to relate verbal labels to tactile or tactile-kinesthetic stimuli. It is evident that the mechanical mode of stimulation in all the DIP tasks requires a more astute perception of figure-ground ability, spatial directionality, and visual memory than the manually stimulated tasks in the PH and BOH categories. The discontinuous tactile impulses of the DIP tasks present the added problem of deducing letter forms from fragmented parts. The strict time framework of stimulus presentation in the DIP technique forces the child to attend more keenly than he usually does to letter directionality and

Fig. 1. SCHEMATIC REPRESENTATION OF THREE LOWER-CASE LETTERS, *b, i, t,* AS THEY APPEAR ONE-BY-ONE ON THE TACTILE MATRIX.

The circled dots in Figure 1 indicate the pegs which are activated in succession, with a 60-msec time interval between each. The directionality of each letter agrees with the way the children are taught to draw the letters. Thus, the motion descends for the first segment of *b*, and is then completed by the semicircle descending. The *i* first has the descending motion and then is completed with the dot. The *t* first has the descending motion and then the cross bar from left to right. As soon as one peg appears, the pressure of the palm against the tactile matrix forces the peg to recede. Thus, only one peg protrudes at a time.

sequence. The brisk interpoint rate is 60 msec, and the relatively short interval between letters in the serial ordering skills is only 1 sec.

The PH tasks bring into play the kinesthetic element in conjunction with the tactile. Now the child analyzes the external space through the movement he is involuntarily making as his fingertip glides over the flat surface. He must keep in mind how each letter relates to a verbal label. As the task becomes more difficult, he is required to recall the temporal order of pairs of letters; and, finally, in one PH task he must execute and replicate the motor actions his own forefinger just made involuntarily with another person's guidance.

The BOH tasks are a simpler version of tactile letter decoding than the DIP series. In these the child attends to the manual stimulus on the back of his hand. The rate at which each letter is "drawn" is fairly slow: similar to the speed with which a teacher would draw a letter on the blackboard. The child is not required to force his attention on the fractional elements of the movement and spatial relationships; nor is he required to decode sequential tactile letters at a brisk predetermined rate used in DIP technique.

Within the DIP, PH, and BOH categories are sets of skills designed to assess the reading-disabled child's cross-modal processing skills by tactile stimulation under a variety of conditions. The tasks were designed to answer questions about serial-spatial order, transfer ability in ideomotor recognition of letters, age-related facility, the relative ease in which the child can decode BOH versus PH and DIP skills, the effect of poor visual memory skills on serial ordering, and the comparison of visual with verbal responses.

DIP Tasks

Ten Letters: Naming for Left and Right Hand. This involves identifying by name the single letters after perceiving the series of dots on the palm by the DIP mechanical instrumentation. The right and left hands are tested separately. A total of 10 letters is presented to each hand: NL (naming for left) and NR (naming for right).

Ten Letters: Visual Matching. The tactile movement of the DIP technique is matched to appropriate visual representations, without naming the letters. The same series of 10 lower-case letters is used for stimulation as in naming. Each hand is tested separately: VL (visual left) and VR (visual right).

Serial Ordering. This task involves serial ordering of the letters *c* and *l* for children between 5 and 7 years of age, and serial ordering of the letters *c, l,* and *s* for children between 7 and 9 years of age. This is the only task that has an easier version for the younger group and a more difficult version for the older group. Two versions were used because the disabled child under 7 years had difficulty in serial recall of a chain containing three different letters, whereas the older child could keep this many in storage. In the stimulus dimension the sequence was timed by the DIP computer. Each letter occurred on the palm in 1-sec intervals. The sequences started with two or three characters and increased in length to five characters in randomized order for the young children using only the letters *c* and *l*, to seven characters in a chain for the older children using the letters *c, l,* and *s.*

Two kinds of responses were required. In each one the child was required to decode and store in his memory the tactile letter order of the characters which he was told he would feel. The first ordering task required an oral-naming response, SERN (serial naming). The child named the entire chain of letters. The next serial-ordering task required a visual-matching response, SERV (serial visual). Here the response was a visual matching of the entire chain after each timed sequence. In this task the response required a left-to-right visuospatial matching of the temporal order of tactile letters. For response, the child selected one visual pattern from a multiple array. The shift from a temporal to a spatial organization in this task was to test the relationship of serial order and visuospatial imagery.

PH Tasks

The passive hand task with single letters was called PHS. The teacher steered the left hand, specifically the forefinger, over the flat surface to draw 10 lower-case letters. For response the child must name each letter as it was drawn passively. His sight was occluded. This task was given to assess the relationship of age-related factors to training—specifically to test the hypothesis that young children easily develop an ideomotor image of letter movement through DIP tactile training. The task was used also to assess the strong bond of verbal imagery interacting with ideomotor imagery. At the end of the study this task was assessed.

PHP.   This task, involving the passive motor action of a pair of letters (PHP), differs from the preceding task only by the fact that two letters are used in the tactile-kinesthetic stimulus instead of one. The child analyzed the temporal order of his own passive movement in finger-drawing pairs of letters as the teacher steered his hand on a flat surface. He must recall both the letter names in correct order; sight was occluded.

PHMM.   The third version of the passive motor action of the hand is the most difficult of the PH tasks. Here the child must reproduce from memory and by his own voluntary finger action the letter forms he has just made by the passive action of his hand: PHMM (passive-hand motor memory). The stimulus contained patterns of letters in groups of two and three. Thus the task required ideomotor imagery, serial-order recall, and ability to reconstruct and program appropriate movements for forming the succession of letters. This task was introduced to assess how levels of visual memory might influence the response which required a temporal-spatial-motoric image of multiple letters.

BOH Tasks

Two types of BOH tasks were used. The simpler task consisted of tactile discrimination of single letters manually drawn with a stylus or a similar instrument on the back of the hand (BOHS); sight was occluded. The child identified the continuous movement of the blunted instrument by naming the letter drawn. The stimulus consisted of 10 single lower-case letters. A more difficult version of the preceding task consisted of presenting pairs of letters in the tactile stimulus instead of single letters. The child must name the specified pairs in correct temporal order (BOHP).

The BOH tasks, which are easier than the DIP tasks, were given as transfer skills halfway through the experiment (after only 5 hr of specific training of the DIP technique). The BOH tests were given to assess the correlation of visual memory skills and to assess the relative ease with which children could decode letters by this method, as opposed to the mechanized DIP method.

METHODS AND PROCEDURES

Reading-Disabled Children

The original total number of reading-disabled subjects for this study was 162, including 96 children who were specifically trained on the tactile mechanism (TT) and 66 children not trained (NT). In one task (DIP naming of letters), a pre- and posttest were administered to the TT group. In this instance their pretest scores were compared to their posttest scores. In all other tasks the TT group was tested only after 3½ months of specific training. As a basis of comparison, a control group of reading-disabled children was selected to match the experimental group 1 year after the experimental group had been trained and tested. Only right-handed children were used in the analysis.

The disabled subjects in the TT group were selected from the school populations of the Cornman School for Learning Disabilities and from two satellite schools in the Philadelphia Public School System. All children were given a battery of psychological tests by school authorities; neurologists gave many of these children a neurologic screening as well. All of the children had specific reading problems. Among them at least six had expressive language problems, and another six had severe visuomotor problems. The remainder had varying degrees of dysfunction in auditory, visual, and motor skills. None had hearing loss, blindness, or primary emotional disorders. All of the disabled children were in special classes for the reading-disabled, and it was presumed that these children would be mainstreamed within 4 years of that special instruction.

The fairly small subsample comparing the two segments of disabled readers (TT and NT) resulted only after two consecutive years of testing; there were not enough children under 7 years of age during the first year to designate a control group. Therefore, the selection of a control group of disabled readers was delayed until the second year of the program. The disabled children within the experimental and control groups were well matched according to numbers, sex, IQ, age, race, and general socioeconomic background (middle class). They had been screened by the same psychologists and were receiving classroom instruction from the same teachers. They were tested on the tactile tasks by the same aides and psychologists. They were all right-handed after being tested on 10 informal measures of hand preference, hand-writing, and relative motor accuracy in tracing skills with both hands (Ayres Motor Accuracy Test, 1972).

All children in the study had at least a score of 80 on the Performance Score of the Wechsler Intelligence Scale for Children (1949). The mean full score for each group was 96. Within the TT group at Cornman there were 16 subjects between 5 and 7 years of age, and 28 subjects between 7 and 9 years of age. There were 33 boys and 11 girls in the sample, or a proportion of 3:1 between boys and girls. The NT group contained 18 subjects between 5 and 7 years, and 33 subjects between 7 and 9 years of age. There were 37 boys and 15 girls in the NT group. There were 12 Blacks in the TT group and 10 in the NT group. Their IQ ranged between 90 and 110. The remaining subjects were all Caucasian. The children between the ages of 5 and 7 were virtually nonreaders. In a preliminary alphabet-recognition test more than half of them knew only the letter symbols of their own first name. The children between the ages of 7 and 9 had a first-grade average in reading, as shown by standardized reading tests.

One of the problems in initiating early intervention programs is the scarcity of children diagnosed and screened out as high risk before 7 years of age. The present investigation took place in a large city school district where children are carefully screened. Fewer than 30 children under 7 years were designated as potentially learning-disabled, and all were at the Cornman School.

Normal Children

A normal sample of children was used as a means of comparing the performance of the reading-disabled. The normal sample was selected from one private and three public schools in Philadelphia. The public schools children were from the second, third, and fourth grades, and those from the private school comprised almost all of its kindergarten and first-grade children. No child had a history of reading disabilities. On the other hand, no child in the normal sample was selected who was superior in reading. Each was selected by teachers as being average in reading ability. Each child was within grade level in standardized reading tests administered by the school district. No IQ measures were available for the normal sample. The schools served a middle-class community, similar to the backgrounds of the children in the disabled groups. The final number of normal children who were right-handed was 109. Of this total group, 63 were trained in tactile letter decoding for 3 months, and 46 were tested but not trained. The division between boys and girls in the trained group was (young) 7 boys and 6 girls; and (old) 17 boys and 15 girls. The division between the sexes in the untrained group was (young) 8 boys and 6 girls, and (old) 17 boys and 15 girls.

Two sets of statistical analyses were made. The first set compared TT and NT subjects within the disabled-reading group, and again within the normal-reading group. The number of subjects reported constituted the within-group comparisons for the disabled and normal groups. In these kinds of comparisons, the TT and NT children came from one school within the disabled group, and from another school within the normal group. The second set of analyses contrasted normal and reading-disabled children within the trained categories. Here the groups were somewhat enlarged and included normal and disabled children from other elementary schools, as well as the ones used in the first set of analyses. Tables 1 to 3 refer to the smaller groups of children used in within-group comparisons. Tables 4 to 8 refer to the larger groups of trained children used in between-group comparisons.

The Tactile Training Groups

For approximately 3½ months each child in the normal and disabled groups received tactile training by coming to the tactile laboratory in each school for one 15-min session twice a week. The children between 5 and 7 years of age were trained to recognize the following letters: *m, e, b, a, s, o, n, i, t,* and *c*. These letters were taught in pairs so that the child could distinguish salient features of the letters and compare them with each other. Whenever possible, the letter pairs formed words such as *no, so, it, is, be, me,* and *at*. Children between 7 and 9 years of age also learned to recognize the specified 10 letters in pairs. In addition they learned the tactile forms for *p, a, h, d,* and *k*. Subjects were trained to match visual sequences with the tactile in word formations such as *mat mad*, or *cat sat*. All lessons were mimeographed for replicability. The TT children (in the disabled and normal samples) received a total of approximately 10 hr of tactile training by two teachers, two aides, and two psychologists.

Tactile Training on the Left Hand

During the 3½-month period between the pre- and posttests all the tactile training was done only on the child's left palm. Thus, his right hand was left free to write the letters that his left hand was feeling when the task required a written response. The tactile decoding was unfamiliar to the child and fairly difficult to decipher in aspects of directionality and form discrimination. The left hand decoded, and the right hand interpreted.

The rationale in using the left hand for tactile training was based primarily on the practical considerations that it was easy for the child to have his right hand free to select visual cards with the appropriate word patterns or to write the response while his left hand remained fixed on the tactile box. Findings have suggested that the learning-disabled child is superior in left-hand tactile manipulation of letter shapes (Witelson, 1976), and that unsighted children are superior on their left hands in Braille decoding (Hermelin and O'Connor, 1971). Tactile shape discrimination has been shown to depend primarily on the contralateral or crossed somesthetic functions (Sperry, Gazzaniga, and Bogen, 1969). Inasmuch as the child probably would first figure out the tactile shape and reduce the moving series of dots to a gestalt, he would be using the right-hemisphere processes even before the left. In a pilot study of a subsample of normal subjects (not used in this project), half were trained on their right, and the other half were trained on their left hands.

The findings indicated no significant differences with either hand between the two groups. We do not know whether there would be a significant difference between hands for those trained on the left as opposed to the right within a reading-disabled group, since no comparisons in training hand were made for that group. A recent study pertaining to left-handed LD children between 7 and 9 years of age (Schevill, in press) suggests that training on the nonpreferred hand facilitates bilateral tactile learning, and that left-handers are more accurate in tactile decoding on their untrained preferred hand than on the trained one. The study showed that the same kind of discrepancy between hands did not occur for right-handed children with adequate or with poor visual memory. They were equally accurate on both hands within levels of visual memory skills.

Tests

At the conclusion of the experimental training period, all children were given the series of tests individually to assess tactile decoding and ideomotor imagery with and without verbalization in the response.

The children from the normal and disabled groups who received no tactile training (NT) were given a practice session with the tactile mechanism before any official test. When specific pairs of letters were to be named or recalled in sequential patterns, the NTs were given a short preliminary period of drill in seeing, naming, and feeling the specified pair of letters. All testing was individually administered in the tactile laboratory in each school. Only one test was given during a session. If both hands were tested in specific tests, half of the children were first tested on the right, and the other half on the left hands.

STATISTICAL ANALYSES, RESULTS, AND IMPLICATIONS

Hypothesis 1: Ideomotor and Visual Matching Concepts

Passive hand task. The main method used to assess the results between young and old reading-disabled children in visual matching and in ideomotor imagery was through analysis of variance. For the PHS task in the disabled group there were two main factors: Age and Training. Only the left hand was tested for this task within the disabled group, and so no comparison of Side was made. (Both hands were tested within the normal group for the PHS task.) A mixed design analysis of variance was carried out with two between factors, Age and Training, and one within factor, left and right side. Table 1 enumerates the main effects as well as the interaction terms for the two analyses of variance in the passive hand task for normal and disabled readers.

The only main effect shown for the reading-disabled group was Training ($df = 1/92$, $F = 6.07$, $p < .05$). Since the young and old segments of the trained disabled subsample achieved the same error scores, there was no main effect for Age. Accuracy increased with training similarly for the young trained normal group as it did for the disabled group. The old trained normal group reached criterion level on both hands, and the young trained normal group almost reached criterion level on the left but not on the right hand. Comparisons using simple main effects of differences between sides within the trained and untrained groups indicated that there were fewer errors for the young group on the left than on the right hands ($df = 1/85$, $F = 11.25$, $p < .01$). There was no difference between the young and old on the left side. Right-hand scores did not differ significantly between the trained and untrained young segments.

Visual matching tasks.   The second task in which it was anticipated that the young high-risk child could perform relatively well was in the tactile-visual matching of single letters (VR and VL). Here both hands were tested for the disabled and for the normal. Within each group the left and right hands were analyzed as a within factor, Side; and Training and Age were analyzed as between factors in two analysis of variance designs. The results from both the reading-disabled and the normal groups' analyses are summarized in Table 2.

Table 1

PASSIVE HAND RECOGNITION OF SINGLE LETTERS (PHS): MEAN ERROR SCORES FOR NORMAL AND DISABLED READERS

	Normal Readers							
	Trained			Untrained			Total	N
	Right Hand	Left Hand	N	Right Hand	Left Hand	N		
Young	.20	.08	13	.27	.28	15	.21	28
Old	.01	.01	20	.12	.12	41	.08	61
Total	.08	.04	33	.16	.16	56		

Summary of Analyses of Variance for Normal Readers:
Significant Main Factors and Interaction Effects

Age:	$df = 1/85$, $F = 32.06$, $p < .001$
Training:	$df = 1/85$, $F = 23.15$, $p < .001$
Side by Age by Training:	$df = 1/85$, $F = 4.89$, $p < .05$

	Disabled Readers							
	Right Hand	Left Hand	N	Right Hand	Left Hand	N	Total	N
Young		.18	16		.37	18	.28	34
Old		.18	28		.21	34	.20	62
Total		.18	44		.27	52		

Summary of Analyses of Variance for Disabled Readers:
Significant Main Factor

Training:	$df = 1/92$, $F = 6.07$, $p < .05$

Table 2

TACTILE TO VISUAL MATCHING OF SINGLE LETTERS (VR, VL): MEAN ERROR SCORES FOR NORMAL AND DISABLED READERS

Normal Readers

| | Trained | | | Untrained | | | | |
	Right Hand	Left Hand	N	Right Hand	Left Hand	N	Total	N
Young	.20	.15	13	.28	.29	15	.23	28
Old	.07	.08	20	.20	.16	41	.17	61
Total	.12	.11	33	.22	.19	56		

Summary of Analyses of Variance for Normal Readers:
Significant Main Factors

Training:	$df = 1/85, F = 12.14, p < .001$
Age:	$df = 1/85, F = 11.31, p < .001$

Disabled Readers

| | Trained | | | Untrained | | | | |
	Right Hand	Left Hand	N	Right Hand	Left Hand	N	Total	N
Young	.43	.36	16	.61	.55	18	.49	34
Old	.39	.40	28	.35	.34	34	.37	62
Total	.40	.39	44	.44	.43	52		

Summary of Analyses of Variance for Disabled Readers:
Significant Main Factors and Interaction Effects

Age:	$df = 1/92, F = 8.79, p < .01$
Training by Age:	$df = 1/92, F = 21.67, p < .001$

The findings from the disabled group in the VR/VL performance indicate a significant interaction of Age and Training. The young trained segment "caught up" with the old segment; the only difference between the young and old was within the untrained subsample ($df = 1/92$, $F = 21.67$, $p < .001$). The findings from the normal group in the same task indicate a significant main effect for Age ($df = 1/85$, $F = 11.31$; $p < .001$), and a significant main effect for Training ($df = 1/85$, $F = 12.14$; $p < .001$).

Implications.   In both tasks, the PHS and the VR/VL, the young disabled readers displayed vigor in acquiring cross-modal skills through tactile training, whereas the old disabled readers showed a kind of lassitude. In both tasks the young normal readers displayed a spurt of learning as a result of the tactile training, and the old normals either reached criterion level or reached almost that point after training. This set of analyses showed similar trends for the young segments in the normal and disabled groups, and dissimilar trends for the old segments.

Clearly these analyses indicate the powerful effect of the mechanized tactile stimulation for the young high-risk child. These findings strongly imply that training in the DIP technique activates intersensory functioning with concentration on the spatial dimensions of letters. By contrast, the old reading-disabled child might be less concerned with the spatial analysis of each letter than with wondering, "What letter is this?"

In a comparison of the normal sample with the reading-disabled, two findings are noteworthy. First, the old segment of normal children responded to tactile training in these simple cross-modal skills and was consistently better than the young segment. By contrast, the old segment of reading-disabled children was not consistently better than the young group in the two single cross-modal tasks after DIP training. Second, the fact that both the young disabled and the young trained normal groups made successful transfer to the PHS task signifies that there is a strong bond between the tactile and kinesthetic modalities. The fact that transfer occurred specifically on the left hand for the young normal group implies that this particular age level is using a greater degree of spatial than verbal processing for this task. Since only the left hand was tested in the PHS task within the group of disabled readers, no firm assumptions can be made about the relative sensitivity of one hand versus the other for the disabled groups.

Research in cross-modal matching implies that differences exist between the backward reader and the normal even when the subjects are all within the normal range (Muehl and Kremenak, 1966). Although the difference in cross-modal matching between the normal and disabled is a significant issue, it is less important than the finding that the young disabled reader can learn basic intersensory skills using the tactile, kinesthetic, and visual modalities in mediation for verbal decoding.

This is the first report that describes a method of tactile instruction for eliciting ideomotor imagery as a transfer skill. In an informal pilot study where disabled readers were trained in tactile letter decoding on the back of the hand, there was no carry-over to ideomotor imagery, even though the experimental group received almost perfect scores in the tactile tasks themselves. The concentration on the fragmented moving line projected by the DIP mechanical instrumentation probably is responsible for the elicitation of ideomotor images of letter movement and formation.

It is impressive to watch a young disabled child selectively focus his attention on the DIP tactile, then on the ideomotor, visual, and auditory dimensions of individual letters, word beginnings and word endings. Since reading-related skills require a shift from one modality to another, the findings thus far indicate that DIP training would be valuable in developing facility and flexibility in intersensory processing, using spatial dimension as a point of reference. These skills provide the basis for better integration of spatial and notational elements in more complex reading and spelling.

The findings have significance for the educator as well as for the psychologist. For the psychologist the findings imply that the young disabled child cognitively relates external tactile movement to external space—that he can internalize external movement and analyze kinesthetic passive movement in terms of notational labels. For the educator the findings imply that the young disabled child is responsive to tactile DIP training, and that one of its benefits is stress on ideomotor imagery and associations of letter names. Thus, passive ideomotor action can be used interchangeably in future curricula with tactile stimulation in evoking cross-modal associations with visual, auditory, and kinesthetic processes in visual matching, reading, and writing exercises.

Little research has been done to demonstrate how sensory-integrative processes using tactile stimuli can be developed as a result of training. The findings of this study provide data which educators such as Montessori (1964) and Fernald (1943) knew intuitively in their remarkable teaching in the fields of special education and learning disabilities—namely, that tactile/kinesthetic practice fosters intersensory associations with visual and auditory information. The findings lend support to leading educators' wisdom in dealing with remediation for the young disabled child. Myklebust (1975) writes;

In some children rather than attempting to raise the level of function in a given area of deficit, it is necessary to raise the level of intercommunication among cognitive systems. By doing so, a higher level of integration of all experience is obtained, which in turn increases the ability to function with depth of meaning (p. 107).

Hypothesis 2: Serial Order and Poor Visual Memory

The second group of hypotheses referred to the kinds of serial-ordering tasks in which the disabled child with deficient visual memory might be less proficient than the disabled child with adequate visual memory. An analysis of variance was performed on each task in the DIP, PH, and BOH categories, with the three main factors, Age by Training by Levels of Visual Memory. If the factor of Visual Memory was significant in serial-ordering tasks requiring a serial-spatial synthesis and not for those requiring a verbal recall, the findings would support the assumption that the deficits in serial ordering for children with poor copying skills are correlated with a spatial factor.

The data in Table 3 corroborate the assumption that tasks that involve conversion of a serial order to a spatial context are difficult for the child with poor visual memory. Specifically serial ordering of tactile letters with a visual-matching response (SERV) required such a conversion. This task was relatively more difficult for the subgroup with poor visual retention than for the group with adequate visual retention. Serial order of letters in passive hand movement with a written motor response (PHMM) also required such a conversion, and was especially difficult for the subgroup with poor visual memory.

Implications.   The findings imply that within the training group of disabled readers the serial-ordering skills, requiring either a visual matching (SERV) or a finger-written response (PHMM) were sensitive to differences in visual retention. By contrast, SERN, another serial-ordering skill with a verbal response, was not sensitive to these differences. Two other serial-ordering tasks also required a verbal response. One task was identifying, in correct order, pairs of letters drawn manually on the back of the hand (BOHP), and the other task was identifying pairs of letters drawn with the childs' own passive hand movement (PHP). There was no difference between the disabled readers with adequate and deficient memory skills in these serial-ordering skills with a verbal response. Finally, there was no difference between subgroups in any of the simpler single letter tasks except the tactile naming of the left hand using the DIP system of stimulation. In that one task, (DIP NL) children with adequate visual memory were more accurate than children with deficient visual memory.

Table 4 enumerates the mean error scores for the three tactile tasks in which visual memory was a significant main factor. An inspection of the mean scores indicates that those children with deficient visual memory were not consistently poor in tactile decoding. The old with deficient visual memory skills were almost as competent as the old with adequate visual memory. By contrast the young with deficient visual memory were less accurate in tactile decoding than the young with adequate visual memory. Young children with deficient visual memory were at a disadvantage in letter decoding through the tactile sense. They had not yet learned the letters by visual recognition, and could not rely on tactile decoding as a strategy to evoke verbal associations. The problem was accentuated in serial-ordering skills requiring a temporal-spatial synthesis.

These results have a negative implication. They imply that children with poor visual retention skills will have poor spatial orientation in tactile decoding, just as they have in visual decoding. Tactile practice in serial-ordering processing will not correct reversal

Table 3

EFFECTS OF VISUAL MEMORY, AGE, AND TRAINING ON DISABLED READERS' TACTILE PERFORMANCE: SUMMARY OF ANALYSES OF VARIANCE

| | Main Effects | | | | | | Benton Visual Memory | | | Interaction Effects Age by Training | | |
| | Training | | | Age | | | | | | | | |
Task	d/f	F	p	d/f	F	p	d/f	F	p	d/f	F	p
DIP naming, right	1/72	21.23	.01	1/72	13.18	.01						
DIP naming, left	1/72	14.70	.001	1/72	10.64	.01	1/72	5.46	.01	1/88	7.33	.01*
DIP visual matching, right				1/88	14.73	.000				1/88	6.76	.01*
DIP visual matching, left												
DIP serial order, naming	1/67	58.99	.001	Implicit in difference in content								
DIP serial order, visual matching	1/67	16.39	.001	Implicit in difference in content			1/67	4.86	.05			
Passive hand, single letters	1/88	6.75	.05	1/88	7.69	.01						
Passive hand, pairs				1/67	14.15	.001	1/67	6.34	.01			
Passive hand, motor memory	1/88	5.26	.05	1/88	5.54	.05						
Back-of-hand, single letters	1/88	6.25	.01	1/88	7.40	.01						
Back-of-hand, pairs of letters												

*No difference between young and old in trained group.

164

Table 4

MEAN ERROR SCORES FOR DISABLED READERS: DIP NAMING-LEFT, SERIAL-VISUAL, PASSIVE HAND-MOTOR MEMORY

Age	Adequate Visual Memory				Deficient Visual Memory			
	Trained	N	Untrained	N	Trained	N	Untrained	N
DIP Naming, Left Hand								
Young	.66	12	.79	12	.81	4	.88	4
Old	.39	34	.69	34	.39	26	.59	26
Total	.46	46	.72	46	.45	30	.63	30
Serial-Visual								
Young	.40	12	.58	5	.58	4	.73	6
Old	.33	14	.63	12	.44	14	.65	8
Total	.36	26	.62	17	.47	18	.68	14
Passive Hand-Motor Memory								
Young	.56	12	.56	5	.74	4	.65	6
Old	.41	14	.44	12	.57	14	.44	8
Total	.48	26	.48	17	.61	18	.53	14

problems in reading. Children with poor visual retention might be able to decode successive letters such as *no* through DIP training and transduce the two letters to the appropriate word when no visual model is supplied or where no written response is required. Yet these children will be likely to point to the word *on* when they match a visual representation to the temporal succession of letters just perceived on the tactile box.

Hypothesis 3: Limited Integration of Spatial and Verbal Elements

The third set of assumptions considered two approaches in evaluating the integration of spatial and verbal cognitive systems in tactile decoding. In the first approach, it was anticipated and found that the disabled reader's weakest skill was in naming letters with DIP mechanical stimulation. In the second approach it was anticipated that a common underlying factor in tactile task correlations was the integration of spatial and verbal components. Results indicated that the pattern of intercorrelation for the disabled reader with adequate visual memory was different for the disabled reader with deficient visual memory. These findings imply that within the disabled group adequate visual memory was a positive cognitive factor in tactile decoding by making a connection with the verbal system. Thus adequate spatial analysis could account for a limited source of integration between the nonverbal and verbal cognitive systems.

Task and Group Comparisons in Analyses of Variance

The first approach, evaluating the unevenness in cognitive processing skills for the reading-disabled, was by analysis of variance. The variables, Tasks by Groups by Sex, were the main factors in ANOVAS performed separately for the young and old trained groups of normal and reading-disabled children. The first set of analyses of variance compared the children's scores in three sets of letter-naming tasks: (a) DIP tasks when the stimulation occurred mechanically by the discontinuous tapping impulses on the left and right hands; (b) PH tasks, by the passive hand movement in evoking an ideomotor image of the letter; and (c) BOH taskes, by manual tracing of letters on the back of the hand. In each instance, the response was the oral naming of 10 single letters.

The findings shown in Table 5 indicate a significant main effect for Group—namely that normal readers were more accurate in task performance than disabled readers and a significant main effect for Task. There were no main effects for Sex.

Duncan Multiple Range Tests (1955) qualified the main effects and revealed that for the old normal readers the mechanized DIP tactile naming task was more difficult ($p<.01$) than either the back-of-the-hand or passive-hand tasks. The findings also indicated for the old normal readers that the passive-hand task was the easiest of the naming tasks. For the old disabled readers, the passive-hand and back-of-the-hand tasks were equally easy and both easier than the DIP naming task. The Group-by-Task interaction effect, when further analyzed for the old group, showed that the normal readers surpassed the disabled beyond the .01 level of significance in all naming tasks except the back of the hand in single letters.

Passive hand: $df = 1/89;$ $F = 26.66;$ $p<.01$
Naming for right hand: $df = 1/89;$ $F = 48.09;$ $p<.01$
Naming for left hand: $df = 1/89;$ $F = 113.81;$ $p<.01$

Within the young trained sample the Duncan Multiple Range Tests showed no differences among naming tasks for the normal readers. There were differences, however, among tasks for the disabled group; the PHS task was the easiest, and the DIP naming task

Table 5

NAMING SINGLE LETTERS: MEAN ERROR SCORES FOR TRAINED NORMAL AND DISABLED READERS

		Normal Readers						Disabled Readers					
		Young Mean			Old Mean			Young Mean			Old Mean		
Task	Sex	Error	SD	N	Error	SD	N	Error	SD	N	Error	SD	N
DIP	M	.32	.24	7	.17	.19	17	.72	.26	10	.48	.23	48
Naming right	F	.27	.19	6	.14	.11	16	.64	.16	6	.53	.20	12
DIP	M	.29	.20	7	.17	.13	17	.63	.27	10	.47	.22	48
Naming left	F	.22	.50	6	.18	.18	16	.81	.16	6	.49	.27	12
Passive hand	M	.26	.35	7	.05	.09	17	.22	.21	10	.21	.17	48
Naming left	F	.13	.28	6	.05	.07	16	.12	.12	6	.22	.17	12
Back of hand	M	.36	.14	7	.33	.19	17	.42	.27	10	.28	.16	48
Naming left	F	.28	.12	6	.34	.17	16	.37	.24	6	.24	.20	12

Summary of Analyses of Variance:
Significant Main Factors and Interaction Effects

Old Readers
Group	$df = 1/89,$	$F = 43.21,$	$p<.001$
Task	$df = 3/267,$	$F = 23.36,$	$p<.001$
Group by Task	$df = 1/277,$	$F = 23.36,$	$p<.001$

Young Readers
Group	$df = 1/25,$	$F = 11.74,$	$p<.01$
Task	$df = 3/75,$	$F = 20.60,$	$p<.001$
Group by Task	$df = 3/75,$	$F = 13.94,$	$p<.001$

was the most difficult. The Group-by-Task analysis, when further analyzed for the young sample, indicated that between the normal and disabled readers a highly significant difference existed in the mechanical DIP naming. Normals were superior to the disabled on the left hand ($df = 1/25$; $F = 27.50$; $p<.001$) and on the right hand ($df = 1/25$; $F = 47.00$; $p<.001$). There was no difference between the young normal and young disabled, however, in the PH and BOH naming tasks.

The second set of analyses of variance, summarized in Table 6, itemizes the results when the two DIP single-letter-naming tasks for the left and right hands were compared with the DIP visual matching of single letters for the left and right hands. The results indicate a significant main effect for Group. In each analysis the normal reader surpassed the disabled. No Sex differences were found. The main effects for Task were qualified by interaction effects of Group by Task. Duncan Multiple Range Tests showed Group differences between the tasks. The disabled readers, both young and old, were significantly more competent in the visual matching than in the verbal naming. The old normal readers were as competent in the naming as they were in the visual matching. The young normal readers were more competent in the visual matching on the left hand than in naming on the right hand. Otherwise their scores between tasks were similar.

From the evidence in Table 6, we see that the reading-disabled child is able to make intersensory associations in tactile visual processing but has difficulty in naming tactile letters. The normal child, when trained, is just as accurate, however, in naming letters as in pointing to the visual representation.

Implications. When compared to skills focusing only on spatial information, the oral-naming tactile tasks were extremely difficult for the reading-disabled child. The findings imply that an enormous gap exists between the two cognitive systems: spatial and verbal processing. In the present experiment the tactile training was reinforcing the disabled reader's spatial skills. DIP training did not develop an adequate facility in spatial-language integration. DIP training for the normal reader, however, did facilitate the integration of the visual system with the verbal. He could perform the more difficult naming tasks almost as well as the visual-matching skills.

The implications from these findings are that the disabled readers are using visual imagery skills in the DIP mechanized tactile decoding process because for most disabled readers these are their cognitive strengths when compared to letter-naming skills. If the tactile visual-matching skills were adapted in regular curricular activities to contain language cues, disabled children could be learning spatial-language integration and would not be so limited in tactile processing of both of these elements.

Table 7 summarizes serial-ordering skills with a naming and visual response when the stimulus is the timed sequence of letters with the DIP instrumentation. Group by Task by Sex analyses of variance showed significant main Group and Task effects for young and old. The normal were significantly more accurate than the disabled, and the visual-matching response was consistently easier than the naming response. There were no significant main effects for Sex.

Intercorrelation Measures for
Three Groups

The second approach of evaluating underlying cognitive processes was by comparing intercorrelation measures. The DIP tasks, using mechanical stimulation, were correlated with tasks using manual stimulation, BOH and PH, in Pearson r analyses. In analyzing the

Table 6

NAMING COMPARED TO VISUAL MATCHING RESPONSE: MEAN ERROR SCORES FOR TRAINED NORMAL AND DISABLED READERS

| | | Normal Readers | | | | | | Disabled Readers | | | | | |
| | | Young Mean Error | SD | N | Old Mean Error | SD | N | Young Mean Error | SD | N | Old Mean Error | SD | N |
Task	Sex												
DIP	M	.28	.25	8	.16	.17	23	.67	.24	15	.47	.24	43
Naming right	F	.27	.19	6	.09	.10	29	.64	.16	6	.53	.20	12
DIP	M	.27	.20	8	.17	.13	23	.64	.24	15	.45	.22	43
Naming left	F	.22	.21	6	.11	.16	29	.81	.15	6	.49	.27	12
Visual	M	.23	.07	8	.15	.12	23	.40	.17	15	.33	.19	43
Right	F	.17	.12	6	.11	.12	29	.45	.22	6	.40	.18	12
Visual	M	.20	.15	8	.17	.15	23	.37	.20	15	.32	.22	43
Left	F	.08	.11	6	.12	.13	29	.37	.34	6	.33	.21	.12

Summary of Analyses of Variance:
Significant Main Factors and Interaction Effects

Old Readers
Group $df = 1/103$, $F = 81.86$, $p < .001$
Task $df = 3/309$, $F = 8.09$, $p < .001$
Group by Task $df = 3/309$, $F = 11.14$, $p < .001$

Young Readers
Group $df = 1/31$, $F = 31.12$, $p < .001$
Task $df = 3/93$, $F = 20.33$, $p < .001$
Group by Task $df = 3/93$, $F = 6.21$, $p < .001$

Table 7

SERIAL ORDERING WITH A VISUAL MATCHING OR NAMING RESPONSE: MEAN ERROR SCORES FOR TRAINED NORMAL AND DISABLED READERS

| | | Normal Readers | | | | | | Disabled Readers | | | | | |
| | | Young Mean Error | SD | N | Old Mean Error | SD | N | Young Mean Error | SD | N | Old Mean Error | SD | N |
Task	Sex												
SERV	M	.17	.16	7	.17	.23	23	.49	.24	10	.34	.23	48
(Visual Response)	F	.20	.17	6	.13	.18	27	.37	.26	6	.35	.22	12
SERN	M	.17	.16	7	.31	.24	23	.48	.27	10	.45	.23	48
(Naming Response)	F	.20	.17	6	.27	.18	27	.63	.26	6	.44	.22	12

Summary of Analyses of Variance:
Significant Main Factors

Old Readers
Group $d/f = 1/106$, $F = 23.81$, $p < .001$
Task $d/f = 1/106$, $F = 26.99$, $p < .001$

Young Readers
Group $d/f = 1/25$, $F = 21.37$, $p < .001$

intercorrelations, the disabled readers were subdivided according to their scores in the Benton Visual Memory Test. Table 8 itemizes the significant correlations within the two subgroups of disabled readers, and within the normal sample. Table 9 presents the mean error scores of the two samples of disabled readers and the normal group. All of the children's scores in this set of hypotheses were evaluated only after the period of specific tactile training. In Table 9 the scores are different for the normal and disabled, but not generally different for the two subgroups of disabled readers. Nevertheless, the patterns of correlations differed almost as much between the adequate and deficient visual memory subgroups of disabled readers as between normal and disabled readers. The number of correlations, shown in Table 7, vary strikingly among the three groups.

The findings indicated that there were 17 significant correlations for the normal readers, 7 significant correlations for the disabled readers with adequate visual memory skills, and only 2 significant correlations for the disabled readers with deficient visual memory. These patterns of correlations imply that normal readers bring a strong underlying communal factor to the tactile-decoding process, and that for the disabled readers this factor is weak and depends, in part, on level of comptence in visual-memory skills during the training period.

Spatial-Language Integration

An inspection of the correlations suggests that the highest level of intercorrelation is between tasks that require serial-spatial integration with tasks that require an oral-naming response. Implicit in the cognitive processing required for the serial-spatial integration task is verbal and spatial memory. Implicit in the cognitive processing required for the oral-naming tasks is ability to convert the spatial dimensions of the tactile stimulus to the notational. The nature of the intercorrelations thus implies that the integration of spatial and language imagery is an underlying communal factor in tactile letter decoding. The normal readers were intact in both visual-memory and verbal-memory processes. The level of intercorrelation was exceedingly high among tactile tasks for this subgroup. The disabled readers with adequate visual memory used primarily visual-memory skills in tactile decoding. The tactile tasks were amenable to this kind of processing, and the children were using their cognitive strengths. The number of intercorrelations was moderate in this subgroup. The disabled readers with deficient visual memory were unable to apply adequate spatial analytic skills in the tactile decoding, were approaching each tactile task as a separate entity, and relied little on spatial cues as a means of identifying letter shapes and names. The level of intercorrelation among tasks was low for this subgroup.

In summary, the total findings from the third hypothesis support the conclusions of others who have investigated cognitive processing and learning. Myklebust, et al. (1971) and Guthrie (1973) found the patterns of intercorrelations to vary for normal and disabled readers in IQ and in reading tests. This investigation found the pattern of intercorrelations to vary for normal and disabled readers in tactile tasks. In addition, this investigation defined one underlying factor, visual memory, as a significant variable to account for differences between subgroups of disabled readers. The pattern of intercorrelations was greater in tactile decoding skills for disabled children with adequate visual memory than for those with deficient visual memory, suggesting that within these subgroups adequate visual memory facilitated integration with the verbal system.

Implications. The findings manifested that normal children are more competent than disabled children in tactile processing, just as they are in auditory and visual processing. The central processing system in spatial-verbal memory is dependent upon an

Table 8

PATTERNS OF CORRELATIONS AMONG TACTILE TASKS FOR TRAINED GROUPS OF NORMAL
AND DISABLED READERS

		DIP Naming Right	DIP Naming Left	DIP Visual Matching Right	DIP Visual Matching Left	DIP Serial Visual	DIP Serial Naming
Passive hand, single letter naming	N	.43**	.46**			.36**	
	LD₁						
	LD₂						
Passive hand, double letter naming	N	.33*	.43**		.38**	.37*	.34**
	LD₁						
	LD₂						
Back of hand, single letter naming	N		.41**	.29**	.30**		
	LD₁		.37**	.47**		.35**	
	LD₂						
Back of hand, double letter naming	N		.33**			.31*	
	LD₁		.35**				
	LD₂						
Passive hand, motor memory	N	.44**	.42**	.33**		.46**	
	LD₁	.36**		.36**		.31*	
	LD₂	.57**	.44**				

*$p < .01$.
**$p < .005$.
N = Normal; LD₁ = Disabled, adequate visual memory; LD₂ = Disabled, deficient visual memory.

integrative network of cognitive systems which subserve analysis, storage, recall, and interpretation of sensory information. The normal child probably has an image of letter shape, notation, and sound even before he begins the tactile practice. He brings central processing skills to the tactile task, whereas the disabled child probably brings a one-sided cognitive proficiency to the tactile learning.

The task comparisons implied that the DIP training might have greater potential in intervention work when used alternately with other modes and with other versions of the tactile mode than when used as a system substitution "method" by itself. The PH and BOH strategies, which do not require complex visual memory skills and figure-ground deductions, might be used for simpler kinds of recognition tasks in multisensory training for a large cross-section of disabled children.

Each kind of tactile stimulation has its own merit in developing intersensory associations for the disabled reader. The DIP equipment has a built-in timing factor which forces the child to attend to each letter stimulus within a prescribed interval. This form of intervention also develops direct intercommunication systems with the visual and kinesthetic modalities, which in turn evoke oral-naming responses. On the other hand, the PH and BOH strategies used either in conjunction with DIP technique or independently have the advantage that they are generally simpler than the DIP tasks and do not significantly restrict the child with poor visual memory and inadequate copying skills.

Table 9

TOTAL MEAN ERROR SCORES FOR TACTILELY TRAINED DISABLED AND NORMAL READERS

Task	Disabled, Adequate Visual Memory (N = 46)		Disabled, Deficient Visual Memory (N = 30)		Normal, Adequate Visual Memory (N = 60)	
	$\bar{x}$	SD	$\bar{x}$	SD	$\bar{x}$	SD
Passive hand, single letter naming (PASSS)	.18	.16	.24	.18	.09	.19
Passive hand, double letter naming (PASSD)	.33	.22	.38	.22	.08	.10
Back of hand, single letter naming (BOHS)	.30	.20	.29	.19	.26	.18
Back of hand, double letter naming (BOHD)	.48	.31	.44	.29	.29	.22
Passive hand, motor memory (PHMM)	.50	.20	.57	.19	.23	.18
DIP naming, right (NR)	.51	.25	.58	.21	.16	.17
DIP naming, left (NL)	.46	.24	.62	.24	.16	.16
DIP visual matching, right (VR)	.35	.20	.40	.16	.14	.12
DIP visual matching, left (VL)	.29	.21	.40	.22	.15	.14
Serial visual (SERV)	.46	.24	.48	.24	.16	.15
Serial naming (SERN)	.32	.19	.43	.22	.27	.20

CONCLUSIONS

This study is only an initial step in assessing ways in which the tactile modality can be used by the reading-disabled child. We have limited answers to such questions as, ''What child would benefit the most from such a program?'', ''Which kinds of tasks are easiest and which are most difficult?'', or ''How can tactile tasks be adapted to reinforce the child's cognitive deficiencies?'' The study has singled out a few tasks which could be incorporated into a more global curriculum. The method used for studying variations in tactile learning isolated three models: a developmental cognitive model of intersensory integration; a model that reveals a syndrome of deficiencies in serial-order cognitive processing; and a model of spatial adequacy as a means of facilitating integration with the verbal system.

The first model illustrates how children of between 5 and 7 years develop associations in kinesthetic and visual recognition by training in analysis of a moving tactile stimulus. The second model illustrates how deficiencies in spatial analysis affect serial ordering in tactile letter decoding. The third model identifies relative levels of correlation between spatial and verbal systems in tactile decoding as a reflection of the integration in these cognitive systems. The first model validates the assumption that children between the ages of 5 and 7 respond favorably to spatial emphasis in early tactile training. The second model indicates that children with poor copying skills may be deficient in complex tactile tasks of serial-spatial integration. The third model implies that tactile training can increase verbal and visual integration when disabled children use visual memory as a cognitive strength.

Findings from the three cognitive processing models suggest that the spatial factor is an important component in either facilitating or limiting tactile learning for the disabled child, and its effectiveness depends on individual differences in visual memory, tactile training, and the nature of the stimulation. Tactile letter decoding facility is not a unitary ability. It requires competence in cross-modal spatial-verbal integration, visual imagery, verbal recall, figure-ground imagery, and ideomotor imagery.

The findings of the study emphasize that lower-level cross-modal associations can and should be developed by a combined DIP, BOH, and PH curriculum for the reading-disabled child. Other research might establish that verbalization with PH practice is helpful for the subsample of children with visuomotor deficiencies. Meanwhile, it seems that a modified tactile curriculum with highly structured tasks in verbal categorization of pairs of letters brings the tactile and verbal systems into closer interaction. Alternation of DIP, BOH, and PH strategies with visual and auditory cues and classification tasks might assist in developing association between symbol and sound, a necessity for the disabled child. This could reach the child with poor visual memory skills as well as the child with other kinds of deficits in verbal-spatial processing.

REFERENCES

Ayres, A. *Southern California Sensory Integration Tests.* Los Angeles: Western Psychological Services, 1972.

Benton, A. *Benton Revised Visual Retention Test.* New Jersey: The Psychological Corporation, 1974.

Benton, A. Developmental dyslexia: neurological aspects. *In* W. J. Friedlander, ed., *Advances in Neurology,* Vol. VII. New York: Raven Press, 1975.

Boder, E. Developmental dyslexia: prevailing diagnostic concepts and a new diagnostic approach. *In* H. Myklebust, ed., *Progress in Learning Disabilities,* Vol. II. New York: Grune & Stratton, 1971.

Duncan, D. Multiple range and multiple F tests. *Biometrics,* 1955, 11:1–42.

Fernald, G. *Remedial Techniques in Basic School Subjects.* New York: McGraw-Hill, 1943.

Gibson, E. Learning to read. *In* H. Singer and R. Ruddell, eds., *Theoretical Models and Processes of Reading.* Newark: International Reading Association, 1971.

Guthrie, J. Models of reading and reading disability. *Journal of Educational Psychology,* 1973, 65:9–18.

Hermelin, B., and O'Connor, H. Functional asymmetry in the reading of Braille. *Neuropsychologia,* 1971, . 9:431–435.

James, W. *The Principles of Psychology,* Vol II. New York: Dover, 1950.

Johnson, D., and Myklebust, H. *Learning Disabilities: Educational Principles and Practices.* New York: Grune & Stratton, 1967.

Kinsbourne, M. Cerebral dominance, learning, and cognition. *In* H. Myklebust, ed., *Progress in Learning Disabilities,* Vol. III. New York: Grune & Stratton, 1975.

Konorski, J. *Integrative Activity of the Brain.* Chicago: University of Chicago Press, 1970.

Luria, A. *Restoration of Function After Brain Injury.* B. Haigh, trans. London: Pergamon Press, 1963.

Monroe, M. *Children who Cannot Read.* Chicago: University of Chicago Press, 1932.

Montessori, M. *The Montessori Method.* A. E. Goerge, trans. Cambridge, Mass.: Robert Bentlet, 1964.

Muehl, S., and Kremenak, S. Ability to match information within and between auditory and visual sense modalities and subsequent reading achievement. *Journal of Educational Psychology,* 1966, 57:230–239.

Myklebust, H. Nonverbal learning disabilities: assessment and intervention. *In* H. Myklebust, ed., *Progress in Learning Disabilities*, Vol. III. New York: Grune & Stratton, 1975.

Myklebust, H., Bannochie, M., and Killen, J. Learning disabilities and cognitive processes. *In* H. Myklebust, ed., *Progress in Learning Disabilities,* Vol. II. New York: Grune & Stratton, 1971.

Orton, S. *Reading, Writing, and Speech Problems in Children*. New York: Norton, 1937.

Sandor, F., ed., *Musical Education in Hungary*. Budapest: Corvina, 1966.

Satz, P., Rardin, D., and Ross, J. An evaluation of a theory of specific developmental dyslexia. *Child Development,* 1971, 42:2009–2021.

Schevill, H. Tactile learning, handedness, and reading disability. *In* J. Herron, ed. *The Sinistral Mind*. New York: Academic Press, in press.

Sperry, R., Gazzaniga, M., and Bogen, J. Interhemispheric relationships: the neocortical commisures; syndromes of hemisphere disconnection. *In* P. J. Vinken and G. Bruyn, eds. *Handbook of Clinical Neurology*, Vol. IV. New York: Wiley and Sons, 1969.

Wechsler, D. *Wechsler Intelligence Scale for Children*. New York: Psychological Corporation, 1949.

Witelson, S. Abnormal right hemisphere specialization for developmental dyslexia. *In* R. Knights and D. Bakker, eds. *The Neuropsychology of Learning Disorders*. Baltimore: University Park Press, 1976.

VII.   Reading Disabilities and Cognitive Disturbances

JAMES R. KILLEN

Children with learning disabilities present a wide variety of learning problems, and disorders in reading permeate many of these specific disabilities (Myklebust, Bannochie, and Killen, 1971). Myklebust (1973) has noted that reading disabilities may result from lack of appropriate schooling, emotional disturbance, visual impairment, specific brain dysfunctions, or dyslexia. If we view reading as a highly complex series of cognitive processes, we can develop an understanding of reading deficiencies separate from the context of etiologies. The purpose of this chapter is to describe reading as cognitive processes and to relate how disturbances in those processes affect development of appropriate reading skills.

THE READING PROCESSES

Reading has been defined as a *verbal* process rather than a *visual* process (Neisser, 1967), implying that it is primarily an activity by which meaning is derived from visual symbols. We may conclude that a child is reading when the printed materials convey significance and meaning to him. We must, however, consider what is meant by "meaning." When is the printed word, sentence, or paragraph meaningful? What is it that allows one child to read with comprehension, but another is unable to gain significance from the selection?

Reading for meaning can occur only when a child has the experiential background that allows him to relate to the content in a personal way. His personal experiences become internalized both as real events and as representational activities (Myklebust, 1965; Neisser, 1967; Shepard, 1978). Thus, building a doghouse, for example, is an event that is stored in experiential memory. But, more importantly, it also becomes symbolic of a family of activities—construction, dogs, tools, companionship, and others. These representational meanings are then available to the child and allow him to read with comprehension a story about the construction of a multistory office building. Note that the child has not had the direct experience of constructing with steel and glass, but the symbolic meanings of his doghouse activity bridge the meaning gap, so he gains an understanding of how such massive projects are completed, all from the vicarious experience of reading.

For the child to attain such comprehension it is necessary for him to acquire the basic skills by which the printed word becomes internalized. Perception, storage, and retrieval of letter, word, and phrase configurations, and ability to relate the printed word to its spoken equivalents are essential (Luria, 1969; Neisser, 1967; Sokolov, 1969). These processes, although essential, exist to permit the child to complete the essence of reading—acquisition of meaning through relating content to internalized representational experiences.

Symbol Systems

If we view reading as a symbolic activity of relating written words to representational experiences, then we must consider the nature of symbol systems, the processes and learning that build our complex structures of symbolic meanings.

Research into the acquisition of language by young children has identified cognitive development that contributes to a primary system of symbolic meanings (Luria, 1969; Myklebust, 1965, 1973; Piaget, 1967; Sokolov, 1969). In the infant, initial sound production is the experimental manipulation of maturing cognitive and speech systems, which later enable the child to express himself. As these expressions are reinforced by particular vocal sounds produced by others when talking to the child, and as the processes of auditory discrimination become more acute, "random" babbling becomes focused upon the production of speech units standard to the language being received; the child acquires ability to direct the production of imitative vocalizations.

Concurrent with the development of these abilities is growth in the internalization of activities and events. At first the infant can only relate to what is present in his sensory field, and an object hidden from view is an object that does not exist. Soon, however, he is able to store and retrieve these experiences, and seeks out an object that has disappeared. This internalization of the *experiential* event becomes the basis for internalization of the *representational* event, and new activities are learned—not just by doing but also by relating them with other experiences symbolically. When the symbolic event becomes cognitively linked with the appropriate imitative vocalization, the child is able to verbalize inner meanings; true communicative language begins.

This initial form of verbal expression often is not easily understood, because both the stored words to be expressed and the expressive system itself lack maturity, and distortions in word choice and speech are common. Continued development of the meaning system as well as maturation of the speech mechanisms eventually lead to effective communicative, or social language (Farnham-Diggory, 1972; Slobin, 1973).

A second and more important result of this initial verbalization occurs as the child acquires a larger listening and speaking vocabulary. Through use of the heard and spoken word, experiences become symbolic verbally, as compared to earlier and parallel experiential or nonverbal content. Because words can have a symbolic content more generic than nonword symbols, the verbal symbol system becomes the most highly developed form of cognitive thought, particularly for the higher level processes of divergent thinking and evaluation, as shown by studies on the deaf (Myklebust, 1964). We observe this in the egocentric speaking of children engaged in a meaningful activity. Their "conversation" at play is self-directed and serves to internalize the experience in verbal symbolic meanings (Luria, 1969; Sokolov, 1969; Vygotsky, 1962). Through practice and maturation this egocentric speech extinguishes as the child acquires the ability to internalize experiences directly in word (verbal) symbols without the need for auditory speaking. This inner verbal system becomes the primary form for storage of experiential meanings; thus, a symbol system is acquired, verbal in content and auditory in form.

Reading, as a symbolic activity, does not directly employ the primary symbol system by which meanings are stored. Only when the child acquires ability either to relate the visual form to its auditory equivalent, or when the visual symbol develops its own meaning, can comprehension occur. In fact, both of these methods are used by the advanced reader. Initially the beginning reader must translate the visual symbol into its auditory equivalent—the word form that carries meaning for him. By this translation of the graphemic elements to their phonemic equivalents, the child is able to access his primary meaning system, and gradually the visual symbols acquire their own direct meanings. Translation of familiar words and phrases is no longer required; a secondary (visual) system for meaning is developing. Continued practice leads to a well-developed visual symbol system, more limited than the auditory, but serviceable for most reading tasks. When new words or difficult passages are met, however, even the adult reader will revert to "sounding out" or reading aloud (auditorizing) the word or sentence in order to use the primary symbol system for meaning.

Oral Expression and Reading

An activity related to the acquisition of meaning from the visual symbol is that of oral expression, either of the symbol directly (oral reading) or of the meaning derived from reading. Oral reading, the exact auditory expression of written language, includes the tasks already discussed. Appropriate visual perception and memory must be completed rapidly and accurately. The sight-sound relations must be formed, not only for the graphemic-phonemic equivalents for auditory production but also morphemic-phonemic relations for phrasing and production of meaning. Correct auditory formulation and expression of the speech sounds also is required for fluent and acurate oral production. For the beginning reader this adds up to a formidable task, indeed.

Oral expression is involved also in relating meaning derived from silent or oral reading. The child must relate the printed word to a symbol system for meaning—either the auditory, the visual, or both. These meanings are then used to formulate appropriate responses; either oral statements or the selection of appropriate written responses. At the highest level the meaning derived from a number of readings must be integrated to develop new concepts for thinking and expression. When we ask a child to give some indication of comprehension, then, we are asking for ability to comprehend what has been read and ability to express those meanings in appropriate responses.

This is the nature of reading, always involving acquisition of meaning from printed symbols, but including activities and processes for development of a meaning system, for relating the printed form to that meaning, and for expressing the content and substance of the read word.

READING AND COGNITIVE PROCESSES

Cognitive learning systems are organizations of learning processes closely interrelated in function (Johnson and Myklebust, 1967). These learning systems are based on the neurology of learning but relate to the psychological events resulting from that neurological structure. We can identify three such learning systems: systems for modalities of learning, systems for the contents of learning, and systems involving the levels of learning (Killen, 1975).

Modality Systems

The modality systems for learning involved in reading relate to the primary input and output modalities and the interrelations of those modalities. Auditory intramodality learning includes the reception and expression of oral language. New vocabulary drill often requires a child to listen to the word spoken by the teacher and then to repeat it orally. The auditory processes enable the child to perceive and store the heard word as well as to formulate and express the spoken word. A vocal-motor action is required for speaking, but that act is monitored by auditory matching. Hence, the entire task is processed by the auditory cognitive system, and dysfunctions in that system will prevent the child from successfully completing this reading activity.

Similarly, visual intramodality processes involve a single learning system. A reading task of having children match a vocabulary word printed on a card to a duplicate included in a deck of other written words is an example of this system. Here the visual processes permit the child to perceive correctly the stimulus word and to discriminate its match from the response deck. Dysfunctions in the visual system will prevent the child from completing this task with accuracy or speed.

Both the visual and auditory systems together are involved in many reading lessons. Reading out loud involves the visual system for processing written words; visual perception and reception are required for adequate input. Auditory expression uses the processes of reauditorization and vocal-motor expression to provide for spoken output. The two modality systems must interrelate so that the results of the visual processes of reception are transduced into their auditory equivalents for expression. Disabilities in one or more of the three essential steps—visual reception, visual to auditory transducing, and auditory expression—will result in reduced performance in oral reading of words or paragraphs.

Sometimes the transducing process requires translating auditory information into visual equivalents. For example, children may be asked to listen to a word and then locate it in a written list. Here the auditory processes provide for reception of information, and the visual processes control the output; auditory to visual transducing is required. Note that each direction of processing—auditory to visual, and visual to auditory—is a distinct and unique process. As before, dysfunctions in the auditory, visual, or auditory to visual processes will prevent children from completing this selection task adequately.

These systems become more complex when we introduce tactile or kinesthetic components, such as in tracing letters or word configurations or in following a moving target to develop left to right eye movements. Tactile-kinesthetic (T-K) intramodality learning, as well as the intermodality transducing processes of T-K to visual, T-K to auditory, auditory to T-K, and visual to T-K, all require integrities in these systems for success in learning to read by tactile and kinesthetic methods.

We have shown that a reader receives meaning from a selection when he relates to the printed content in a personal way; the materials being read have significance based on experience. This experiential base for reading comprehension is not dependent on one modality alone or even on the translation of information from one modality to another. Rather, it involves all modalities simultaneously, so that input through any modality is able to relate to the entire experience. This integration of the modality processes, or integrative learning, is the cognitive system used for reading and listening comprehension. Any dysfunction in one of the modality systems causes incomplete integration, and the resultant meaning is deficient. Further, a disability in the integrative process itself prevents a child from reading with comprehension, though the receptive and expressive processes may be intact; a child may have good skills in word calling and oral reading but be unable to read with meaning.

Content Systems

Reading also involves the content systems for learning—systems related to verbal and nonverbal processes. Nonverbal intrahemispheric processes include many of the reading and readiness skills: figure-ground selection, visual and auditory discrimination and recognition, and recall of objects in a set. Here all learning is accomplished by the nonverbal systems, and dysfunctions in these processes result in failure to perform these tasks necessary to the development of reading skills. Reading is primarily a series of verbal intrahemispheric processes, including silent and oral reading, development of reading vocabulary, and word attack skills. Verbal disabilities, therefore, affect the primary reading tasks, resulting in serious deficits in acquiring reading skills.

Some reading activities require, in addition to verbal or nonverbal processes, the ability to transduce between the content systems. Preliminary surveys before reading a selection require children to interpret context pictures in terms of verbal symbols, an interhemispheric process of nonverbal to verbal transducing. In other tasks children are asked to select a picture from a series that relates to a word or paragraph; the verbal to nonverbal interhemispheric process is involved here. A dysfunction in one or both of these transducing processes will result in deficits in relating nonverbal and verbal symbol systems appropriately, even though the disabled child may be able to process information within each content system adequately.

Integrative learning, like that involving the modalities for learning, permits the acquisition of meaning; simultaneous use of both verbal and nonverbal contents relate to the experiential meanings of significance to the reader. Serious reading problems result when integrative learning is disturbed, for the child is unable to relate the printed word to his own experiences, and the reading content is comprehended only from its own context and not from any personal meaning. Thus, the child may be able to answer questions about factual content but will be deficient in inferential meanings.

Systems for Levels of Learning

Reading involves all levels of learning—perception, imagery, symbolism, and conceptualization. At the perceptual level the child is required to complete auditory discriminations to hear the differences in phonemic units and to discriminate visually between graphemic elements. These perceived sounds and print may be stored at the level of imagery for use in drill activities or to form the mental images needed for matching the graphemic and phonemic units. These two lower levels of learning are nonverbal in content, even though the child may be processing "word" units, since at these cognitive levels the processes do not involve symbolic meaning.

The activities of word attack, reading comprehension, reading out loud, and oral responses to the reading are all performed at the level of symbolism. The printed "word" now represents personal experiences and becomes a verbal symbol to the reader. The highest level of learning—conceptualization—includes those processes related to creative and critical reading. Manipulation of ideas derived from the reading context permit the child to create new meanings and interpretations or to compare the reading contents with earlier knowledge.

Dysfunctions in these processes can affect reading achievement. Perceptual errors result in an inability to cognitively see or hear differences in words, thereby disturbing the development of efficient word recognition or word attack skills. Disabilities in imagery prevent short-term storage of perceived events, vital to processing at a symbolic level. Both word attack and comprehension are affected by symbolic disorders, and conceptual disabilities interfere with processes related to concrete and abstract operations.

Reading, then, is an activity requiring complex combinations of the cognitive learning systems. Dyslexia, or disturbances of the learning systems, result in serious disabilities in learning to read.

A Processing Approach

Teachers and reading specialists traditionally have viewed the task of learning to read as acquisition of skills: left-to-right orientation, letter discrimination, initial consonant sounds, sight vocabulary, rhyming words, syllabication, and reading for main ideas, to list but a few. Thus, reading difficulties were seen as a failure to achieve these skills, thereby interrupting or distorting sequential reading. If we relate these skills to the underlying cognitive systems, it becomes apparent that failure to achieve a skill may be due to a breakdown in any number of learning processes. Further, a dysfunction in an underlying process may affect more than one skill area, and we conclude that there is not a close correlation between skill and process. For example, the acquisition of a sight vocabulary means that the child will be able to give an appropriate auditory response to a visual word.

Many learning systems are related to this skill. Intramodality learning of nonverbal visual information includes the processes of selective attention, perceptual organization, recognition, and short-term memory. These functions enable the reader to process initially and to store the sensory information being received when a printed word is presented. The intramodality system for verbal visual information includes the process of symbolic reception of the perceived meaning unit. The received visual symbol is converted to its auditory equivalent by the intermodality process of visual to auditory transducing. The auditory model for speaking is created by the intramodal reauditorization process, and this internal model is used to formulate the correct vocal-motor expression, a verbal auditory intramodal process. And if the child is able to apply his experience to the words being learned, integrative learning in the form of verbal inner language is also used.

This example shows that failure to learn a specific skill is dependent on complex systems of underlying learning processes. Further, these processes also can affect other areas of learning to read or even interfere with learning other school subjects. The reauditorization process, for example, is also important to achievement in oral language, spelling, written language, and arithmetic.

The processing approach views reading disabilities as failures in how children learn to read and considers that these failures may be manifested in other areas of learning. Remediation must be directed to the processing dysfunctions if we are to effect real and permanent improvement. The failure of intensive efforts to improve reading skills might be due to failure to recognize and deal with the cognitive disabilities underlying these reading deficiencies.

How are we to accomplish this match between process disturbances and remediation? Basically we must learn how to translate reading into its cognitive components through analysis of the learning tasks involved. We can analyze the task of reading aloud for comprehension, for example, by relating the task contents to learning systems. The input task is reading of the visual symbol and involves these learning systems: verbal content, visual modality, and the levels of perception, imagery, and symbolism. The output task of speaking the auditory symbol includes cognitive systems for verbal content, auditory modality, and the levels of imagery and symbolism. And meaning is internalized by relating the verbal symbols to experiences, processes involving the verbal and nonverbal contents, the level of symbolism, and integration for meaning. The overall task of reading out loud with comprehension, then, includes all of these systems and the intermodal and interhemispheric processes: verbal and nonverbal contents; verbal and nonverbal transducing; visual and auditory modalities; visual and auditory transducing; the level of perception, imagery, and symbolism; and integrative learning.

A failure in oral reading for meaning might be due to a breakdown in any one or more of these systems. By utilizing a battery of tests designed to isolate specific processes, the cognitive dysfunctions underlying poor oral reading comprehension can be determined. Thus, through cognitive analysis of the reading tasks, we are able to isolate the processing dysfunction(s). In the same manner we can identify the learning integrities. By knowing both the cognitive deficits and abilities we are able to develop an appropriate remedial program to improve oral reading comprehension, as well as to improve other areas of learning that require these same processes. Note that we are not relating performance to skill levels; we are identifying dysfunctions in processes that cause these learning deficits.

COGNITIVE DYSFUNCTIONS AND READING DISABILITIES

We have suggested some of the cognitive processes involved in a few reading tasks. The overall reading activity requires integrities in a number of *direct* cognitive functions. As we have seen, where these processes are not intact, reading disabilities will be evident. And because reading is not an isolated activity but is based on a series of readiness and related skills, there are also *indirect* processes which must be intact for normal reading development.

Direct Processes of Reading

The cognitive processes directly involved in learning to read are those that relate to the primary tasks of auditory and visual reception, intermodal transducing, inner thought for meaning, and auditory expression. Verbal auditory reception enables the reader to receive the heard verbal symbols as meaning units. A dysfunction in this process results in disorders in receiving the perceived auditory meaning unit for use in symbolic language.

This *auditory dyslexia* is a disability in the primary symbol system and prevents the child from using auditory analysis for decoding words. Verbal visual reception is a parallel process in the visual modality, permitting the reception of read verbal symbols as meaning units. A learning disability in this process, *visual dyslexia,* results in an inability to receive the perceived visual unit for use in symbolic language. This deficit in the secondary symbol system interferes with the development of a reading vocabulary.

The verbal visual to auditory transducing process converts the received visual symbol into its auditory equivalent, thereby permitting use of the primary symbol system for meaning. A dysfunction in this process results in errors in making the grapheme-phoneme equivalents, a fundamental problem in developing phonetic analysis and word-recognition skills.

The cognitive process of verbal inner language provides for inner thought to relate word symbols to representational meaning. Word-calling is the result of a disability in this process, since the received symbol cannot be comprehended in terms of inner meaning. Finally, vocal-motor production of spoken words is the function of the process of verbal auditory expression; errors in reading aloud due to improper motor formulation will result from a dysfunction in this process.

These direct processes support the development of reading skills, and specific dysfunctions in one or more of these cognitive operations cause critical deficiencies in learning to read, deficiencies that must be remediated not by teaching to the deficient skill but by teaching to the underlying learning problem.

Indirect Processes of Reading

The reading task not only involves the direct processes for reception, meaning, and expression, but it also requires support from lower-level processes that perceive and store information for the symbolic tasks and from related nonverbal symbolic learning.

Adequate perception of visual and auditory information is prerequisite to higher level reception. The tasks of selection, organization, and recognition of visual and auditory data provide for initial decoding and preparation for higher processing. Errors in visual figure-ground, interference from background sounds, inability to discriminate properly the visual or auditory information, and agnosias for visual or auditory data may result from perceptual dysfunctions.

Perceived visual and auditory information is stored in imagery processes, both in short-term memory of the products of perception and in long-term memory of the perceptual processes. Short-term storage and retrieval permits the child to remember for immediate use the visual experience in terms of its content and spatial dimensions, and the content and sequence of the auditory information. Dysfunctions in recall cause errors in these activities, errors that may distort the retrieved image or preclude its retrieval. Thus, the child with these disabilities will have problems in remembering words just drilled or in temporarily storing information until it can be processed at higher levels of cognition.

Long-term imagery provides for the recreation of an experience so that the child is able mentally to "see" and "hear" the event as it occurred and to use this revisualized or reauditorized image as an internal model for auditory and visual expression. A learning disability in these processes will prevent success in learning to create the proper auditory model for oral reading or the correct visual model for writing words presented orally.

Nonverbal inner language is the process of representational inner thought for nonverbal experiences. Personal experiences initially are represented nonverbally, and the verbal symbol systems must draw upon these stored meanings to develop their own meaning content. A disability in nonverbal inner language may prevent the development of adequate meaning for nonverbal experiences in the areas of body image and self-perception, spatial orientation, social perception, or quantity, thereby affecting the development of adequate verbal symbolic meanings for these experiences. Further, interhemispheric learning is essential to conversion of meaning in the nonverbal content to its equivalent in verbal symbols. A dysfunction in nonverbal to verbal transducing will prevent the necessary transfer of data even though the processes of verbal and nonverbal inner language are intact.

The processes defined here and their application to reading are presented in terms of our present knowledge about learning. What we know about the psychology of learning of the handicapped is far from complete, however; there is a critical need to reach better understandings of learning in general and of reading disabilities in particular. Our present investigations into the cognitive processes of reading, presented on the pages following, promise to enhance these understandings.

STUDIES OF READING PROCESSES

Our continuing investigations into the nature of learning by handicapped children have provided significant research findings about reading and disabilities in learning to read. Our premise has been that studies of reading processes by children with learning disabilities will provide critical insights into the nature of childhood dyslexia. Moreover, they further our understanding of the cognitive processes of normal children as well.

The Sample and Instrumentation

For our research we chose a population of third- and fourth-grade children in four Chicago suburban school districts (Myklebust and Boshes, 1969). From a screening population of 2767 children, 627 children were selected for intensive individual evaluations. A total of 394 children passed the sensory, psychodynamic, and motor screenings, and were accepted as the study sample. Table 1 describes the subjects by sex and grade.

Table 1

DISTRIBUTION OF SUBJECTS BY SEX AND GRADE

Sex	Grade 3	Grade 4	Total
Male	167	152	319
Female	78	69	147
Total	245	221	466

An intensive psychoeducational evaluation was completed on the study sample. It included 15 standardized tests with a total of 45 separate tests and subtests, as listed in Table 2.

The learning quotient (LQ) (Johnson and Myklebust, 1967; Myklebust, 1968; Myklebust and Boshes, 1969; Myklebust, 1973a) has been found to be an effective measure of impaired learning and was used to differentiate the normal and learning disability children in this study. The tests administered were divided into six learning areas: auditory reception, auditory expression, reading, written language, arithmetic, and nonverbal. A learning quotient was calculated for each learning area for each child. Learning efficiency of 90% (LQ of 90) was considered minimal integrity for normal learning [the normal (N) group]; children with an LQ below 90 in any one or more of the six learning areas were defined as children with learning disabilities. Further, learning-disabled children with a minimal learning efficiency of 85% (LQ of 85 to 89) in one or more of the six learning areas were classified as borderline learning disabled [the borderline (B) group], while those with a learning quotient below 85 in any one or more of the six learning areas were classified as more severely learning disabled [the learning-disability (LD) group]. The distribution of subjects according to learning group is shown in Table 3. As can be seen from Table 3, many of the subjects who were classified as experimentals (borderline or learning-disability groups) were not disabled in reading, and selection of subjects solely on the basis of learning groups would bias studies of reading processes. Therefore, the subjects were divided into subgroups related to the reading area. Those subjects, N, B, or LD, who had a learning quotient of 90 or above in the reading area, were placed in the Pass group and those with a learning quotient below 90 in the reading area were placed in the Fail group. This resulted in four reading groups: Normal, Borderline/Pass, Learning Disability/Pass, and Experimental (borderline plus learning disability)/Fail. This distribution of subjects is shown in Table 4.

Validation of the Learning Quotient

The learning quotient is a measurement of educational achievement derived from measures of actual and expected achievement (Myklebust, 1968, 1973a). To validate its use in this study it was necessary to examine the predictability of actual reading achievement age (AA) from the four age measures employed in the formula: chronological age (CA), mental age (MA), grade age (GA), and reading expectancy age (EA), the computed performance "norm" for each child. A stepwise multiple regression procedure was used to determine the amount of variance in reading achievement age accounted for by each age variable. Table 5 reports the variable chosen for each regression step and the R^2 value for that variable.

This procedure demonstrated that of the four age measures related to the learning quotient, the expectancy age is the most consistent predictor of actual achievement. Since

Table 2

PSYCHOEDUCATIONAL TEST BATTERY

Test	Subtest
Gates-MacGinitie Reading Tests Primary C, Forms 1 and 2 Primary D, Forms 1 and 2	Reading Speed and Accuracy Reading Comprehension Reading Vocabulary
Gates-McKillop Reading Diagnostic Test Form 1	Word Parts Nonsense Words Syllabication
Metropolitan Achievement Test Elementary Level	Arithmetic Computation Spelling
Gates-Russell Spelling Diagnostic Test	Oral Words One-Syllable Words Two-Syllable Words
Picture Story Language Test	Total Words Total Sentences Words per Sentence Syntax Abstract-Concrete
Detroit Tests of Learning Aptitude	Free Association Verbal Opposites Auditory Attention Span for Unrelated Words Auditory Attention Span for Related Syllables Oral Directions Visual Attention Span for Letters Orientation Designs
Oral Picture Story Language Test	Words per Sentence Abstract-Concrete
Leiter International Performance Scale	
Healy Pictorial Completion Test I	
Vineland Social Maturity Scale	
Kent Emergency Scale D	
Heath Railwalking Test	
Goodenough-Harris Draw-A-Man Test	
Wechsler Intelligence Scale for Children	Information Comprehension Arithmetic Similarities Vocabulary Digit Span Picture Completion Picture Arrangement Block Design Object Assembly Coding Mazes
Wide Range Achievement Test	Reading

Table 3

DISTRIBUTION OF SUBJECTS BY LEARNING GROUPS

Learning Area	Learning Group			Total
	N	B*	LD*	
Auditory reception	412	38	16	466
Auditory expression	450	10	6	466
Reading	349	54	63	466
Written language	402	35	29	466
Arithmetic	379	71	15	465
Nonverbal	391	39	35	465
All areas	237	116	113	466

*Some children were classified as B or LD in more than one learning area.

Table 4

DISTRIBUTION OF SUBJECTS BY READING GROUPS

Reading Group	N
Normal	237
Borderline/Pass	74
Learning Disability/Pass	38
Experimental/Fail	117

Table 5

REGRESSION OF ACHIEVEMENT AGE IN READING

Sample		Step	Normals		B/Pass		LD/Pass		EXP/Fail*	
			Age	R^2	Age	R^2	Age	R^2	Age	R^2
SEX:	M	1	EA	.578	EA	.545	EA	.192	EA	.956
GD:	3&4	2	GA	.011	GA	.008	MA	.019	GA	.003
		3	CA	.002	CA	.000	GA	.001	CA	.000
		4	MA	.002	MA	.000	CA	.000	MA	.000
SEX:	F	1	EA	.513	EA	.552	MA	.365	EA	.855
GD:	3&4	2	MA	.008	GA	.005	CA	.067	CA	.058
		3	GA	.005	MA	.026	EA	.044	MA	.002
		4	CA	.001	CA	.000			GA	.007
SEX:	M&F	1	EA	.399	MA	.519	EA	.353	EA	.901
GD:	3	2	MA	.008	CA	.022	CA	.008	MA	.002
		3	CA	.000	EA	.010	GA	.008	CA	.001
		4	GA	.000	GA	.013	MA	.009	GA	.002
SEX:	M&F	1	EA	.421	EA	.487	EA	.108	EA	.837
GD:	4	2	GA	.018	GA	.011	MA	.004	MA	.036
		3	CA	.001	CA	.002	CA	.002	CA	.000
SEX:	M&F	1	EA	.551	EA	.540	EA	.203	EA	.947
GD:	3&4	2	MA	.006	CA	.005	MA	.000	MA	.003
		3	CA	.003	GA	.002			GA	.000
		4	GA	.000	MA	.000			CA	.000

*Includes only subjects with reading LQ values between 85 and 89.

the learning quotient is a ratio of achievement age to expectancy age, use of the LQ as a valid criterion for selecting normal and experimental subjects was accepted. Further, the learning quotient, because it is sensitive to chronological growth, mental maturation, and learning experience, is accepted as a valid descriptor for inferential statistical analyses, as described below.

Factor Analytic Studies

The purpose of this investigation was to isolate the ways in which children learn to read and to delineate differences among normal children, children with learning disabilities who were normal in reading, and the reading disabled. Each of the direct reading processing systems was selected for examination. The psychoeducational tests that involved processes related to each direct system were included in factor studies of that system, along with the variables of sex and grade. Table 6 lists the tests and the abbreviations used in the factor matrix tables. Principle factoring with iteration was then completed to determine inferred factors related to the shared variance among the independent variables; these inferred factors would indicate the nature of the processing activities used to complete each of the psychoeducational tests. Varimax orthogonal rotation was then used to maximize the variance of the loadings for each inferred factor, thereby simplifying analysis of each factor.

The rotated factor matrices presented in Tables 7 through 23 show the significant factors (determined by eigenvalues ≥ 1.0) and the factor loading for each variable included. The sex variable was coded with a value of one for male and two for female; positive factor loadings for sex therefore favor the female subjects. Significant factor loadings were determined by testing the Pearson correlation coefficients at the $p = .05$ (two-tail) level.

Interpretation of these factor results considers that the N, B/Pass, and LD/Pass groups all completed the reading tasks adequately; positive factor loadings for the relevant variables are indicative of inferred factors leading to learning success. Conversely, since the Experimental/Fail group reflects reading disabilities, positive loadings relate to inferred factors contributing to reading failure. The first three study groups, then, are positively related to the factors, while the variables for the Fail group have an inverse relation to the inferred factors.

Analysis of Direct Processes for Reading

The results for the tests related to *auditory reception* are shown in Tables 7 through 10. The primary factor for the N group, accounting for nearly half of the variance, is auditory reception of words relating to verbal meaning. This factor is also primary to the B/Pass group, and for both groups there is a positive correlation with grade, indicating the positive role of age and experience. For the LD/Pass group, however, the primary factor is correlated with verbal input related to nonverbal meaning, indicating a deficit in the verbal meaning system. This is also true in the subjects failing reading; the primary factor is correlated with verbal meaning, showing that children with reading disabilities have a deficit in verbal language.

The secondary factors for the N group show a decreasing role of auditory reception for conversion to visual memory, direct verbal meanings, and auditory memory. We may conclude that the process of auditory reception is most highly developed by the normals for the receipt of oral language related to personal verbal meanings. Though the relative factor weights are somewhat rearranged for the B/Pass group, the pattern is generally

Table 6

FACTOR ANALYSIS VARIABLES AND ABBREVIATIONS

Variable	Abbreviation
Sex	SEX
Grade	GD
Gates-MacGinitie: Reading Accuracy	GMGACC
Gates-MacGinitie: Reading Comprehension	GMGCOM
Gates-MacGinitie: Reading Vocabulary	GMGVOC
Gates-McKillop: Word Parts	GMKWPT
Gates-McKillop: Nonsense Words	GMKNON
Gates-McKillop: Syllabication	GMKSYL
Metropolitan: Arithmetic	METARI
Metropolitan: Spelling	METSPL
Gates-Russell: Oral Words	GRLOWD
Gates-Russell: One-Syllable Words	GRLONE
Gates-Russell: Two-Syllable Words	GRLTWO
Picture Story Language Test: Total Words	PSLTTW
Picture Story Language Test: Total Sentences	PSLTTS
Picture Story Language Test: Words per Sentence	PSLTWS
Picture Story Language Test: Syntax	PSLTSN
Picture Story Language Test: Abstract-Concrete	PSLTAC
Detroit: Free Association	DETFRA
Detroit: Verbal Opposites	DETVOP
Detroit: Auditory Attention Span—Words	DETAAW
Detroit: Auditory Attention Span—Sentences	DETAAS
Detroit: Oral Directions	DETODR
Detroit: Visual Attention Span—Letters	DETVAL
Detroit: Orientation	DETORT
Detroit: Designs	DETDES
Oral PSLT: Words per Sentence	OPSLWS
Oral PSLT: Abstract-Concrete	OPSLAC
Leiter	LEITER
Healy I	HEALYI
Vineland Social Maturity	VINELD
Kent Scale D	KENTED
Heath Railwalking	HEATHR
Goodenough-Harris Draw-A-Man	GHDRMN
WISC: Information	WISINF
WISC: Comprehension	WISCOM
WISC: Arithmetic	WISART
WISC: Similarities	WISSIM
WISC: Vocabulary	WISVOC
WISC: Digit Span	WISDSP
WISC: Picture Completion	WISPCP
WISC: Picture Arrangement	WISPAR
WISC: Block Design	WISBKD
WISC: Object Assembly	WISOBA
WISC: Coding	WISCOD
WISC: Mazes	WISMAZ
Wide Range Achievement Test: Reading	WRATRD

JAMES R. KILLEN

Table 7

VARIMAX ROTATED FACTOR MATRIX
AUDITORY RECEPTION
NORMAL SUBJECTS

Variable	N	Factor* 1	2	3	4	5
SEX	237				288	
GD	237	686		−232		
GRLOWD	237		616			256
GRLONE	237		678			−230
GRLTWO	237		622		213	
DETVOP	237			650		
DETAAW	237				631	
DETAAS	237				765	
DETODR	237				293	
DETORT	237			345		268
KENTED	237			557		
WISINF	237					296
WISCOM	237	972				
WISART	237	692		355		
WISSIM	237	438				
WISVOC	237	631				
WISDSP	237	516		445		
% Variance		42.6	26.9	14.1	10.5	5.8

*Decimal points are omitted from the correlation coefficients.
Critical value at $p = .05$: $r = .195$
                $p = .01$: $r = .254$

intact, indicating a similar integrity for auditory reception of verbally meaningful data. The LD/Pass group results show a greater integrity for auditory reception that relates more to nonverbal meanings and visual memory than to verbal inner thought, though significant ability for reception of verbally meaningful information is present. The reading disabled, however, demonstrate relatively higher integrities for auditory reception of information to be used for tasks other than verbal meaning, suggesting a greater dependence on nonverbal visual experiences.

When we examine the results for tests of *visual reception* (see Tables 11 to 14), a similar pattern in evident. The primary inferred factor for the N and B/Pass groups relates most significantly to the Gates-McKillop tests—tests that require decoding of the visual symbol without inherent meaning. For these groups the visual reception taks is primarily one of processing for conversion to auditory symbols and not for direct meaning of the visual unit itself. The LD/Pass group relates most to the Metropolitan Spelling and Detroit Visual Attention for Letters test, both of which use the visual image directly at a level of imagery and not with any signficant meaning, indicating that visual symbol processing serves lower-level cognitive operations. The Experimental/Fail group shows high loadings on the primary factor for word decoding and memory, suggesting that reading failure is a result of inability to complete the initial processing necessary for conversion to the auditory symbol or for comparison with revisualized word images.

Secondary inferred factors relate to word meaning for the N and B/Pass groups and to speed and accuracy of the reception process for the LD/Pass and Experimental/Fail groups, though these are less important to reading success for the experimental subjects. A

Table 8

VARIMAX ROTATED FACTOR MATRIX
AUDITORY RECEPTION
BORDERLINE/PASS SUBJECTS

Variable	N	Factor* 1	2	3	4	5
SEX	74		253	−242	−291	
GD	74	694				
GRLOWD	74		649		−249	
GRLONE	74		766			
GRLTWO	74		865			
DETVOP	74	236	210	354	375	
DETAAW	74					546
DETAAS	74					854
DETODR	74			298		300
DETORT	74			968		
KENTED	74	278	−252	433	554	
WISINF	74				−436	
WISCOM	74	943			263	
WISART	74	536		359	535	226
WISSIM	74	676				
WISVOC	74	563				317
WISDSP	74	499			593	
% Variance		46.8	23.2	14.5	9.5	5.9

*Decimal points are omitted from the correlation coefficients.
Critical value at $p = .05$: $r = .222$
$p = .01$: $r = .289$

grade loading is noted for the LD/Pass group, suggesting that maturation will improve functioning of the visual reception process.

The results for tests involving *auditory-visual transducing,* Tables 15 to 18, show that the grapheme-phoneme relationship is dependent on skill in breaking the visual code. High loadings for factor 1 for all groups suggest that auditory-visual transducing is related most highly to tasks involving syllabication or other visual-decoding skills and to transducing of the resultant graphemic units to their auditory equivalents. The reverse process, auditory reception and auditory-to-visual transducing, is important to the good reader as a secondary ability, as shown by high loadings on WISC Arithmetic. Intermodal processing requiring meaning transfer from nonverbal to verbal contents (the Oral Picture Story Language Test) is significant for the N, B/Pass, and Experimental/Fail groups, suggesting that good readers with little or no learning disability are able to transduce simultaneously between contents and modalities, but that a severe learning problem precludes this more complex processing. A significant grade effect is present in the Experimental/Fail group, indicating the intermodal transducing deficits more severely affect the older nonreader.

Factor loadings for tests of *verbal inner language* are shown in Tables 19 to 22. The primary factor for the N and B/Pass groups has high loadings for verbal meaning closely related to personal experience (WISC Comprehension), showing that for these normal and near-normal readers verbal inner language is primarily a process for storing and retrieving personal units of experience. For the LD/Pass group the primary factor relates to meanings derived from the received symbols, and loadings related to personal meaning are relatively unimportant. The poor readers seem to be affected by inability to receive and store

Table 9

VARIMAX ROTATED FACTOR MATRIX
AUDITORY RECEPTION
LEARNING DISABILITY/PASS SUBJECTS

Variable	N	Factor* 1	2	3	4	5
SEX	38					−691
GD	38	−634				
GRLOWD	38		561	−382		
GRLONE	38		823			
GRLTWO	38		870			
DETVOP	38	615				−342
DETAAW	38				700	
DETAAS	38				813	
DETODR	38	529				
DETORT	38	790				
KENTED	38	380	270			378
WISINF	38		−422			
WISCOM	38	−641		760		
WISART	38			547		
WISSIM	38			620		
WISVOC	38		483	479		
WISDSP	38		345			
% Variance		34.7	24.3	21.0	12.9	7.1

*Decimal points are omitted from the correlation coefficients.
Critical value at $p = .05$: $r = .316$
$p = .01$: $r = .373$

information or to attach meaning to received symbols. A negative factor loading for WISC Comprehension on factor 2 for this group suggests that inner meaning may be intact, but it is not readily accessible through the reception processes. Significant loadings on the Picture Story Language Test (Myklebust, 1965), Total Words for all groups, indicates the importance of inner language for word expression in reading success. Thus, good readers are able to access a well-developed system of personal inner thought, while children with severe learning problems and poor readers either have a deficit in verbal inner language or are unable to utilize it effectively.

The results for *auditory expression* shown in Tables 23 to 26 indicate that expression of inner meaning is the most significant process for all groups, suggesting that poor readers are affected by basic deficits in verbal inner language. Repetition of received input is a secondary factor for the N, B/Pass groups, showing that these children are also able to relate directly the auditory reception and expression process, though this is more effective for the LD group when the information received is less readily related to inner thought. Relatively high loadings in this area are also seen for the Fail group, suggesting that reading deficits may also relate to inability to receive and store information needed for expression. A sex effect positive for the female subjects is shown for the N and B/Pass groups.

These studies of the direct reading processes show that readers (Pass groups) and nonreaders (Fail group) do process information in different ways. Further, the more severe learning-disability children (LD/Pass group) have basic dysfunction in higher level pro-

Table 10

VARIMAX ROTATED FACTOR MATRIX
AUDITORY RECEPTION
EXPERIMENTAL/FAIL SUBJECTS

Variable	N	Factor* 1	2	3	4	5
SEX	117					−479
GD	117	608				282
GRLOWD	117	−437	597		242	−228
GRLONE	116		848	228		
GRLTWO	116		702			
DETVOP	117			316	540	
DETAAW	117			691		
DETAAS	117			750		
DETODR	117			247		230
DETORT	117				746	
KENTED	117				613	260
WISINF	117					436
WISCOM	117	859				321
WISART	117	600		208	337	
WISSIM	117	427				
WISVOC	117	457		281		248
WISDSP	117	460	236	339	211	
% Variance		37.8	30.0	13.8	11.0	7.3

*Decimal points are omitted from the correlation coefficients.
Critical value at $p = .05: r = .195$
$p = .01: r = .254$

cesses and in more complex processing systems. These children learn more effectively when the content is nonverbal or where processing is restricted to perception or imagery levels. Moreover, when presented with verbal information the children with more severe learning problems attempt to process the data in terms of its perceptual content rather than its symbolic meaning. These children, who are successful in reading, are able to learn to decode the visual symbol and to relate it to its inherent meaning, but basic deficits in symbol manipulation and verbal inner meaning preclude the development of truly independent reading.

Disabilities in reading are due to a number of processing problems; dysfunctions in visual reception, auditory reception, and verbal inner language permeate the patterns demonstrated in these analyses. The process of visual reception, important for decoding of the printed symbol, is less than intact for the nonreader. Difficulties in breaking the visual code in terms of syllabication and recognition of word parts are due to this disability. Further, inability to process the visual symbol prevents its conversion to the equivalent auditory unit for meaning. The processes of relating the visual or auditory symbol to inner language and of accessing inner meaning for oral expression are also deficits for the reading-disabled child. There appear to be problems in the recall and revisualization processes, resulting in loss or distortion of received data before it can be processed at the symbolic level and in creating mental images from reading. Finally, the nonreader is disabled in complex intersystems tasks. Reading instruction should avoid tasks requiring simultaneous use of verbal, nonverbal, auditory, and visual systems.

Table 11

VARIMAX ROTATED FACTOR MATRIX
VISUAL RECEPTION
NORMAL SUBJECTS

Variable	N	Factor* 1	Factor* 2	Factor* 3
SEX	237			356
GD	237	−572	338	279
GMGACC	154		523	460
GMGCOM	155		696	
GMGVOC	154		841	
GMKWPT	237	897		
GMKNON	237	788		
GMKSYL	237	755		
METSPL	155	527	390	343
DETVAL	237	241	244	197
WRATRD	237	341	272	568
% Variance		50.2	40.5	9.3

*Decimal points are omitted from the correlation coefficients.
Critical value at $p = .05$: $r = .195$
$p = .01$: $r = .254$

Table 12

VARIMAX ROTATED FACTOR MATRIX
VISUAL RECEPTION
BORDERLINE/PASS SUBJECTS

Variable	N	Factor* 1	Factor* 2	Factor* 3
SEX	74	237		291
GD	74		246	487
GMGACC	54		406	560
GMGCOM	54		725	
GMGVOC	54		975	
GMKWPT	74	856		
GMKNON	74	584		
GMKSYL	74	838		
METSPL	54	646	310	282
DETVAL	74		376	
WRATRD	74			694
% Variance		53.7	32.0	14.3

*Decimal points are omitted from the correlation coefficients.
Critical value for $N=74$ at $p = .05$: $r = .222$
$p = .01$: $r = .289$
Critical value for $N=54$ at $p = .05$: $r = .266$
$p = .01$: $r = .345$

192

Table 13

VARIMAX ROTATED FACTOR MATRIX
VISUAL RECEPTION
LEARNING DISABILITY/PASS SUBJECTS

| Variable | N | Factor* | | |
		1	2	3
SEX	38	341		
GD	38			733
GMGACC	28		902	
GMGCOM	28		777	−372
GMGVOC	28	494	444	
GMKWPT	38	753		
GMKNON	38	701		−343
GMKSYL	38	817		
METSPL	28	911		
DETVAL	38	387		
WRATRD	38			
% Variance		56.9	23.8	19.3

*Decimal points are omitted from the correlation coefficients.
Critical value for $N=38$ at $p = .05$: $r = .316$
$p = .01$: $r = .373$
Critical value for $N=28$ at $p = .05$: $r = .367$
$p = .01$: $r = .471$

Table 14

VARIMAX ROTATED FACTOR MATRIX
VISUAL RECEPTION
EXPERIMENTAL/FAIL SUBJECTS

| Variable | N | Factor* | | |
		1	2	3
SEX	117		246	236
GD	117			
GMGACC	96		878	
GMGCOM	96	350	426	
GMGVOC	97	506	402	
GMKWPT	116	761	196	
GMKNON	117	707		
GMKSYL	116	740	247	
METSPL	97	757	448	
DETVAL	117	333		
WRATRD	117			991
% Variance		65.1	22.3	12.7

*Decimal points are omitted from the correlation coefficients.
Critical value for $N>100$ at $p = .05$: $r = .195$
$p = .01$: $r = .254$
Critical value for $N=97$ at $p = .05$: $r = .199$
$p = .01$: $r = .259$
Critical value for $N=96$ at $p = .05$: $r = .200$
$p = .01$: $r = .260$

Table 15

VARIMAX ROTATED FACTOR MATRIX
AUDITORY-VISUAL TRANSDUCING
NORMAL SUBJECTS

Variable	N	Factor* 1	2	3	4	5
SEX	237			440	235	
GD	237	−333	418		372	232
GMKWPT	237	857	−278			
GMKNON	237	612	−508			
GMKSYL	237	740				−263
GRLOWD	237	710				
GRLONE	237	627		176		334
GRLTWO	237	555		224		277
DETODR	237				378	
DETVAL	237	338		189	305	
OPSLWS	237					−504
OPSLAC	236	196		499		
WISART	237		787		199	
WRATRD	237		279		563	175
% Variance		56.4	20.8	9.0	7.3	6.5

*Decimal points are omitted from the correlation coefficients.
Critical value at $p = .05$: $r = .195$
$p = .01$: $r = .254$

Table 16

VARIMAX ROTATED FACTOR MATRIX
AUDITORY-VISUAL TRANSDUCING
BORDERLINE/PASS SUBJECTS

Variable	N	Factor* 1	2	3	4	5
SEX	74		−304		480	
GD	74		333	243	470	
GMKWPT	74	825				
GMKNON	74	535	−466			
GMKSYL	74	808				
GRLOWD	74	743	−222			
GRLONE	74	767	247			−291
GRLTWO	74	742				
DETODR	74		302	−307		518
DETVAL	74	296				
OPSLWS	74					497
OPSLAC	74			784		
WISART	74		846			
WRATRD	74				587	
% Variance		49.6	19.0	12.1	10.0	9.3

*Decimal points are omitted from the correlation coefficients.
Critical value at $p = .05$: $r = .222$
$p = .01$: $r = .289$

Table 17

VARIMAX ROTATED FACTOR MATRIX
AUDITORY-VISUAL TRANSDUCING
LEARNING DISABILITY/PASS SUBJECTS

Variable	N	Factor* 1	2	3	4	5
SEX	38					323
GD	38		477			730
GMKWPT	38	721			394	
GMKNON	38	732				
GMKSYL	38	793				
GRLOWD	38	853				
GRLONE	38	370			712	
GRLTWO	38	455			824	
DETODR	38					602
DETVAL	38	416				
OPSLWS	38		−605			
OPSLAC	38			512		
WISART	38			951		
WRATRD	38		848			
% Variance		48.7	19.1	14.3	9.8	8.0

*Decimal points are omitted from the correlation coefficients.

Critical value at $p = .05$: $r = .316$

$\qquad p = .01$: $r = .373$

Table 18

VARIMAX ROTATED FACTOR MATRIX
AUDITORY-VISUAL TRANSDUCING
EXPERIMENTAL/FAIL SUBJECTS

Variable	N	Factor* 1	2	3	4	5
SEX	117			545		
GD	117		809		−255	
GMKWPT	116	783				
GMKNON	117	664				
GMKSYL	116	721				
GRLOWD	117	−660	−354		286	
GRLONE	116	790				687
GRLTWO	116	665		202		
DETODR	117					
DETVAL	117	319			574	
OPSLWS	117		473		325	270
OPSLAC	117	196		598		
WISART	117					
WRATRD	117					
% Variance		54.1	18.0	12.5	8.0	7.4

*Decimal points are omitted from the correlation coefficients.

Critical value at $p = .05$: $r = .195$

$\qquad p = .01$: $r = .254$

Table 19

VARIMAX ROTATED FACTOR MATRIX
VERBAL INNER LANGUAGE
NORMAL SUBJECTS

Variable	N	Factor* 1	2	3	4	5	6
SEX	237						
GD	237	765			−268		
GMGACC	154	465					394
GMGCOM	155	266					727
GMGVOC	154	274					694
PSLTTW	237		890				
PSLTTS	236		886				
PSLTWS	237						
PSLTSN	237						
PSLTAC	237		368			495	
DETFRA	237		199	209			
DETVOP	237				490		
DETAAW	237			669			
DETAAS	237			724	196		
DETODR	237						
DETVAL	237			607			
DETORT	237				470		
OPSLWS	236						
OPSLAC	236					823	
KENTED	237				409		373
WISINF	237	234					
WISCOM	237	931					
WISART	237	628				365	
WISSIM	237	296					
WISVOC	237	597					
WISDSP	237	474			328		360
% Variance		32.7	20.0	12.1	10.1	6.7	6.1

*Decimal points are omitted from the correlation coefficients.

Critical value at $p = 05$: $r = .195$

$p = .01$: $r = .254$

IMPLICATIONS FOR EDUCATION

Our investigations demonstrate the potential for developing a greater understanding of dyslexia and other cognitive learning disorders. Disabilities in learning to listen and speak, to write, to perform quantitative operations, and to relate to the spatial, social, and directional world appropriately may all be investigated by analysis of the cognitive process differences between normal and disabled children. These studies, however, can only relate to the learning processes as they are demonstrated by the psychoeducational tests employed. These tests typically are designed to measure specific cognitive outcomes rather than processing systems, and the cognitive processes employed for each task are often complex interactions among the learning systems for modalities, contents, and levels of learning. For example, short-term auditory memory or recall is evaluated by such tests as the WISC Digit Span, Detroit Auditory Attention Span, and ITPA Auditory Sequential Memory tests, all of which employ meaningful symbols. The cognitive pro-

Table 20

VARIMAX ROTATED FACTOR MATRIX
VERBAL INNER LANGUAGE
BORDERLINE/PASS SUBJECTS

Variable	N	Factor*					
		1	2	3	4	5	6
SEX	74		256		393		
GD	74	431		345	432		
GMGACC	54	553	395			465	
GMGCOM	54	650					−320
GMGVOC	54	648	390				
PSLTTW	74		830				
PSLTTS	74		834				−263
PSLTWS	74						262
PSLTSN	74			327			
PSLTAC	74		682	−305			
DETFRA	74		350	250			320
DETVOP	74	600				266	
DETAAW	74			430		−442	
DETAAS	74	516		375		−428	277
DETODR	74	294		396			
DETVAL	74		284	550			
DETORT	74	402	−281	324	−382		
OPSLWS	74				−257		314
OPSLAC	74		635	311	−304		312
KENTED	74	579	−346				
WISINF	74	−287		286	312		
WISCOM	74	814		−350	−292		
WISART	74	865					
WISSIM	74	734					
WISVOC	74	571					
WISDSP	74	674	−239	−287			
% Variance		35.9	21.6	12.1	8.2	7.1	6.0

*Decimal points are omitted from the correlation coefficients.
Critical value for $N=74$ at $p = .05$: $r = .222$
$p = .01$: $r = .289$
Critical value for $N=54$ at $p = .05$: $r = .266$
$p = .01$: $r = .345$

cesses used to evaluate this area of learning are a combination of nonverbal imagery and verbal symbolic processes; differentiation of specific cognitive operations used by a child to complete this task is not possible. Future research into the nature of cognitive disorders will be dependent on the development of test instruments designed to assess specific cognitive learning systems free from confounding process interactions.

Just as complete diagnosis is dependent upon assessment of specific cognitive processes, remediation is dependent upon knowledge of individual cognitive learning deficits and integrities. Our ability to measure the learning processes directly will enable us to construct more valid diagnostic summaries that relate to how each child learns or fails to learn. Knowing this, we will be able to develop appropriate remedial objectives that address the cognitive dysfunctions, and we will be able to define our educational program in terms of learning rather than of behaviorally demonstrated skill achievements. Further,

Table 21

VARIMAX ROTATED FACTOR MATRIX
VERBAL INNER LANGUAGE
LEARNING DISABILITY/PASS SUBJECTS

Variable	N	Factor*					
		1	2	3	4	5	6
SEX	38		459				
GD	38	−507			563		
GMGACC	28			−400	483		
GMGCOM	28	788		−476			
GMGVOC	28	559			446		
PSLTTW	38		785				
PSLTTS	38		672	508			
PSLTWS	38		609				−376
PSLTSN	38						
PSLTAC	38			556			
DETFRA	38		−426			492	
DETVOP	38	574					
DETAAW	38		370			531	
DETAAS	38	333				668	
DETODR	38			333	−522		
DETVAL	38						597
DETORT	38	842					
OPSLWS	38		491				
OPSLAC	38	526	425				
KENTED	38	382	−324				
WISINF	38						−342
WISCOM	38	−325	−477	473	563		
WISART	38			586			
WISSIM	38		−477				−393
WISVOC	38		−388		393		
WISDSP	38	374		364			
% Variance		22.5	20.0	13.7	11.9	9.5	8.5

*Decimal points are omitted from the correlation coefficients.

Critical value for $N=38$ at $p = .05$: $r = .316$

$p = .01$: $r = .373$

Critical value for $N=28$ at $p = .05$: $r = .367$

$p = .01$: $r = .471$

Table 22

VARIMAX ROTATED FACTOR MATRIX
VERBAL INNER LANGUAGE
EXPERIMENTAL/FAIL SUBJECTS

Variable	N	Factor* 1	2	3	4	5	6
SEX	117		285			462	
GD	117		−526	506	195		
GMGACC	96	229	490		384	240	
GMGCOM	96		444		462		
GMGVOC	97	443	316		316		
PSLTTW	117	422	488	658			
PSLTTS	117	418	372	456	−333		
PSLTWS	117		204				−203
PSLTSN	117	319				−250	
PSLTAC	117	470	230	264	−285		−282
DETFRA	117			−293		212	
DETVOP	117	538		−246			
DETAAW	117	384		−357	−335		332
DETAAS	117	542		−406	−243		231
DETODR	117	290					
DETVAL	117	262		−260			
DETORT	117	414			335	−399	
OPSLWS	117		204				−217
OPSLAC	117	448	304				−318
KENTED	117	523			200	−472	
WISINF	117		−224		−196	−272	
WISCOM	117		−752	495			
WISART	117	570	−374		224		
WISSIM	117		−338				
WISVOC	117	528	−344				
WISDSP	117	541	−417				−420
% Variance		26.2	21.0	14.9	9.8	8.0	6.2

*Decimal points are omitted from the correlation coefficients.

Critical value for $N > 100$ at $p = .05$: $r = .195$

$p = .01$: $r = .254$

Critical value for $N = 97$ at $p = .05$: $r = .199$

$p = .01$: $r = .259$

Critical value for $N = 96$ at $p = .05$: $r = .200$

$p = .01$: $r = .260$

Table 23

VARIMAX ROTATED FACTOR MATRIX
AUDITORY EXPRESSION
NORMAL SUBJECTS

Variable	N	Factor*				
		1	2	3	4	5
SEX	237				450	
GD	237	670				−388
GMKNON	237	−638				227
DETFRA	237				470	
DETVOP	237			625		
DETAAW	237		624			
DETAAS	237		670	232	294	
DETVAL	237		589			
OPSLWS	236		−268	198		
OPSLAC	236					498
WISINF	237		−236			−241
WISCOM	237	980				
WISART	237	734		365		
WISSIM	237	459				
WISVOC	237	627				
WISDSP	237	476		553		
WRATRD	237	506			434	−228
% Variance		49.6	24.9	12.4	7.0	6.1

*Decimal points are omitted from the correlation coefficients.

Critical value at $p = .05$: $r = .195$

$p = .01$: $r = .254$

Table 24

VARIMAX ROTATED FACTOR MATRIX
AUDITORY EXPRESSION
BORDERLINE/PASS SUBJECTS

Variable	N	Factor* 1	2	3	4	5	6
SEX	74			560			
GRADE	74	556		326			
GMKNON	74	−578			318		
DETFRA	74					600	
DETVOP	74	424					298
DETAAW	74		588				
DETAAS	74	312	810				238
DETVAL	74		531			237	
OPSLWS	74						629
OPSLAC	74				724	326	
WISINF	74				−432		
WISCOM	74	970					
WISART	74	765					
WISSIM	74	749					
WISVOC	74	531	272	252	332		
WISDSP	74	712		−279		−239	
WRATRD	74			540			
% Variance		46.6	17.5	12.9	11.4	6.3	5.3

*Decimal points are omitted from the correlation coefficients.

Critical value at $p = .05$: $r = .222$

$p = .01$: $r = .289$

Table 25

VARIMAX ROTATED FACTOR MATRIX
AUDITORY EXPRESSION
LEARNING DISABILITY/PASS SUBJECTS

Variable	N	Factor*					
		1	2	3	4	5	6
SEX	38					316	
GD	38	591				441	
GMGNON	38	−618		−384		328	
DETFRA	38		386		370		
DETVOP	38	−400	380				
DETAAW	38		−678				
DETAAS	38		585	418	529		
DETVAL	38	−363					
OPSLWS	38	−531					
OPSLAC	38			410	−376	385	
WISINF	38			552			
WISCOM	38	747					
WISART	38		521		−401	340	
WISSIM	38	443	396		−328		−380
WISVOC	38	351	397	336			
WISDSP	38		524				
WRATRD	38	729					
% Variance		31.1	24.5	14.2	13.0	10.7	6.6

*Decimal points are omitted from the correlation coefficients.

Critical value at $p = .05$: $r = .316$

$\qquad\qquad p = .01$: $r = .373$

our knowledge of individual cognitive patterns will enable us to adopt strategies for learning that take advantage of a child's processing capabilities while attending to the learning dysfunctions.

Evaluation of the remediation program is essential as a check on the child's progress and on the remedial program design. If our goal is to improve processing disabilities, our evaluation plan must make provision for measurement of changes in cognitive functioning. Further, our evaluation methods must be consistent with the educational strategies adopted for each child. If we employ a general evaluation method for a group of reading-disabled children with differences in cognitive dysfunctions, the results obtained may be more diagnostic of the learning problems than they will be evaluative of the learning program. Hence, individualization of all facets of the remediation program is essential to the education of dyslexic children.

Education of the child with cognitive disabilities releated to reading is complex. We must determine the nature of the processing problems, relate our learning tasks to the individual cognitive deficits and integrities, and evaluate the educational plan in terms of growth in processing abilities. Yet we believe this to be the most effective educational approach. As we learn more about the nature of cognitive disabilities, this methodology increasingly will become significant for the education of dyslexic children.

Table 26

VARIMAX ROTATED FACTOR MATRIX
AUDITORY EXPRESSION
EXPERIMENTAL/FAIL SUBJECTS

Variable	N	Factor*					
		1	2	3	4	5	6
SEX	117				545		
GD	117	718					
GMKNON	117					810	
DETFRA	117			198	378		
DETVOP	117		494	257			
DETAAW	117			846			
DETAAS	117		334	639			
DETVAL	117			327		282	
OPSLWS	117	−209					217
OPSLAC	117		343			238	
WISINF	117						574
WISCOM	117	933					
WISART	117	393	601				
WISSIM	117	256	343				
WISVOC	117	460	304	256			
WISDSP	117		756				318
WRATRD	117	388	−215	−245	688		
% Variance		33.2	28.5	12.9	10.7	7.8	6.8

*Decimal points are omitted from the correlation coefficients.
Critical value at $p = .05$: $r = .195$
$\quad\quad\quad\quad p = .01$: $r = .254$

REFERENCES

Farnham-Diggory, S. *Cognitive Processes in Children: A Psychological Preparation for Teaching and Curriculum Development.* New York: Harper & Row, 1972.

Johnson, D., and Myklebust, H. *Learning Disabilities: Educational Principles and Practices.* New York: Grune & Stratton, 1967.

Killen, J. A learning systems approach to intervention. *In* H. Myklebust, ed., *Progress in Learning Disabilities,* Vol. III. New York: Grune & Stratton, 1975.

Luria, A. Speech development and the formation of mental processes. *In* M. Cole and I. Maltzman, eds., *A Handbook of Contemporary Soviet Psychology.* New York: Basic Books, 1969.

Myklebust, H. *The Psychology of Deafness: Sensory Deprivation, Learning, and Adjustment* (2nd ed.). New York: Grune & Stratton, 1964.

Myklebust, H. *Development and Disorders of Written Language: Picture Story Language Test,* Vol. I. New York: Grune & Stratton, 1965.

Myklebust, H. Learning disabilities: definition and overview. *In* H. Myklebust, ed., *Progress in Learning Disabilities,* Vol. I. New York: Grune & Stratton, 1968.

Myklebust, H. *Development and Disorders of Written Language: Studies of Normal and Exceptional Children,* Vol. II. New York: Grune & Stratton, 1973.

Myklebust, H. Indentification and diagnosis of children with learning disabilities: an interdisciplinary study of criteria. *In* S. Walzer and P. Wolff, eds., *Minimal Cerebral Dysfunction in Children.* New York: Grune & Stratton, 1973a.

Myklebust, H., Bannochie, M., and Killen, J. Learning disabilities and cognitive processes. *In* H. Myklebust, ed., *Progress in Learning Disabilities,* Vol. II. New York: Grune & Stratton, 1971.

Myklebust, H., and Boshes, B. *Minimal Brain Damage in Children*. Washington, D.C.: Department of Health, Education and Welfare, USPHS, 1969.

Neisser, U. *Cognitive Psychology*. New York: Appleton-Century-Crofts, 1967.

Piaget, J. *Six Psychological Studies*. New York: Random House, 1967.

Shepard, R. The mental image. *American Psychologist,* 1978, 33:125–137.

Slobin, D. Cognitive prerequisities for the development of grammar. *In* C. Ferguson and D. Slobin, eds. *Studies of Child Language Development*. New York: Holt, Rinehart & Winston, 1973.

Sokolov, A. Studies of the speech mechanisms of thinking. *In* M. Cole and I. Maltzman, eds., *A Handbook of Contemporary Soviet Psychology*. New York: Basic Books, 1969.

Vygotsky, L. *Thought and Language*. Cambridge, Mass.: MIT Press, 1962.

VIII.   Reading Disabilities:
Problems of Rule Acquisition and Linguistic Awareness

DORIS J. JOHNSON AND PAMELA EVANS HOOK

Children with reading problems have long concerned educators, psychologists, neurologists, and other professionals. The nature of the problems varies, however, with the populations studied and the theoretical frames of reference used. In recent years it has become increasingly clear that broad-based multidisciplinary studies are necessary to determine as much as possible about the nature of the disturbance. Specialists in learning disabilities, psychoneurology, psycholinguistics, and various branches of medicine including genetics, psychiatry, and ophthalmology all contribute to our understanding of reading and its disorders.

Research and observations indicate many causes for reading problems including sensory impairments, mental retardation, central nervous system disturbance, and lack of stimulation or instruction. Consequently, the management and educational programs should be designed to meet individual needs. The group of children with whom we are concerned primarily have many integrities; they have adequate hearing, vision, and intelligence but have difficulty decoding or interpreting the printed word. Because of the complexity of the reading process and the various cognitive skills required, we find it necessary to complete a comprehensive psychoeducational evaluation to define the child's strengths and weaknesses. Our basic frame of reference is one that views the child as an active "information processor" who has multiple modalities for input and output of information and potential for a network of complex integrative skills. In addition to a detailed study of the child's reading behavior, the evaluation assesses modes of input and output to ascertain which are intact or deficient (Johnson and Myklebust, 1967). Further analyses are done to determine whether impairments result from disturbances in intrasensory, intersensory, or multisensory learning (Birch and Belmont, 1964; Chalfant and Scheffelin, 1969; Hebb, 1963; Myklebust, 1967; Zigmond, 1966). Tasks are selected or designed to determine the level of the breakdown—that is, whether the disturbance occurs at the level of perception, imagery, symbolization, or conceptualization (Myklebust, 1964; Johnson and Myklebust, 1967; Myklebust, Bannochie, and Killen, 1971).

Several studies have enhanced our understanding of cognitive processes in relation to reading disabilities (Vellutino, 1977; Vernon, 1977); however, not all are conclusive. Those related to phonemic discrimination, in particular, have yielded various results (Hammill and Larsen, 1974). This is due in many respects to the varied populations and instruments used for research. Wepman (1960) and Harris (1970) reported that children who fail to detect differences in sounds of words may have difficulty reading. Their hypotheses were confirmed by Flynn and Byrne (1970) who found that retarded readers had more difficulty with auditory discrimination of words, nonsense syllables, and musical pitches than did advanced readers in the third grade. Atchison (1975) found that a group of first-grade learning-disability children performed significantly below the controls on various measures of phonemic discrimination but a small subgroup contributed to most of the difference. Phonemic discrimination performance did not correlate significantly with reading achievement for either group of children.

Various memory disturbances have been observed among dyslexic children. In a descriptive study of 60 dyslexic children, Johnson and Myklebust (1965) found that auditory verbal memory disturbances were more pronounced than visual impairments. The dyslexics were particularly deficient on the Auditory Attention Span for Words subtest of the Detroit Tests of Learning Aptitude (Baker and Leland, 1967). Their performance also was poor on the Auditory Attention Span for Syllables subtest. The latter task involves repetition of sentences, and therefore might assess some aspects of syntax as well as memory span.

Many investigations have indicated that reading-disabled children have difficulty with temporal sequencing (Vellutino, 1977; Vernon, 1977). Ability to order information is critical for many facets of language including syntax and formulation of ideas. In addition, reading requires integration of an auditory temporal sequence with a visuospatial pattern. In our studies we have attempted to determine whether the child has a sensory specific problem of sequencing or whether he has generalized problems of ordering. Burns (1975) examined sequential memory according to various modalities of input and output among good and poor readers. Subjects were given sets of digits auditorily, visually, and bisensorily; with each set of inputs they were asked to give oral and written responses. She found that the reading-disabled subjects had difficulty with sequential memory irrespective of mode of input or output.

Johnson and Myklebust(1965) observed other auditory sequencing problems in a group of 60 dyslexics. Only 13 of the group were able to say the months of the year in order. Our recent clinical experience with adolescents and young adults with learning disabilities suggests that many have problems with memory for the alphabet, days of the week, and other series.

Word-retrieval problems also have been found among many children with language and learning disabilities (Johnson and Myklebust, 1967; Rutherford, 1977; Vellutino, 1977). They use circumlocutions, word substitutions, sound effects or pantomime in order to communicate. Some have difficulty with oral reading tasks. They may recognize letter names or sounds but cannot recall the names. Some substitute words with similar meanings such as "cake" for "cookie." Some have extensive pauses or latencies before speaking or reading words. These problems of picture-naming and letter-naming were found to be highly predictive of reading failures in studies done by Jansky and deHirsch (1972). Mattis, French, and Rapin (1975) isolated a subgroup of dyslexic adolescents who had language disorders and retrieval problems. Although German (1976) did not study a specific group of subjects with reading problems she found that a population of 8- to 10-year-old learning-disabled boys had more word-retrieval problems than the control group. These studies suggest the continued need to analyze cognitive processes in relation to reading. Longitudinal research of both efficient and inefficient readers is necessary to determine which processes are most crucial for various aspects of reading acquisition.

RULE ACQUISITION AND READING

The primary purpose of this chapter is to review current research related to acquisition and application of certain linguistic rules necessary for efficient reading. Disturbances of perception or memory may interfere with a child's ability to read, but one of the most critical factors pertains to abstraction of the rule systems needed for oral language and reading. The process of language acquisition is one of learning rules (Gibson and Levin, 1975). Initially, the child learns phonological, syntactic, and semantic rules for oral communication. Later, when reading is introduced, he abstracts sets of rules related to orthography and written texts.

Studies of children with oral language disorders indicate that many youngsters are delayed in acquiring one or more sets of these rules (Morehead and Morehead, 1976; Lenneberg and Lenneberg, 1975). Various researchers reported that speech-defective children use rules not typically found among normal children; thus, in some instances the problem may be one of difference rather than delay (Menyuk, 1964; Lee, 1966). Our clinical studies of young language-impaired children revealed inconsistent rule usage. In a study of normal and language-delayed preschoolers, Johnson and Kohner (1973) found that the latter group were far less predictable in use of plural rules than normal children.

When a child enters school he has acquired considerable competence in the basic use of oral communication. Language usage has become nearly automatic and he has a high degree of skill and mastery over the necessary rules. He brings considerable knowledge to the reading process. Goodman (1967) highlights the relationship between reading and oral language by referring to the reading process as a "psycho-linguistic guessing game." The reader predicts what the next word will be from the preceding words using his previous knowledge of language and the grapho-phonemic, semantic, and syntactic cues. An experienced reader relies more heavily on the syntactic and semantic cues, while the beginning reader is more dependent on the grapho-phonemic cues. The child with language disorders has a less efficient basis for making accurate predictions. A recent study by Blalock (1977) indicated that children with learning disabilities were less adept in making predictions forming hypotheses than were normal children.

Both oral language and reading tasks involve abstraction and application of rules. Gibson and Levin (1975) developed a theory of information processing in relation to reading which supports this hypothesis. They assert that there are two basic assumptions about reading: first, that reading is a cognitive process that starts at the perceptual and ends at the conceptual level; and second, the basis of language (and therefore reading) is abstraction. The child must learn that objects have distinctive features relative to each other and that events are invariant and occur over time. From establishing the relationship between the distinctive feature and invariants, the child forms higher order structures or hierarchies. These hierarchies are sets of rule systems which the child uses to organize his world. The processes through which the child must learn include the abstracting of essential characteristics (the features and invariants) through differentiation, filtering out or ignoring irrelevant characteristics, and developing progressively better strategies for abstracting and filtering. As learning progresses, the child becomes more specific with regard to features that can be abstracted; hence there is greater economy in the information processing. For example, in reading, the child becomes more able to use larger units in his processing, moving from the single letter, to words, phrases, and clauses.

Wardaugh (1969) stresses that a definition of reading must include the understanding of at least two concepts. First, there is a connection between English orthography and the phonological system. Secondly, sentences have meanings that can be accounted for in terms of syntactic and semantic rules. The first of these could be considered as similar to decoding the surface structure level of language and the second as analogous to a combination of structural and semantic analysis at the deep structure levels as described in Ruddell's (1970) systems of communication model.

Perfetti (1977) suggests that a higher level of processing is necessary for complete comprehension, which involves an integrative analysis and synthesis of the sentence with the context and with previous knowledge or experience. A breakdown in ability to establish the sound/symbol correspondence, or to decode the word at the surface structure level, hinders comprehension or analysis of syntactic and semantic components at the deep structure level. Difficulty in using semantic cues also inhibits correct decoding of words as well as disrupts comprehension (Goodman, 1967). The beginning or inefficient reader must deduce meaning from the surface structure or grapho-phonemic cues, but the fluent reader can use his developing semantic knowledge at the deep structure level as a tool to predict what the surface structure will be (Smith, 1971).

Chall (1974) states that the reading process goes through structural, qualitative changes rather than merely quantitative changes. At all stages, reading is a problem-solving behavior but the problem is transformed over time. The first stage can be thought of as the Decoding stage (Chall, 1974) or Transfer stage (Fries, 1963). The major problem to be solved at this stage is "cracking the code" or transferring from "the auditory signs" for language signals which the child already knows to new visual signs for the same signals. This stage generally occurs in grade one and the first part of grade two.

Fries describes the second stage, encompassing grades two and three, as the time when responses to visual patterns become "habits" and are so automatic that the graphic shapes themselves sink below the threshold of attention. It is at this stage that the child is becoming an "automatic" rather than merely "accurate" reader, as described by LaBerge and Samuels (1974). Chall emphasizes the role of this stage in developing fluency in use and application of skills. She says that the content of what a child reads in second and third grade is not new; the stories are about real life or fanciful characters and the ideas are familiar. The child reads for confirmation of things he already knows. The language level of the written material is well below his oral language level.

By the third stage, beginning around fourth grade, the child has reached the point where reading is so automatic that it is used equally, or more than, oral language in acquiring experience (Fries, 1963). Chall emphasizes that, at this stage, the child must use reading as a vehicle for learning. The vocabulary level and syntactic complexity of the sentences increases substantially until it reaches and extends beyond the oral language level of the child.

Control of language is important at all stages and, depending upon the type of problem a child has, various difficulties appear at each stage. Problems in "cracking the code" interfere with progression to stages II and III. Although a child may not have marked difficulty at stage I, he may have problems developing the automaticity that allows him to attend to the meaning.

LaBerge and Samuels (1974) have developed a model of the reading process based on attention and automatic processing which helps to explain the difficulties encountered by children who have a learning disability in reading. The attention of the efficient reader is on the meaning of what he is reading rather than on the surface structure grapho-phonemic associations and syntax, It is therefore necessary to develop automaticity in the application of word-attack skills so that these skills no longer require attention and the reader can concentrate on meaning. Proficient readers have developed a high degree of automaticity in application of phonic word-attack skills. When they do not recognize a word automatically they are able, with moderate attention, to give a relatively accurate approximation of the actual word. Children who have a learning disability in reading however, have not developed automaticity in decoding of words and, to be successful, must focus much more attention on application of phonic word-attack skills. Their attempts at phonic analysis have not progressed to an accurate level and their errors often bear little resemblance to the actual word.

LINGUISTIC AWARENESS AND READING

Although children have a relatively good language base by the age of 6, they continue to develop and refine their language skills. One area of continued development is in the awareness of the rule system governing language and applying these rules when learning to read.

Venezky (1972) states that young children are unaware of the purpose or nature of reading. They do not know that letters represent sounds, that sounds can be blended into words, and words into sentences. He stresses that to master reading they must learn to treat sounds as individual units and manipulate them—"rhyming, matching words by initial or final sounds, or by attaching sounds to letters and blending them into words" (p. 16). Francis (1972) emphasizes that much of the child's confusion is due to "unfamiliarity with an analytical approach to language" (p. 17).

It is the child's ability to treat language "analytically" that is of importance in learning to read (Venezky, 1972). There must be a minimum level of linguistic awareness needed for reading—for, as Warren (1971) points out, if a child has not abstracted the set of features that make up the phonemes of his language, the establishment of grapheme/phoneme correspondence will be impossible. Everyone, however, is not sufficiently aware of the phonological units nor can they easily acquire this awareness even by being taught (Cazden, 1973). Children beginning school are still developing awareness of aspects of their own speech that are necessary to learn phonics (Karpova, 1955; Bruce, 1964; Lieberman, Shankweiler, Fischer and Carter, 1974). Cazden (1973) labels this difficulty as lack of metalinguistic awareness, which she defines as "the ability to make language forms opaque and attend to them in and for themselves." She views this as "a special kind of language performance, one which makes special cognitive demands, and seems to be less easily and less universally acquired than the language performances of speaking and listening" (p.3).

Vygotsky (1962) stresses the interrelationship between learning to read and developing metalinguistic awareness. The child has only an unconscious command of the grammar and phonetic composition of words of his native language.

> If you ask a child to produce a combination of sounds, for example *sk*, you will find that its deliberate articulation is too hard for him, yet within a structure, as in the word Moscow, he pronounces the same sounds with ease . . . the child realizes for the first time in learning to write that the word *Moscow* consists of the sounds m-o-s-k-o-w and learns to pronounce each one separately. (pp. 101–102)

The attention of the listener is not on speech sounds, words, or syntactic patterns but on the meaning of the utterance or the intention of the speaker. Language forms are basically transparent—one sees through them to the meaning (Cazden, 1973). However, the person can become aware of synthesizing and can reflect on the linguistic experience in the same way he can reflect on other experiences (Mattingly, 1972; Cazden, 1973). Conscious awareness of the rules governing language comprehension and use are not developed evenly across all aspects of language. There is much greater awareness of phonological and phonetic elements (surface structure) than of syntactic or semantic elements (deep structure or transformational history). Words, syllables, and short phrases appear to be the most obvious minimal units, and isolated phonological segments or phonemes are less so. Many studies have been done to determine the minimal unit, but results have been inconclusive (Liberman, Cooper, Shankweiler, et al., 1967; Savin and Bever, 1970; Day, 1970; Bond, 1971; McNeill and Lindig, 1973).

Linguistic awareness is the basis for many language-based skills which require isolation and manipulation of phonological elements. There appears to be a neurologic basis for this difference between the act of synthesis and awareness of the elements being synthesized. The Russian neurologist, Konorski (1967), has developed a theory of neurologic organization which supports this premise that metalinguistic awareness requires ability to analyze existing structures. He hypothesizes that perceptions are formed into single higher order units (gnostic areas) made up of lower order receptions (transit units) but do not "know" from which components they have been synthesized. The transit stimulus patterns no longer participate as separate items but are amalgamated into the whole and lose their individuality. These gnostic units are described as the biologically meaningful stimulus patterns that are used in associative processes and behavior. The process of perceiving the patterns represented in lower levels (e.g., phonemes) is not done by returning to lower levels but requires formation of special perceptive units at the highest level. He stresses that the simplicity is only apparent and that the act is even more sophisticated because it is not a natural perceptive experience. As Anglin (1970) points out, employing principles and being aware of them may reflect different cognitive capacities.

A breakdown in conscious awareness of the separate elements that make up the rule systems for intonation, phonology, and grammar in oral language might be expected in children who have difficulty applying phonic word-attack skills. Since these rules probably have been developed to a greater extent intuitively, it is believed that their performance will be better on material with semantic cues and will deteriorate on nonmeaningful material where more conscious awareness (isolation and abstraction) and generalization are necessary. They can be expected to have difficulty applying knowledge of intonation and grammar as well as of phonology when reading orally.

Awareness of Segmentation

Ability to segment the speech flow into isolated words is essential for reading acquisition and appears to be developmental. Holden and MacGinitie (1973) stress that language acquisition in early childhood is unconscious and perhaps similar to sensorimotor learning at the preoperational period. Awareness of language may require more conceptual and cognitive processes associated with operational thought and may be "based more and more on conscious awareness of laws, rules, or relationships that permit manipulations of abstract concepts" (p. 7). The results of their study on kindergarten and first-grade children showed a rapid increase in word awareness at about age 6 and a .68 correlation (adjusted for reliability) with the development of Piagetian type of seriation. A developmental progression of awareness of words was noted. First graders did better on all tasks but found awareness of a word inserted into a list easier than a word inserted into a sentence; both tasks were easier than those requiring the child to be aware that a word changed the grammatical structure of the sentence.

Huttenlocher (1964) studied 4½ to 5-year-olds in their ability to separate two-word sequences and their ability to reverse the order of words. The children had most difficulty separating words that were commonly said together such as *it is* and *red apple*, whereas items such as *man table* were much easier. Karpova (1955) found that Russian children aged 3½ to 7 generally could not divide a sentence into its lexical units. They could distinguish nouns and make a simple division between the complete subject and predicate but had most difficulty in isolating prepositions and conjunctions. Gibson and Levin (1975) describe the stages of ability to segment words in sentences hypothesized by

Karpova (1955): (a) the child considers the meaning of a sentence independently of its structure; (b) the child divides sentences into meaning units, usually nouns; and (c) the child segments the sentences into subject and predicate groups and identifies almost all words although he may still have difficulty with prepositions and conjunctions.

Somewhat similar stages of awareness of words when making up sentences with word cards were found by Mackay and Thompson (1968). They were summarized by Cazden (1972) in the following manner. The child first makes lists of words with no apparent connection and reads them as isolated units. He then composes telegraphic sentences but reads them as complete sentences, and finally realizes that words are missing and either adds them at the end or selects the missing words after the nouns and verbs but inserts them in the correct order. Cazden says this sequence of development appears to indicate that at "five or six years old, children recapitulate at a metalinguistic level of conscious awareness and the development from telegraphic to complete sentence that they went through when they were two to three years old at the linguistic level of nonconscious oral speech" (pp. 86–87).

Results of studies comparing children's ability to segment speech in oral and written form have been somewhat inconsistent. Kingston, Weaver, and Figa (1971) found that first graders could segment sentences containing nonsense words and real words equally well and used primarily the visual cues of the spaces between words. When asked to put out a block for each word in a sentence, the children did better with a visual stimulus (sentence typed on a primary typewriter) than either of two auditory stimuli (sentence read by examiner or via a tape recording). They tended to overestimate the number of words in the visual presentation and to underestimate them in the auditory. It is difficult to determine, however, whether difficulty with auditory memory was as important a factor as the lack of visual cues.

Figa (1973), in a study of the relationship between perception of oral and written sentence segmentation of first graders, found that those who had trouble orally also had trouble with written segmentation. The children who did not have difficulty with oral segmentation had fewer problems with written material. She concluded that ability to segment sentences orally precedes ability to segment sentences presented graphically. However, since she initially divided her groups on the basis of whether or not they could segment sentences orally, it seems that these skills might simply be correlated with one another.

Holden and McGinitie (1973) studied kindergarten children's conceptions of word boundaries in speech and print. They also found that when segmenting phrases and short sentences into words, function words were more difficult to isolate and were generally compounded with the following content word. In choosing a visual representation of the sentence based on their oral segmentation, no children consistently chose the conventional representation if they did not segment it correctly auditorily. Several children were able to base their response on a correspondence between their oral segmentation and the visual representation. There were many, however, who did not respond consistently in choosing a visual segmentation that corresponded with their auditory segmentation.

It was concluded that children's conceptions of word boundaries often reflect intuitive linguistic features such as rhythm rather than conventional definitions of words and that many children often reflect intuitive linguistic features such as rhythm rather than conventional definitions of words, and that many children at the end of kindergarten are not familiar with printing conventions. Ability to identify words in context might not coincide with beginning reading instruction for all children and reading may be more difficult for those who can respond to utterances only globally rather than analytically. Ability to segment oral sentences has been found to correlate fairly highly (.47) with total reading achievement of children in the first grade (McNinch, 1974).

McNeill and Lindig (1973) feel that none of these experiments reveal the perceptual units of speech. They criticize Savin and Bever (1970) by pointing out that, when comparing response times to recognition of phonemes versus syllables, the same search list was used and it contained only syllables. Thus phoneme targets were being compared to syllable search lists. McNeill hypothesizes that the longer response time to phonemes was due to a mismatch between linguistic level of the target and level of the search list. His study revealed that the level producing the minimal response time can equally be the phoneme, syllable, word, or sentence depending on the levels being compared. In accord with Cazden (1973), McNeill discusses this phenomenon in terms of linguistic transparency. Ordinarily the listener is not aware of phonological and grammatical structures even though they are "perceived." When the target and the search list are on different linguistic levels, attention must be divided between two mutually transparent objects—the further apart the levels, the more difficult the task. What is "perceptually real" is what is "opaque" or what one focuses one's attention on; in speech, it is the meaning. None of the levels are focused unless a conscious effort is made.

Whatever the most natural unit of language is, children must learn to isolate phonemes within words in order to apply phonics as a word-attack strategy.

> An ability to hear each separate sound in a word, to separate it clearly from the one next to it, and to know out of which sound the word is composed, i.e., the ability to analyze word sound composition, is a very important precondition for correct training in literacy. (Zaporozhets and Elkonin, 1971, p. 169)

This ability, however, is not always learned spontaneously. Cazden (1972) and Calfee, Chapman, and Venezky (1972) emphasize that the difficulty in developing conscious awareness does not usually lie at the perceptual level. Eimas, Siqueland, Jusczyk, et al. (1971) have shown that even infants respond to changes in phonemes. Messer (1967) found that children aged 3.1 to 4.5 years had implicit knowledge of phonology and were able to differentiate words that violated English phonology from those that conformed. Menyuk (1968) also found that by age 4 children were able to distinguish English from non-English phonological rules. Tests attempting to measure auditory discrimination, defined by Wepman as the capacity to distinguish between phonemes or individual sounds used in speech, have been found to be significantly correlated with beginning reading ability (Wepman, 1960; Christine and Christine, 1964; deHirsch, Jansky, and Langford, 1966).

Most of these tests, however, require the child to compare two words and therefore to reflect on sounds in words and make conscious judgments about them. These tests thus require more than perceptual discrimination. As Wepman points out, ability to accurately compare words develops at different rates in children but most children have developed adequate awareness by 8 years of age. Further support for the hypothesis that word comparisons require more than auditory discrimination at the perceptual level is found in research that indicates nonsense or unfamiliar words are more difficult to differentiate than familiar words for kindergarten and first-grade children (Elenbogen and Thompson, 1972; Atchison, 1975).

There continues to be controversy over whether these kinds of "auditory discrimination" tests are helpful in identifying areas of deficit in children with reading problems above the age of 8. Larsen, Rogers, and Sowell (1976) compared learning disability children to normal children aged 8 to 10 on Wepman's Auditory Discrimination Test (1973) and found no significant differences. Hook (1976) tested 9- and 10-year-old proficient and learning disabled readers using a modified version of Wepman's test and a test involving pairs of nonsense words based on the same contrasts present in real words. No significant differences were found between the groups on the real words but significant differences were present on the nonsense words. It is possible that, although difficulties in comparing real words tend to decrease as the child grows older and are less correlated with reading in the upper grades, the same underlying problem might appear in somewhat more difficult tasks of language analysis.

Although ability to distinguish between minimally contrasting pairs of words has been found to correlate with reading in the early grades, it has been shown that, even in first through third graders, the ability to identify specific sounds is more important (Risko, 1973). Ability to segment words into parts also appears to be developmental. Liberman, Shankweiler, Fischer, et al. (1974) make an interesting analogy between the segments first abstracted by the child and the development of writing systems. The first writing system to develop used meaningful units (words), then use of meaningless units (syllables) was devised, and finally the alphabetic system using segments of phonemic size was developed.

Meaningful words are the first units abstracted by the child, then syllables, and finally phonemes. This is the order of increasing difficulty and the order of appearance in development. Liberman's study on the ability of nursery school, kindergarten, and first-grade children to segment words into syllables and phonemes, found the following progression: in nursery school, no children could segment by phonemes but 46% could segment by syllables; by kindergarten, 17% could segment by phonemes and 48% by syllables; and by the end of first grade, 70% by phonemes and 90% by syllables. Phonemes are more difficult because, for example, a word with three phonemic segments has only one acoustic segment while each syllable within a word has a vocalic nucleus and a peak of acoustic energy which provides an audible cue to segmentation.

Bruce (1964) found developmental progression in ability of 5- to 7.6-year-olds to isolate and manipulate sounds in a task requiring deletion of sounds from words. The children were asked to say what word would be left if a particular letter (beginning, middle, or end) were taken away. Children with a mental age below 7.0 had great difficulty with the task. They generally either repeated the test word (9.6%) or gave a single sound or letter name (84.6%). Strategies of the children became progressively more analytic. Children with a mental age of 5+ had little appreciation that sounds and words are related, and children with the mental age of 6+ used phonetic resemblance rather than analysis and gave answers that shared phonetic characteristics, such as *han-d/land* or *pin-k/wink*. By the metal age of 7+, the children were able to achieve closer approximations; their failures became more analytic.

The position of the phoneme within the word was also significant. Analysis of the beginning of the word is easiest, and the middle hardest. Even by the mental age of 8+ and 9+, some children still had trouble deleting sounds in the middle. Bruce outlines the child's progression toward more accurate phonetic analysis in the following way:

1. Recognize that words and sounds are interrelated.
2. Acquire criteria of what constitutes analysis
3. Achieve positional differentiation
4. Overcome the cohesiveness of the word sound pattern in their experience.

Zhurova (1963–1964) found that when required to abstract the relationship between two words beginning with the same sound, many children from age 5 to 6 years and most from 4 to 5 years could not complete the task. By the age of 6 to 7, however, they could generalize the relationship to new situations. Calfee, et al. (1972) studied the ability of kindergarten children to learn paired associates based on segmentation during a training period and to transfer this knowledge. Some segmentation resulted in real words and some in nonsense words. The real word list produced more correct responses, but this was not related to transfer performance. The children seemed to learn a concept based on phonological relations; their errors were phonologically similar to the stimulus word. There was a bimodal distribution on both the training and the transfer tasks. The children either grasped the concept (reached criterion on the training task) and were able to transfer it or they did not reach criterion and could not do the transfer task.

Rosner (1975) developed a test of a child's ability to isolate and manipulate sounds in words. The task begins with omitting one part of a compound word. Then the task becomes more difficult, requiring omission of the beginning sound, the ending sound, and finally, a sound within a consonant blend. By third grade, all of the tasks should be easily accomplished. Difficulty with this type of phonetic analysis contributes to difficulty in learning to read (Rosner, 1974). Word reading correlated .53 among first graders and .49 among second graders with this test (Rosner and Simon, 1971).

This difficulty in segmenting and manipulating sounds in words appears to continue throughout elementary school for many disabled readers. Hook (1976) found significant differences between proficient and learning-disabled readers, aged 9 and 10, on a series of tasks requiring ability to isolate and manipulate sounds in words. The task that was the best predictor of group membership was learning a code language similar to Pig Latin, which involved ability to isolate and manipulate sounds in words and to apply rules. This task accounted for 100% of group memberships for both groups. None of the learning-disabled readers were able to effectively perform the task and all of the proficient readers could. In addition, even if a learning-disabled child was able to complete one item correctly, he was unable to consistently apply the rules to subsequent words, whereas once the proficient readers mastered the rules, they could consistently apply them even to multisyllabic words. These results are in keeping with the results of a major project conducted by Myklebust, Bannochie, and Killen (1971) on learning disability and normal children. The test that best differentiated the two groups of children was syllabication (reading nonsense words).

Our observations of adolescent and adult dyslexics indicate that many have persistent problems with segmenting and manipulating sounds in words. In a study of adults who were learning secret languages, Day (1973) found two distinct groups: language-bound and stimulus-bound. The language-bound subjects had more difficulty applying the rules of the "secret language" and tended to give more global than sequential responses. They had more difficulty judging temporal order of dichotically presented stimuli and "heard" the natural order of English blends more often even when stimuli were presented in the opposite order (e.g.; they heard the *b* before the *l* even when *l* was presented first). They also tended to show a high level of dichotic fusion—if *banket* was sent to one ear and *lanket* to the other, they felt they heard *blanket* more often than the stimulus-bound group. Implications of this difficulty for learning a foreign language were suggested by Day. This study has relevance for learning-disabled youth since many of them have problems in foreign language learning as they grow older, even after they have overcome many of their reading problems.

Awareness of Syntax

Although Lefevre (1964) acknowledges the importance of awareness of the phonological level of language in developing adequate reading skills, he emphasizes that he considers the last two levels of language analysis (morphemic and syntactic) as most important. The most significant signalling systems for these language analyses are (a) intonation, (b) function order in the sentence; (c) structure words; and (d) word form changes.

Intonation is considered by Lefevre (1964) to be the most important of these language devices and is the first learned by the child. Lewis (1936) outlines three stages in the development of language: broad discrimination between different patterns of expression in intonation, followed by a stage where the total pattern—both the phonetic form and the intonational form—is attended to but the intonational form dominates and finally, the phonetic pattern becomes the dominant feature but the function of the intonational pattern continues to be important. Lieberman (1967) has hypothesized that linguistic use of intonation reflects an innately determined and highly organized system. There are two basic pitch contours—falling contour at the end of a sentence, and rising to mark a question. The child first learns the intonation pattern for statements and then questions. Armstrong and Ward (1926) have defined these contours as two tunes. *Tune I* starts on a medium pitch and continues on this pitch with some upward variation on the stressed syllables until the end of the sentence when the pitch falls rapidly. This is found in statements and imperatives. *Tune II* starts at either a high or middle pitch and gradually falls but ends with a rising or level pitch. This is used in yes/no questions or to imply uncertainty. It is believed that pitch phonemes constitute separate morphemes and carry their own meaning independent of the words (Bloomfield, 1933).

Children with reading problems have more difficulty than normal readers in recognizing the intonational pattern marking a question. Vogel (1972) reported second-grade dyslexic children to have significantly more difficulty than normal children recognizing a question versus a statement melody pattern when nonsense words were used. Results of a study comparing 9- and 10-year-old learning-disabled readers and proficient readers indicated that older elementary-aged children continue to have difficulty recognizing the question contour and have trouble abstracting the rule that any declarative statement can be transformed into a question by using this marked contour (Hook, 1976). Hook also found that learning-disability children had more difficulty applying the rule than in recognizing it.

These findings support results of studies that recognition of rules was easier than application in young children (Anisfeld and Tucker, 1967). Application of a rule requires complete awareness of the principle while recognition can be based on intuitive knowledge. The proficient readers did equally well on both recognition and application subtests, indicating complete understanding of the rule.

Children with learning defects, on the other hand, had more difficulty with application, possibly indicating a relatively stronger intuitive awareness than conscious awareness. It should be noted, however, that on the recognition items it is possible to guess with a 50% chance of being correct. Many of the children with learning disabilities said they were unsure of the answer but guessed correctly. It is difficult to determine whether they were guided by their intuitive knowledge or were fortunate in their choices. Their confusion and failure to *apply* the rule governing intonation, however, indicates a deficiency in the development of rule generalization and application. The learning-disabled children and the proficient readers also appeared to approach the tasks differently in terms of problem-solving behavior and hypothesis-testing strategies. The proficient readers some-times needed to do several items before they understood the principle involved, but once they grasped the rule, they applied it consistently. The learning-disabled readers, on the other hand, often indicated that the task was impossible to solve and either guessed when possible or changed the nature of the task by not following the directions. For example, one of the tasks involved repeating phrases such as, "I eat dinner," first as a statement and then as a question, without changing the word order or adding or subtracting any words. Some learning-disabled children could think of no alternate strategy than to form a question such as "Did I eat dinner?" When told this was not a permissible response, they tended to give up or continue with similar incorrect responses.

The development of awareness of the last three signalling systems involved in mor-phemic and syntactic language analysis discussed by Lefevre (1964)—function order in the sentence, structure words, and word form changes—is also related to reading achievement and appears to increase with age. By 6 years of age, most children have developed control over the most important syntactic elements of their oral language (McNeill; 1970). Although use of syntax continues to be refined, all English inflectional morphemes are present in the vocabulary of first graders (Berko; 1958), and preschool children use all the grammatical sentence types used by adults (Menyuk, 1971). Gibson and Levin (1975) point out, however, that the features of grammar, like phonology, are opaque. The child uses grammatical rules intuitively before he has the ability to abstract the rules and apply them in novel situations.

Children are able to apply correct morphological endings to real words that they are unable to apply to nonsense words (Berko, 1958; Newfield and Schlanger, 1968). Berko feels that the children have memorized these words in a rote manner rather than having learned the grammatical rule. It is suggested, however, that children do know the rules, but at an implicit nonconscious level, and do not have sufficient linguistic awareness to apply them in nonmeaningful situations. Further support is given to this theory by the finding that first graders are able to recognize the correct form of nonsense words before they are able to produce it themselves (Anisfeld and Tucker, 1967). The use of mor-phological rules to nonsense words appears to be developmental, and increases from preschool to first grade (Berko, 1958).

The child's awareness of the syntax of his language continues to develop throughout the early elementary school grades (Palermo and Molfese, 1972). As use of syntax develops in children, the tendency to associate words by part of speech and to abstract the syntactic characteristics of nonsense words increases (Brown and Berko, 1960). Children tend to respond with associations to words from different syntactic classes until about the age of 8 when syntactic similarity becomes a more important determiner (Gibson and Levin, 1975). Brown and Berko conclude that the change to words associated syntacti-cally and the ability to make correct grammatical use of new words "are two manifesta-tions of the child's developing appreciation of English syntax" (p. 13).

A child's control and awareness of syntactic and morphologic elements of oral language appears to be significantly related to reading achievement. Weinstein and Rabinovitch (1971) compared good and poor fourth-grade readers in memorization of lists of unstructured and syntactically structured nonsense words. There was no difference in being able to retain the unstructured material, but good readers learned the structured lists easily, whereas poor readers did not. Poor readers were not able to use the syntactic cues that were implicit in the structured lists to facilitate recall. Rudell's (1973) scores of beginning first graders on the Berry-Talbott (Berry, 1966), a test of ability to apply morphologic rules to nonsense words, and Bellugi and Brown's Test of Syntax, correlated significantly with their scores on reading achievement tests at the end of the year.

According to Vogel, (1975) the Berry-Talbott was one of three tests most responsible for the variance between her group of normals and her group of dyslexic 7- and 8-year-olds (.001 level of significance). It is interesting, however, that Vogel did not find differences between her groups in the recognition of correct grammatical usage. This lends support to the theory that there is developmental progression from skill in recognizing grammaticality to applying it in a structured non-spontaneous situation, to finally being able to apply this knowledge to nonsense words. This is similar to the findings on the development of linguistic awareness of phonology and intonation discussed above. Similar difficulties on the Berry-Talbott have been found in upper elementary 9- and 10-year-old learning-disabled children with reading problems (Hook, 1976).

Vogel and Hook also found significant differences on the Illinois Test of Psycholinguistic Abilities Grammatic Closure subtest, which involves applying morphologic endings to real words. Hook emphasizes, however, that although these results indicate that learning-disabled readers have difficulty with applying morphologic endings to both real and nonsense words, it should be noted that the tasks on the ITPA Grammatic Closure and the Berry-Talbott are not directly parallel. The Grammatic Closure subtest contains a high percentage of irregular words, and the Berry-Talbott is based primarily on regular words. The errors of the children in both groups on the Grammatic Closure subtest did not involve knowledge of regular endings or words (Hook, 1976). The largest number of errors occurred on irregular past-tense verbs, noun plurals, and pronouns. The learning-disability children made more errors in each of the categories of irregular words but failed no items that involved words with regular endings.

The difficulty in remembering and applying irregular forms may be related to the problems in rule abstraction discussed above. Although it appears that many children with learning disabilities by age 9 often have adequately mastered regular syntactic rules, they have not yet abstracted the more specific rules needed for correct usage when dealing with irregular words. This may be less a function of memory than a failure to recognize and note irregularities when they occur. Normally developing children often "overgeneralize" syntactic rules to irregular words previously used correctly. Since meaning is not significantly interfered with by this overgeneralizing, the learning-disability child might have a tendency to overlook the surface structure syntax and never focus on the fine distinctions, which are easily noted and assimilated by the normal child after sufficient practice with the rule system. This seems to indicate a weakened syntactic base in that the learning-disabled readers have not developed the automatic ability to apply irregular endings in a structured situation. Some of their mistakes, however, indicated possible interference from the testing format. For example, children who responded with *childs* as the plural for *child* would probably use the correct form in their spontaneous speech. This area needs further investigation.

Results of other studies analyzing expressive language support a relationship between reading and language ability. Strickland (1962) studied the relationship between children's spontaneous oral language and reading in second and sixth grades. He found that poorer readers used a larger proportion of short utterances and employed the most common syntactic patterns less frequently. There were trends toward greater use of movable elements in sentences (statements of time, place, cause, etc.), subordination, and elaboration among better readers, but it was felt that no strong conclusions could be made.

Harris (1975), using a structured task requiring the children to formulate oral and written responses illustrating various syntactic patterns, found a significant correlation between oral and written syntax and reading achievement in second graders. Use of syntax was significantly superior to intelligence as a predictor of reading achievement. Again, it appears that proficiency in applying knowledge of grammar in a structured situation is related to reading achievement.

SUMMARY

The purpose of this chapter was to review research related to language processes, linguistic awareness, and reading. Since oral language cues are directly related to the cuing systems used in reading, it is important to include many auditory processes in the diagnosis of learning-disabled children (Johnson, 1977). It is equally important to study the child's ability to abstract and apply linguistic rules in novel situations. Both recognition and application of principles should be assessed to plan appropriate remediation. To provide the most beneficial instruction it also is helpful to observe the ways in which a child acquires new rules and principles. Some can induce rules following repeated instances but others may need to be given more explicit rules. The clinician needs to provide ample opportunities for rule application so that language patterns become automatic.

REFERENCES

Anglin, J. *The Growth of Word Meaning*. Cambridge: M.I.T. Press, 1970.

Anisfeld, M., and Tucker, G. English pluralization rules of six-year-old children. *Child Development*, 1967, 38:1201–1217.

Armstrong, L., and Ward, I. *Handbook of English Intonation*. Berlin: B.G. Teubner, 1926.

Atchinson, M. Variables influencing phonemic discrimination performance in normal and learning-disabled first-grade-age children. Unpublished doctoral dissertation, Northwestern University, 1975.

Baker, H., and Leland, B. *Detroit Tests of Learning Aptitude*. Indianapolis: Bobbs-Merrill Company, 1967.

Berko, J. The child's learning of English morphology. *Word*, 1958, 14:150–177.

Berry, M. *Berry-Talbott Language Tests 1. Comprehension of Grammar*. Rockford, Ill.: 1966.

Birch, H., and Belmont, I. Auditory-visual integration in normal and retarded readers. *American Journal of Orthopsychiatry*, 1964, 34:852–861.

Blalock, J. A study of conceptualization in preschool normal and learning disabled children. Unpublished doctoral dissertation, Northwestern University, 1977.

Bloomfield, L. *Language*. New York: Holt, 1933.

Bond, Z. Units in speech perception. *Working Papers in Linguistics*, No. 9, viii–112. Computer and Information Science Research Center Technical Report Series. The Ohio State University, Columbus, Ohio. OSU-CISRC-TR-71-8. ERIC, ED 060686, 1971.

Brown, R., and Berko, J. Word associations and the acquisition of grammar. *Child Development*, 1960, 31:1–14.

Bruce, D. Analyses of word sounds by young children. *British Journal of Educational Psychology*, 1964, 34:158–169.

Burns, S. An investigation of the relationship between sequential memory and oral reading skills in normal and learning disabled children. Unpublished doctoral dissertation, Northwestern University, 1975.

Calfee, R., Chapman, R., and Venezky, R. How a child needs to think to learn to read. *In* L. Gregg, ed., *Cognition in Learning and Memory*. New York: Wiley, 1972.

Cazden, C. *Child Language and Education*. New York: Holt, Rinehart and Winston, 1972.

Cazden, C. Play with language and metalinguistic awareness: one dimension of language experience. Bank Street College of Education. Paper presented at the Second Lucy Sprague Mitchell Memorial Conference, 1973.

Chalfant, J., and Scheffelin, M. Central processing dysfunctions in children: A review of research. *National Institute of Neurological Diseases and Stroke Monograph*, 1969, 9.

Chall, J. A proposal for reading stages. Paper presented at Harvard University Institute on Reading and Learning Disabilities, 1974.

Christine, D., and Christine, C. The Relationship of auditory discrimination to auditory defects and reading retardation. *Elemenatary School Journal,* 1964, 65:97–100.

Day, R. Temporal order judgments in speech: Are individuals language-bound or stimulus-bound? (St. Louis). Paper presented at the 9th Annual Meeting of the Psychonomic Society, 1969. *Haskins Laboratory Report,* SR-21/22, 1970, 71–87. Cited in I. Lehiste, Units of speech perception. *Working Papers in Linguistics,* No. 12, June, 1972. The Ohio State University, Columbus, Ohio. OSU-CIRC-TR 72-6.

Day, R. On learning secret languages. *Haskins laboratory status report.* SR-34-73, 1973, 141–150.

de Hirsch, K., Jansky, J., and Langford, W. *Predicting Reading Failure.* New York: Harper & Row, 1966.

Eimas, P., Siqueland, E., Jusczyk, P., and Vigoreto, J. Speech perception in infants. *Science,* 1971, 171:303–306.

Elenbogen, E., and Thompson, G. Comparison of social class effects in two tests of auditory discrimination. *Journal of Learning Disabilities,* 1972, 5:209–212.

Elkonin, D. The psychology of mastering the elements of reading. *In* B. Simon and J. Simon, eds., *Educational Psychology in the U.S.S.R.* Stanford: Stanford University Press, 1963.

Figa, L. (University of Georgia) Empirical factors involving the perception of oral and written word unit segmentation by first grade children. *Dissertation Abstracts International,* 1973, 33:3378.

Flynn, P., and Byrne, M. Relationship between reading and selected auditory abilities of third-grade children. *Journal of Speech and Hearing Research,* 1970, 13:731–740.

Francis, H. Sentence structure and learning to read. *British Journal of Educational Psychology,* 1972, 42:113–119.

Fries, C. *Linguistics and Reading.* New York: Holt, Rinehart and Winston, 1963.

Germand, D. A Study of word finding abilities in normal and learning disabled children. Unpublished doctoral dissertation, Northwestern University, 1976.

Gibson, E., and Levin, H. *The Psychology of Reading.* Cambridge: M.I.T. Press, 1975.

Goodman, K. Reading: a psycholinguistic guessing game. *Journal of the Reading Specialist,* 1967, 6:126–135.

Hammill, D., and Larsen, D. The relationship of selected auditory perceptual skills and reading ability. *Journal of Learning Disabilities,* 1974, 7:429–436.

Harris, A. *How to Increase Reading Ability* (5th ed.). New York: David McKay Co., 1970.

Harris, M. Second grade syntax attainment and reading achievement. Paper presented at the Annual Meeting of International Reading Association, 1975. ERIC, ED 106764.

Hebb, D. The semi-autonomous process: its nature and nurture. *American Psychologist,* 1963, 18:16.

Holden, M., and MacGinitie, W. Metalinguistic ability and cognitive performance in children from five to seven. Paper presented at Annual Meeting of the American Educational Research Association, 1973.

Hook, P. A study of metalinguistic awareness and reading strategies in proficient and learning disabled readers. Unpublished doctoral dissertation, Northwesteren University, 1976.

Huttenlocher, J. Children's language: word-phrase relationship. *Science,* 1964, 143:264–265.

Jansky, J., and deHirsch, K. *Preventing Reading Failure.* New York: Harper & Row, 1972.

Johnson, D. Psycho-educational evaluation of children with learning disabilities: study of auditory processes. *In* G. Millichap, ed., *Learning Disabilities and Related Disorders.* Chicago: Yearbook Medical Publishers, 1977.

Johnson, D., and Kohner, P. A study of plural rules in preschool normal and learning disabled children. Paper presented at the Annual Meeting of the Council for Exceptional Children, 1973.

Johnson, D., and Myklebust, H. Dyslexia in childhood. *In* J. Hellmuth, ed., *Learning Disorders,* Vol. I. Seattle: Special Child Publications, 1965.

Johnson, D., and Myklebust, H. *Learning Disabilities: Educational Principles and Practices.* New York: Grune & Stratton, 1967.

Karpova, S. The preschooler's realization of the lexical structure of speech. *Voprosy Psikhologii,* 1955, 4:43–55. Abstract in D. Slobin. Abstracts of Soviet Studies of Child Language. In N. Smith and G. Miller, eds., *The Genesis of Language.* Cambridge: M.I.T. Press, 1966.

Kingston, A., Weaver, W., and Figa, L. Experiments in children's perceptions of words and word boundaries. Yearbook of the National Reading Conference, 1971, 21:91–99.

Konorski, J. *Integrative Activity of the Brain.* Chicago: University of Chicago Press, 1967.

LaBerge, D., and Samuels, S. Toward a theory of automatic information processing in reading. *Cognitive Psychology,* 1974, 6:293–323.

Larsen, S., Rogers, D., and Sowell, V. The use of selected perceptual tests differentiating between normal and learning disabled children. *Journal of Learning Disabilities,* 1976, 9:85–90.

Lee, L. Developmental sentence types: a method for comparing normal and deviant syntactic development. *Journal of Speech and Hearing Disorders,* 1966, 31:311–330.

Lefevre, C. *Linguistics and the Teaching of Reading.* New York: McGraw-Hill, 1964.

Lennenberg, E., and Lennenberg, E. *Foundations of Language Development*, Vol. 2. New York: Academic Press, 1975.

Lewis, M. *Infant Speech, a Study of the Beginnings of Language*. New York: Basic Books, 1936.

Liberman, A., Cooper, F., Shankweiler, D., and Studdert-Kennedy, M. Perception of the speech code. *Psychological Review*, 1967, 74:431–461.

Liberman, I., Shankweiler, D., Fischer, F., and Carter, B. Explicit syllable and phoneme segmentation in the young child. *Journal of Experimental Child Psychology*, 1974, 18:201–212.

Mackay, D., and Thompson, B. The initial teaching of reading and writing: some notes toward a theory of literacy. Programme in linguistics and English teaching, Paper No. 3. London: University College and Longmans, 1968. Cited in C. Cazden *Child Language and Education*. New York: Holt, Rinehart and Winston, 1972.

Mattingly, I. Reading, the linguistic process, and linguistic awareness. *In* J. Kavanagh and I. Mattingly, eds., *Language by Ear and by Eye*. Cambridge: M.I.T. Press, 1972.

Mattis, S., French, J., and Rapin, I. Dyslexia in children and young adults: three independent neuropsychological syndromes. *Developmental Medicine and Child Neurology*, 1975, 17:150–163.

McNeill, D. The development of language. *In* P. Mussen, ed., *Carmichael's Manual of Child Psychology*, Vol. 1 (3rd ed.). New York: John Wiley and Sons, 1970.

McNeill, D., and Lindig, K. The perceptual reality of phonemes, syllables, words and sentences. *Journal of Verbal Learning and Verbal Behavior*, 1973, 12:419–430.

McNinch, G. Awareness of aural and visual word boundary within a sample of first graders. *Perception and Motor Skills*, 1974, 38:1127–1134.

Menyuk, P. Comparison of grammar of children with functionally deviant and normal speech. *Journal of Speech and Hearing Research*, 1964, 7:109–121.

Menyuk, P. Children's learning and production of grammatical and nongrammatical phonological sequences. *Child Development*, 1968, 39:849–859.

Menyuk, P. *The Acquisition and Development of Language*. Englewood Cliffs, N.J.: Prentice-Hall, 1971.

Messer, I. Implicit phonology in children. *Journal of Verbal Learning and Verbal Behavior*, 1967, 6:609–613.

Morehead, D., and Morehead, A. *Normal and Deficient Child Language*. Baltimore: University Park Press, 1976.

Myklebust, H. *Psychology of Deafness*. New York: Grune & Stratton, 1964.

Myklebust, H. Learning disabilities in psychoneurologically disturbed children. *In* P. Hoch and J. Zubin, eds., *Psychopathology of Mental Development*. New York: Grune & Stratton, 1967.

Myklebust, H., Bannochie, M., and Killen, J. Learning disabilities and cognitive processes. *In* H. Myklebust, ed., *Progress in Learning Disabilities*, Vol. II. New York: Grune & Stratton, 1971.

Newfield, M., and Schlanger, B. The acquisition of English morphology by normal and educable mentally retarded children. *Journal of Speech and Hearing Research*, 1968, 11:693–706.

Palermo, D., and Molfese, D. Language acquisition from age five onward. *Psychological Bulletin*, 1972, 78:409–428.

Perfetti, C. Language comprehension and fast decoding: some psycholinguistic prerequisites for skilled reading comprehension. *In* J. Guthrie, ed., *Cognition, Curriculum and Comprehension*. Newark, Del.: International Reading Association, 1977.

Risko, V. Relate auditory discrimination to reading achievement. *Reading World*, 1973, 13:43–51.

Rosner, J. Auditory analysis training with prereaders. *Reading Teacher*, 1974, 27:379–384.

Rosner, J. *Helping Children Overcome Learning Difficulties*. New York: Walker, 1975.

Rosner, J., and Simon, D. The auditory analysis test: An initial report. *Journal of Learning Disabilities*, 1971, 4:384–392.

Ruddell, R. Psycholinguistic implications for a system of communication model. *In* H. Singer, ed., *Theoretical Models and Processes of Reading*. Newark, Del.: International Reading Association, 1970.

Ruddell, R. The relationship of grapheme-phoneme correspondences and of language structure to achievement in first-grade reading. *In* K. Goodman, ed., *The Psycholinguistic Nature of the Reading Process*. Detroit: Wayne State University Press, 1973.

Rutherford, D. Speech and Language Disorders and M.B.D. *In* G. Millichap, ed. *Learning Disabilities and Related Disorders*. Chicago: Yearbook Medical Publishers, 1977.

Savin, H., and Bever, T. The nonperceptual reality of the phoneme. *Journal of Verbal Learning and Verbal Behavior*, 1970, 9:295–302.

Smith, F. *Understanding Reading*. New York: Holt, Rinehart and Winston, 1971.

Strickland, R. The language of elementary school children. *Bulletin of School of Education*, Indiana University, 1962, 38:No. 4.

Vellutino, F. Alternative conceptualizations of dyslexia: evidence in support of a verbal deficit hypothesis. *Harvard Educational Review,* 1977,47:334–354.

Venezky, R. *Language and cognition in reading.* Technical Report No. 188. Wisconsin University, Madison, Research and Development Center for Cognitive Learning, 1972. ERIC ED 067647.

Vernon, M. Varieties of deficiency in the reading process. *Harvard Educational Review,* 1977, 47:396–410.

Vogel, S. An investigation of syntactic abilities in normal and dyslexic children. Unpublished doctoral dissertation, Northwestern University, 1972.

Vogel, S. *An Investigation of Syntactic Abilities in Normal and Dyslexic Children.* Baltimore: University Park Press, 1975.

Vygotsky, L. *Thought and Language.* Cambridge: M.I.T. Press, 1962.

Wardaugh, R. The teaching of phonics and comprehension: a linguistic evaluation. *In* K. Goodman and J. Fleming *Psycholinguistics and the Teaching of Reading.* Newark, Del.: International Reading Association, 1969.

Warren, R. Identification times for phonemic components of graded complexity and for spelling of speech. *Perception and Psychophysics,* 1971, 9:345–349.

Weinstein, R., and Rabinovitch, M. Sentence structure and retention in good and poor readers. *Journal of Educational Psychology,* 1971, 62:25–30.

Wepman, J. Auditory discrimination, speech and reading. *The Elementary School Journal,* 1960, 60:325–333.

Wepman, J. *Auditory Discrimination Test.* Chicago: Language Research Associates, 1973.

Zaporozhets, A., and Elkonin, D. *The Psychology of Preschool Children.* Cambridge: M.I.T. Press, 1971.

Zhurova, L. The development of analyses of words into their sounds by preschool children. *Soviet Psychology and Psychiatry,* 1963–1964, 2:17–27.

Zigmond, N. Intrasensory and intersensory processes in normal and dyslexic children. Unpublished doctoral dissertation, Northwestern University, 1966.

IX. Education for Children with Reading Disabilities

JOHN T. GUTHRIE AND MARY SEIFERT

Education may be the most frequently discussed topic in the field of learning disabilities. At the same time, it is a topic on which there is a small amount of research-based information. The focus of this chapter will be on (a) educational viewpoints of reading disablities, (b) alternative conceptual frameworks for teaching children with learning disabilities, (c) educational research on effective teaching practices, (d) a review of cognitive deficiencies of poor readers, and (e) principles of instruction.

At the most general level, education consists of choices about what is taught to whom and how it should be accomplished. Decisions about these matters are deeply rooted in the cultural heritage of the community. For example, 8- to 10-year-old boys in aboriginal Australia have been found to be superior in draw-a-person and Bender-Gestalt tests (Money and Nurcombe, 1974). Aboriginal boys fare better than American boys and also better than girls in their own communities. The reason is that boys learn to paint in preparation for a circumcision ceremony at 8 to 10 years old. At that time, each boy discloses his totemic body painting on his chest and abdomen to the village as part of the rites of passage into manhood.

A second factor profoundly influencing education is historical precedent. Many educational ideas are practiced today as they were in the past. For instance, having children read aloud in the beginning stages of instruction is as common today as it was in the 18th century. A medical parallel described by Eisenberg (1977) is tonsillectomy and adenoidectomy. The practice of surgically removing tonsils and adenoids when they are infected is extremely widespread, about 1 million cases per year, with about 60 fatalities resulting from the surgery. And yet, this practice prevails without a single shred of scientific evidence. Having become usual and customary, it is not subject to the scrutiny of an experimental design. The practice may be well advised, but it is based on tradition rather than scientific evidence. The same is true of many, many educational practices.

The what and how of teaching are strongly influenced by how the community perceives the content to be learned, and the nature of the learner. These forces have shaped, or as we shall argue misshaped, the field of reading disabilities. Among all sorts of concerned professionals, it is widely known that there is a strong influence from the field of medicine in reading disabilities. Certainly, it was a medically trained ophthalmologist, Hinshelwood, who in 1895 first gave popularity to the idea of word blindness. And Samuel Orton, a medically trained neurologist of the 1920s, eloquently drew attention to the mystery of intelligent children who had not learned to read. Stemming from these and many other sources, the prevailing picture of children who have problems learning to read is drawn in medical language. We are dominated by a conception that relates reading disabilities to disease.

Portions of this chapter have appeared in the following articles and are reprinted with permission:

Guthrie, J. Metaphors for reading failure. *The Reading Teacher,* 1978, 31 (7): 852–854.

Guthrie, J., and Tyler, S. Cognition and instruction of poor readers. *Journal of Reading Behavior,* in press.

Disease Metaphor

A disease can first be described in terms of its symptoms, but the symptoms them-selves are only a sign, not the real problem. Direct treatment of symptoms alone is rare except in the case of a headache, which is not a disease. For example, thessalemia involves swelling of the joints, but it would do little good to wrap the patient's joints with gauze to prevent swelling. After presentation of the symptoms comes a critical step, diagnosis. In this stage the particular subtype of the problem is located. Special tests are conducted to locate the underlying cause. For thessalemia, which results from disorders of globin chain synthesis, the malfuction is located by means of laboratory tests made on blood of the patient. Treatment is directed toward the underlying cause, and if properly selected, it provides reasonably quick and permanent relief. The patient is restored to health and maintained at that level in most cases.

The metaphor of disease for reading goes like this. The child's lack of ability to read well is noticed by the parent or teacher and presented to a professional clinician. The child's mumbling, stuttering approach to printed words is taken by the clinician as a symptom. The failure to read is not the problem. The problem is a basic factor such as visual memory impairment, auditory closure dysfunction, or sensorimotor immaturity. From the disease model we know that biological functions are independent. A person might be anemic although he will remain intelligent, his brain functioning adequately. A person may have a liver problem, but his arm will still perform normally. So reading problems are divided into separate independent components. Factors such as visual se-quential memory are separable from the rest of reading and isolable as the problem for a child. When reading problems are viewed as diseases, extensive diagnosis is needed before treatment can begin. Treatment must be targeted directly to the particular cause identified. If it is well chosen, the treatment will have marked effects, and the child can resume his normal life. If remediation for the reading problem is not immediately effec-tive, it is because the real cause could not be accurately identified or the proper treatment has not been sufficiently developed to countervail the child's difficulty.

Canoeing Metaphor

From an educational standpoint, a far more apt metaphor for learning to read is learning to canoe in the South Pacific. Margaret Mead reports that for Samoans and other islanders in the South Pacific, traveling by canoe is one of life's essentials. In Samoa the daily bread is fish. Fishing requires canoes, and canoes require canoeing. A young boy learns at his father's side that canoes are vital, even sacred. Excellent canoeists are prestigious in the community, and those who fail to learn are relegated to a low place.

Learning to canoe entails learning two relatively distinct abilities—paddling and navigating. Paddling may be initiated in preliminary forms and is improved by physical coordination and strength. Navigating requires knowledge about goals for a trip; direc-tional markers in nature; conditions of weather, water, and wind; and qualities of the craft. While a person who is paddling can be readily observed, a person sitting in a boat navigating may be thinking, planning, or observing landmarks without any behavior visible to an outsider.

Failure to learn canoeing in Samoa is a failure of acquisition. One never attains proficiency in the first place. It may result from a failure in either paddling or navigating, or both. Though causes of canoeing failure may include genetic, physiologic, and emo-tional factors, the largest influence is education. Children who have large amounts of observation, teaching, and practice in canoeing will be superior to those who stay on shore and mend the nets. For those who are educated, there will be normal distribution of attainment—a bell-shaped curve of canoeing ability. Some few will be excellent, many average, and some few very low.

From an educational standpoint, the most effective means to teach canoeing for those who have not learned would involve task analysis and teaching the components to the highest possible level of proficiency. Two distinct aspects are paddling and navigating. But the processes making up these abilities will probably be highly integrated. In paddling, the person who is relatively good at the fast stop will also be good at the sharp left turn. In navigating, there is an inherent connection between understanding the ultimate destination, the relationship between landmarks needed to reach the destination, and the detection of any single landmark. As a result, the many aspects of canoeing will have to be taught together, although one of them might be emphasized for a brief period of time. Proficiency will require long hours and years of diligent and purposeful practice.

As in canoeing, there are two fundamental processes of reading—word recognition (decoding) and comprehension. The skills in each of these areas are highly integrated. A child who is low in one aspect of the skill is usually low in many aspects, and may be characterized as having a slow rate of learning on a wide range of processes. Like paddling, word-recognition processes are reasonably observable during oral reading. But like navigation, comprehension is more difficult for an outsider to see. A child sitting at a table in front of a book may be highly active, but the action is invisible, at least to the naked eye. For children who have not learned, teaching must be focused on particular components and yet also broadly designed and interconnected. Education programs last many years, and any amount of improvement is useful to the student.

VIEWPOINTS OF READING DISABILITIES

Learning Disabilities

Our perception of educational needs for disabled readers is often shaped by our definitions of the population. Who are the children for whom a different form of education may be needed? One authority in the disabilities movement is Lerner (1975). She proclaimed that the field of learning disabilities

> focuses on children of normal intelligence who may be failing in any of a number of learning areas, including arithmetic, language skills, writing, motor development, social skills, as well as reading. But the cause is not primarily due to emotional disturbance, mental retardation, sensory handicap, or educational deprivation. The problem for these children relates to a central nervous system dysfunction. (p. 120)

This definition is rather widely adopted. For instance, Vellutino (1977), a psychologist, used it as the foundation for a review of research on cognitive language and perceptual theories of learning disability. The pervasiveness of this view among practitioners is illustrated by its use as the basis for an article in *Today's Education,* which circulates to 1.8 million members of the National Education Association (Kessinger and Singleton, 1977).

Reading Specialists

Professionals in the reading field, those recognized as authorities by reading teachers and remedial reading specialists, have held a slightly different view. According to Harris (Harris and Sipay, 1975), it is important to distinguish between (a) disabled readers who are unable to function academically at grade level because of poor reading ability; (b) underachievers whose reading ability is sufficient for grade-level requirements, although well below their own expectancy; and (c) slow learners whose reading ability is below age level but in keeping with their somewhat limited learning capacity. In this view, disabled readers are children who cannot read well enough to learn from written materials in school and who seem to have a potential to read more proficiently. For details, specific formulas for calculating expectancies are available from Harris and Sipay (1975). A similar definition of reading disabilities is outlined by Bond and Tinker (1973). In contrast to Lerner's definition, these do not include presumptions about central nervous system dysfunction or exclusions on the basis of social, emotional, or sensory factors.

It should be noted that several noted authorities in reading do not provide any definition at all. Spache (1976) wrote a volume of more than 450 pages on reading disabilities without one. Durkin (1976) includes a chapter on "diagnostic teaching" in her book *Teaching Young Children to Read* with no conceptual framework for reading disabilities. She says that for children who need to become better readers, there are instructional decisions concerned with classroom organization, selection of materials, and goals for lessons. The notion of potential for learning, the level of reading ability compared to other abilities, and the relative importance of different reading skills are ignored. Of course, it may not be necessary for a teacher to know or comprehend an abstract definition to be an effective educator. The relationship between knowledge and teaching effectiveness has not been established.

Similarities

Concensus about the definition of reading disabilities would seem to be unlikely. However, a close inspection of contemporary statements of authorities from different disciplines reveals a surprising similarity. Cruikshank (1977) says that reading disability is a result of perceptual processing deficiency. He then gives a broad definition of perceptual processing as

> mental processes through which the child acquired his basic alphabets of sounds and forms. [A] perceptual handicap refers to inadequate ability in such areas as the following: recognizing fine differences between auditory and visual discriminatory features underlying the sounds used in speech and the orthographic forms used in reading; retaining and recalling those discriminated sounds and forms sequentially, but in short and long term memory; ordering the forms and sounds sequentially, both in sensory and motor acts. (p. 54)

This definition brings the focus to processes used in spoken and written language. It avoids global factors, such as auditory processing, that might include music, train whistles, sentence memory, or following a logical argument.

From the perspective of educational psychology, Williams (1978) construes reading disability as a failure to learn decoding skills at a normal rate. In their word-recognition processees, disabled readers show reversals and transpositions of letters, adding or dropping of phonemes or syllables, substituting one word for another with a similar meaning, confusing similar letter sounds, and inability to blend or analyze word parts. The operations that the children cannot perform are similar to those outlined by Cruikshank, although Williams gives concrete examples of the tasks, rather than abstract formulations of the processes those tasks may entail.

Recommended by Haring and Bateman (1977) is the position that reading disability refers to children who "are failing to learn reading as readily as it seems they should" (p.

126). These authors contend that with minor exceptions the terms "learning disabled" and "reading disabled" apply to the same children, those who are not learning to read according to expectation. Differences in definition of the problem, beliefs about major causes, and training of personnel do little to change this fact. The basic question is what kind of teaching and teacher should be provided for a child who is having an inordinate struggle in learning to read.

While this chapter is oriented primarily to elementary school children, older students also have reading difficulties. From his perch as a reading coordinator in a New York City high school, Shapiro has remarked that his students show a "higher" form of illiteracy (Shapiro and Kriftcher, 1976). By this he means "a limitation in one's ability to understand relationships between ideas imbedded in language symbols and the world of real objects, persons, and events . . . the inability to think constructively about the urgent, complex problems presented by the contemporary world" (p. 382). Such a limitation is awesome in its pervasiveness and in its implications for democratic society. Although the problem is general and not well articulated, educators are deeply concerned about the relationships between background knowledge, reading proficiency, written expression, and logical thinking. Regrettably, research on these problems is at its most primitive stage, and the consequence of failing to learn these abilities has not yet been analyzed in any depth (Kirsch and Guthrie, 1978).

Legal

For some professionals the only real definition is legal—the one that defines who will receive funds for evaluation and teaching of children. According to Public Law 94-142, a specific learning disability

> means a disorder in one or more of the basic psychological processes involved in understanding or in using language, spoken or written, which may manifest itself in an imperfect ability to listen, think, speak, read, write, spell, or do mathematical calculations. The term includes such conditions as perceptual handicaps, brain injury, minimal brain dysfunction, dyslexia, and developmental aphasia. The term does not include children who have learning problems which are primarily the result of visual, hearing, or motor handicaps, of mental retardation, of emotional disturbance, or of environmental, cultural, or economic disadvantage. (*Federal Register,* 1977, p. 65083)

The rules and regulations issued by the Office of Education include criteria for determining the existence of a specific learning disability. From these regulations, a team may determine a child has a specific learning disability if the child does not achieve commensurate with his/her age and ability levels in one or more of the areas—oral expression, listening comprehension, written expression, basic reading skills, reading comprehension, mathematics calculation, or mathematics reasoning. The discrepancy between ability and achievement must not result from: (1) a visual/hearing or motor handicap; (2) mental retardation; (3) emotional disturbance; or (4) environmental, cultural, or economic disadvantage. Regardless of whether this law benefits children, professionals should be skeptical of its truth value. It is unthinkable that government, by fiat, could define the problem so precisely as to preclude the need for future research or innovation.

There is a confluence among leading professionals from diverse fields about defining reading disability. This movement is toward specific tasks, such as basic reading skill and oral expression, that children cannot perform and that are inherently useful for their functioning in school and later life. The movement is away from a definition based on etiology—that is, a neurologic dysfunction or perceptual handicap. The movement retains the concept of a discrepancy betwen expectation and achievement, which was supported by Harris, although it has been deemphasized by other authorities, as Cruikshank, Williams, Haring, Bateman, and Lerner.

CONCEPTUAL FRAMEWORKS FOR INSTRUCTION

Basic Factors

The first volume of *Progress in Learning Disabilities* carried a chapter by Frostig (1968) on education. It stands as a sound statement for this viewpoint, although it has also been well expressed by many other writers. Frostig suggested that children who have learning difficulties must first be evaluated. Tests should be administered to determine the child's strengths and weaknesses. She recommended four tests, including the Illinois Test for Psycholinguistic Abilities (ITPA), the Wechsler Intelligence Scale for Children (WISC), the Wepman Test for Auditory Discrimination, and the Frostig Developmental Test of Visual Perception. These furnish measures of visual perception, auditory perception, higher thought processes, and language functions.

Frostig (1968) contended that, "Training for children with learning disabilities as nearly as possible should be geared to the test results, using areas of strength to provide experience of success, and attempting to train the areas of weakness" (p. 245). She went on to explain that "visual perception plays a significant role in all school learning, including reading. . . . Clinical observation clearly shows that for perceptually deficient children, the process of learning to read is laborious, and requires the investment of much energy. The institution of preventive remedial perceptual training therefore is of utmost importance" (p. 249). "Training in auditory perception involves helping the child to pay attention to auditory stimuli, to discriminate sounds, and to interpret what he hears. The preliminary training is concerned with sounds other than speech sounds...[including musical rhythms, clapping, and animal noises]" (p. 251). Further, children can be taught higher thought processes by learning to sort and classify two and three dimensional objects, learn visualization and memory for visual stimuli, and translating one code into another, e.g., in using picture writing and Morse code.

In the basic factors approach to remediation, a child's cognitive, perceptual, sensorimotor, and other faculties are assessed by a variety of psychoeducational instruments. Patterns of relatively high and low functioning are identified on factors that are correlated with reading disability. Although a causal role for these deficits is often specifically disavowed (Kirk, 1972), remedial programs to reduce the deficits are planned, nevertheless, on the belief that the child's reading will be improved.

Educational practices that issue from this conceptual framework are diverse (Bryan and Bryan, 1975). For example, with regard to visual perception activities, Lerner (1976) recommends that "direct teaching of visual perceptual skills appears to be a promising approach" (p. 190). Activities in an educational program might include (a) pegboard designs—reproducing colored, visual, geometric patterns to form the design on a pegboard; (b) finding shapes in pictures—finding all the round objects or designs in a picture; (c) bead designs—copying or reproducing designs with beads on a string; (d) puzzles—putting them together; (e) letters in numbers—visual perception and discrimination of letters, and (f) rate of perception—using a tachistoscope of flash cards to reduce the time acquired to recognize pictures, figures, numbers, and words. Similar activities are recommended for auditory functioning, haptic perception, cross-modal perception, auditory memory, and visual memory.

To illustrate that these recommendations or similar recommendations made by other authorities are widespread, consider two examples. An article in *Today's Education* (Kessinger and Singleton, 1977), official magazine of the National Education Association, carries a case of a learning-disabled boy. The child was admitted to the program for learning disabilities because of lwo scores on ITPA-like tests. The remedial teacher claimed that "reading was the high priority area" for the child. The boy was taught pegboard skills, colored block arrangements, letter sound correspondences, configuration keys for words, and tracing a variety of forms. In another article in the *Instructor*, which circulates to 300,000 teachers monthly, a reading counselor reported a case of one disabled reader (Peltzman, 1977). At 9 years of age, "he could not read and was a dismal failure in school." The teacher used the "Fernald method," which consists of having a child dictate words to the teacher, the teacher writes the words on file cards, and the child traces them and reads them. Four years later, the child was claimed to be in a regular seventh grade and doing well. He was reported to have self-confidence and hopes of a music education in college. The author does not report the reading level of the child following the tutoring program. But since it is stated that the child presently cannot decode any unknown words nor take any examinations in written form, his reading ability could hardly exceed the third grade level. Yet the teacher was faithful that the long educational struggle had helped the child..

Critique of Basic Factors Approach

Four shortcomings of the basic factors approach to instruction will be outlined here. The first is conceptual. It is possible that the advocates of basic factors were unable to resist the temptation of correlated deficits. Because children who cannot read also have an inadequate memory for a sequence of geometric forms, they should be trained to remember geometric forms. It seems unlikely that a nonsequitur so flagrant would have given rise to a massive educational movement, but it is possible.

It may also be that the supporters of this view overgeneralized each of the factors— that is, visual perception is a process required for reading, or at least word recognition. And visual perception is also a process required to remember a sequence of geometric forms. If one assumed that these two visual processes were the same, then educating children to perceive geometric forms might be assumed to improve word recognition. However, the two sets of processes—those needed to perceive words and those needed to perceive geometric forms—are different. Tests of the two show low correlations, and many cognitive operations—such as perception of redundancy and pronunciation, which are required for word recognition—are absent in abstract pattern perception (Guthrie, Goldberg, and Finucci, 1972; Kolers, 1975).

A second shortcoming is psychometric. The tests used to differentiate strengths and weaknesses in poor learners are inadequate for that purpose. First, the measures are often standardized on inappropriate populations. The Peabody Picture Vocabulary Test (PPVT) was standardized on 4000 white middle-class children around Nashville, Tennessee. The Slossen Intelligence Test was standardized on children from gifted, normal, and retarded classes, and adults from professional groups and county jails, many of whom had neurologic disorders. For other tests, such as the Gates-McKillip Diagnostic Reading Test, it is not known on whom the tests were standardized (Ysseldyke, 1977).

Low subtest reliability is a feature of diagnostic scales often used to estimate learning disabilities or reading disabilities. For example, the test-retest reliability of the Developmental Test of Visual Perception subtests range from .29 to .70. The ITPA subtest reliabilities range from .21 to .89 (Ysseldyke and Salvia, 1974). With such low reliabilities, one's likelihood of predicting whether a child is high or low in a given factor, such as visual perception, auditory reception, or grammatical closure, barely exceeds chance. Further, it is inherent in the diagnostic philosophy that strengths and weaknesses will be examined. But this implies that different scores will be identified. The reliability of a different score is known to be substantially lower than the reliability of either score taken separately, which means that a subtest profile is not likely to be repeated for a given child from one testing to the next.

The problem of validity can hardly be addressed psychometrically, since the reliability of the subtests has not been established clearly. But were the reliability sufficient, we face unanswered questions about (a) how to predict who is achieving less than their potential, (b) a meaningful description of strengths and weaknesses which implies independence among components, and (c) how to predict who will benefit from special teaching, the essential educational problem. In short, the available tests are reasonably useful for comparing an individual to a large group for screening and placement purposes on some occasions. The tests are inadequate, however, as a foundation for instruction.

A third shortcoming is the lack of support for one critical assumption about diagnosis. The assumption is that the separate factors being measured are independent. If a specific child shows a profile with large discrepancies, it is assumed that the differences are not solely attributable to measurement error. This problem was examined by Carroll (1972) in the *Seventh Mental Measurements Yearbook*. In a review of more than 250 references on the ITPA, he found there were only three main factors, although the testing included 12 subtests. These factors are verbal comprehension, immediate memory span, and auditory-visual processing. In other words, the differences for certain individuals in separate subtests are most likely a consequence of measurement error. Further, Carroll found there was no pattern of high or low scores, which are characteristic of children with reading disabilities. From this we may conclude that a program of training specific abilities based on the ITPA tests would rest on fairly shaky ground. In other words, if these basic factors exist, they cannot be measured precisely enough and are not sufficiently independent as a basis for separate activities in an educational program.

A fourth criticism of the basic factors approach is that it lacks supporting empirical evidence from comparative studies. The visual perception factor has received the most attention, due to the availability of the Frostig curriculum for visual perception. In a review of 25 educational experiments, Hammill (1972) concluded that the evidence was largely negative. In 23 cases a treatment program designed to improve the factor of visual perception was compared to a control in which those activities were excluded. In no case did the experimental group increase reading scores compared to the control group, although in several cases it increased the scores on the Frostig Test of Visual Perception. A thorough evaluation cannot be reported for auditory perception, higher order processes, or language skills, as there are insufficient experimental comparisons to provide a clear conclusion.

A citation of merit should be given to Marianne Frostig for her contribution to the conceptual development of the field of reading disability. While her conceptual framework and educational program have been largely discredited on logical and empirical grounds, she emerges as the major figure. Her viewpoint was articulated with sufficient precision, and her curriculum developed with enough appeal to attract research and educational tryouts. Their failure is a natural part of the process. We must agree with Isidor Rabi, the physicist, who said, "As soon as you answer one thing, you uncover more questions. Theories are shown to be wrong and new theories are proposed. Just imagine if theories didn't turn out to be wrong, and physics came to an end. It would be a very sad thing'' (Raeburn, 1977, p. 6).

Reading Skills

The second conceptual framework for education is oriented to instruction in reading skills. One of the more insightful and objective proponents of this rationale is Harris. In the book, *How to Increase Reading Ability,* first published in 1940, Harris formulates this viewpoint (Harris and Sipay, 1975). After cautioning the reader with several caveats, Harris defines reading as ''the meaningful interpretation of written or printed verbal symbols. . . . Reading is an extension of oral communication and builds upon listening and speaking skills'' (p. 5). He goes on to say that

> Effective reading requires both that words be identified immediately at sight and that the reader can, when necessary, decode unfamiliar words. To identify or recognize a written or printed word means to say aloud a spoken word it represents, to have an auditory image of the word while reading silently, or in very rapid silent reading to become aware of the meaning of the word without necessarily having an auditory image of it. (p. 353).

He continues by claiming that, ''In most reading disabilities, deficiencies in recognizing, decoding and recalling printed words are central'' (p. 390). To improve word recognition it is suggested that visual discrimination practice be given, emphasizing similarities and differences in letters, letter groups, and words, and auditory discrimination should stress phonemes and spoken words. Correspondences between the two should be the focus. Remedial lessons should be aimed directly at the specific errors made by children in their reading. A widespread teaching dilemma is the mismatch between the phonic skills of the children and phonics lessons provided by teachers.

Harris' definition of reading emphasizes meaningful interpretation. He notes that poor comprehension can result from a variety of causes, and the nature of remedial work to be employed depends on the source of difficulty. When low comprehension results from poor word recognition or a deficient oral vocabulary, instruction should begin on those skills. In other cases, inadequate comprehension seems to be the primary difficulty and needs to be improved directly. Harris contends that

> Many of the shortcomings in comprehension that are discovered in the upper grades are caused by the absence of any previous instruction to help to develop the missing skill. Remedial education often consists of providing instruction that never took place with a child at a younger age. Often it is necessary to break a comprehension skill down into simple components. For instance, if a child cannot summarize a paragraph clearly, the teacher may need to check for decoding errors, word meanings, and sentence comprehension, asking a child to develop the structure or sequence of the paragraph in sections which are finally integrated to form a whole. (p. 502)

A substantial number of authorities in reading education believe that remedial instruction is very similar to excellent developmental instruction. The differences are that in remedial instruction more emphasis is given to adequate time, sufficient materials, and lower teacher-pupil ratios. From Otto's viewpoint, all instruction entails five main elements: (a) identify essential skills to be learned; (b) state objectives for instruction; (c) examine individual skill development; (d) identify appropriate teaching-learning activities and materials; and (e) evaluate the results (Otto, Peters, and Peters, 1977). A specific outline of the skills to be taught and procedures for instruction may be found in Otto (1977).

Many teachers and other professionals who work with children who have not learned to read up to their expectation use the conceptual framework of task analysis. Haring and Bateman (1977) outline this procedure as containing four basic components: "(1) describing desired outcomes in behavioral terms; (2) naming skills and knowledge involved in the task; (3) naming, classifying, and measuring the functions named in the second step; and (4) development of the course of action" (p. 224). Several advocates of the experimental-analysis-of-behavior approach to education have extended the systematic approach to instruction by constructing a program based on (a) direct measurement of the behavior to be taught, (b) daily measurement, (c) individual analysis of the performance of each child, and (d) experimental control, which consists of determining whether any specific teaching activity has influenced the child's performance level on the scale of interest. Further details about these approaches can be found in Haring and Bateman (1977) and Hansen and Lovitt (1977).

Educational Practices in Reading Skills Approach

The most frequently adopted goals and procedures for teaching children who have not learned to read have been presented by Howlett and Weintraub (1978). Their findings derive from a nationwide study of compensatory reading programs, those designed for children who were one or more years behind in reading. More details about the study can be found in the *Compensatory Reading Survey* (Calfee and Drum in press). Goals differ slightly for primary and intermediate grades. For grade two, about 90% of the teachers included the following as major goals: phonics/structural analysis, developing visual discrimination, and developing auditory discrimination. Less than 80% of the teachers in grade six held these as major goals. In both second and sixth grade, more than 90% of compensatory reading teachers held as major goals the development of comprehension and the improvement of attitudes toward reading.

For sixth-grade teachers, relatively higher emphasis was spent on developing study skills and improving comprehension. These changes and goals fairly accurately reflect the changes in reading skills that are learned during the elementary school years. These data suggest that the sixth-grade children who are in compensatory reading programs are perceived as reading to learn comprehension skills and to develop more positive attitudes toward reading. While decoding and word-recognition skills are not likely to be completely developed, they are not the primary source of difficulty for children at this age. Most frequently, the time invested by teachers, according to their own reports, was consistent with the goals for reading skills. One major exception was apparent. Improvement of student attitudes was a major goal for over 90% of the teachers, but only about 45% of the teachers reported that reading for enjoyment was an activity in which "a great deal" of time was spent.

Programs of instruction vary widely. But to illustrate the two trends for primary and intermediate level instruction presented in the previous paragraph, the following two programs seem representative. Wallach and Wallach (1976) designed, implemented, and thoroughly reported a program for first graders who were found to be "at high risk." Children who scored below the 15th percentile in the Metropolitan Readiness Test during the first month of first grade were provided tutoring as a supplement to their regular educational program. Adult volunteer tutors from the local community were trained to provide tutoring for ½ h/day, 5 days/week, for the school year. Children were first taught to recognize individual letters and the sound that most frequently corresponds to the letter. The sounds for vowels were those that have been called "short"—that is, *a* in *bat, e* in *bet, u* in *but, i* in *bit,* and *o* in *cot.* Letters were then combined to form (cvc) words such as *f-a-t.* After learning to "sound out" simple words, children read short stories. For a given story, all words were first learned separately. Then children read words in the passage context with correction for each word in which a mistake was made. By the end of the program, children were reading about four pages per day in "pre-primers," the simplest stories with a limited set of words to be recognized.

Does such a program, such as the Wallach and Wallach (1976), benefit children who are likely to become disabled readers? As an evaluation, the authors conducted an experiment. In the beginning of the school year, children from below the 15th percentile were randomly assigned a regular program or regular program and tutoring supplement. Test results in the spring, using the Spache Diagnostic Scales, showed that (a) in word recognition, 61% of the tutored group were at 1.8 grade level or higher, whereas 25% of the matched control group were 1.8 or higher; and (b) in comprehension, 25% of the tutored group were 1.8 or higher, whereas 11% of the control group were at that level. With inferential statistics, the authors demonstrated that the gains were not attributable to chance, and many educators would view these results as functionally beneficial to the children. This evidence supports the tutoring program as a supplement. However, it does not support the specifics of the method. A different tutoring program emphasizing sight words and comprehension skills may have had equal effects.

As an illustration of a program at a slightly higher level, the Graves and Patberg (1976) report is useful. In their scheme, seventh and eighth graders reading at the 1.6 to 5.5 grade level were tutored by college students. The tutors were supervised by a professor and two graduate students in English education and reading. Students at the lower range of skills were taught words on the Dale list of 769 easy words. Individual words were grouped into simple (vc + cvc) and complex (vcc + cvcc) vowel patterns for instruction. Substantial practice was given with these words. Students read simple passages, games were played with words, and tutors read to students each session. For higher level students (3.5 to 5.5), background was first given on each passage to be read. Students read selections from a short anthology, short plays, and high-interest easy-reading novels, and skill exercises, and listened to records accompanying stories with emphasis on certain comprehension skills. Vocabulary games, word-attack exercises, and comprehension activities were included. Students received five sessions per week, including three 45-min periods of individual tutoring. The average duration of the program was 6.6 months, with an average gain of 1.4 years on the Spache Diagnostic Scales. This is an increase of about 2 years reading gain for 1 year in school under these conditions. This gain has been found to be representative of other programs (Guthrie, Seifert, and Kline, 1978).

Educational Research on Reading Skills

What do we know with a reasonable degree of certainty about teaching reading skills? Which instructional variables increase achievement in programs designed to teach reading skills to children who have not learned according to expectation? Among educational researchers there is a concurrence that "academic engaged time" correlates highly with reading achievement. Academic engaged time refers to student attention to reading materials in which they may be expected to learn skills or content. The importance of this variable for children who are learning at normal rates was examined in a review of the literature by Bloom (1976). He found that correlations of student attention with student gain were about .40 to .50. For students who have not learned according to expectation, the Stallings (1975) analysis is informative. For individual reading groups across a large range of classrooms, time spent in reading yielded higher correlations (.3 to .6) with achievement than large number of other variables investigated.

Substantial surveys of research on teaching have been made by Medley (1977) and Rosenshine (1976) to locate instructional variables consistently associated with high reading achievement. Their reveiws reveal a pattern of variables that increase academic engaged time, and, consequently, increase achievement. The instructional model is teacher-centered, the teacher making decisions about goals and materials and activities. Since teacher monitoring is important, group work in about sizes of three to seven is more effective than total individualization. Children spend about half of their time doing reading lessons in private seatwork interacting with reading materials. Teachers pose simple questions, relatively low on Bloom's taxonomy. Teachers provide assistance when needed and infrequently criticize students.

To attempt to determine which aspects of teaching programs make them effective, the authors conducted an exhaustive review of published reports about remedial reading programs (Guthrie, et al.; 1978). Reports were selected from 1969 to 1975, on children who had not learned to read between the ages of 7 and 15, for whom reading tests had been given at the beginning and end of an instructional program, for which the total duration of the program was reported in hours or weeks. With these criteria, 15 programs were located. The major variable distinguishing the more from the less effective was tutoring. In programs in which one teacher enjoyed the luxury of one to three children in a group, the rate of gain was 3.7 years of reading level for each year of instruction. In groups where there were more than four children for one teacher, the rate of learning was 1.7 years for a year of teaching. A substantial number of other variables could not be validated as important, including age of entrance into the program, professional training of the tutor, and the method of instruction.

Although the improvement of student attitudes toward reading is a nearly universal goal among teachers, little research attention has been devoted to it. The affective domain has simply not been investigated with enough rigor to discuss the relationship of educational variables to attitude development.

Critique of Reading Skills Approach

The approach to instruction, advocated by most professionals in reading, entails the teaching of the following skills: letter-sound correspondences, blending, phonics/structural analysis, word recognition, word meaning, sentence meaning, passage (story) structure, study skills, and content-area reading. In the primary grades, the first of these are emphasized slightly more than the latter, whereas in the intermediate grades the latter are predominant. The one generalization about teaching that might be agreed upon is that the more time children spend engaged with materials in which these skills might be learned, the more proficient they become. Tutoring is one highly effective means of insuring engagement.

An assumption in the reading-skills approach is that educators know what is learned by students as they become able readers. One claim is that word recognition is learned, which consists of saying a word out loud when it is presented in print. This skill may be classified as a performance. It is a behavior (saying a word) in the presence of a stimulus (the printed word). What is learned is the performance of saying words when they are presented in writing. Yet there is clear evidence that learning to recognize words is not simply learning a large number of stimulus-response associations. The phenomenon that calls the reading-skills approach into serious question is that children can recognize nonsense words. At the early age of 7, many children are able to correctly pronounce written words that they have never seen before. Such an accomplishment must be based on a covert set of rules. In some sense, the child must know rules that relate spelling patterns of printed words to phonological patterns of spoken language. Note that children can seldom verbalize these rules, no more than they can verbalize the grammatical rules of the language they use relatively well. It is these rules that are learned, not stimulus-response bonds. What children learn is not a performance, but a process of applying unverbalized rules of orthographic correspondence to written language (Guthrie and Seifert, 1977; Venezky, 1976).

Advocates of the reading-skills approach to instruction construe comprehension as correct answers to questions after presentation of a written passage. If students can give appropriate replies to reasonable questions after reading a passage at their level of difficulty, they are said to comprehend. Yet it is in no way possible for comprehension to simply amount to specific answers to specific questions over specific paragraphs. First, the question is usually new for the students, and they have not had occasion to learn a verbatim answer to that exact question. Rather, the student must learn a large set of covert processes. For example, suppose the following comprehension item: "Jim belongs to the Boy Scouts. The Scouts in Jim's troop come from poor families." Question: Does Jim come from a poor family? Several component stages are involved in answering this question, and Frase's (1977) model of comprehension may be used to outline them.

The first stage consists of encoding the information. The content of the two sentences must be represented in the child's memory. This might also entail a maintenance operation like rehearsal, which is a second stage. A third stage at the time of testing involves retrieval of appropriate information from each sentence. Occasionally information may be stored in memory, but is not easily retrieved upon demand. A fourth stage involves relating the two sentences. Information from both of them must be combined to produce a new unit of information for answering the question. These processes are covert and not readily observable while students are in the act of answering a question. Yet it is these processes that are learned when a student learns reading comprehension.

Children who have not learned to read have failed to acquire fundamental cognitive processes; as a result, their performance is deficient. To attempt to improve performances during remedial instruction may provide some benefit to the student. But it can never be optimal, since it is the set of cognitive processes that needs to be improved. The reading-skills approach to remediation succeeds by being appropriately targeted to performances that are deficient. However, it fails by underanalyzing the complexity of learning to read.

Cognitive Framework

The basic-factors and reading-skills frameworks for reading instruction previously discussed differ on two fundamental dimensions. According to the basic-factors model, what is learned in early acquisition are faculties such as auditory perception, visual perception, sequential memory, auditory visual integration, and so on. The basic-factors advocates hold a Platonistic view that these factors are primarily learned by exercise. Children are led to engage in the factor, such as visual perception, by being given tasks which require visual perception. They respond by seeing figures, shapes, and features, and seem to learn as a result of activity.

In the reading-skills framework, what is learned are performances, such as word recognition, giving synonyms for words, supplying paraphrases for sentences, and answering questions based on a passage. One primary means for learning these performances is reinforcement: exposure to the stimuli, the child's active responses, and reinforcements in the form of teacher approval, self-recognition of correct performance, or the satisfaciton of grasping a meaning.

From a cognitive view, what children learn in reading, or fail to learn, is knowledge. One form of knowledge is the representation of meaning. Children learn about objects in the physical world and their relationships. they may also learn abstract formulations about the physical world. This form of knowing is knowledge "that"—"that" rats are rodents, "that" Bill is taller than Jill, and "that" fire is a transformation of energy from solid to heat. Much of what children learn, or fail to learn, is "content area" subject matter of this form.

Granted that children have at least some knowledge, it is necessary for them to have a means for acquiring it. There must be operations whereby children come to know that rats are rodents, and Bill is taller than Jill. A suitable term for these mysterious talents is cognitive process. (*Cognition* means knowing, and *process* implies an operation that has to do with knowing.) Examples par excellence are the cognitive processes that lead to word recognition. When the child knows "how" to decode printed symbols into an oral language counterpart, new meanings are accessible.

Likewise, knowing "how" to perceive sentence structure during reading or to grasp the relations among major ideas in passages are means children use to learn about the outside world. Free of specific content, these processes effect a transaction between the thoughts and intentions of an author and the knowledge and purposes of a reader. These means are knowing "how," rather than knowing "that."

In a cognitive process framework for instruction, children learn how to read by means of search, discovery, and construction. Recently, Stauffer (1977) observed that

> Every artifact, whether it be words or things, is a man-made product endowed with a purpose. A hammer, or the word *hammer*, is man-made and attests to a conscious and rational intention . . . one can conclude that purpose for reading, like intention in thinking, is crucial to comprehension. This being so, a teacher is obliged to nurture the inquiry process so that readers develop an active intelligence capable of projecting, weighing evidence, making critical decisions, and doing constructive research. (p. 242)

In a different vein, there is accumulating evidence that when children listen to language or read, they search for large structural units. At 6 to 8 years, a child most likely will remember the critical aspects of a fable, such as *The Shepherd Boy and the Wolf* (Smiley, Oakley, Worthen, et al., 1977). Since a child recalls the story in terms of its structure, he must possess an abstract form of the structure in memory before the story is presented. The child must also be searching while he is listening or reading. The listener must be in some sense aware of the important events when they occur or immediately after they occur to relate them to other events and aid memory for them. Awareness implies that the child expects events to be coming as he listens or reads and that he is searching for knowledge or relationships in the story.

A substantial amount of the "how" in reading is learned by construction. The cognitive operations needed for word recognition and comprehension are devised because they are efficient. For reasons of economy, children develop rules of orthographic correspondence, sentence structure, and passage organization. In this way, they can cope more quickly and accurately with the myriad bits of stimuli that impinge on their eyes and ears.

An example of the constructive process can be shown in children's learning of addition. Groen and Resnick (1977) illustrated that children can invent the principle of commutativity in addition. They presented preschool children addition problems, such as 1 + 3, with a pile of toy blocks to be used in counting. On their own, the children soon learned to select a larger number (3, since it is larger), count those blocks, then count the smaller number cumulatively (1 additional block makes 4). This implies the recognition that 1 + 3 is the same as 3 + 1, the principle of commutativity. This principle is fundamental to mathematics, and children seem to construct it while they are working on specific tasks where it will be useful.

Children's capability for construction in learning to read must be prodigious, since they command such a wide range of operations for relating the written language to the spoken language and perceiving structure in sentences and paragraphs. Seldom are these operations taught explicitly. For instance, there is a phonetic rule for the relations that the letter *o* is sounded "long" when followed by final *ll* or medial *l* and a consonant, as in *cold, bolt,* and *polka.* This rule is learned inductively by most children after being given several examples. Rarely is the rule verbalized, nor should it be. But the intraword dependencies are picked up by the successful and not perceived by the less skilled readers (Katz, 1977).

What are the cognitive processes in reading—the ones that poor readers fail to acquire? Regrettably, there is no easy consensus. The number of suggested processes is enormous, and their interrelationships are only beginning to be explored. What is clear is that children can learn without teachers having a validated theory of acquisition. Two thousand years ago, some people learned to read when there were no theories whatever. But a problem arises in our day of universal education when some people do not learn normally. The ability to invent reading is not possessed equally by everyone. As a consequence, we must find ways to support low achievers.

A reading program stemming from the cognitive view should be based on a careful analysis of what is to be learned. As we mentioned previously, what children learn is knowledge—knowledge "that" and knowledge "how." Learning to read is rooted in both of these. For example, to read a story about the little red hen, a child must know "that" hens can walk to see their friends, "that" cooking takes several steps, "how" to recognize words, "how" to recognize a story's climax. A challenge for future research is to specify these cognitive processes and their relationships.

Materials read by the child must be so designed as to help the child construct the processes needed. Words, sentences, and stories will be needed that are geared directly to what information is new from moment to moment and what information can be remembered by the child.

A prime characteristic of knowledge is that it is organized. It is often structured in hierarchies of networks of interrelationships. Knowing about the little red hen is related to knowing about other animals, farms, and children who want to engage in cooking or other projects. The operations needed for word recognition, sentence perception, and story comprehension on one passage are related to operations in reading and thinking about other stories, words, and sentences. That is to say, planning the structure in which new information is to be placed is critical for a good program (Carroll, 1976).

Finally, it is important to understand and be able to direct the childs attention to features of the text that are relevant to a new construction. Directed attention is needed to recognize a pattern in a series of concrete examples, which is the basis for invention of generalized cognitive process.

Cognitive processes cannot be transferred to children like gifts, nor can they be performed by the teacher for the child to observe. But children can be led through tasks that help them invent reading for themselves. When children fail to learn, their lack of invention is often the main obstacle. And when educators fail to teach them effectively, a lack of understanding about invention is often the major limitation.

COGNITIVE PROCESSES IN READING

To pursue the cognitive view of education, we now review recent studies that may suggest what cognitive processes seem not to be learned by children who have not learned to read according to expectation. Development of optimal reading instruction for children who have not achieved a normal level of reading proficiency may be improved by taking into account cognitive characteristics of these children. We present some of the salient cognitive qualities of poor readers that may be valuable for thinking about teaching.

It should be noted that a variety of noncognitive variables are important in learning to read, although they will not be considered here in detail. For instance, emotional instability often has been suggested as a cause and as a result of reading failure (Vernon, 1971). The expectations of children about whether they will excel or have difficulty in learning to read has been reported recently by Entwisle (1976) as a causal factor in reading achievement. It has been widely documented that socioeconomic status (Whiteman and Deutsch, 1968) is correlated about .5 to .6 with reading achievement in grades four to six, although the specific sources of this influence have not been traced fully. Numerous analyses of neurologic functioning, including dichotic listening (Bryden, 1970; Kimura, 1961), visual evoked responses (Preston, Guthrie, and Childs, 1974), and postmortem examinations (Benson, 1976) have confirmed that neurologic dysfunction cannot be discounted as a source of reading difficulty for some individuals. These factors are usually thought to be less amenable to educational change than cognitive processes. One cannot modify a child's socioeconomic level easily, nor readily alter the neurologic structure of the brain. Cognitive deficiencies, on the other hand, may be open to improvement through education.

To examine aspects of cognitive functioning that are relevant to reading instruction, one must study tasks that are specific to reading. Many investigators have attempted to study analogs of reading. One of the most common is the dot pattern task (Kahn and Birch, 1968). It requires the child to match a series of dots printed on paper with spaces between them of varying widths to a series of tones presented auditorally with time intervals between them of varying lengths. This "auditory visual association task" is thought to be an analog for reading. However, there is no reason to believe that the cognitive operations needed to perform this task are similar to those of reading. The dots on the page do not contain critical features like letters or orthographic rules like words. Auditory tones that are few in number and meaningless bear little resemblance to complex meaningful spoken language. The reported correlations of about .3 between performance on the dot pattern task and reading achievement lead only to the inference that reading involves auditory visual association, a fact that is inherent in reading any alphabetic writing system. Another shortcoming of an analog is that it does not provide useful prescriptive information. To know that a child is low on a dot pattern task does not provide any indication about what kind of teaching to give in reading, since we would never give training in associating dot patterns or training in serial memory for tones. The same problems occur for the use of hieroglyphs as stimuli and cvc trigrams as responses, or pictures as stimuli and words as responses that have been used by several investigators

(Vellutino, Steger, Harding, et al., 1975). Consequently, we have not included studies that do not contain tasks that may be found commonly when people are reading.

While these arguments for an analysis of reading-specific tasks have been mainly rational, there is also empirical support. Following a review of alternate theories of reading disability, Vellutino (1977) concludes that (a) the perceptual deficit theory is doubtful, (b) intersensory integration theory is not supported, (c) and the temporal order perception hypothesis lacks evidence. He contends that reading disability is due to "one or more aspects of linguistic functioning. . . the semantic, syntactic, and phonological components of language [are] possible areas of difficulty" (p. 348). We agree, but now proceed to more detail about these linguistic aspects.

References in this review will be made to children who are low achievers in reading or poor readers. We are referring to children whose reading achievement is lower than would be expected based on relatively normal intelligence; children with IQs below 80 are excluded from these generalizations. We are also referring to low achievers in reading as a group, since there is little conclusive systematic evidence that subtypes of poor readers can be reliably distinguished. Although it is intuitively compelling that there should be many reasons for a child to fail to learn a skill as complex as reading and that different children should fail for different reasons, systematic evidence on this point is notably absent. Satz (Satz, Rardin, and Ross, 1971) presented a theory that the causes of reading failure were different for children of different chronological ages. He suggested that inadequate perceptual and memory processes would be the source of poor reading for children in the 7-to-8-year range, whereas language processes would be the source of reading for children in the 11-to-12-year range. However, his data did not unequivocally support the notion. Language problems were evident for both age groups on his tests and a motor component in the perceptual tasks made the results difficult to interpret (Saltz, et al., 1971). Most important, this theory does not treat the essential issue that poor readers of the same age fall into subgroups.

One proposal that merits further study is that some children comprehend written material poorly, due to inadequate sight vocabulary, whereas other children comprehend poorly due to inadequate skill in organizing and reasoning with complex relationships in discourse (Cromer, 1970). Many reading teachers and clinicians testify that some children have difficulties with word recognition, while others seem to identify words correctly without being able to garner meaning from the sentences. There is an indication that the latter group is relatively insensitive to syntactic constraints within sentences (Isakson and Miller, 1976) and benefits from organizational prompts, such as the uses of imagery (Levin, 1973). While these subgroups merit further study and will likely require differential teaching emphasis, the distinction cannot be sustained for the remainder of this review, due to a dearth of relevant investigations.

Low achievers in reading often have been divided into those who have a reading deficiency and those who have a general learning deficiency based on intelligence or listening comprehension. Children who read below grade level but have normal intelligence and/or listening skills are thought to be distinguishable from children who are relatively low in both reading and listening. The former are said to have a reading problem and the latter to have a language problem (Critchley, 1970; Symmes and Rapoport, 1972; Sticht, Beck, and Hauke, 1974). This division is defensible if the groups also differ on variables other than intelligence and/or listening, such as other cognitive processes or instructional needs. Unfortunately, there is no evidence to support the cognitive and instructional differences of these subgroups. Supporters of this method of subgrouping contend that low reading achievement is "explained" by a relatively low intelligence or a relatively general learning deficiency. This is appellation, rather than explanation. The term *dyslexia* may be a useful description of a syndrome, but it does not serve as scientific explanation for the phenomena it describes. In any case, the available literature on cognitive processes in poor readers does not permit the distinction between reading deficiency and general learning deficiency. In the majority of studies, good and poor readers were identified on the basis of a median split in a regular classroom. Under these conditions, poor readers usually are slightly lower than good readers in intelligence and/or listening comprehension (Calfee, Venezky, and Chapman, 1969). Consequently, we refer to high achievers in reading as good readers and low achievers in reading as poor readers.

A corollary to the proposition that there are subtypes of poor readers is that there are also different types of instruction that are optimal for teaching these different types of learners. The available evidence on this point is extremely thin, but nevertheless negative. For instance, Robinson (1972) divided children into one group with visual aptitudes and another group with auditory aptitudes. Half of each group were taught with a sight method emphasizing words and sentences; the others were taught with a phonics emphasis, which included teaching letter sounds, blending, oral reading, and so on. Only 11% of the children were either high-visual–low-auditory or low-visual–high-auditory, indicating that extreme discrepancies in modality aptitudes were rare. There were no consistent differences between the methods of instruction, nor were there any significant interactions between instructional approach and modality aptitudes. In other words, previous research has not identified a means by which to subdivide poor readers into different groups so as to allocate instruction differentially and increase the efficiency of teaching.

CHARACTERISTICS OF PRIMARY LEVEL DISABLED READERS

In examining the processes of reading that are not easily learned by children who are poor readers, it is sensible to separate children into different age groups. The processes that are undergoing rapid acquisition may differ at different age levels. For example, perceptual, memory, and decoding skills may be demanded heavily and acquired rapidly in early stages of reading, which often occur in first and second grade, whereas language comprehension and the application of previous knowledge ot the content of written material may be heavily demanded and undergo rapid acquisition during later years in grades four through six. Consequently, primary and intermediate levels will be examined separately in this review.

A substantial amount of variability in reading achievement of the population appears at an early age. Newman (1972) conducted a longitudinal study of 230 children from first through sixth grades. The children were average in intelligence, but the group contained a disproportionately large number that were lower than average in reading readiness at the beginning of first grade. Despite this restricted range, the correlation of word recognition—namely, the word reading subtest of the Stanford Achievement Test—and reading comprehension at sixth grade—namely, reading subtest of the Iowa Test of Basic Skills—was .52. Word study skills at the end of first grade correlated .58 with reading comprehension at the end of sixth grade. In other words, about 25% of the variance in achievement at the end of sixth grade could be accounted for by achievement at the end of first grade. Mackworth and Mackworth (1974) report another reason for investigating the reading problems of children at a young age. In a cross-sectional design, they administered an identical test to children in grades one, two, four, and six. The measure required the identification of upper- and lower-case letters and judgments about whether word pairs sounded the same. The words were identical *(cup-cup)*, different *(pain-pair)*, or homophones *(bear-bare)*. Children at each grade were divided into good and poor readers based on reports from the teachers. There were very few errors, for anyone, on the identical items. However, on the homophones, poor readers made more errors than good readers at all grade levels from first through sixth. Both good and poor readers improved in proficiency, but the poor readers were consistently worse than good readers at all levels. Speed of decoding was measured by judging the reaction time on each word pair. On all categories of words, poor readers were slower than good readers, at all grade levels. Poor readers and good readers both improved as grade levels increased, but poor readers were worse by a constant amount. In other words, the problem of decoding that occurs in first grade appears to persist until the end of elementary school.

Is achievement at the end of first grade highly related to measures of readiness taken before the entrance to school? The widely circulated study of Jansky and deHirsch (1972) reported that letter naming in kindergarten correlated .54 with reading achievement at the end of second grade; word matching correlated .45 with achievement, and the similarity subtest of the WISC correlated .53 with end of second grade achievement. Other evidence from Newman (1972) is that the WISC verbal scores correlated .45 with word recognition at the end of first grade and that was superior to Metropolitan Readiness Test or the Murphy-Durrell Analysis of Reading Difficulty Subscales in predictive power. First, we may note that the correlations between performance in kindergarten and end of first grade are in the moderate range, accounting for about 20% of the variance. Second, we may note that the most powerful predictors during kindergarten include (a) the WISC verbal subscore, a measure of intelligence, (b) the Metropolitan Readiness Test, a global assessment of school readiness, and (c) letter naming. The only variable specific to reading is letter naming, which is notable. Possibly, letter naming predicts reading achievement, due to the joint influence of socioeconomic status on both. These indications are that the important antecedents to reading are global factors that relate to all school achievement, and specific cognitive precursors to reading failure have not been identified. What is clear is that what is learned or not learned during first grade facilitates or inhibits reading proficiency at later ages. Since later achievement seems highly related to early proficiency, it seems prudent to give emphasis to study of processes that are not easily acquired during early stages of reading acquisition.

Decoding Accuracy

The term *decoding* is used to refer to the process of rendering printed language into spoken language. It includes whole-word-recognition, word-analysis, and word-attack skills.

Characteristic strategies of children learning to read in first grade have been studied by the examination of oral reading errors. The strengths and weaknesses of good and poor readers may also be examined with this procedure. Weber (1970) systematically collected the oral reading errors of 43 first-grade children over a 5-month period. At the end of the year, the children were divided into those with relatively high reading achievement, about 2.6 grade level on the word knowledge subtest of the Metropolitan Achievement Test, and those who had relatively low reading achievement, about 1.8 on the word knowledge subtest. The extent to which children possess appropriate language comprehension processes and deploy these operations during the course of reading can be judged by the grammatical acceptability of the oral reading errors. Good and poor readers did not differ on this count. The high achievers in reading had 93% of the errors grammatically accept-able in the context of the sentence preceding the error. Low achievers in reading had 89% of the errors grammatically acceptable to the preceding context. In a replication of the study, the results were the same. Apparently, all children, regardless of reading level, use the grammatical cues that precede a word in the sentence for identification of that word.

One might also ask how frequently good and poor readers make errors that are grammatically inconsistent with the entire sentence. Using the criterion that an error must be grammatically acceptable with the context occurring before and after the error within the sentence, good and poor readers seem not to differ significantly. Among high achiev-ers, 68% of the errors were consistent with the entire sentence; and among low achievers, 56% of the errors met this criterion.

Confirmation of these findings have been reported by Biemiller (1970). He developed a criterion of contextual acceptability, which required that an error be both grammatically and semantically acceptable in terms of the preceding context of the sentence. Using this criterion, children at high, medium, and low achievement levels in reading at the end of first grade had the following percentages of errors that were contextually acceptable: 84, 84, and 81. In other words, the extent to which children use grammatical and semantic cues in identifying words is equally high, regardless of reading ability level at the end of first grade. Biemiller also found that contextual acceptability of errors is consistently high throughout first grade. In the earliest stages of reading for all first graders in his study, the contextual acceptability for the high, average, and low ability groups were 86%, 62%, and 78% correct. This implies that children enter first grade with language capabilities that are sufficient for the task of reading, and that they perceive reading as a languaging activity, regardless of reading proficiency level. For children who speak English as a first language and who do not have another obstacle to learning to read, such as a gross neurologic dysfunction, problems in early reading acquisition do not appear to be the result of inadequate language capacity or usage.

The extent to which first graders attend to graphic and phonological cues for word identification was also estimated by Weber (1970). She reported a graphic similarity index which was used to code each error in terms of the similarity of the graphic features of the error to the original word. This index was based on number of shared letters, similarity of length, and appropriate weights for these variables. Low achievers in reading at the end of first grade had a mean of 256.47, whereas high achievers had a mean of 407.87—that is, the graphic similarity of errors for high achievers was higher than for low achievers. This suggests that high achievers attend more closely to the graphic cues in words and give oral responses that are more consistent with the rules of pronunciation that may be used for written words in English. Using a simpler index of graphic similarity, Biemiller (1970) illustrated that good and poor readers differ at the end of first grade in the graphic similarity of their oral reading errors. In later stages of acquisistion, he reported the high-ability group had 50% errors that were graphically similar, whereas the low-ability group had 26% graphically similar errors. The lower group had not improved over the course of first grade, although the high-ability group had increased their graphic similarity scores. This suggests that the primary process that is acquired in the first year of learning to read is decoding proficiency. The speed at which children learn to read seems to be related primarily to the time required to learn proficient decoding strategies. These strategies include learning letter-sound correspondences and orthographic rules (such as permissible letter sequences), which are useful for rendering printed words into spoken language.

A Prerequisite for Reading

Assuming that acquisition of proficient decoding represents the major problem in early stages of reading, we may next ask what cognitive processes lead to difficulty in learning to decode. Following a review of 75 studies on this problem, Williams (1977) takes the position that "auditory skills" represent the major hurdle for young readers. These skills are said to include auditory discrimination, memory, sequencing ability, analysis, and synthesis. Williams notes that a proliferation of correlational studies was initiated by Monroe (1932), illustrating a relationship between auditory discrimination and reading level. Other correlational studies have pointed to the importance of distinguishing separate sounds in words or phonemic segmentation. Blending sounds to one another, blending phonemes to syllables, and other tasks requiring the manipulation of sound sequences are important. Williams notes that there have been two studies illustrating the impact of training in auditory skills on reading achievement. In one, identifying phonemes in words by counting them individually was found to facilitate word analysis—for example, pronouncing unfamiliar words. It seems reasonable that a child must be able to segment the sounds in the stream of speech into units of subword length if decoding is to be learned. Since decoding requires the acquisition of rules that map letters and letter sequences to sounds and syllable units, the child must be capable of locating the constituents in the visual and auditory domain (Shankweiler and Liberman, 1976). It appears that the visual discriminations and segmentations are fairly simple, in comparison to the auditory analysis that is necessary for a child to learn orthographic structure and rules for decoding (Liberman, Shankweiler, Liberman, et al., 1976).

Opponents of this position (Hammill and Larsen, 1971) argue that the low to moderate correlations between auditory skills and reading do not provide a basis for instructional development. The relationships are too weak and not sufficiently established as causal to provide a basis for instruction. We suggest that what is needed is more evidence from intervention and training studies, indicating that instruction in "auditory skills" facilitates learning to read. Then these processes can be called prerequisites to decoding, and confidently incorporated into curriculum designs.

Instructional Effects

The problems of poor readers may also be examined by identifying instructional variables that are particularly important for low achievers in reading. If a certain instructional practice—for example, emphasis on phonic skills—has a decided benefit for low achievers, it is reasonable to conclude that low achievers are characterized by inadequate phonics and word-analysis skills. The content of instruction, among other variables, in 15 published reports of teaching programs for remedial readers was examined by Guthrie, et al. (1978). However, contents of the programs and methods of instruction were described at such a superficial level that comparisons could not be made with any confidence. Locating and communicating critical features of instructional programs need further development.

Despite some opinion to the contrary, we believe that the first-grade studies may be at least partially conclusive in regard to instructional effects in first-grade reading (Bond and Dykstra, 1967). Since this investigation included several program comparisons at each of 27 project sites, multiple dependent variables, statistical control for previous achievement, and extensive statistical control for previous achievement and extensive statistical analyses, it merits some attention. However, the authors' conclusions deviate from their findings. Consequently, we reanalyzed this study to interpret the results.

We invoked the following series of decision rules: (a) Only the word-reading and paragraph-meaning subtests of the Stanford Achievement Test were used. Other dependent variables were not included. (b) Analyses of covariance were interpreted and the analyses of variance were not examined. For a given contrast—for example, between basal and basal plus phonics—two analyses of covariance were conducted: one with all of the readiness measures and pretests combined as the covariate, and a second with the readiness measure or pretest that was most strongly correlated with the posttest as a single covariate. For a given comparison, say between basal and phonics plus basal, several project sites were included. Examining across project sites, it was decided that if either analysis of covariance illustrated that there was no difference between the treatment groups and there was no interaction between the treatment groups and project sites, the contrast would be regarded as not having produced a significant difference. In other words, if differences that might have been present could be eliminated by either system of covariance analysis, the difference was regarded as negligible. (c) For a given contrast, if both covariances showed a treatment effect in the same direction and there was no disordinal interaction with projects, the treatment effect—that is, the difference between methods of instruction—was considered to be present.

Using these decision rules, several conclusions emerged. First, children learned decoding as measured by the word-reading subtest of the SAT more efficiently by a skills method than by a language-oriented approach. For example, when word reading was used as the criterion, two skill-oriented methods, one emphasizing "stuctural linguistics" and the other emphasizing "phonics and structural lingustics," were both superior to a basal method. It should be noted that the basal readers contained more stories and fewer skill-oriented lessons than those used currently. Two language-oriented approaches—for example, language experience approach and basal—were not different in their impact on word reading. In addition to the apparent benefits of skill-based approaches over basal for word recognition, we found that combining phonics and basal was noticeably superior to basal alone for teaching word reading.

When the paragraph-meaning subtest of the SAT was used for the dependent variable, employing the same decision rules, there were no consistent differences between skill-based and language-based approaches to instruction. Linguistic and basal approaches did not differ; phonic/linguistic was superior to basal; language experience and basal did not differ; and basal combined with phonics was superior to basal alone. Language and comprehension-oriented approaches to instruction were no more effective than decoding and skill-oriented approaches for teaching reading comprehension.

These findings are consistent with the results of the oral reading error studies. First, the oral reading error studies suggested that it is decoding that is learned primarily during the course of first grade. The first-grade studies illustrated that skill-based instruction, which emphasizes decoding, had an edge in efficiency over language-based approaches in teaching word recognition and decoding. Second, since comprehension is not an area that needs a dramatic amount of improvement in first grade according to the oral reading error studies, it follows that instructional variations should not influence reading comprehension. This prediction was confirmed by our reexamination of the first-grade studies.

Another instructional variable that may shed light on the characteristics of poor readers is amount of teaching time. Harris and Serwer (1966) showed that the amount of time spent engaged in explicit instructional activities pertinent to reading correlated .56 with the word-reading subtest of the SAT and .55 with the paragraph-meaning subtest of the SAT. In contrast, other more peripheral activities, such as general discussion, art, or dramatization, had no significant relationship to achievement. Needless to say, the investment of time itself will not increase reading achievement. Time must be spent in fruitful ways. Amount of time spent in a language-experience approach in which a considerable amount of time was spent in field trips and writing, but little time in reading activities, did not correlate significantly with reading achievement. Another illustration is provided by Ball and Bogatz (1973). They reported that increasing the exposure of children to the Sesame Street program, which emphasizes letter sound correspondences and other "phonics" skills, increased reading achievement in first grade markedly.

Hypotheses about the relationships between amount of instructional time and characteristics of students and reading achievement have been forwarded recently by Wiley and Harnischfeger (1974). An update of the Carroll (1963) model of school learning suggests that achievement is determined by (a) total time needed for a child to learn a task and (b) the total time the child spends learning the task. In other words, achievement is a function of time required for instruction and time allocated for instruction. Their data illustrate globally that exposure, in terms of hours of schooling per year, is related to achievement in reading comprehension. They concluded that "in schools where students receive 24 percent more schooling, they will increase their average gain in reading comprehension by two-thirds. . . the amount of schooling a child receives is a highly relevant factor for his achievement" (p. 9). Implicit in this model is the proposition that children who need a large amount of time to learn reading will benefit more from increases of instructional time than children who need less time for learning to read. It has recently been found that children who read poorly benefit more from increases in amount of time spent in learning and teacher-student interaction than children who are learning to read normally (Rosenshine, 1976). Consequently, it is possible to characterize poor readers as needing larger amounts of learning time than average. Poor readers require larger than average amounts of teaching and interaction with written material to learn to read.

CHARACTERISTICS OF INTERMEDIATE LEVEL DISABLED READERS

Decoding Accuracy

Our next section presents some of the reading problems that are present for children in the intermediate grades four through six, as revealed in current research. A first issue raised is whether children who are low achievers in reading at this age are proficient in decoding. One simple approach to this problem is to identify a group of 10-year-olds in fifth grade who are high and low achievers. Belmont and Birch (1966) identified such groups. The poor readers were 1.5 grade equivalents below the normal readers who were reading at the grade level appropriate for their age and intelligence on the Metropolitan Achievement Test:Reading, which requires comprehension. For these groups, the performance on the word-knowledge subtest was compared. This subtest requires matching a single word to several other single-word alternatives. It demands decoding and semantic recognition of single words and is less complex than answering questions over paragraphs, as the reading subtest requires. The poor readers were 2.0 years in grade equivalent behind the good readers who were at the expected grade level for their age and intelligence on the word-knowledge subtest, indicating that the poor readers were about as far behind their peers in decoding and recognizing meanings of single words as they were in reading comprehension. It should be noted that these two subtests are norm-referenced separately. They are not based on the same psychometric scales, and absolute comparisons should not be made.

Investigators have illustrated that decoding accuracy is a distinct problem for low readers in the intermediate grade levels. Among them, Guthrie (1973) compared normal fourth graders with children in fourth grade who performed at about the second-grade level on standardized reading comprehension measures. The poor comprehenders were noticeably lower in decoding eight categories of words and syllable units. In fact, the poor readers were virtually identical to a younger group of 7-year-old children reading at about the second-grade level. In other words, proficiency of decoding among children who are poor comprehenders in fourth grade is very similar to the decoding level of younger children who are matched with them on comprehension. By making comparison across three independent studies, Smiley, Pasquale, and Chandler (1976) showed that the absolute level of proficiency in decoding words, such as *strip, speak, thank,* and *floss,* among low-reading seventh graders was about 80% correct. The absolute proficiency of normally achieving fifth-grade children was 90%, and normal second graders were about 68% accurate. Low readers in the 9-to-12-year age group are usually inadequate in decoding, or word recognition.

Decoding is dependent on the acquisition of rules. For example, as illustrated by Calfee, et al. (1969), when the letter *c* is followed by *e* or *i,* it is pronounced with the *s* sound, whereas when *c* is followed by *a, o,* or *u,* it is pronounced with the sound *k.* Synthetic words that are governed by these rules are pronounced more accurately by sixth graders than third graders. Furthermore, it has been shown (Guthrie and Seifert, 1977) that complexity of the letter-sound correspondence rules determine their learning for both disabled readers at age 12 and normal children at age 7 to 9. Simple rules are learned before more complex rules, irrespective of instruction, and the same orthographic regularities must be learned by normal and low readers.

Acquisition of decoding may be construed as the learning of rules, and poor readers are inferior to good readers in this cognitive process. In addition, rule learning in these terms continues into 11th and 12th grades of high school (Doehring, 1976). It seems that decoding proficiency increases throughout the intermediate grades and later. Decoding is not acquired and mastered at an early stage and then followed by rapid acquisition of comprehension processes. Decoding accuracy continues to develop to the end of elementary school and beyond.

Decoding Speed

Low readers at the intermediate level have often been observed by teachers to decode slowly, and there is clear evidence that response speed is a major factor in acquisition of decoding from 1st to 12th grades (Doehring, 1976). If slow decoding is widespread and frequent among poor readers, it may have inhibitive effects beyond those of trying the patience of teachers. There is current theorizing (LaBerge and Samuels, 1974; Perfetti, 1977) that slow decoding and inefficient verbal processing of sentences may be interconnected. If children have a limited capacity for cognitive processing and a substantial amount of their processing space is consumed by decoding, then the comprehension of sentences and discourse may be reduced. While these hypotheses have yet to be confirmed, rapid decoding is a potentially important cognitive operation.

Rapid decoding was found to be correlated with reading comprehension by Perfetti and Hogaboam (1975). Fifth graders who achieved poorly on a reading comprehension test were slower in pronouncing isolated words than fifth graders who performed normally in comprehension. This is similar to the finding reported by Mackworth and Mackworth (1974) reviewed earlier in this paper. The outcome was substantiated by Steinheiser and

Guthrie (1978), who illustrated that word matching based on sound, which requires decoding, was slower for poor comprehenders than good comprehenders, despite the fact that word matching based on visual features alone was similar for the two groups. These are associated cognitive operations, and the direction of causality is based on conceptual rather than experimental evidence. Some authors (LaBerge and Samuels, 1974; Perfetti, 1977) contend that slow decoding consumes processing space and reduces the amount of attention available for semantic processing, thus limiting comprehension; however, it is also plausible that fluent semantic processing facilitates decoding, since words may be decoded partly on the basis of their meaning as well as their letter-sound correspondences. To help us choose between these alternatives, we need learning experiments in which one process is learned to a criterion and the effects on other processes are observed.

Orthographic Regularity

An aspect of reading that is allied with decoding is the perception of orthographic regularity. As outlined by Gibson and Levin (1975) and others, orthographic regularity refers to intraword redundancy, rules for permissable letter sequences, and the preservation of meaning in the spelling patterns for words. The lexical similarity of two words, for instance, *grace* and *gracious,* is maintained in the phonological structure (pronunciation) and in the orthographic structure (spelling) of the two words. There is some modest evidence that intermediate-aged poor readers have not acquired orthographic structure as fully as good readers at this age level. Barganz (1974) found that fifth-grade children who were low achievers in reading were worse than good readers at the same grade level in using orthographic structure for word identification. In the study, children were presented two spoken sentences with the last word omitted. For example, "To discuss a topic is to talk about it. If a group of students talked about a topic, it would be a _____." Four visual alternatives were presented: (a) discushun, (b) discussion, (c) discushion, and (d) discuzion. Good readers were more facile than the poor readers in selecting the correct visual alternative, illustrating their utilization of morphophonemic mapping rules as described by Venezky (1967).

Another dimension of orthographic regularity is positional frequency (Mason, 1975) that good and poor readers at the sixth-grade level are different in their abilities to use positional redundancy of letters. Mason found for all readers that a letter is identified more rapidly in highly frequent than less frequent positions. For example, the letter *s* is more easily identified in "somled" than "sdelmo," since the *d* and the *o* in the former occur in usual or redundant locations. However, good readers showed a larger facilitation for spatial redundancy than poor readers, suggesting the rules for permissable letter positions were less well learned by poor readers. This effect could be due to interletter transition information or single-letter positional redundancy alone. Evidence supporting the latter, but not discounting the former has been found (Katz, 1977). These lines of research are only beginning, but they point to abstract rules that are cognitive hurdles for low achievers in reading.

Segmenting

Inasmuch as the comprehension of spoken language requires semantic and syntactic processing, the comprehension of written material should also engage the reader in these cognitive operations. The ability to segment written language and process its constitutents separately would seem to be useful for comprehension. To examine this segmentation in poor readers, Guthrie and Tyler (1976) compared the immediate recall of meaningful, anomalous, and random word strings during reading and listening for good and poor readers. These types of word strings were used since the difference between the recall of meaningful and anomalous word strings is thought to reflect semantic processing, and the difference between the recall of anomalous and random strings is thought to be an index of syntactic processing (McNeil, 1970). Good and poor readers who were of the same age and intelligence performed at the same level on the listening tasks, with recall of meaningful superior to anomalous, which were superior to random word strings. In reading, the good readers performed at a higher level than poor readers on all tasks. For both groups, the order of difficulty was meaningful, anomalous, random. Poor readers seemed to benefit from syntactic and semantic cues as much as good readers in both reading and listening. In these tasks the syntactic and semantic cues are highly salient, and the same results might not occur for more subtle aspects of language.

While poor readers certainly process the most salient semantic properties of written sentences (Guthrie and Tyler, 1976), and isolated words in print (Golinkoff and Rosinski, 1976), there is evidence that poor readers are nevertheless weaker in processing more subtle semantic features. For example, Samuels, Begy, and Chen (1976) illustrated that poor readers were inferior to good readers on filling in the spaces when presented with a stimulus of black c__ __ or deep sn__ __. This may be interpreted as indicating that poor readers were inferior in using the lexical cue "black" that was available to assist in the identification of the word *cat*. In a study of semantic processing sentences, Steinheiser and Guthrie (1974) found that poor readers were weaker than good readers in locating target words of a semantic category within written paragraphs.

That poor readers may be inferior to good readers in processing syntactic aspects of sentences was suggested by Isakson and Miller (1976). Oral reading errors of good readers increased when syntactic violations were placed in sentences, but the oral reading errors of poor readers were not influenced by syntactic violations. Additional support for the general notion is provided by Weinstein and Rabinovitch (1971), who demonstrated that poor readers may not use the constraints of word order in sentences as efficiently as normals in learning an oral sentence repetition task. Poor readers do not seem to use syntactic characteristics of sentences, such as word order constraints and syntactic markers (*ing*, plural *s*) to facilitate processing. A problem with this study for our purposes is that it contained listening tasks but not reading tasks. The only observation that can be made with this limited evidence is that processing of semantic and syntactic properties of sentences during reading is a probable weakness for poor readers at the intermediate grade levels and merits further study.

Constructing

Another type of processing that should be considered here is the constructive, referring to how children build semantic representations. During reading, information from the written material and the reader's previous knowledge are combined by constructive processes of memory and inference. For children at the intermediate grade levels, it has been suggested that poor readers are worse than good readers in their ability to recall information from multiclause sentences or recall information from a sentence in a paragraph that precedes the sentence the child is reading at any given moment (Perfetti and Goldman, 1976). This occurred despite the fact that poor readers were equal to good readers in recalling information from a long single-clause sentence. Apparently, poor readers were relatively weak in combining information from separate parts (sentences) of the message into a well-organized unit. While the findings are limited, this area of cognitive processing deserves closer examination as a potential distinction among good and poor readers (Frase, 1975).

Semantic representation of a narrative passage is also thought to require constructive processes in addition to perceptual operations. Most narrative stories, folk tales, and myths contain a thematic structure with a hierarchy of important ideas or propositions. Poor readers are worse than good readers in the reconstruction of such thematic structures. In free recall of stories presented in spoken or written form, poor readers show lower memory in general and less distinction between information that is central and peripheral to the theme than good readers. Comprehension for reading and listening alike seems to rely on perception and recreation of story structure (Smiley, et al., 1977).

An aspect of constructing that is receiving increased attention from psycholinguists is inference. There is an accumulation of evidence that children derive and retain inferred relationships from prose. It has been claimed that children spontaneously infer presuppositions, consequences, and means-ends relations in stories that are read to them. Elaborations of sentences consisting of inferred instruments of actions—that is, he hit the nail "with a hammer"—are frequent, although developmental trends from 6 to 12 years are evident (Paris and Lindauer, 1976). The role of inference in reading achievement is suggested by evidence that good readers identified true inferences more accurately after being presented written sentences than poor readers. This occurred despite the fact that true premises were recognized equally by the two groups. The groups were matched on age, intelligence, and sex. Apparently, semantic elaboration and inference increased with reading achievement (Waller, 1976).

From this review, it is apparent that good and poor readers at the intermediate grade levels may be distinguished in terms of several levels of processing related to reading. Low achievers seem to be inferior to higher achievers on (a) decoding accuracy, (b) decoding speed, (c) perception of orthographic regularity, (d) semantic segmentation, and (e) semantic construction. There is at least tentative evidence that none of these levels of processing should be discounted as a source of problems for poor readers at the intermediate grade levels. What we have here is a list of cognitive processes that seem to be important for reading and seem to distinguish good from poor readers. Survey data support this interpretation (Hazlett, Arhmann, and Johnson, 1972).

INSTRUCTION FOR DISABLED READERS

As we discussed previously, a cognitive framework for instruction requires a detailed analysis of what is to be learned. Knowledge about subject matter contents and operations needed to learn these contents are both acquired. We have reviewed operations that disabled readers seem to lack—decoding accuracy, decoding speed, perception of orthographic regularity, semantic segmentation, and semantic construction. These are "how" children understand meanings from print, rather than "what" they comprehend. Scientific study of children's acquisition of subject matter is still in its infancy, and little empirical basis for instruction can be provided in this latter area.

Before suggesting the instructional concepts, it should be noted that evidence presented so far has been largely correlational; reading performance is concomitant with cognitive process X. The question we ask is what instructional principles might be developed bearing this evidence in mind. This evidence does not compel the instructional principles logically or empirically, but it is nevertheless provocative. The concepts presented here are not likely to be sufficient for a total program. Lack of detail and oversimplification are prominent, a shortcoming that may be remedied by educational research of the future that will link the knowledge base of cognitive science with teaching practice (Guthrie, 1977).

Primary Level

The development of instructional implications from the review is based on the finding that, at the primary level, disabled readers are characterized mainly by inadequate decoding. Acquisition of letter-sound correspondences and other orthographic rules that allow accurate rendition of printed words into spoken words is slower for poor readers. The most plausible curricular implication is that decoding accuracy should be a major goal in teaching primary-level reading for poor readers. Instructional materials and activities should be arranged to insure that decoding is learned to a high level of proficiency. Since decoding English is a performance based on learning correspondence rules, early reading materials should present words governed by a few simple rules at first, which are followed by the more complex. This is not to say that correspondence rules should be verbalized, but rather that decoding performance that is based on rules should be taught. In selecting a commercial reading program for poor readers, the following characteristics should be regarded as desirable: regularity of letter-sound correspondences, blending sounds into words, abstracting letters/sounds from words, introduction of new decoding elements by the teacher, and ample time and incentive for decoding activities. This emphasis should not exclude other important activities, such as silent reading, listening to stories, answering questions, writing, spelling, and so forth. Curricular emphasis on decoding activities is likely to be effective, since the basic problem at this level is the acquisition of decoding skills.

There are many unanswered questions in curriculum design for poor readers at the primary level. If we accept that a decoding emphasis is sensible, what is the appropriate combination of "decoding" and "comprehension" as an instructional goal? How should the teacher present demands for processing meaning with demands for accurate decoding in a coordinated program? In the decoding instruction, what is the optimal method for assuring that children learn to segment spoken words into phonemes and syllables and printed words into letters? How much time and emphasis should be given to construction of spoken words (blending sounds into words) and printed words (spelling)? What are the appropriate sequences for segmentation and constructing activities? Curricular designers and teachers make decisions about these issues frequently on the basis of teaching experience, but there is little scientific basis for their judgments. Answers to these questions, we hope, will be provided by future research and will help in establishing better guidelines for curriculum development in early reading.

Intermediate Level

A number of cognitive processing constructs emerged from the literature as distinguishing good from poor readers at this level of development in reading. These included decoding accuracy, decoding speed, perception of orthographic regularity, semantic segmentation, and semantic construction. This is a group of associated cognitive components of reading. There is no compelling evidence that causal relations exist among them, or that a hierarchy is present. We do not know, for instance, that teaching rapid decoding facilitates semantic construction. Experimental evidence on the relationships between these constructs is needed.

Reading programs for poor readers at the intermediate level should assure that the cognitive processes presented in the previous paragraph are included as goals of instruction. Usually the most effective means for attaining an instructional goal is to teach it directly, and these processes probably should be taught with well-planned activities. These may not be the only cognitive processes that poor readers at this level need to be taught. There are probably other processes that have not been studied and should be included. However, this represents a minimum set and a starting point for development and evaluation of programs.

A question that is often raised by teachers and curriculum designers is how much emphasis to place on spoken language instruction outside of reading. In terms of our constructs, should semantic segmenting and constructing be taught through reading or listening activities or both? If a child or a group performs a sentence-comprehension task well in listening and poorly by reading, the answer is teach by reading. If the group performs the task poorly in both modalities, teaching probably should include both. There may be many occasions where a language skill can be improved most efficiently in reading activities. For example, segmenting a sentence into its major (syntactic) constituents may be taught best with written materials. In print, the sentence can be scanned, reviewed, divided, and redivided quite easily. Language lessons may be optimized in reading activities. We know they are basically language rather than reading lessons if the students cannot perform the task more proficiently by listening than by reading. An advantage of using written materials is that they can be used to teach processes specific to reading, such as orthographic regularity, as well as processes general to language, such as semantic constructing.

Unanswered questions in curriculum design abound at the intermediate level. For instance, in teaching decoding in fourth grade, how difficult should the words be that are given, and what level accuracy should be expected of the children? If decoding speed is important, what specific criteria for speed can be used? What levels of meanings should be taught for words, sentences, and stories? How long and complex should be the stories that are given, and what kinds of responses should be requested from children (summaries, reactions, imitations, evaluations, etc.) to facilitate the many facets of comprehension? Most published reading curricula that are used for low readers have treated these issues, but almost no other basic research has been conducted.

Principles of Instruction

From the literature on cognitive characteristics of good and poor readers, a set of general instructional principles may be developed.

1. Direct instruction toward deficient cognitive processes. The first principle, is based on the fact that not all poor readers are deficient in all cognitive processes that are needed for reading. For example, primary-level children usually lack decoding skills while having adequate language processes during readings. Therefore, teaching language—for example, semantic segmentation—will not likely improve reading. Furthermore, the deficient cognitive processes of poor readers—for example, decoding accuracy—cannot be somehow circumvented and another process substituted, since they are all necessary for normal reading.

2. Provide simultaneous instruction in as many cognitive processes as need improvement. The second principle is needed, since poor readers are often deficient in several cognitive processes, and there is no evidence for a hierarchy among them. For example, for intermediate-level poor readers, several processes must be improved, and we do not know that teaching one will improve the others. Since instruction in one process—

that is, rapid decoding—may not improve another process—that is, semantic segmentation—both are needed for reading, and both should be taught to children who are deficient in them. Further, since these processes are likely to be interdependent and mutually facilitative in good readers, it is reasonable to teach them simultaneously, rather than sequentially. Attempts should be made to improve all deficient cognitive processes at about the same rates.

3. Integrate instruction on deficient components into purposeful reading for pleasure or information. As Frase (1975) has shown with adults, a person's purpose for reading influences what is comprehended and remembered. In other words, cognitive processes operate at the direction of the reader's purpose. Since children need to learn the role of purpose in reading, newly learned cognition processes, such as rapid decoding or semantic segmentation, should be required to occur under conditions of realistic purposes. This will enable the reader to call up these processes when they are useful for his purpose in a practical reading situation.

4. Commit a substantial amount of time to formal reading instruction. The fourth principle, the value of substantial amounts of reading instruction, is as important as good instructional design. There is evidence that poor readers are inferior to good readers in the rate of learning essential processes. To a considerable extent, we all acquire similar reading skills, but poor readers learn them more slowly (Calfee, et al., 1969; Mackworth and Mackworth, 1974; Guthrie and Seifert, 1977). Consequently, poor readers should benefit from large amounts of instructional time. This expectation was confirmed in a nationwide study of follow-through programs (Stallings, 1975). Poor readers were found to benefit more from time committed to direct instruction. A well-designed instructional program can have an impact only if it is given a substantial amount of time and space in the curriculum.

REFERENCES

Ball, S., and Bogatz, G. Research on Sesame Street: some implications for compensatory education. *In* J. Stanley, ed., *Compensatory Education for Children, Ages 2 to 8.* Baltimore: Johns Hopkins University Press, 1973.

Barganz, R. Phonological and orthographic relationships to reading performance. *Visible Language,* 1974, 8:101–122.

Belmont, L., and Birch, H. The intellectual profile of retarded readers. *Perceptual and Motor Skills,* 1966, 22:787–816.

Benson, D. F. Alexia. *In* J. T. Guthrie, ed., *Aspects of Reading Acquisition.* Baltimore: Johns Hopkins University Press, 1976.

Biemiller, A. The development of the use of graphic and contextual information as children learn to read. *Reading Research Quarterly,* 1970, 6:75–96.

Bloom, B. *Human Characteristics and School Learning.* New York: McGraw-Hill, 1976.

Bond, G. L., and Dykstra, R. The cooperative research program in first-grade reading instruction. *Reading Research Quarterly,* 1967, 2:5–142.

Bond, G. and Tinker, M. *Reading Difficulties: Their Diagnosis and Correction* (3rd ed.). New York: Meredith Corporation, 1973.

Bryan, T., and Bryan, J. *Understanding Learning Disabilities.* Port Washington, N.Y.: Alfred Publishing, 1975.

Bryden, M. Laterality effects in dichotic listening: relations with handedness and reading ability in children. *Neuropsychologia,* 1970, 8:443–450.

Calfee, R., and Drum, P. *Compensatory Reading Survey.* Newark, Del.: International Reading Association, in press.

Calfee, R., Venezky, R., and Chapman, R. *Pronunciation of synthetic words with predictable and unpredictable letter-sound correspondences* (Tech. Rep. 71). Wisconsin Research Development Center for Cognitive Learning, 1969.

Carroll, J. A model for school learning. *Teachers College Record*, 1963, 64:723–733.

Carroll, J. Review of Illinois Test of Psycholinguistic Abilities (rev. ed.). *In* O. Buros, ed., *Seventh Mental Measurements Yearbook* (Vol. 1). Highland Park, N.J.: Gryphon Press, 1972.

Carroll, J. Promoting language skills: the role of instruction. *In* D. Klahr, ed., *Cognition and Instruction.* Hillsdale, N.J.: Lawrence Erlbaum Associates, 1976.

Critchley, M. *The Dyslexic Child.* Springfield, Ill.: Charles C. Thomas, 1970.

Cromer, W. The difference model: a new explanation for some reading difficulties. *Journal of Educational Psychology,* 1970, 61:471–483.

Cruikshank, W. Myths and realities. *Journal of Learning Disabilities,* 1977, 10(1):51–58.

Doehring, D. Acquisition of rapid reading responses. *Monographs of the Society for Research in Child Development,* 1976, 41(2, Serial No. 165).

Durkin, D. *Teaching Young Children to Read* (2nd ed.). Boston: Allyn & Bacon, 1976.

Eisenberg, L. The social imperatives of medical research. *Science,* 1977, 198(4322):1105–1110.

Entwisle, D. Young children's expectations for reading. *In* J. Guthrie, ed., *Aspects of Reading Acquisition.* Baltimore: Johns Hopkins University Press, 1976.

Federal Register, 42(250), December 29, 1977, pp. 65082–65085.

Frase, L. Prose processing. *In* G. Bower, ed., *The Psychology of Learning and Motivation.* New York: Academic Press, 1975.

Frase, L. Comments on an applied behavior analysis approach to reading comprehension. *In* J. Guthrie (ed.), *Cognition, Curriculum, and Comprehension.* Newark, Del.: International Reading Association, 1977.

Frostig, M. Education for children with learning disabilities. *In* H. Myklebust, ed., *Progress in Learning Disabilities,* Vol. I. New York: Grune & Stratton, 1968.

Gibson, E., and Levin, H. *The Psychology of Reading.* Cambridge, Mass.: MIT Press, 1975.

Golinkoff, R., and Rosinski, R. Decoding, semantic processing, and reading comprehension skill. *Child Development,* 1976, 47:252–258.

Graves, M., and Patberg, J. A tutoring program for adolescents seriously deficient in reading. *Journal of Reading Behavior,* 1976, 8(1):27–35.

Groen, G., and Resnick, L. Can preschool children invent addition algorithms? *Journal of Educational Psychology,* 1977, 69(6):645–652.

Guthrie, J. Models of reading and reading disability. *Journal of Educational Psychology,* 1973, 65:9–18.

Guthrie, J., ed. *Cognition, Curriculum, and Comprehension.* Newark, Del.: International Reading Association, 1977.

Guthrie, J., Goldberg, H., and Finucci, J. Independence of abilities in disabled readers. *Journal of Reading Behavior,* 1972, 4(2):129–138.

Guthrie, J., and Seifert, M. Letter-sound complexity in learning to identify words. *Journal of Educational Psychology,* 1977, 69(6):686–696.

Guthrie, J., Seifert, M., and Kline, L. Clues from research on programs for poor readers. *In* S. Samuels, ed., *What Research Has to Say About Reading Instruction.* Newark, Del.: International Reading Association, 1978.

Guthrie, J., and Tyler, S. Psycholinguistic processing in reading and listening among good and poor readers. *Journal of Reading Behavior,* 1976, 8:415–426.

Guthrie, J., and Tyler, S. Cognition and instruction of poor readers. *Journal of Reading Behavior,* 1978,

Hammill, D. Training visual perceptual processes. *Journal of Learning Disabilities,* 1972, 5(10):552–559.

Hammill, D., and Larsen, S. Relationship of selected auditory perceptual skills and reading ability. *Journal of Learning Disabilities,* 1971, 1:40–46.

Hansen, C., and Lovitt, T. An applied behavior analysis approach to reading comprehension. *In* J. Guthrie, ed., *Cognition, Curriculum, and Comprehension.* Newark, Del.: International Reading Association, 1977.

Haring, N., and Bateman, B. *Teaching the Learning Disabled Child.* Englewood Cliffs, N.J.: Prentice-Hall, 1977.

Harris, A., and Serwer, B. The CRAFT Project: instructional time in reading research. *Reading Research Quarterly,* 1966, 2:27–57.

Harris, A., and Sipay, E. *How to Increase Reading Ability: A Guide to Developmental and Remedial Methods* (6th ed.). New York: David McKay Company, 1975.

Hazlett, J., Arhmann, J., and Johnson, G. *Reading: Summary, National Assessment of Educational Progress* (Report 02-R-00). Denver, Col.: Education Commission of the States, May 1972.

Hinshelwood, J. *Congenital Word-Blindness.* London: Lewis, 1917.

Howlett, N., and Weintraub, S. Instructional procedures. *In* R. Calfee and P. Drum, eds., *Compensatory Reading Survey.* Newark, Del.: International Reading Association, in press.

Isakson, R., and Miller, J. Sensitivity to syntactic and semantic cues in good and poor comprehenders. *Journal of Educational Psychology*, 1976, 68:787–792.

Jansky, J., and deHirsch, K. *Preventing Reading Failure.* New York: Harper & Row, 1972.

Kahn, D., and Birch, H. Development of auditory-visual integration and reading achievement. *Perceptual and Motor Skills,* 1968, 27:459–468.

Katz, L. Reading ability and single-letter orthographic redundancy. *Journal of Educational Psychology,* 1977, 69(6):653–659.

Kessinger, D., and Singleton, J. I don't do this on purpose! *Today's Education,* November-December 1977, pp. 36–39.

Kimura, D. Cerebral dominance and the perception of verbal stimuli. *Canadian Journal of Psychology,* 1961, 15:166–171

Kirk, S. *Educating Exceptional Children.* Boston: Houghton Mifflin, 1972.

Kirsch, I., and Guthrie, J. The concept and measurement of functional literacy. *Reading Research Quarterly,* 1978, 13:   –

Kolers, P. Specifity of operations in sentence recognition. *Cognitive Psychol 1975, 7(3):239–06.*

LaBerge, D., and Samuels, S. Toward a theory of automatic information processing in reading. *Cognitive Psychology,* 1974, 6:293–323.

Lerner, J. Remedial reading and learning disabilities: are they the same or different? *Journal of Special Education,* 1975, 9(2):119–131.

Lerner, J. *Children with Learning Disabilities* (2nd ed.). Boston: Houghton Mifflin, 1976.

Levin, J. Inducing comprehension in poor readers: a test of a recent model. *Journal of Educational Psychology,* 1973, 65:19–24.

Liberman, I., Shankweiler, D., Liberman, A., Fowler, C., and Fischer, F. Phonetic segmentation and recoding in the beginning reader. *In* A. Reber and D. Scarborough, eds., *Reading: Theory and Practice.* Hillsdale, N.J.: Lawrence Erlbaum Associates, 1976.

Mackworth, J., and Mackworth, N. How children read: matching by sight and sound. *Journal of Reading Behavior,* 1974, 6:295–305.

Mason, M. Reading ability and letter search time: effects of orthographic structure defined by single-letter positional frequency. *Journal of Experimental Psychology: General,* 1975, 104:146–166.

McNeil, D. The development of language. *In* P. Mussen, ed., *Carmichael's Handbook of Child Psychology.* New York: Wiley & Sons, 1970.

Medley, D. *Teacher Competence and Teacher Effectiveness: A Review of Process-Product Research.* Washington, D.C.: American Association of Colleges for Teacher Education, 1977.

Money, J., and Nurcombe, M. Ability tests and cultural heritage? The draw-a-person and Bender tests in Aboriginal Australia. *Journal of Learning Disabilities,* 1974, 7(5):297–303.

Monroe, M. *Children Who Cannot Read.* Chicago: University of Chicago Press, 1932.

Newman, A. Later achievement study of pupils underachieving in reading in first grade. *Reading Research Quarterly,* 1972, 7:477–508.

Orton, S. *Reading, Writing and Speech Problems in Children.* London: Chapman & Hall, 1937.

Otto, W. Design for developing comprehension skills. *In* J. Guthrie, ed., *Cognition, Curriculum, and Comprehension.* Newark, Del.: International Reading Association, 1977.

Otto, W., Peters, N., and Peters, C. *Reading Problems: A Multidisciplinary Perspective.* Reading, Mass.: Addison-Wesley, 1977.

Paris, S., and Lindauer, B. The role of inference in children's comprehension and memory for sentences. *Cognitive Psychology,* 1976, 8:217–227.

Peltzman, B. Josh—A disabled reader and how he was helped: a case study. *Instructor,* 1977, 6(86):151–153.

Perfetti, C. Language comprehension and fast decoding. *In* J. Guthrie, ed., *Cognition, Curriculum, and Comprehension.* Newark, Del.: International Reading Association, 1977.

Perfetti, C., and Goldman, S. Discourse memory and reading comprehension skill. *Journal of Verbal Learning and Verbal Behavior,* 1976, 14:33–42.

Perfetti, C., and Hogaboam, T. Relationship between single word decoding and reading comprehension skill. *Journal of Educational Psychology,* 1975, 67:461–469.

Preston, M., Guthrie, J., and Childs, B. Visual evoked responses in normal and disabled readers. *Psychophysiology,* 1974, 11:452–457.

Raeburn, P. I. Rabi: Columbia's scientist-statesman. *Columbia Today,* winter 1977, pp. 4–6.

Robinson, H. Visual and auditory modalities related to methods for beginning reading. *Reading Research Quarterly,* 1972, 8:7–39.

Rosenshine, B. Classroom instruction. *In* N. Gage, Ed., *The Psychology of Teaching Methods* (75th Yearbook of the National Society for the Study of Education). Chicago: University of Chicago Press, 1976.

Samuels, S., Begy, G., and Chen, C. Comparison of word recognition speed and strategies of less skilled and more highly skilled readers. *Reading Research Quarterly*, 1976, 11:72–86.

Satz, P., Rardin, D., and Ross, J. An evaluation of a theory of specific developmental dyslexia. *Child Development*, 1971, 42:2009–2021.

Shankweiler, D., and Liberman, I. Exploring the relations between reading and speech. *In* R. Knights and D. Bakker, eds., *The Neuropsychology of Learning Disorders*. Baltimore: University Park Press, 1976.

Shapiro, N., and Kriftcher, N. Combatting the lower and higher illiteracies. *Journal of Reading*, 1976, 19(5): 381–386.

Smiley, S., Oakley, D., Worthen, D., Campione, J., and Brown, A. Recall of thematically relevant material by adolescent good and poor readers as a function of written versus oral presentation. *Journal of Educational Psychology*, 1977, 69(4):381–387.

Smiley, S., Pasquale, F., and Chandler, C. The pronunciation of familiar, unfamiliar and synthetic words by good and poor adolescent readers. *Journal of Reading Behavior*, 1976, 8(3):289–297.

Spache, G. *Investigating the Issues of Reading Disabilities*. Boston: Allyn & Bacon, 1976.

Stallings, J. Implementation and child effects of teaching practices in Follow Through classrooms. *Monographs of Society for Research in Child Development*, 1975, 40(7–8) (No. 163).

Stauffer, R. Cognitive processes fundamental to reading instruction. *In* J. Guthrie, ed., *Cognition, Curriculum, and Comprehension*. Newark, Del.: International Reading Association, 1977.

Steinheiser, F., and Guthrie, J. Scanning times through prose and word strings for various targets by normal and disabled readers. *Perceptual and Motor Skills*, 1974, 39:931–938.

Steinheiser, F., and Guthrie, J. Reading ability and efficiency of graphemic-phonemic encoding. *Journal of General Psychology*, 1970, 00:000–000.

Sticht, T., Beck, L., and Hauke, R. *Auding and Reading: A Developmental Model*. Alexandria, Va.: Human Resources Research Organization, 1974.

Symmes, J., and Rapoport, J. Unexpected reading failure. *American Journal of Orthopsychiatry*, 1972, 42:82–91.

Vellutino, F. Alternative conceptualizations of dyslexia: evidence in support of a verbal-deficit hypothesis. *Harvard Educational Review*, 1977, 47(3):334–354.

Vellutino, F., Steger, J., Harding, C., and Phillips, F. Verbal vs. non-verbal paired associates learning in poor and normal readers. *Neuropsychologia*, 1975, 13:75–82.

Venezky, R. English orthography: its graphical structure and its relation to sound. *Reading Research Quarterly*, 1967, 2:75–105.

Venezky, R. *Theoretical and Experimental Base for Teaching Reading*. The Hague, The Netherlands: Mouton, 1976.

Vernon, M. *Reading and its Difficulties*. Cambridge, Mass.: Cambridge University Press, 1971.

Wallach, M., and Wallach, L. *Teaching All Children to Read*. Chicago: University of Chicago Press, 1976.

Waller, T. Children's recognition memory for written sentences: a comparison of good and poor readers. *Child Development*, 1976, 47(1):90–95.

Weber, R. First-graders' use of grammatical context in reading. *In* H. Levin and J. Williams, eds., *Basic Studies on Reading*. New York: Basic Books, 1970.

Weinstein, R., and Rabinovitch, M. Sentence structure and retention in good and poor readers. *Journal of Educational Psychology*, 1971, 62:25–30.

Whiteman, M., and Deutsch, M. Social disadvantages as related to intellective and language development. *In* M. Deutsch, I. Katz, and A. Jensen, eds., *Social Class, Race and Psychological Development*. New York: Holt, Rinehart and Winston, 1968.

Wiley, D., and Harnischfeger, A. Explosion of a myth: quantity of schooling and exposure to instruction, major educational vehicles. *Educational Researcher*, 1974, 3(4):7–13.

Williams, J. Building perceptual and cognitive strategies into a reading curriculum. *In* A. Reber and D. Scarborough, eds., *Toward a Psychology of Reading*. Hillsdale, N.J.: Lawrence Erlbaum Associates, 1977.

Williams, J. The ABDs of reading: a program for the learning-disabled. *In* L. Resnick and P. Weaver, eds., *Theory and Practice of Early Reading*. Hillsdale, N.J.: Lawrence Erlbaum Associates, 1978.

Ysseldyke, J. *Assessing the learning disabled youngster: The state of the art* (Res. Rep. #1). Minneapolis: Institute for Research on Learning Disabilities, University of Minnesota, November 1977.

Ysseldyke, J., and Salvia, J. Diagnostic-prescriptive teaching: two models. *Exceptional Children*, 1974, 41(3):181–185.

Index